second edition

Research Methods

Knowledge Base

William M. K. Trochim
Cornell University

ATOMICDOGPUBLISHING.COM

THOMSON™

The Research Methods Knowledge Base 2e
William M.K. Trochim

Executive Editors:
Michele Baird, Maureen Staudt, and
Michael Stranz

Project Development Manager
Linda de Stefano

Sr. Marketing Coordinators:
Lindsay Annett and Sara Mercurio

Production/Manufacturing Supervisor
Donna M. Brown

Premedia Services Supervisor:
Dan Plofchan

Custom Production Editor:
Julie M. Niesen

Rights and Permissions Specialists:
Kalina Ingham Hintz, Connee Draper

Cover Image:
© 2007 Getty

Composition House:
International Typesetting and
Composition

The Adaptable Courseware Program
consists of products and additions to
existing Thomson products that are
produced from camera-ready copy.
Peer review, class testing, and
accuracy are primarily the responsibility
of the author(s).

ISBN 0-97013-859-8
978-0-9701385-9-0

International Divisions List

Asia (Including India):
Thomson Learning
(a division of Thomson Asia Pte Ltd)
5 Shenton Way #01-01
UIC Building
Singapore 068808
Tel: (65) 6410-1200
Fax: (65) 6410-1208

Australia/New Zealand:
Thomson Learning Australia
102 Dodds Street
Southbank, Victoria 3006
Australia

Latin America:
Thomson Learning
Seneca 53
Colonia Polano
11560 Mexico, D.F., Mexico
Tel (525) 281-2906
Fax (525) 281-2656

Canada:
Thomson Nelson
1120 Birchmount Road
Toronto, Ontario
Canada M1K 5G4
Tel (416) 752-9100
Fax (416) 752-8102

UK/Europe/Middle East/Africa:
Thomson Learning
High Holborn House
50-51 Bedford Row
London, WC1R 4LR
United Kingdom
Tel 44 (020) 7067-2500
Fax 44 (020) 7067-2600

Spain (Includes Portugal):
Thomson Paraninfo
Calle Magallanes 25
28015 Madrid
España
Tel 34 (0)91 446-3350
Fax 34 (0)91 445-621

Contents

Preface vii

Part 1

Foundations 1

Chapter 1

Foundations 3

1-1 The Language of Research 4
  1-1a Five Big Words 4
  1-1b Types of Studies 5
  1-1c Time in Research 5
  1-1d Types of Relationships 6
    The Nature of a Relationship 6
    Patterns of Relationships 6
  1-1e Variables 8
  1-1f Hypotheses 9
  1-1g Types of Data 11
  1-1h The Unit of Analysis 13
  1-1i Two Research Fallacies 13
1-2 Philosophy of Research 14
  1-2a Structure of Research 14
    Components of a Study 15
  1-2b Deduction and Induction 17
  1-2c Positivism and Post-Positivism 18
  1-2d Introduction to Validity 20
1-3 Ethics in Research 23
  1-3a The Language of Ethics 24
1-4 Conceptualizing 25
  1-4a Problem Formulation 25
    Where Research Topics Come From 25
    Feasibility 26
    The Literature Review 27
  1-4b Concept Mapping 27
1-5 Evaluation Research 30
  1-5a Introduction to Evaluation 30
    Definitions of Evaluation 30
    The Goals of Evaluation 31

    Evaluation Strategies 31
    Types of Evaluation 32
    Evaluation Questions and Methods 33
  1-5b The Planning Evaluation Cycle 34
  1-5c An Evaluation Culture 34

Part 2

Sampling 39

Chapter 2

Sampling 41

2-1 External Validity 42
  2-1a Threats to External Validity 43
  2-1b Improving External Validity 43
2-2 Sampling Terminology 44
2-3 Statistical Terms in Sampling 45
  2-3a The Sampling Distribution 46
  2-3b Sampling Error 47
  2-3c The 65, 95, 99 Percent Rule 48
2-4 Probability Sampling 50
  2-4a Some Definitions 50
  2-4b Simple Random Sampling 50
  2-4c Stratified Random Sampling 51
  2-4d Systematic Random Sampling 53
  2-4e Cluster (Area) Random Sampling 54
  2-4f Multi-Stage Sampling 55
2-5 Nonprobability Sampling 55
  2-5a Accidental, Haphazard, or Convenience
    Sampling 56
  2-5b Purposive Sampling 56
    Modal Instance Sampling 56
    Expert Sampling 57
    Quota Sampling 57
    Heterogeneity Sampling 58
    Snowball Sampling 58
Summary 58

Part 3

Measurement 61

Chapter 3

The Theory of Measurement 63

3-1 Construct Validity 64
   3-1a Measurement Validity Types 65
      Translation Validity 66
      Criterion-Related Validity 67
   3-1b Idea of Construct Validity 69
   3-1c Convergent and Discriminant Validity 71
      Convergent Validity 72
      Discriminant Validity 72
      Putting It All Together 73
   3-1d Threats to Construct Validity 75
      Inadequate Preoperational Explication
         of Constructs 75
      Mono-Operation Bias 75
      Mono-Method Bias 75
      Interaction of Different Treatments 76
      Interaction of Testing and Treatment 76
      Restricted Generalizability Across Constructs 76
      Confounding Constructs and Levels
         of Constructs 77
      The Social Threats to Construct Validity 77
   3-1e The Nomological Network 78
   3-1f The Multitrait-Multimethod Matrix 79
      Principles of Interpretation 81
      Advantages and Disadvantages of MTMM 83
      A Modified MTMM —Leaving Out the Methods
         Factor 83
   3-1g Pattern Matching for Construct Validity 84
      The Theory of Pattern Matching 84
      Pattern Matching and Construct Validity 86
      Advantages and Disadvantages of Pattern
         Matching 88
3-2 Reliability 88
   3-2a True Score Theory 89
   3-2b Measurement Error 90
      What Is Random Error? 90
      What Is Systematic Error? 91
      Reducing Measurement Error 91
   3-2c Theory of Reliability 92
   3-2d Types of Reliability 96
      Inter-Rater or Inter-Observer Reliability 96
      Test-Retest Reliability 97
      Parallel-Forms Reliability 98
      Internal Consistency Reliability 99
   3-2e Reliability and Validity 101
3-3 Levels of Measurement 103
   3-3a Why Is Level of Measurement Important? 104
Summary 105

Chapter 4

Survey Research and Scaling 107

4-1 Survey Research 108
   4-1a Types of Surveys 108
      Questionnaires 108
      Interviews 109
   4-1b Selecting the Survey Method 109
      Population Issues 109
      Sampling Issues 110
      Question Issues 111
      Content Issues 111
      Bias Issues 112
      Administrative Issues 112
   4-1c Constructing the Survey 113
      Types of Questions 113
      Question Content 117
      Response Format 119
      Question Wording 122
      Question Placement 124
   4-1d The Golden Rule 125
   4-1e Interviews 125
      The Role of the Interviewer 125
      Training the Interviewers 126
      The Interviewer's Kit 127
      Conducting the Interview 127
   4-1f Advantages and Disadvantages of Survey
      Methods 132
4-2 Scaling 132
4-3 General Issues in Scaling 133
   4-3a Purposes of Scaling 134
   4-3b Dimensionality 134
   4-3c Unidimensional or Multidimensional? 136
   4-4d The Major Unidimensional Scale Types 136
4-4 Thurstone Scaling 136
   4-4a The Method of Equal-Appearing Intervals 136
   4-4b The Other Thurstone Methods 145
4-5 Likert Scaling 145
   4-5a Example: The Employment Self-Esteem Scale 147
4-6 Guttman Scaling 147
Summary 150

Chapter 5

Qualitative and Unobtrusive Measures 151

5-1 Qualitative Measures 152
   5-1a The Qualitative/Quantitative Debate 154
      Qualitative and Quantitative Data 154
      All Qualitative Data Can Be Coded
         Quantitatively 155
      All Quantitative Data Is Based on Qualitative
         Judgment 157
      Qualitative and Quantitative Assumptions 158
   5-1b Qualitative Data 159
   5-1c Qualitative Approaches 159

Ethnography 159
Phenomenology 159
Field Research 160
Grounded Theory 160
5-1d Qualitative Methods 161
Participant Observation 161
Direct Observation 161
Unstructured Interviewing 161
Case Studies 161
5-1e Qualitative Validity 162
Credibility 162
Transferability 162
Dependability 162
Confirmability 163
5-2 Unobtrusive Measures 164
5-2a Indirect Measures 164
5-2b Content Analysis 165
5-2c Secondary Analysis of Data 166
Summary 167

A 2 x 3 Example 202
A Three-Factor Example 203
Incomplete Factorial Design 204
7-4 Randomized Block Designs 205
7-4a How Blocking Reduces Noise 206
7-5 Covariance Designs 207
7-5a How Does a Covariate Reduce Noise? 208
7-5b Summary 211
7-6 Hybrid Experimental Designs 211
7-6a The Solomon Four-Group Design 211
7-6b Switching-Replications Design 213
Summary 214

Part 4

Design 169

Chapter 6

Design 171

6-1 Internal Validity 172
6-1a Establishing Cause and Effect 173
Temporal Precedence 173
Covariation of the Cause and Effect 174
No Plausible Alternative Explanations 174
6-1b Single-Group Threats 175
Regression to the Mean 178
6-1c Multiple-Group Threats 182
6-1d Social Interaction Threats 185
6-2 Introduction to Design 186
6-3 Types of Designs 188
Summary 190

Chapter 7

Experimental Design 191

7-1 Introduction to Experimental Design 192
7-1a Experimental Designs and Internal Validity 192
7-1b Two-Group Experimental Designs 193
7-1c Probabilistic Equivalence 195
7-1d Random Selection and Assignment 196
7-2 Classifying Experimental Designs 196
7-3 Factorial Designs 197
7-3a The Basic 2 x 3 Factorial Design 198
The Null Outcome 199
The Main Effects 199
Interaction Effects 200
7-3b Factorial Design Variations 202

Chapter 8

Quasi-Experimental Design 215

8-1 The Nonequivalent-Groups Design 216
8-1a The Basic Design 216
8-1b The Bivariate Distribution 217
Possible Outcome 1 217
Possible Outcome 2 218
Possible Outcome 3 219
Possible Outcome 4 220
Possible Outcome 5 220
8-2 The Regression-Discontinuity Design 221
8-2a The Basic RD Design 222
The Logic of the RD Design 224
The Role of the Comparison Group
in RD Designs 226
The Internal Validity of the RD Design 226
8-2b The RD Design and Accountability 228
8-2c Statistical Power and the RD Design 228
8-2d Ethics and the RD Design 228
8-3 Other Quasi-Experimental Designs 228
8-3a The Proxy Pretest Design 228
8-3b The Separate Pre-Post Samples Design 229
8-3c The Double-Pretest Design 230
8-3d The Switching-Replications Design 231
8-3e The Nonequivalent Dependent Variables (NEDV)
Design 231
The Pattern-Matching NEDV Design 232
8-3f The Regression Point Displacement (RPD)
Design 234
Summary 235

Chapter 9

Advanced Design Topics 237

9-1 Designing Designs for Research 238
9-1a Minimizing Threats to Validity 238
9-1b Building a Design 240
Basic Design Elements 240
Expanding a Design 241
9-1c A Simple Strategy for Design Construction 245
9-1d An Example of a Hybrid Design 245
9-1e The Nature of Good Design 247

9-2 Relationships among Pre-Post Designs 248
9-3 Contemporary Issues in Research Design 250
  9-3a The Role of Judgment 250
  9-3b The Case for Tailored Designs 251
  9-3c The Crucial Role of Theory 251
  9-3d Attention to Program Implementation 252
  9-3e The Importance of Quality Control 252
  9-3f The Advantages of Multiple Perspectives 252
  9-3g Evolution of the Concept of Validity 253
  9-3h Development of Increasingly Complex Realistic
    Analytic Models 253
Summary 254

Part 5

Analysis 255

Chapter 10

Analysis 257

10-1 Conclusion Validity 258
  10-1a Threats to Conclusion Validity 259
    Finding No Relationship When There Is One (or,
      Missing the Needle in the Haystack) 259
    Finding a Relationship When There Is Not One (or
      Seeing Things That Aren't There) 260
    Problems That Can Lead to Either Conclusion
      Error 261
  10-1b Statistical Power 262
  10-1c Improving Conclusion Validity 265
10-2 Data Preparation 266
  10-2a Logging the Data 266
  10-2b Checking the Data for Accuracy 266
  10-2c Developing a Database Structure 267
  10-2d Entering the Data into the Computer 267
  10-2e Data Transformations 268
10-3 Descriptive Statistics 268
  10-3a The Distribution 269
  10-3b Central Tendency 270
  10-3c Dispersion or Variability 271
  10-3d Correlation 272
    Correlation Example 272
    Calculating the Correlation 275
    Testing the Significance of a Correlation 277
    The Correlation Matrix 277
    Other Correlations 278
Summary 279

Chapter 11

Analysis for Research Design 281

11-1 Inferential Statistics 282
11-2 General Linear Model 282
  11-2a The Two-Variable Linear Model 282
  11-2b Extending the General Linear Model
    to the General Case 284
  11-2c Dummy Variables 285
11-3 Experimental Analysis 287
  11-3a The t-Test 287
    Statistical Analysis of the t-Test 289
  11-3b Factorial Design Analysis 292
  11-3c Randomized Block Analysis 293
  11-3d Analysis of Covariance 293
11-4 Quasi-Experimental Analysis 294
  11-4a Nonequivalent Groups Analysis 294
    A Simulation Example 295
    The Problem 296
    The Solution 300
    The Simulation Revisited 303
  11-4b Regression-Discontinuity Analysis 304
    Assumptions in the Analysis 304
    The Curvilinearity Problem 305
    Model Specification 306
    Analysis Strategy 308
    Steps in the Analysis 308
    Example Analysis 311
  11-4c Regression Point Displacement Analysis 313
Summary 315

Chapter 12

Write-Up 317

12-1 Key Elements 318
12-2 Formatting 320
  12-2a Title Page 321
  12-2b Abstract 321
  12-2c Body 321
  12-2d Introduction 321
  12-2e Methods 321
  12-2f Sample 321
  12-2g Measures 321
  12-2h Design 322
  12-2i Procedures 322
  12-2j Results 322
  12-2k Conclusions 322
  12-2l References 322
    Reference Citations in the Text of your Paper 322
    Reference List in Reference Section 323
  12-2m Tables 325
  12-2n Figures 325
  12-2o Appendices 325
12-3 Sample Paper 325

Glossary 345

Index 355

Preface

You can approach the study of research methods in many different ways. Here I'm going to give you two metaphors to use for thinking about how you might work your way through the material in this book.

The Road to Research

Remember all those Bob Hope and Bing Crosby films, such as *The Road to Singapore* and *The Road to Morocco?* Of course you don't; you're much too young! Well, two old guys made a whole bunch of movies just after they started doing talkies, and each of the movies had a "road to" title. These guys always managed to get themselves into a terrible jam (along with their beautiful female companion, Dorothy Lamour), but things invariably worked out both comically and musically (in those days, people actually used to sing in movies). Research is a lot like those old movies. No, really. You're going to have fun. Honest.

Well, I thought it might be useful to visualize the research endeavor sequentially, like taking a trip, like moving down a road—the Road to Research. Figure 1 shows an applied way to view the content of this text that helps you consider the research process as a practical sequence of events. You might visualize a research project as a journey where you pass certain landmarks along your way. Every research project needs to start with a clear problem formulation. As you develop your project, you will find critical junctions where you will make choices about how to proceed. Consider issues of sampling, measurement, design, and analysis, as well as the theories of validity behind each step. In the end, you will need to think about the whole picture and write up your findings. You might even find yourself backtracking from time to time and reassessing your previous decisions! This is a two-way road; planning and reflection are critical and interdependent. Think of the asphalt of the road as the foundation of research philosophy and practice. Without consideration of the basics in research, you'll find yourself bogged down in the mud!

The Yin and the Yang of Research

Another way to look at research is illustrated in Figure 2. The figure shows one way of structuring the material in the Knowledge Base. The left side of the figure refers to the theory of research. The right side of the figure refers to the practice of

Figure 1
The research road map.

research. The yin-yang figure in the center links you to a theoretical introduction to research on the left and to the practical issue of how to formulate research projects on the right.

The four arrow links on the left describe the four types of validity in research. The idea of validity provides a unifying theory for understanding the criteria for good research. The four arrow links on the right point to the research practice areas that correspond with each validity type. For instance, external validity is related to the theory of how to generalize research results. Its corresponding practice area is sampling methodology, which is concerned with how to draw representative samples so that generalizations are possible.

The figure as a whole illustrates the yin and yang of research—the inherent complementarities of theory and practice—that I try to convey throughout this book. If you can come to an understanding of this deeper relationship, you will be a better researcher, one who is able to create research processes, rather than simply use them.

Okay now, it's time for you to sit cross-legged and meditate on the yin and yang of it all as we start down the road to research. . . .

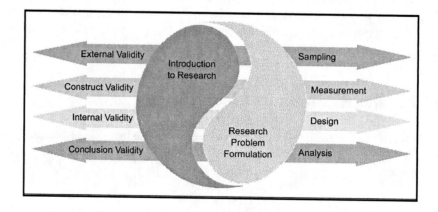

Figure 2
The yin and the yang
of research.

Acknowledgments

This work, as is true for all significant efforts in life, is a collaborative achievement. I want to thank especially the students and friends who assisted and supported me in various ways over the years.

I especially want to thank Dominic Cirillo, who has labored tirelessly over several years on the original web-based and printed versions of *The Research Methods Knowledge Base* and without whom I simply would not have survived. There are also the many graduate teaching assistants who helped me make the transition to a web-based course and contributed their efforts and insights to this work and the teaching of research methods.

Now the *Knowledge Base* has grown from a simple web site to a real text in both electronic and hard-copy versions. For that I need to thank all of my new friends at Atomic Dog Publishing who supplied the enthusiasm and vision to move this effort to the next step. The list must begin with Alex von Rosenberg, who encouraged me to take this step and convinced me that his dog would indeed hunt. Thanks to Dave Hart and Chris Morgan for putting up with all of my questions and concerns. I think I'm finally beginning to get with the program. I'd also like to thank Nicole Bauer for the wonderful graphics work she has done, and I especially want to thank Sydney Jones for her tireless efforts to edit this text into something readable. We do indeed know we live in a digital age when we can collaborate on a project like this without ever having met! You deserve all of the credit and none of the blame.

And, of course, I want to thank all of the students, both undergraduate and graduate, who participated in my courses over the years and used the Knowledge Base in its various incarnations. You have been both my challenge and inspiration.

Atomic Dog publishes unique products that give you the choice of both online and print versions of your text materials. We do this so that you have the flexibility to choose which combination of resources works best for you. For those who use the online and print versions together, we don't want you getting lost as you move between the web and print formats, so we numbered the primary heads and subheads in each chapter the same. For example, the first primary head in Chapter 1 is labeled 1-1, the second primary head in this chapter is labeled 1-2, and so on. The subheads build from the designation of their corresponding primary head: 1-1a, 1-1b, etc.

This numbering system is designed to make moving between the online and print versions as seamless as possible. So if your instructor tells you to read the material in 2-3 and 2-4 for tomorrow's assignment, you'll know that the information appears in Chapter 2 of both the web and print versions of the text, and you can then choose the best way for you to complete your assignment. For your convenience, the Contents for both the web and print versions also show the numbering system.

Part

Foundations

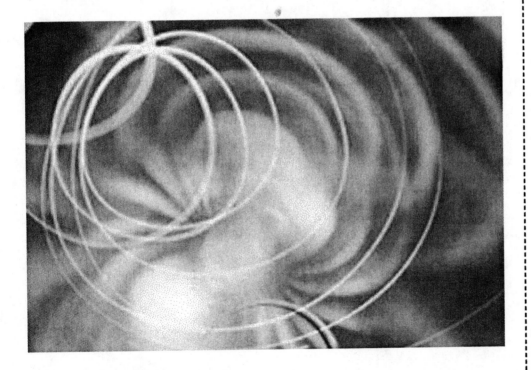

Chapter 1
Foundations

Foundations

You have to begin somewhere. Unfortunately, you can only be in one place at a time and, even less fortunately for you, you happen to be right here right now, so you may as well consider this a place to begin, and what better place to begin than an introduction? Here's where I cover all the stuff you think you already know, and probably should already know, but most likely don't know as well as you think you do.

This chapter begins with the basic language of research, the introductory vocabulary you need to read the rest of the text. With the basic terminology under your belt, I'll show you some of the underlying philosophical issues that drive the research endeavor. Social research always occurs in a social context. It is a human endeavor. I'll point out the critical ethical issues that affect the researcher, research participants, and the research effort generally. For instance, you'll consider how much risk your research participants can be placed under and how you must ensure their privacy. In the section on conceptualization, I answer questions such as where do research problems come from and how do I develop a research question? Finally, I look at a specific, and applied, type of social research known as evaluation research. Evaluation is used to assess the effects of most programs, policies, or initiatives undertaken in government and business.

That ought to be enough to get you started. At least it ought to be enough to get you thoroughly confused. But don't worry, there's stuff that's far more confusing than this yet to come.

Key Terms

alternative
 hypothesis
anonymity
attribute
causal
cause construct
concept maps
conclusion
 validity
confidentiality
constructivisism
correlational
 relationship
critical realism
cross-sectional
deductive
dependent
 variable
ecological
 fallacy
effect construct
empirical
epistemology
exception fallacy
exhaustive
formative
 evaluations
hierarchical
 modeling
hypothesis
hypothetical-
 deductive
 model
idiographic
independent
 variable
inductive
informed
 consent
Institutional
 Review Board
 (IRB)
longitudinal
methodology
mutually
 exclusive

natural selection
theory of
 knowledge
negative
 relationship
nomothetic
null hypothesis
one-tailed
 hypothesis
operationaliza-
 tion
positive
 relationship
positivism
post-positivism
qualitative data
qualitative
 variable
quantitative
 data
quantitative
 variable
relationship
repeated
 measures
Requests For
 Proposals
 (RFPs)
research
 question
right to service
subjectivist
summative
 evaluations
theoretical
third-variable
 problem
threats to
 validity
time series
two-tailed
 hypothesis
unit of analysis
validity
variable
voluntary

1-1 The Language of Research

Learning about research is a lot like learning about anything else. To start, you need to learn the jargon people use, the big controversies they fight over, and the different factions that define the major players. Let's start by considering five really big multisyllable words that researchers sometimes use to describe what they do. I'll only do these five for now, to give you an idea of just how esoteric the discussion can get (but not enough to cause you to give up in total despair). You can then take on some of the major *issues* in research like the types of studies you can perform, the role of time in research, and the different types of relationships you can estimate. Then you have to consider defining some basic terms like variable, hypothesis, data, and unit of analysis. If you're like me, you hate learning vocabulary, so I'll quickly move along to consider two of the major research fallacies, just to give you an idea of how wrong researchers can be if they're not careful. (Of course, there's always a certain probability that they'll be wrong even if they are extremely careful.)

1-1a Five Big Words

Research involves an eclectic blending of an enormous range of skills and activities. To be a good social researcher, you have to be able to work well with a variety of people, understand the specific methods used to conduct research, understand the subject that you are studying, convince someone to give you the funds to study it, stay on track and on schedule, speak and write persuasively, and on and on.

Here, I want to introduce you to five terms that I think help describe some of the key aspects of contemporary social research. (This list is not exhaustive. It's really just the first five terms that came into my mind when I was thinking about this and thinking about how I might be able to impress someone with really big, complex words to describe fairly straightforward concepts.)

I present the first two terms—theoretical and empirical—together because they are often contrasted with each other. Social research is **theoretical**, meaning that much of it is concerned with developing, exploring, or testing the theories or ideas that social researchers have about how the world operates. It is also **empirical**, meaning that it is based on observations and measurements of reality—on what you perceive of the world around you. You can even think of most research as a blending of these two terms—a comparison of theories about how the world operates with observations of its operation.

The next term—**nomothetic**—comes (I think) from the writings of the psychologist Gordon Allport. Nomothetic refers to laws or rules that pertain to the general case (nomos in Greek) and is contrasted with the term **idiographic** which refers to laws or rules that relate to individuals (idiots in Greek???). In any event, the point here is that most social research is concerned with the nomothetic—the general case—rather than the individual. Individuals are often studied, but usually there is interest in generalizing to more than just the individual.

In a post-positivist view of science (see the section on Positivism and Post-Positivism later in this chapter), certainty is no longer regarded as attainable. Thus, the fourth big word that describes much contemporary social research is **probabilistic**, or based on probabilities. The inferences made in social research have probabilities associated with them; they are seldom meant to be considered as covering laws that pertain to all cases. Part of the reason statistics has become so dominant in social research is that it enables the estimation of the probabilities for the situations being studied.

The last term I want to introduce is causal. You have to be careful with this term. Note that it is spelled *causal* not *casual*. You'll really be embarrassed if you write about the "casual hypothesis" in your study! The term **causal** means that most social research is interested (at some point) in looking at cause-effect relationships. This doesn't mean that most research actually studies cause-effect relationships. Some studies simply observe; for instance, a survey might seek to describe the percent of people holding a particular opinion. Many studies explore relationships—for example, studies often attempt to determine whether there is a relationship between gender and salary. Probably the vast majority of applied social research consists of these descriptive and correlational studies. So why am I talking about causal studies? Because for most social sciences, it is important to go beyond simply looking at the world or looking at relationships. You might like to be able to change the world, to improve it and eliminate some of its major problems. If you want to change the world (especially if you want to do this in an organized, scientific way), you are automatically interested in causal relationships—ones that tell how causes (for example, programs and treatments) affect the outcomes of interest.

1-1b Types of Studies

Research projects take three basic forms:

1. **Descriptive** studies are designed primarily to describe what is going on or what exists. Public opinion polls that seek only to describe the proportion of people who hold various opinions are primarily descriptive in nature. For instance, if you want to know what percent of the population would vote for a Democrat or a Republican in the next presidential election, you are simply interested in describing something.
2. **Relational** studies look at the relationships between two or more variables. A public opinion poll that compares what proportion of males and females say they would vote for a Democratic or a Republican candidate in the next presidential election is essentially studying the relationship between gender and voting preference.
3. **Causal** studies are designed to determine whether one or more variables (for example, a program or treatment variable) causes or affects one or more outcome variables. If you performed a public opinion poll to try to determine whether a recent political advertising campaign changed voter preferences, you would essentially be studying whether the campaign (cause) changed the proportion of voters who would vote Democratic or Republican (effect).

The three study types can be viewed as cumulative. That is, a relational study assumes that you can first describe (by measuring or observing) each of the variables you are trying to relate. A causal study assumes that you can describe both the cause and effect variables and that you can show that they are related to each other. Causal studies are probably the most demanding of the three types of studies to perform.

1-1c Time in Research

Time is an important element of any research design, and here I want to introduce one of the most fundamental distinctions in research design nomenclature: cross-sectional versus longitudinal studies. A cross-sectional study is one that takes place at a single point in time. In effect, you are taking a slice or cross-section of whatever it is you're observing or measuring. A *longitudinal* study is one that takes place over time—you have at least two (and often more) waves of measurement in a longitudinal design.

A further distinction is made between two types of longitudinal designs: repeated measures and time series. There is no universally agreed upon rule for distinguishing between these two terms; but in general, if you have two or a few waves of measurement, you are using a ***repeated measures*** design. If you have many waves of measurement over time, you have a ***time series***. How many is many? Usually, you wouldn't use the term time series unless you had at least twenty waves of measurement, and often far more. Sometimes the way you distinguish between these is with the analysis methods you would use. Time series analysis requires that you have at least twenty or so observations over time. Repeated measures analyses aren't often used with as many as twenty waves of measurement.

1-1d Types of Relationships

A ***relationship*** refers to the correspondence between two variables (see the section on variables later in this chapter). When you talk about types of relationships, you can mean that in at least two ways: the *nature* of the relationship or the *pattern* of it.

The Nature of a Relationship

Although all relationships tell about the correspondence between two variables, one special type of relationship holds that the two variables are not only in correspondence, but that one *causes* the other. This is the key distinction between a simple correlational relationship and a causal relationship. A ***correlational relationship*** simply says that two things perform in a synchronized manner. For instance, economists often talk of a correlation between inflation and unemployment. When inflation is high, unemployment also tends to be high. When inflation is low, unemployment also tends to be low. The two variables are correlated; but knowing that two variables are correlated does not tell whether one *causes* the other. It is documented, for instance, that there is a correlation between the number of roads built in Europe and the number of children born in the United States. Does that mean that if fewer children are desired in the United States there should be a cessation of road building in Europe? Or, does it mean that if there aren't enough roads in Europe, U.S. citizens should be encouraged to have more babies? Of course not. (At least, I hope not.) While there is a relationship between the number of roads built and the number of babies, it's not likely that the relationship is a causal one.

This leads to consideration of what is often termed the ***third variable problem***. In this example, it may be that a third variable is causing both the building of roads and the birthrate and causing the correlation that is observed. For instance, perhaps the general world economy is responsible for both. When the economy is good, more roads are built in Europe and more children are born in the United States. The key lesson here is that you have to be careful when you interpret correlations. If you observe a correlation between the number of hours students use the computer to study and their grade point averages (with high computer users getting higher grades), you *cannot* assume that the relationship is causal—that computer use improves grades. In this case, the third variable might be socioeconomic status—richer students, who have greater resources at their disposal, tend to both use computers and make better grades. Resources drive both use and grades; computer use doesn't cause the change in the grade point averages.

Patterns of Relationships

Several terms describe the major different types of patterns one might find in a ***relationship***. First, there is the case of *no relationship* at all. If you know the values on one variable, you don't know anything about the values on the other. For instance, I suspect that there is no relationship between the length of the lifeline on your hand and your grade point average. If I know your GPA, I don't have any idea how long your lifeline is.

Then, there is the ***positive relationship.*** In a positive relationship, high values on one variable are associated with high values on the other and low values on one are associated with low values on the other. Figure 1.1a shows the case where there is no relationship. Figure 1.1b shows an idealized positive relationship between years of education and the salary one might expect to be making.

On the other hand, a ***negative relationship*** implies that high values on one variable are associated with low values on the other. This is also sometimes termed an ***inverse*** relationship. Figure 1.1c shows an idealized negative relationship between a measure of self esteem and a measure of paranoia in psychiatric patients.

These are the simplest types of relationships that might typically be estimated in research. However, the pattern of a relationship can be more complex than this. For instance, Figure 1.1d shows a relationship that changes over the range of both variables, a curvilinear relationship. In this example, the horizontal axis represents dosage of a drug for an illness and the vertical axis represents a severity of illness measure. As the dosage rises, the severity of illness goes down; but at some point, the patient begins to experience negative side effects associated with too high a dosage, and the severity of illness begins to increase again.

Figure 1.1a
No relationship.

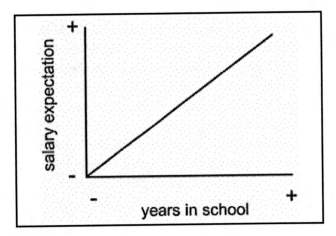

Figure 1.1b
A positive relationship.

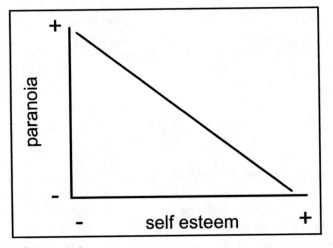

Figure 1.1c
A negative relationship.

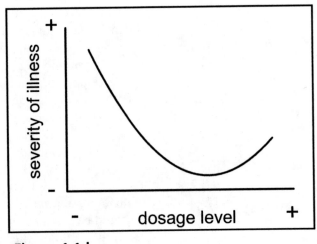

Figure 1.1d
A curvilinear relationship

1-1e Variables

You won't be able to do much in research unless you know how to talk about variables. A *variable* is any entity that can take on different values. Okay, so what does that mean? Anything that can vary can be considered a variable. For instance, *age* can be considered a variable because age can take different values for different people or for the same person at different times. Similarly, *country* can be considered a variable because a person's country can be assigned a value.

Variables aren't always **quantitative** or numerical. The variable *gender* consists of two text values: *male* and *female.* If it is useful, quantitative values can be assigned instead of (or in place of) the text values, but it's not necessary to assign numbers for something to be a variable. It's also important to realize that variables aren't the only things measured in the traditional sense. For instance, in much social research and in program evaluation, the treatment or program is considered to consist of one or more variables. (For example, the cause can be considered a variable.) An educational program can have varying amounts of time on task, classroom settings, student-teacher ratios, and so on. Therefore, even the program can be considered a variable, which can be made up of a number of subvariables.

An **attribute** is a specific value on a variable. For instance, the variable *sex* or *gender* has two attributes: male and female, or, the variable *agreement* might be defined as having five attributes:

- 1 = strongly disagree
- 2 = disagree
- 3 = neutral
- 4 = agree
- 5 = strongly agree

Another important distinction having to do with the term variable is the distinction between an independent and dependent variable. This distinction is particularly relevant when you are investigating cause-effect relationships. It took me the longest time to learn this distinction. (Of course, I'm someone who gets confused about the signs for arrivals and departures at airports—do I go to arrivals because I'm arriving at the airport or does the person I'm picking up go to arrivals because they're arriving on the plane?) I originally thought that an independent variable was one that would be free to vary or respond to some program or treatment, and that a dependent variable must be one that *depends* on my efforts (that is, it's the *treatment*). However this is entirely backwards! In fact *the **independent variable** is what you (or nature) manipulates*—a treatment or program or cause. The **dependent variable** *is what you presume to be affected by the independent variable*—your effects or outcomes. For example, if you are studying the effects of a new educational program on student achievement, the program is the independent variable and your measures of achievement are the dependent ones.

Finally, there are two traits of variables that should always be achieved. Each variable should be **exhaustive**, meaning that it should include all possible answerable responses. For instance, if the variable is *religion* and the only options are *Protestant, Jewish,* and *Muslim,* there are quite a few religions I can think of that haven't been included. The list does not exhaust all possibilities. On the other hand, if you exhaust all the possibilities with some variables—religion being one of them—you would simply have too many responses. The way to deal with this is to explicitly list the most common attributes and then use a general category like *Other* to account for all remaining ones. In addition to being exhaustive, the attributes of a variable should be **mutually exclusive**, meaning that no respondent should be able to have two attributes simultaneously. While this might seem obvious, it is often rather tricky in practice. For instance, you might be tempted to represent the variable *Employment Status* with the two attributes *employed* and *unemployed*. However these **attributes** are not necessarily mutually exclusive—a person who is looking for a second job while employed would be able to check both attributes! But don't researchers often use questions on surveys that ask the respondent to check all that apply and then list a series of categories? Yes, but technically speaking, each of the categories in a question like that is its own **variable** and is treated dichotomously as either checked or unchecked—as attributes that *are* mutually exclusive.

An hypothesis is a specific statement of prediction. It describes in concrete (rather than theoretical) terms what you expect to happen in your study. Not all studies have hypotheses. Sometimes a study is designed to be exploratory (see the section, Inductive Research, later in this chapter). There is no formal hypothesis, and perhaps the purpose of the study is to explore some area more thoroughly to develop some specific hypothesis or prediction that can be tested in future research. A single study may have one or many hypotheses.

1-1f Hypotheses

Actually, whenever I talk about an hypothesis, I am really thinking simultaneously about *two* hypotheses. Let's say that you predict that there will be a relationship between two variables in your study. The way to set up the hypothesis test is to formulate two hypothesis statements: one that describes your prediction and one that describes all the other possible outcomes with respect to the hypothesized relationship. Your prediction is that variable A and variable B will be related. (You don't care whether it's a positive or negative relationship.) Then the only other possible outcome would be that variable A and variable B are *not* related. Usually, the hypothesis that you support (your prediction) is called the **alternative hypothesis**, and the hypothesis that describes the remaining possible outcomes is termed the **null hypothesis**. Sometimes a notation like H_A or H_1 is used to represent the alternative hypothesis or your prediction, and H_O or H_0 to represent the null case. You have to be careful here, though. In some studies, your prediction might well be that there will be no difference or change. In this case, you are essentially trying to find support for the null hypothesis and you are opposed to the alternative.

If your prediction specifies a direction, the null hypothesis is the no-difference prediction *and* the prediction of the opposite direction. This is called a **one-tailed hypothesis**. For instance, let's imagine that you are investigating the effects of a new employee-training program and that you believe one of the outcomes will be that there will be *less* employee absenteeism. Your two hypotheses might be stated something like this:

The null hypothesis for this study is

H_O: As a result of the XYZ company employee-training program, there will either be no significant difference in employee absenteeism or there will be a significant *increase,*

which is tested against the alternative hypothesis:

H_A: As a result of the XYZ company employee-training program, there will be a significant *decrease* in employee absenteeism.

In Figure 1.2, this situation is illustrated graphically. The alternative hypothesis—your prediction that the program will decrease absenteeism—is shown there. The null must account for the other two possible conditions: no difference, or an increase in absenteeism. The figure shows a hypothetical distribution of absenteeism differences. The term one-tailed refers to the tail of the distribution on the outcome variable.

Figure 1.2
A one-tailed hypothesis.

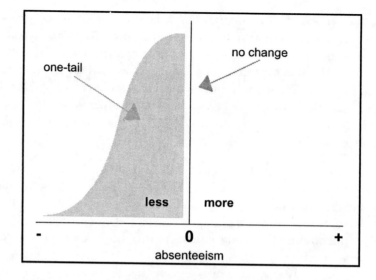

When your prediction does *not* specify a direction, you have a **two-tailed hypothesis**. For instance, let's assume you are studying a new drug treatment for depression. The drug has gone through some initial animal trials, but has not yet been tested on humans. You believe (based on theory and the previous research) that the drug will have an effect, but you are not confident enough to hypothesize a direction and say the drug will reduce depression. (After all, you've seen more than enough promising drug treatments come along that eventually were shown to have severe side effects that actually worsened symptoms.) In this case, you might state the two hypotheses like this:

The null hypothesis for this study is

H_O: As a result of 300mg./day of the ABC drug, there will be no significant difference in depression,

which is tested against the alternative hypothesis:

H_A: As a result of 300mg./day of the ABC drug, there will be a significant difference in depression.

Figure 1.3 illustrates this two-tailed prediction for this case. Again, notice that the term two-tailed refers to the tails of the distribution for your outcome variable.

Figure 1.3
A two-tailed hypothesis.

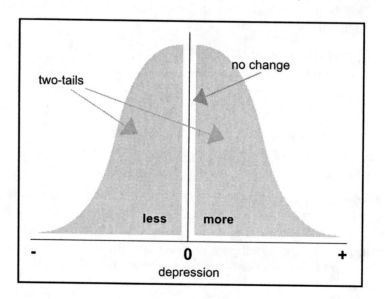

The important thing to remember about stating hypotheses is that you formulate your prediction (directional or not), and then you formulate a second hypothesis that is mutually exclusive of the first and incorporates all possible alternative outcomes for that case. When your study analysis is completed, the idea is that you will have to choose between the two hypotheses. If your prediction was correct, you would (usually) reject the null hypothesis and accept the alternative. If your original prediction was not supported in the data, you will accept the null hypothesis and reject the alternative. The logic of hypothesis testing is based on these two basic principles:

- Two mutually exclusive hypothesis statements that, together, exhaust all possible outcomes need to be developed.
- The hypotheses must be tested so that one is necessarily accepted and the other rejected.

Okay, I know it's a convoluted, awkward, and formalistic way to ask research questions, but it encompasses a long tradition in statistics called the *hypothetical-deductive model*, and sometimes things are just done because they're traditions. And anyway, if all of this hypothesis testing was easy enough so anybody could understand it, how do you think statisticians and methodologists would stay employed?

1-1g Types of Data

Data will be discussed in lots of places in this text, but here I just want to make a fundamental distinction between two types of data: qualitative and quantitative. Typically data is called quantitative if it is in numerical form and qualitative if it is not. Notice that qualitative data could be much more than just words or text. Photographs, videos, sound recordings, and so on, can be considered qualitative data.

Personally, while I find the distinction between qualitative and quantitative data to have some utility, I think most people draw too hard a distinction, and that can lead to all sorts of confusion. In some areas of social research, the qualitative-quantitative distinction has led to protracted arguments with the proponents of each arguing the superiority of their kind of data over the other. The quantitative types argue that their data is hard, rigorous, credible, and scientific. The qualitative proponents counter that their data is sensitive, nuanced, detailed, and contextual.

For many of us in social research, this kind of polarized debate has become less than productive. Additionally, it obscures the fact that qualitative and quantitative data are intimately related to each other. *All quantitative data is based upon qualitative judgments; and all qualitative data can be described and manipulated numerically.* For instance, think about a common quantitative measure in social research—a self-esteem scale. The researchers who developed such instruments had to make countless judgments in constructing them: How to define self-esteem; how to distinguish it from other related concepts; how to word potential scale items; how to make sure the items would be understandable to the intended respondents; what kinds of contexts they could be used in; what kinds of cultural and language constraints might be present, and so on. Researchers who decide to use such a scale in their studies have to make another set of judgments: how well the scale measures the intended concept; how reliable or consistent it is; how appropriate it is for the research context and intended respondents; and so on. Believe it or not, even the respondents make many judgments when filling out such a scale: what various terms and phrases mean; why the researcher is giving this scale to them; how much energy and effort they want to expend to complete it, and so on. Even the consumers and readers of the research make judgments about the self-esteem measure and its appropriateness in that research context. What may look like a simple, straightforward, cut-and-dried quantitative measure is actually based on lots of qualitative judgments made by many different people.

On the other hand, all qualitative information can be easily converted into quantitative, and many times doing so would add considerable value to your research. The simplest way to do this is to divide the qualitative information into categories and number them! I know that sounds trivial, but even that simple nominal enumeration can enable you to organize and process qualitative information more efficiently. As an example, you might take text information (say, excerpts from transcripts) and pile these excerpts into piles of similar statements. When you perform something as easy as this simple grouping or piling task, you can describe the results quantitatively. For instance, Figure 1.4 shows that if you had ten statements and grouped these into five piles, you could describe the piles using a 10 x 10 table of 0's and 1's. If two statements were placed together in the same pile, you would put a 1 in their row-column juncture.

Figure 1.4
Example of how you can convert qualitative sorting information into quantitative data.

		1	2	3	4	5	6	7	8	9	10
	1	1	1	0	0	0	1	0	0	1	0
	2	1	1	0	0	0	1	0	0	1	0
Binary	3	0	0	1	1	0	0	0	0	0	0
Square	4	0	0	1	1	0	0	0	0	0	0
Similarity	5	0	0	0	0	1	0	0	1	0	0
Matrix for the	6	1	1	0	0	0	1	0	0	1	0
sort	7	0	0	0	0	0	0	1	0	0	0
	8	0	0	0	0	1	0	0	1	0	0
	9	1	1	0	0	0	1	0	0	1	0
	10	0	0	0	0	0	0	0	0	0	1

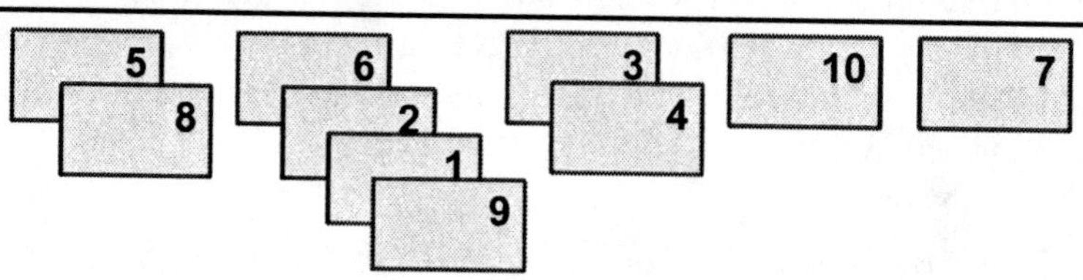

If two statements were placed in different piles, you would use a 0. The resulting matrix or table describes the grouping of the ten statements in terms of their similarity. Even though the data in this example consists of qualitative statements (one per card), the result of this simple qualitative procedure (grouping similar excerpts into the same piles) is *quantitative* in nature. "So what?" you ask. Once you have the data in numerical form, you can manipulate it numerically. For instance, you could have five different judges sort the 10 excerpts and obtain a 0-1 matrix like this for each judge. Then you could average the five matrices into a single one that shows the proportions of judges who grouped each pair together. This proportion could be considered an estimate of the similarity (across independent judges) of the excerpts. While this might not seem too exciting or useful, it is exactly this kind of procedure that I use as an integral part of the process of developing concept maps of ideas for groups of people (something that *is* useful). Concept mapping is described later in this chapter.

One of the most important ideas in a research project is the ***unit of analysis***. The unit of analysis is the major entity that you are analyzing in your study. For instance, any of the following could be a unit of analysis in a study:

- Individuals
- Groups
- Artifacts (books, photos, newspapers)
- Geographical units (town, census tract, state)
- Social interactions (dyadic relations, divorces, arrests)

Why is it called the unit of analysis and not something else (like, the unit of sampling)? Because *it is the analysis you do in your study that determines what the unit is.* For instance, if you are comparing the children in two classrooms on achievement test scores, the unit is the individual child because you have a score for each child. On the other hand, if you are comparing the two classes on classroom climate, your unit of analysis is the group, in this case the classroom, because you only have a classroom climate score for the class as a whole and not for each individual student.

For different analyses in the same study, you may have different units of analysis. If you decide to base an analysis on student scores, the individual is the unit. However you might decide to compare average classroom performance. In this case, since the data that goes into the analysis is the average itself (and not the individuals' scores) the unit of analysis is actually the group. Even though you had data at the student level, you use aggregates in the analysis. In many areas of social research, these hierarchies of analysis units have become particularly important and have spawned a whole area of statistical analysis sometimes referred to as ***hierarchical modeling***. This is true in education, for instance, where a researcher might compare classroom performance data but collect achievement data at the individual student level.

A *fallacy* is an error in reasoning, usually based on mistaken assumptions. Researchers are familiar with all the ways they could go wrong and the fallacies they are susceptible to. Here, I discuss two of the most important.

The ***ecological fallacy*** occurs when you make conclusions about individuals based only on analyses of group data. For instance, assume that you measured the math scores of a particular classroom and found that they had the highest average score in the district. Later (probably at the mall) you run into one of the kids from that class and you think to yourself, 'She must be a math whiz.' Aha! Fallacy! Just because she comes from the class with the highest *average* doesn't mean that she is automatically a high-scorer in math. She could be the lowest math scorer in a class that otherwise consists of math geniuses.

An ***exception fallacy*** is sort of the reverse of the ecological fallacy. It occurs when you reach a group conclusion on the basis of exceptional cases. This kind of fallacious reasoning is at the core of a lot of sexism and racism. The stereotype is of the guy who sees a woman make a driving error and concludes that women are terrible drivers. Wrong! Fallacy!

Both of these fallacies point to some of the traps that exist in research and in everyday reasoning. They also point out how important it is to do research. It is important to determine empirically how individuals perform, rather than simply rely on group averages. Similarly, it is important to look at whether there are correlations between certain behaviors and certain groups.

1-1h The Unit of Analysis

1-1i Two Research Fallacies

1-2 Philosophy of Research

You probably think of research as something abstract and complicated. It can be, but you'll see (I hope) that if you understand the different parts or phases of a research project and how these fit together, it's not nearly as complicated as it may seem at first glance. A research project has a well-known structure: a beginning, middle, and end. I introduce the basic **phases** of a research project in the section titled "Structure of Research." Here, I also introduce some important distinctions in research: the different types of questions you can ask in a research project; and, the major components or parts of a research project.

Before the modern idea of research emerged, there was a term for what philosophers used to call research: logical reasoning. So, it should come as no surprise that some of the basic distinctions in logic have carried over into contemporary research. In the section "Deduction and Induction" later in this chapter, I discuss how two major logical systems, the inductive and deductive methods of reasoning, are related to modern research.

Okay, you knew that no introduction would be complete without considering something having to do with assumptions and philosophy. (I thought I very cleverly snuck in the stuff about logic in the last paragraph.) All research is based on assumptions about how the world is perceived and how you can best come to understand it. Of course, nobody really *knows* how you can best understand the world, and philosophers have been arguing about that question for at least two millennia now, so all I'm going to do is look at how most contemporary social scientists approach the question of how you know about the world around you. Two major philosophical schools of thought are considered—Positivism and Post-Positivism—that are especially important perspectives for contemporary social research. (I'm only considering positivism and post-positivism here because these are the major schools of thought. Forgive me for not considering the hotly debated alternatives like relativism, subjectivism, hermeneutics, deconstructivism, constructivism, feminism, and so on.)

Quality is one of the most important issues in research. I introduce the idea of validity to refer to the quality of various conclusions you might reach based on a research project. Here's where I have to give you the pitch about validity. When I mention validity, most students roll their eyes, curl up into a fetal position, or go to sleep. They think validity is just something abstract and philosophical (and I guess it is at some level). But I think if you can understand *validity*—the principles that are used to judge the quality of research—you'll be able to do much more than just complete a research project. You'll be able to be a virtuoso at research because you'll have an understanding of *why* you need to do certain things to ensure quality. You won't just be plugging in standard procedures you learned in school—sampling method X, measurement tool Y—you'll be able to help create the next generation of research technology.

1-2a Structure of Research

Most research projects share the same general structure. You might think of this structure as following the shape of an hourglass as shown in Figure 1.5. The research process usually starts with a broad area of interest, the initial problem that the researcher wishes to study. For instance, the researcher could be interested in how to use computers to improve the performance of students in mathematics; but this initial interest is far too broad to study in any single research project. (It might not even be addressable in a lifetime of research.) The researcher has to narrow the question down to one that can reasonably be studied in a research project. This might involve formulating a hypothesis or a focus question.

For instance, the researcher might hypothesize that a particular method of computer instruction in math will improve the ability of elementary school students in a specific district. At the narrowest point of the research hourglass, the researcher is engaged in direct measurement or observation of the question of interest.

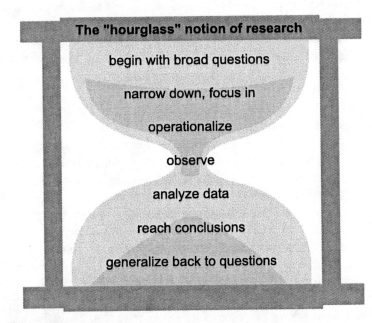

The "hourglass" notion of research

begin with broad questions

narrow down, focus in

operationalize

observe

analyze data

reach conclusions

generalize back to questions

Figure 1.5
The hourglass metaphor for the research process.

Once the basic data is collected, the researcher begins trying to understand it, usually by analyzing it in a variety of ways. Even for a single hypothesis, there are a number of analyses a researcher might typically conduct. At this point, the researcher begins to formulate some initial conclusions about what happened as a result of the computerized math program. Finally, the researcher often will attempt to address the original broad question of interest by generalizing from the results of this specific study to other related situations. For instance, on the basis of strong results indicating that the math program had a positive effect on student performance, the researcher might conclude that other school districts similar to the one in the study might expect similar results.

Components of a Study

What are the basic components or parts of a research study? Here, I'll describe the basic components involved in a causal study. Because causal studies presuppose descriptive and relational questions, many of the components of causal studies will also be found in descriptive and relational studies.

Most social research originates from some general problem or question. You might, for instance, be interested in which programs enable the unemployed to get jobs. Usually, the problem is broad enough that you could not hope to address it adequately in a single research study. Consequently, the problem is typically narrowed down to a more specific *research question* that can be addressed. The research question is often stated in the context of some theory that has been advanced to address the problem. For instance, you might have the theory that ongoing support services are needed to assure that the newly employed remain employed. The research question is the central issue being addressed in the study and is often phrased in the language of theory. For instance, a research question might be:

Is a program of supported employment more effective (than no program at all) at keeping newly employed persons on the job?

The problem with such a question is that it is still too general to be studied directly. Consequently, in most research, an even more specific statement, called an *hypothesis* is developed that describes in *operational* terms exactly what you think will happen in the study (see the section, Hypotheses, earlier in this chapter). For instance, the hypothesis for your employment study might be something like the following:

The Metropolitan Supported Employment Program will significantly increase rates of employment after six months for persons who are newly employed (after being out of work for at least one year) compared with persons who receive no comparable program.

Notice that this hypothesis is specific enough that a reader can understand quite well what the study is trying to assess.

In causal studies, there are at least two major variables of interest, the cause and the effect. Usually the cause is some type of event, program, or treatment. A distinction is made between causes that the researcher can control (such as a program) versus causes that occur naturally or outside the researcher's influence (such as a change in interest rates, or the occurrence of an earthquake). The effect is the outcome that you wish to study. For both the cause and effect, a distinction is made between the idea of them (the construct) and how they are actually manifested in reality. For instance, when you think about what a program of support services for the newly employed might be, you are thinking of the construct. On the other hand, the real world is not always what you think it is. In research, a distinction is made between your view of an entity (the construct) and the entity as it exists (the *operationalization*). Ideally, the two should agree. Social research is always conducted in a social context. Researchers ask people questions, observe families interacting, or measure the opinions of people in a city. The units that participate in the project are important components of any research project. Units are directly related to the question of sampling. In most projects, it's not possible to involve all of the people it is desirable to involve. For instance, in studying a program of support services for the newly employed, you can't possibly include in your study everyone in the world, or even in the country, who is newly employed. Instead, you have to try to obtain a representative sample of such people. When sampling, a distinction is made between the theoretical population of interest and the final sample that is actually included in the study. Usually the term *units* refers to the *people* that are sampled and from whom information is gathered; but for some projects the units are organizations, groups, or geographical entities like cities or towns. Sometimes the sampling strategy is multilevel; a number of cities are selected and within them families are sampled.

In causal studies, the interest is in the effects of some cause on one or more *outcomes*. The outcomes are directly related to the research problem; usually the greatest interest is in outcomes that are most reflective of the problem. In the hypothetical supported-employment study, you would probably be most interested in measures of employment—is the person currently employed, or, what is his or her rate of absenteeism.

Finally, in a causal study, the effects of the cause of interest (for example, the program) are usually compared to other conditions (for example, another program or no program at all). Thus, a key component in a causal study concerns how you decide which units (people) receive the program and which are placed in an alternative condition. This issue is directly related to the research design that you use in the study. One of the central themes in research design is determining how people wind up in or are placed in various programs or treatments that you are comparing. These, then, are the major components in a causal study:

- The research problem
- The research question
- The program (cause)
- The units
- The outcomes (effect)
- The design

In logic, a distinction is often made between two broad methods of reasoning known as the deductive and inductive approaches.

Deductive reasoning works from the more general to the more specific (see Figure 1.6). Sometimes this is informally called a top-down approach. You might begin with thinking up a *theory* about your topic of interest. You then narrow that down into more specific *hypotheses* that you can test. You narrow down even further when you collect *observations* to address the hypotheses. This ultimately leads you to be able to test the hypotheses with specific data—a *confirmation* (or not) of your original theories.

1-2b Deduction and Induction

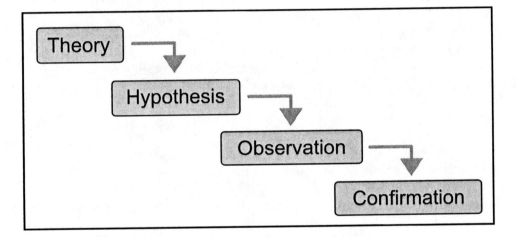

Figure 1.6
A schematic representation of deductive reasoning.

Inductive reasoning works the other way, moving from specific observations to broader generalizations and theories (see Figure 1.7). Informally, this is sometimes called a bottom up approach. (Please note that it's bottom up and *not* bottoms up, which is the kind of thing the bartender says to customers when he's trying to close for the night!) In inductive reasoning, you begin with specific observations and measures, begin detecting patterns and regularities, formulate some tentative hypotheses that you can explore, and finally end up developing some general conclusions or theories.

These two methods of reasoning have a different feel to them when you're conducting research. Inductive reasoning, by its nature, is more open-ended and exploratory, especially at the beginning. Deductive reasoning is narrower in nature and is concerned with testing or confirming hypotheses. Even though a particular study may look like it's purely deductive (for example, an experiment designed to test the hypothesized effects of some treatment on some outcome), most social research involves both inductive and deductive reasoning processes at some time in the project. In fact, it doesn't take a rocket scientist to see that you could assemble the two graphs from Figures 1.6 and 1.7 into a single circular one that continually cycles from theories down to observations and back up again to theories. Even in the most constrained experiment, the researchers might observe patterns in the data that lead them to develop new theories.

Figure 1.7
A schematic representation of inductive reasoning.

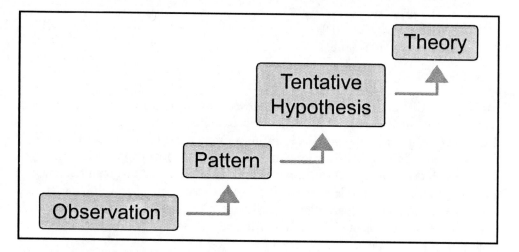

1-2c Positivism and Post-Positivism

Let's start this brief discussion of philosophy of science with a simple distinction between epistemology and methodology. The term *epistemology* comes from the Greek word epistêmê, their term for knowledge. In simple terms, epistemology is the philosophy of knowledge or of how you come to know. *Methodology* is also concerned with how you come to know, but is much more practical in nature. Methodology is focused on the specific ways—the methods—you can use to try to understand the world better. Epistemology and methodology are intimately related: the former involves the *philosophy* of how you come to know the world and the latter involves the *practice*.

When most people in society think about science, they think about some guy in a white lab coat working at a lab bench mixing up chemicals. They think of science as boring, cut-and-dried, and they think of the scientist as narrow-minded and esoteric (the ultimate nerd—think of the humorous but nonetheless mad scientist in the *Back to the Future* movies, for instance). Many of the stereotypes about science come from a period where science was dominated by a particular philosophy—positivism—that tended to support some of these views. Here, I want to suggest (no matter what the movie industry may think) that science has moved on in its thinking into an era of post-positivism where many of those stereotypes of the scientist no longer hold up.

Let's begin by considering what positivism is. In its broadest sense, *positivism* is a rejection of metaphysics (I leave it to you to look up that term if you're not familiar with it). Positivism holds that the goal of knowledge is simply to describe the phenomena that are experienced. The purpose of science is simply to stick to what can be observed and measured. Knowledge of anything beyond that, a positivist would hold, is impossible. When I think of positivism (and the related philosophy of logical positivism) I think of the behaviorists in mid-20th century psychology. These were the mythical rat runners who believed that psychology could only study what could be directly observed and measured. Since emotions, thoughts, and so on can't be directly observed (although it may be possible to measure some of the physical and physiological accompaniments), these were not legitimate topics for a scientific psychology. B. F. Skinner argued that psychology needed to concentrate only on the positive and negative reinforcers of behavior to predict how people will behave; everything else in between (like what the person is thinking) is irrelevant because it can't be measured.

In a positivist view of the world, science was seen as the way to get at truth, to understand the world well enough to predict and control it. The world and the universe were deterministic; they operated by laws of cause and effect that scientists could discern if they applied the unique approach of the scientific method. Science was largely a mechanistic or mechanical affair. Scientists use deductive reasoning to postulate theories that they can test. Based on the results of their studies, they may learn that their theory doesn't fit the facts well and so they need to revise their theory to better predict reality. The positivist believed in *empiricism*—the idea that observation and measurement was the core of the scientific endeavor. The key approach of the scientific method is the experiment, the attempt to discern natural laws through direct manipulation and observation.

Okay, I am exaggerating the positivist position (although you may be amazed at how close to this some of them actually came) to make a point. Things have changed in the typical views of science since the middle part of the 20th century. Probably the most important has been the shift away from positivism into what is termed post-positivism. By post-positivism, I don't mean a slight adjustment to or revision of the positivist position; *post-positivism* is a wholesale rejection of the central tenets of positivism. A post-positivist might begin by recognizing that the way scientists think and work and the way you think in your everyday life are not distinctly different. Scientific reasoning and common sense reasoning are essentially the same process. There is no essential difference between the two, only a difference in degree. Scientists, for example, follow specific procedures to assure that observations are verifiable, accurate, and consistent. In everyday reasoning, you don't always proceed so carefully. (Although, if you think about it, when the stakes are high, even in everyday life you become much more cautious about measurement. Think of the way most responsible parents keep continuous watch over their infants, noticing details that nonparents would never detect.)

One of the most common forms of post-positivism is a philosophy called *critical realism*. A critical realist believes that there is a reality independent of a person's thinking about it that science can study. (This is in contrast with a *subjectivist* who would hold that there is no external reality—each of us is making this all up.) Positivists were also realists. The difference is that the post-positivist critical realist recognizes that all observation is fallible and has error and that all theory is revisable. In other words, the critical realist is *critical* of a person's ability to know *reality* with certainty. Whereas the positivist believed that the goal of science was to uncover the truth, the post-positivist critical realist believes that *the goal of science is to hold steadfastly to the goal of getting it right about reality, even though this goal can never be perfectly achieved.*

Because all measurement is fallible, the post-positivist emphasizes the importance of multiple measures and observations, each of which may possess different types of error, and the need to use *triangulation* across these multiple error sources to try to get a better bead on what's happening in reality. The post-positivist also believes that all observations are theory-laden and that scientists (and everyone else, for that matter) are inherently biased by their cultural experiences, world views, and so on. This is not cause to despair, however. Just because I have my world view based on my experiences and you have yours doesn't mean that it is impossible to translate from each other's experiences or understand each other. That is, post-positivism rejects the relativist idea of the incommensurability of different perspectives, the idea that people can never understand each other because they come from different experiences and cultures. Most post-positivists are *constructivists* who believe that you construct your view of the world based on your perceptions of it. Because perception and observation are fallible, all constructions must be imperfect. So what is meant by *objectivity* in a post-positivist world? Positivists believed that objectivity was a characteristic that resided in the individual scientist. Scientists are responsible for putting aside their biases and beliefs and seeing the world as it really is. Post-positivists reject the idea that any individual can see the world perfectly as it really is. Everyone is biased and all observations are affected (theory-laden). The best hope for achieving objectivity is to triangulate across multiple fallible perspectives. Thus, objectivity is not the characteristic of an individual; it is inherently a social phenomenon. It is what multiple individuals are trying to achieve when they criticize each other's work. Objectivity is never achieved perfectly, but it can be approached. The best way to improve objectivity is to work publicly within the context of a broader contentious community of truth-seekers (including other scientists) who criticize each other's work. The theories that survive such intense scrutiny are a bit like the species that survive in the evolutionary struggle. (This theory is sometimes called the *natural selection theory of knowledge* and holds that ideas have survival value and that knowledge evolves through a process of variation, selection, and retention.) These theories have adaptive value and are probably as close as the human species can come to being objective and understanding reality.

Clearly, all of this stuff is not for the faint of heart. I've seen many a graduate student get lost in the maze of philosophical assumptions that contemporary philosophers of science argue about. Don't think that I believe this is not important stuff; but, in the end, I tend to turn pragmatist on these matters. Philosophers have been debating these issues for thousands of years and there is every reason to believe that they will continue to debate them for thousands of years more. Practicing researchers should check in on this debate from time to time. (Perhaps every hundred years or so would be about right.) Researchers should think about the assumptions they make about the world when they conduct research; but in the meantime, they can't wait for the philosophers to settle the matter. After all, they do have their own work to do.

1-2d Introduction to Validity

Validity can be defined as the best available approximation to the truth of a given proposition, inference, or conclusion. The first thing to ask is: "validity of *what?*" When people think about validity in research, they tend to think in terms of research components. You might say that a measure is a valid one, or that a valid sample was drawn, or that the design had strong validity; but all of those statements are technically incorrect. Measures, samples, and designs don't *have* validity—only propositions can be said to be valid. Technically, you should say that a measure leads to valid conclusions or that a sample enables valid inferences, and so on. It is a proposition, inference, or conclusion that can have validity.

Researchers make lots of different inferences or conclusions while conducting research. Many of these are related to the process of doing research and are not the major hypotheses of the study. Nevertheless, like the bricks that go into building a wall, these intermediate processes and methodological propositions provide the foundation for the substantive conclusions that they wish to address. For instance, virtually all social research involves measurement or observation, and, no matter what researchers measure or observe, they are concerned with whether they are measuring what they intend to measure or with how their observations are influenced by the circumstances in which they are made. They reach conclusions about the quality of their measures—conclusions that will play an important role in addressing the broader substantive issues of their study. When researchers talk about the validity of research, they are often referring to the many conclusions they reach about the quality of different parts of their research methodology.

Validity is typically subdivided into four types. Each type addresses a specific methodological question. To understand the types of validity, you have to know something about how researchers investigate a **research question**. Because all four validity types are really only operative when studying **causal** questions, I will use a causal study to set the context.

Figure 1.8 shows that two realms are involved in research. The first, on the top, is the land of theory. It is what goes on inside your head. It is where you keep your theories about how the world operates. The second, on the bottom, is the land of observations. It is the real world into which you translate your ideas: your programs, treatments, measures, and observations. When you conduct research, you are continually flitting back and forth between these two realms, between what you think about the world and what is going on in it. When you are investigating a cause-effect relationship, you have a theory (implicit or otherwise) of what the cause is (the **cause construct**). For instance, if you are testing a new educational program, you have an idea of what it would look like ideally. Similarly, on the effect side, you have an idea of what you are ideally trying to affect and measure (the **effect construct**). But each of these—the cause and the effect—have to be translated into real things, into a program or treatment and a measure or observational method. The term **operationalization** is used to describe the act of translating a construct into its manifestation. In effect, you take your idea and describe it as a series of operations or procedures. Now, instead of it only being an idea in your mind, it becomes a public entity that others can look at and examine for themselves. It is one thing, for instance, for you to say that you would like to measure self-esteem (a construct). But when you show a ten-item paper-and-pencil self-esteem measure that you developed for that purpose, others can look at it and understand more clearly what you intend by the term self-esteem.

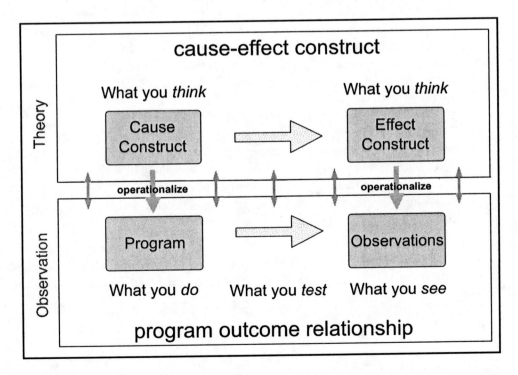

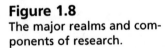

Figure 1.8
The major realms and components of research.

Now, back to explaining the four validity types. They build on one another, with two of them (conclusion and internal) referring to the land of observation on the bottom of Figure 1.8, one of them (construct) emphasizing the linkages between the bottom and the top, and the last (external) being primarily concerned about the range of the theory on the top.

Imagine that you want to examine whether use of a World Wide Web virtual classroom improves student understanding of course material. Assume that you took these two constructs, the **cause construct** (the WWW site) and the **effect construct** (understanding), and **operationalized** them, turned them into realities by constructing the WWW site and a measure of knowledge of the course material. Here are the four validity types and the question each addresses:

- **Conclusion Validity**: In this study, is there a **relationship** between the two variables? In the context of the example, the question might be worded: in this study, is there a relationship between the WWW site and knowledge of course material? There are several conclusions or inferences you might draw to answer such a question. You could, for example, conclude that there is a relationship. You might conclude that there is a positive relationship. You might infer that there is no relationship. You can assess the conclusion validity of each of these conclusions or inferences.

- **Internal Validity**: Assuming that there is a relationship in this study, is the relationship a *causal* one? Just because you find that use of the WWW site and knowledge are correlated, you can't necessarily assume that WWW site use *causes* the knowledge. Both could, for example, be caused by the same factor. For instance, it may be that wealthier students, who have greater resources, would be more likely to have access to a WWW site and would excel on objective tests. When you want to make a claim that your program or treatment caused the outcomes in your study, you can consider the internal validity of your causal claim.

- **Construct Validity**: Assuming that there is a causal relationship in this study, can you claim that the program reflected your *construct* of the program well and that your measure reflected well your idea of the *construct* of the measure? In simpler terms, did you implement the program you intended to implement and did you measure the outcome you wanted to measure? In yet other terms, did you operationalize well the ideas of the cause and the effect? When your research is over, you would like to be able to conclude that you did a credible job of operationalizing your constructs—you can assess the construct validity of this conclusion.

- **External Validity**: Assuming that there is a causal relationship in this study between the constructs of the cause and the effect, can you *generalize* this effect to other persons, places, or times? You are likely to make some claims that your research findings have implications for other groups and individuals in other settings and at other times. When you do, you can examine the external validity of these claims.

Notice how the question that each validity type addresses presupposes an affirmative answer to the previous one. This is what I mean when I say that the validity types build on one another. Figure 1.9 shows the idea of cumulativeness as a staircase, along with the key question for each validity type.

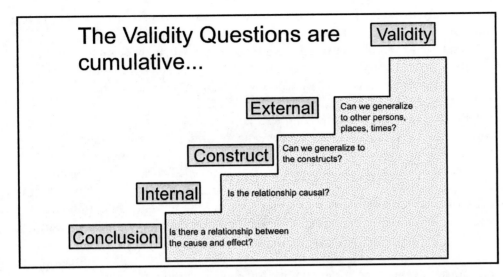

Figure 1.9
The validity staircase, showing the major question for each type of validity.

For any inference or conclusion, there are always possible ***threats to validity***—reasons the conclusion or inference might be wrong. Ideally, you try to reduce the plausibility of the most likely threats to validity, thereby leaving as most plausible the conclusion reached in the study. For instance, imagine a study examining whether there is a relationship between the amount of training in a specific technology and subsequent rates of use of that technology. Because the interest is in a relationship, it is considered an issue of ***conclusion validity***. Assume that the study is completed and no significant correlation between amount of training and adoption rates is found. On this basis, it is *concluded* that there is no relationship between the two. How could this conclusion be wrong—that is, what are the threats to validity? For one, it's possible that there isn't sufficient statistical power to detect a relationship even if it exists. Perhaps the sample size is too small or the measure of amount of training is unreliable. Or maybe assumptions of the correlational test are violated given the variables used. Perhaps there were random irrelevancies in the study setting or random heterogeneity in the respondents that increased the variability in the data and made it harder to see the relationship of interest. The inference that there is no relationship will be stronger—have greater conclusion validity—if you can show that these alternative explanations are not credible. The distributions might be examined to see whether they conform with assumptions of the statistical test, or analyses conducted to determine whether there is sufficient statistical power.

The theory of validity and the many lists of specific threats provide a useful scheme for assessing the quality of research conclusions. The theory is general in scope and applicability, well-articulated in its philosophical suppositions, and virtually impossible to explain adequately in a few minutes. As a framework for judging the quality of evaluations, it is indispensable and well worth understanding.

1-3 Ethics in Research

This is a time of profound change in the understanding of the ethics of applied social research. From the time immediately after World War II until the early 1990s, there was a gradually developing consensus about the key ethical principles that should underlie the research endeavor. Two marker events stand out (among many others) as symbolic of this consensus. The Nuremberg War Crimes Trial following World War II brought to public view the ways German scientists had used captive human subjects as subjects in often gruesome experiments. In the 1950s and 1960s, the Tuskegee Syphilis Study involved the withholding of known effective treatment for syphilis from African-American participants who were infected. Events like these forced the reexamination of ethical standards and the gradual development of a consensus that potential human subjects needed to be protected from being used as guinea pigs in scientific research.

By the 1990s, the dynamics of the situation changed. Cancer patients and persons with AIDS fought publicly with the medical research establishment about the length of time needed to get approval for and complete research into potential cures for fatal diseases. In many cases, it is the ethical assumptions of the previous thirty years that drive this go-slow mentality. According to previous thinking, it is better to risk denying treatment for a while until there is enough confidence in a treatment, than risk harming innocent people (as in the Nuremberg and Tuskegee events). Recently, however, people threatened with fatal illness have been saying to the research establishment that they *want* to be test subjects, even under experimental conditions of considerable risk. Several vocal and articulate patient groups who wanted to be experimented on came up against an ethical review system designed to protect them from being the subjects of experiments!

Although the last few years in the ethics of research have been tumultuous ones, a new consensus is beginning to evolve that involves the stakeholder groups most affected by a problem participating more actively in the formulation of guidelines for research. Although it's not entirely clear, at present, what the new consensus will be, it is almost certain that it will not fall at either extreme: protecting against human experimentation at all costs versus allowing anyone who is willing to be the subject of an experiment.

1-3a The Language of Ethics

As in every other aspect of research, the area of ethics has its own vocabulary. In this section, I present some of the most important language regarding ethics in research.

The principle of **voluntary participation** requires that people not be coerced into participating in research. This is especially relevant where researchers had previously relied on captive audiences for their subjects—prisons, universities, and places like that. Closely related to the notion of voluntary participation is the requirement of **informed consent**. Essentially, this means that prospective research participants must be fully informed about the procedures and risks involved in research and must give their consent to participate. Ethical standards also require that researchers not put participants in a situation where they might be at *risk of harm* as a result of their participation. Harm can be defined as both physical and psychological. Two standards are applied to help protect the privacy of research participants. Almost all research guarantees the participants **confidentiality**; they are assured that identifying information will not be made available to anyone who is not directly involved in the study. The stricter standard is the principle of **anonymity**, which essentially means that the participant will remain anonymous throughout the study, even to the researchers themselves. Clearly, the anonymity standard is a stronger guarantee of privacy, but it is sometimes difficult to accomplish, especially in situations where participants have to be measured at multiple time points (for example in a pre-post study). Increasingly, researchers have had to deal with the ethical issue of a person's **right to service**. Good research practice often requires the use of a no-treatment control group—a group of participants who do *not* get the treatment or program that is being studied. But when that treatment or program may have beneficial effects, persons assigned to the no-treatment control may feel their rights to equal access to services are being curtailed.

Even when clear ethical standards and principles exist, at times the need to do accurate research runs up against the rights of potential participants. No set of standards can possibly anticipate every ethical circumstance. Furthermore, there needs to be a procedure that assures that researchers will consider all relevant ethical issues in formulating research plans. To address such needs most institutions and organizations have formulated an *Institutional Review Board (IRB)*, a panel of persons who reviews grant proposals with respect to ethical implications and decides whether additional actions need to be taken to assure the safety and rights of participants. By reviewing proposals for research, IRBs also help protect the organization and the researcher against potential legal implications of neglecting to address important ethical issues of participants.

1-4 Conceptualizing

One of the most difficult aspects of research—and one of the least discussed—is how to develop the idea for the research project in the first place. In training students, most faculty members simply assume that if students read enough of the research in an area of interest, they will somehow magically be able to produce sensible ideas for further research. Now, that may be true. And heaven knows that's the way researchers have been doing this higher education thing for some time now; but it troubles me that they haven't been able to do a better job of helping their students learn *how* to formulate good research problems. One thing they can do (and some texts at least cover this at a surface level) is to give students a better idea of how professional researchers typically generate research ideas. Some of this is introduced in the discussion of problem formulation that follows.

But maybe researchers can do even better than that. Why can't they turn some of their expertise in developing methods into methods that students and researchers can use to help them formulate ideas for research. I've been working on that area intensively for over a decade now, and I came up with a structured approach that groups can use to map out their ideas on any topic. This approach, called *concept mapping* (see section on concept mapping later in this chapter) can be used by research teams to help them clarify and map out the key research issues in an area, to help them *operationalize* the programs or interventions or the outcome measures for their study. The concept-mapping method isn't the only method around that might help researchers formulate good research problems and projects. Virtually any method that's used to help individuals and groups think more effectively would probably be useful in research formulation; but concept mapping is a good example of a structured approach and will introduce you to the idea of conceptualizing research in a more formalized way.

"Well begun is half done" —Aristotle, quoting an old proverb

1-4a Problem Formulation

Where Research Topics Come From

So how do researchers come up with the idea for a research project? Probably one of the most common sources of research ideas is the experience of *practical problems in the field*. Many researchers are directly engaged in social, health, or human service program implementation and come up with their ideas based on what they see happening around them. Others aren't directly involved in service contexts, but work with (or survey) people to learn what needs to be better understood. Many of the ideas would strike the outsider as silly or worse. For instance, in health services areas, there is great interest in the problem of back injuries among nursing staff. It's not necessarily the thing that comes first to mind when you think about the health care field; but if you reflect on it for a minute longer, it should be obvious that nurses and nursing staff do an awful lot of lifting while performing their jobs. They lift and push heavy equipment, and they lift and push heavy patients! If 5 or 10 out of every hundred nursing staff were to strain their backs on average over the period of one year, the costs would be enormous and that's pretty much what's happening. Even minor injuries can result in increased absenteeism. Major ones can result in lost jobs and expensive medical bills. The nursing industry figures this problem costs tens of millions of dollars annually in increased health care. Additionally, the health-care industry has developed a number of approaches, many of them educational, to try to reduce the scope and cost of the problem. So, even though it might seem silly at first, many of these practical problems that arise in practice can lead to extensive research efforts.

Another source for research ideas is the *literature in your specific field*. Certainly, many researchers get ideas for research by reading the literature and thinking of ways to extend or refine previous research. Another type of literature that acts as a source of good research ideas is the **Requests For Proposals (RFPs)** that are published by government agencies and some companies. These RFPs describe some problem that the agency would like researchers to address; they are virtually handing the researcher an idea. Typically, the RFP describes the problem that needs addressing, the contexts in which it operates, the approach they would like you to take to investigate to address the problem, and the amount they would be willing to pay for such research. Clearly, there's nothing like potential research funding to get researchers to focus on a particular research topic.

Finally, let's not forget the fact that many researchers simply *think up their research* topic on their own. Of course, no one lives in a vacuum, so you would expect that the ideas you come up with on your own are influenced by your background, culture, education, and experiences.

Feasibility

Soon after you get an idea for a study, reality begins to kick in and you begin to think about whether the study is feasible at all. Several major considerations come into play. Many of these involve making *tradeoffs between rigor and practicality*. Performing a scientific study may force you to do things you wouldn't do normally. You might want to ask everyone who used an agency in the past year to fill in your evaluation survey only to find that there were thousands of people and it would be prohibitively expensive. Or, you might want to conduct an in-depth interview on your subject of interest only to learn that the typical participant in your study won't willingly take the hour that your interview requires. If you had unlimited resources and unbridled control over the circumstances, you would always be able to do the best quality research; but those ideal circumstances seldom exist, and researchers are almost always forced to look for the best tradeoffs they can find to get the rigor they desire.

When you are determining the project's feasibility, you almost always need to bear in mind several practical considerations. First, you have to think about *how long the research will take* to accomplish. Second, you have to question whether any important *ethical constraints* require consideration. Third, you must determine whether you can acquire the *cooperation* needed to take the project to its successful conclusion. And finally, you must determine the degree to which the costs will be manageable. Failure to consider any of these factors can mean disaster later.

The Literature Review

One of the most important early steps in a research project is the conducting of the literature review. This is also one of the most humbling experiences you're likely to have. Why? Because you're likely to find out that just about any worthwhile idea you will have has been thought of before, at least to some degree. I frequently have students who come to me complaining that they couldn't find anything in the literature that was related to their topic. And virtually every time they have said that, I was able to show them that was only true because they only looked for articles that were *exactly* the same as their research topic. A literature review is designed to identify related research, to set the current research project within a conceptual and theoretical context. When looked at that way, almost no topic is so new or unique that you can't locate relevant and informative related research.

Here are some tips about conducting the literature review. First, *concentrate your efforts on the scientific literature.* Try to determine what the most credible research journals are in your topical area and start with those. Put the greatest emphasis on research journals that use a blind or juried review system. In a blind or juried review, authors submit potential articles to a journal editor who solicits several reviewers who agree to give a critical review of the paper. The paper is sent to these reviewers with no identification of the author so that there will be no personal bias (either for or against the author). Based on the reviewers' recommendations, the editor can accept the article, reject it, or recommend that the author revise and resubmit it. Articles in journals with blind review processes are likely to have a fairly high level of credibility. Second, *do the review early* in the research process. You are likely to learn a lot in the literature review that will help you determine what the necessary tradeoffs are. After all, previous researchers also had to face tradeoff decisions.

What should you look for in the literature review? First, you might be able to find a study that is quite similar to the one you are thinking of doing. Since all credible research studies have to review the literature themselves, you can check their literature review to get a quick start on your own. Second, prior research will help ensure that you include all of the major relevant constructs in your study. You may find that other similar studies routinely look at an outcome that you might not have included. Your study would not be judged credible if it ignored a major construct. Third, the literature review will help you to find and select appropriate measurement instruments. You will readily see what measurement instruments researchers used themselves in contexts similar to yours. Finally, the literature review will help you to anticipate common problems in your research context. You can use the prior experiences of others to avoid common traps and pitfalls.

1-4b Concept Mapping

Social scientists have developed a number of methods and processes that might help you formulate a research project. I would include among these at least the following: brainstorming, brainwriting, nominal group techniques, focus groups, affinity mapping, Delphi techniques, facet theory, and qualitative text analysis. Here, I'll show you a method that I have developed, called **concept mapping**, which is especially useful for research problem formulation and illustrates some of the advantages of applying social-science methods to conceptualizing research problems.

Concept mapping is a general method that can be used to help any individual or group to describe ideas about some topic in a pictorial form. Several methods currently go by names such as concept mapping, mental mapping, or concept webbing. All of them are similar in that they result in a picture of someone's ideas; but the kind of concept mapping I want to describe here is different in a number of important ways. First, it is primarily a group process and so it is especially well suited for situations where teams or groups of researchers have to work together. The other methods work primarily with individuals. Second, it uses a structured facilitated approach. Specific steps are followed by a trained facilitator in helping a group articulate its ideas and understand them more clearly. Third, the core of concept mapping consists of several state-of-the-art multivariate statistical methods that analyze the input from all of the individuals and yield an aggregate group product. Finally, the method requires the use of specialized computer programs that can handle the data from this type of process and accomplish the correct analysis and mapping procedures.

Although concept mapping is a general method, it is particularly useful for helping social researchers and research teams develop and detail ideas for research. It is especially valuable when researchers want to involve relevant stakeholder groups in the act of creating the research project. Although concept mapping is used for many purposes—strategic planning, product development, market analysis, decision making, measurement development—I concentrate here on its potential for helping researchers formulate their projects.

So what is concept mapping? Essentially, concept mapping is a structured process, focused on a topic or construct of interest, involving input from one or more participants, that produces an interpretable pictorial view (concept map) of their ideas and concepts and how these are interrelated. Concept mapping helps people to think more effectively as a group without losing their individuality. It helps groups capture complex ideas without trivializing them or losing detail (see Figure 1.10).

Figure 1.10
The steps in the concept-mapping process.

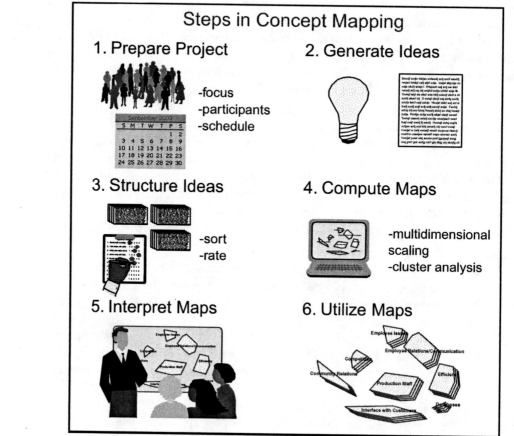

A concept-mapping process involves six steps that can take place in a single day or can be spread out over weeks or months depending on the situation. The process can be accomplished with everyone sitting around a table in the same room or with the participants distributed across the world using the Internet. The steps are as follows:

- **Preparation.** Step one accomplishes three things. The facilitator of the mapping process works with the initiator(s) (those who requested the process initially) to identify who the participants will be. A mapping process can have hundreds or even thousands of stakeholders participating, although there is usually a relatively small group of between 10 and 20 stakeholders involved. Second, the initiator works with the stakeholders to develop the focus for the project. For instance, the group might decide to focus on defining a program or treatment, or it might choose to map all of the expected outcomes. Finally, the group decides on an appropriate schedule for the mapping.
- **Generation.** The stakeholders develop a large set of statements that address the focus. For instance, they might generate statements describing all of the specific activities that will constitute a specific social program, or generate statements describing specific outcomes that could result from participating in a program. A variety of methods can be used to accomplish this including traditional brainstorming, brainwriting, nominal group techniques, focus groups, qualitative text analysis, and so on. The group can generate up to 200 statements in a concept-mapping project. This is a software limitation, in most situations, around 100 statements is the practical limit in terms of the number of statements they can reasonably handle.
- **Structuring.** The participants do two things during structuring. First, each participant sorts the statements into piles of similar statements. They often do this by sorting a deck of cards that has one statement on each card; but they can also do this directly on a computer by dragging the statements into piles that they create. They can have as few or as many piles as they want. Each participant names each pile with a short descriptive label. Then each participant rates each of the statements on some scale. Usually the statements are rated on a 1-to-5 scale for their relative importance, where a 1 means the statement is relatively unimportant compared to all the rest; a 3 means that it is moderately important, and a 5 means that it is extremely important.
- **Representation.** This is where the analysis is done; this is the process of taking the sort and rating input and representing it in map form. Two major statistical analyses are used. The first—multidimensional scaling—takes the sort data across all participants and develops the basic map where each statement is a point on the map and statements that were piled together by more people are closer to each other on the map. The second analysis—cluster analysis—takes the output of the multidimensional scaling (the point map) and partitions the map into groups of statements or ideas, into clusters. If the statements describe program activities, the clusters show how to group them into logical groups of activities. If the statements are specific outcomes, the clusters might be viewed as outcome constructs or concepts.
- **Interpretation.** The facilitator works with the stakeholder group to help develop its own labels and interpretations for the various maps.

- **Utilization**. The stakeholders use the maps to help address the original focus. On the program side, stakeholders use the maps as a visual framework for operationalizing the program; on the outcome side, the maps can be used as the basis for developing measures and displaying results.

The concept-mapping process described here is a structured approach to conceptualizing. However, even researchers who do not appear to be following a structured approach are likely to be using similar steps informally. For instance, all researchers probably go through an internal exercise that is analogous to the brainstorming step described previously. They may not actually brainstorm and write their ideas down, but they probably do something like that informally. After they've generated their ideas, they structure or organize them in some way. For each step in the formalized concept-mapping process you can probably think of analogous ways that researchers accomplish the same task, even if they don't follow such formal approaches. More formalized methods like concept mapping most certainly have benefits over the typical informal approach. For instance, with concept mapping there is an objective record of what was done in each step. Researchers can be both more public and more accountable. A structured process also opens up new possibilities. With concept mapping, it is possible to imagine more effective multiple researcher conceptualization and involvement of other stakeholder groups such as program developers, funders, and clients.

1-5 Evaluation Research

One specific form of social research—evaluation research—is of particular interest here. The following section, Introduction to Evaluation Research, presents an overview of what evaluation is and how it differs from social research generally. I also introduce several evaluation models to give you some perspective on the evaluation endeavor. Evaluation should not be considered in a vacuum. Here, evaluation is viewed as embedded within a larger planning-evaluation cycle.

Evaluation can be a threatening activity. Many groups and organizations struggle with how to build a good evaluation capability into their everyday activities and procedures. This is essentially an organizational culture issue. In the following sections, some of the issues a group or organization needs to address to develop an evaluation culture that works in their context are considered.

1-5a Introduction to Evaluation

Evaluation is a methodological area that is closely related to, but distinguishable from, more traditional social research. Evaluation utilizes many of the same methodologies used in traditional social research; but because evaluation takes place within a political and organizational context, it requires group skills, management ability, political dexterity, sensitivity to multiple stakeholders, and other skills that social research in general does not rely on as much. In the following sections, I introduce the idea of evaluation and some of the major terms and issues in the field.

Definitions of Evaluation

Probably the most frequently given definition of evaluation is *the systematic assessment of the worth or merit of some object.* This definition is hardly perfect. Many types of evaluations do not *necessarily* result in an assessment of worth or merit—descriptive studies, implementation analyses, and formative evaluations, to name a few. Better perhaps is a definition that emphasizes the information-processing and feedback functions of evaluation. For instance, one might say that *evaluation is the systematic acquisition and assessment of information to provide useful feedback about some object.*

Both definitions agree that evaluation is a systematic endeavor and both use the deliberately ambiguous term *object*, which could refer to a program, policy, technology, person, need, activity, and so on. The latter definition emphasizes acquiring and assessing information rather than assessing worth or merit because all evaluation work involves collecting and sifting through data, making judgments about the validity of the information and of inferences derived from it, whether or not an assessment of worth or merit results.

The Goals of Evaluation

The generic goal of most evaluations is to provide useful feedback to a variety of audiences including sponsors, donors, client groups, administrators, staff, and other relevant constituencies. Most often, feedback is perceived as useful if it aids in decision making; but the relationship between an evaluation and its impact is not a simple one; studies that seem critical sometimes fail to influence short-term decisions, and studies that initially seem to have no influence can have a delayed impact when more congenial conditions arise. Despite this, the broad consensus is that the major goal of evaluation should be to influence decision making or policy formulation through the provision of empirically driven feedback.

Evaluation Strategies

The term, evaluation strategies, means broad, overarching perspectives on evaluation. These strategies encompass the most general groups or camps of evaluators; although, at its best, evaluation work borrows eclectically from the perspectives of all these camps. Four major groups of evaluation strategies are discussed here:

- **Scientific-experimental models** These are probably the most historically dominant evaluation strategies. Taking their values and methods from the sciences—especially the social sciences—they prioritize on the desirability of impartiality, accuracy, objectivity, and the validity of the generated information. Included under scientific-experimental models would be the tradition of experimental and quasi-experimental designs; objectives-based research that comes from education; econometrically oriented perspectives including cost-effectiveness and cost-benefit analysis; and the recent articulation of theory-driven evaluation.

- **Management-oriented systems models** Two of the most common of these are the Program Evaluation and Review Technique (PERT) and the Critical Path Method (CPM). Both have been widely used in business and government in this country. It would also be legitimate to include the Logical Framework or Logframe model developed at U.S. Agency for International Development and general systems theory and operations research approaches in this category. Two management-oriented systems models were originated by evaluators: the UTOS model where U stands for Units, T for Treatments, O for Observing Observations, and S for Settings; and the CIPP model where the C stands for Context, the I for Input, the first P for Process, and the second P for Product. These management-oriented system models emphasize comprehensiveness in evaluation, placing evaluation within a larger framework of organizational activities.

- **Qualitative/anthropological models** These models emphasize the importance of observation, the need to retain the phenomenological quality of the evaluation context, and the value of subjective human interpretation in the evaluation process. Included in this category are the approaches known in evaluation as naturalistic or Fourth-Generation evaluation; the various qualitative schools; critical theory and art criticism approaches; and the grounded-theory approach of Glaser and Strauss among others.

- **Participant-oriented models** As the term suggests, these models emphasize the central importance of the evaluation participants, especially clients and users of the program or technology. Client-centered and stakeholder approaches are examples of participant-oriented models, as are consumer-oriented evaluation systems.

With all of these strategies to choose from, how do you decide which to use? Debates that rage within the evaluation profession—and they do rage—are generally battles between these different strategists, with each side claiming the superiority of its position. In reality, most good evaluators are familiar with all four categories and borrow from each as the need arises. There is no inherent incompatibility between these broad strategies; they each bring something valuable to the evaluation table. In fact, in recent years attention has increasingly turned to how one might integrate results from evaluations that use different strategies, carried out from different perspectives, and using different methods. Clearly, there are no simple answers here. The problems are complex, and the methodologies required will and should be varied.

Types of Evaluation

There are many different types of evaluations depending on the object being evaluated and the purpose of the evaluation. Perhaps the most important basic distinction in evaluation types is that between formative and summative evaluation. *Formative evaluations* strengthen or improve the object being evaluated; they help form it by examining the delivery of the program or technology, the quality of its implementation, and the assessment of the organizational context, personnel, procedures, inputs, and so on. *Summative evaluations*, in contrast, examine the effects or outcomes of some object. They summarize it by describing what happens subsequent to delivery of the program or technology; assessing whether the object can be said to have caused the outcome; determining the overall impact of the *causal* factor beyond only the immediate target outcomes; and estimating the relative costs associated with the object.

Formative evaluation includes several evaluation types:

- **Needs assessment** determines who needs the program, how great the need is, and what might work to meet the need.
- **Evaluability assessment** determines whether an evaluation is feasible and how stakeholders can help shape its usefulness.
- **Structured conceptualization** (for example, concept mapping) helps stakeholders define the program or technology, the target population, and the possible outcomes.
- **Implementation evaluation** monitors the fidelity of the program or technology delivery.
- **Process evaluation** investigates the process of delivering the program or technology, including alternative delivery procedures.

Summative evaluation can also be subdivided:

- **Outcome evaluations** investigate whether the program or technology caused demonstrable effects on specifically defined target outcomes.
- **Impact evaluation** is broader and assesses the overall or net effects—intended or unintended—of the program or technology as a whole.
- **Cost-effectiveness and cost-benefit analysis** address questions of efficiency by standardizing outcomes in terms of their dollar costs and values.
- **Secondary analysis** reexamines existing data to address new questions or use methods not previously employed.

- **Meta-analysis** integrates the outcome estimates from multiple studies to arrive at an overall or summary judgment on an evaluation question.

Evaluation Questions and Methods

Evaluators ask many different kinds of questions and use a variety of methods to address them. These are considered within the framework of formative and summative evaluation as presented in the previous section. In formative research the major questions and methodologies are as follows:

- **What is the definition and scope of the problem or issue, or what's the question?** Formulating and conceptualizing methods might be used, including brainstorming, focus groups, nominal group techniques, Delphi methods, brainwriting, stakeholder analysis, synectics, lateral thinking, input-output analysis, and *concept mapping.*
- **Where is the problem and how big or serious is it?** The most common method used here is needs assessment, which can include: analysis of existing data sources, and the use of sample surveys, interviews of constituent populations, qualitative research, expert testimony, and focus groups.
- **How should the program or technology be delivered to address the problem?** Some of the methods already listed apply here, as do detailing methodologies like simulation techniques, or multivariate methods like multi-attribute utility theory or exploratory causal modeling; decision-making methods; and project planning and implementation methods like flow charting, PERT/CPM, and project scheduling.
- **How well is the program or technology delivered?** Qualitative and quantitative monitoring techniques, the use of management information systems, and implementation assessment would be appropriate methodologies here.

The questions and methods addressed under summative evaluation include the following:

- **What type of evaluation is feasible?** Evaluability assessment can be used here, as well as standard approaches for selecting an appropriate evaluation design.
- **What was the effectiveness of the program or technology?** One would choose from observational and correlational methods for demonstrating whether desired effects occurred, and quasi-experimental and experimental designs for determining whether observed effects can reasonably be attributed to the intervention and not to other sources.
- **What is the net impact of the program?** Econometric methods for assessing cost effectiveness and cost/benefits would apply here, along with qualitative methods that enable you to summarize the full range of intended and unintended impacts.

Clearly, this introduction is not meant to be exhaustive. Each of these methods, and the many not mentioned, is supported by an extensive methodological research literature. This is a formidable set of tools; but the need to improve, update, and adapt these methods to changing circumstances means that methodological research and development needs to have a major place in evaluation work.

1-5b The Planning Evaluation Cycle

Often, evaluation is construed as part of a larger managerial or administrative process. Sometimes this is referred to as the *planning-evaluation cycle* (see Figure 1.11). The distinctions between planning and evaluation are not always clear; this cycle is described in many different ways with various phases claimed by both planners and evaluators. Usually, the first stage of such a cycle—the planning phase—is designed to elaborate a set of potential actions, programs, or technologies, and select the best for implementation. Depending on the organization and the problem being addressed, a planning process could involve any or all of these stages: the *formulation* of the problem, issue, or concern; the broad *conceptualization* of the major alternatives that might be considered; the *detailing* of these alternatives and their potential implications; the *evaluation* of the alternatives and the selection of the best one; and the *implementation* of the selected alternative. Although these stages are traditionally considered planning, a lot of evaluation work is involved. Evaluators are trained in needs assessment; they use methodologies—such as the **concept mapping** one presented earlier—that help in conceptualization and detailing, and they have the skills to help assess alternatives and make a choice of the best one.

Figure 1.11
The planning-evaluation cycle.

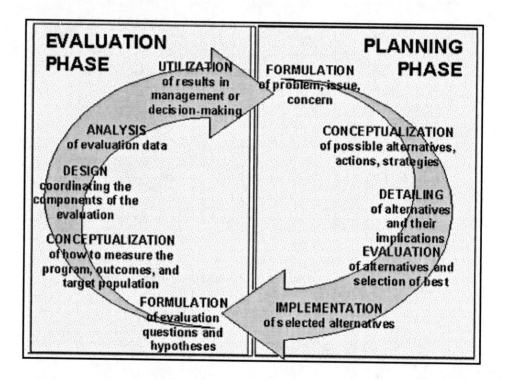

The evaluation phase also involves a sequence of stages that typically include the *formulation* of the major objectives, goals, and **hypotheses** of the program or technology; the *conceptualization* and **operationalization** of the major components of the evaluation (the program, participants, setting, and measures); the *design* of the evaluation, the *details* of how these components will be coordinated; the *analysis* of the information, both qualitative and quantitative; and the *utilization* of the evaluation results.

1-5c An Evaluation Culture

When you begin to practice applied social research or become a program evaluator, you are entering a community of social researchers, a culture of its own. What are the values of the culture? Or, perhaps more importantly, what *should* its values be? Here I provide a vision of the types of values I would like to see become an integral part of twenty-first century thought in general, and of the applied research community in particular. There is no special order of importance to the way these ideas are presented; I'll leave that ordering to subsequent efforts. As you read this discussion, ask yourself how similar these values are to your own. What values do you think the applied research community should adopt? Here are my views.

First, an evaluation culture will embrace an *action-oriented* perspective that actively seeks solutions to problems, trying out tentative ones, weighing the results and consequences of actions, all within an endless cycle of supposition-action-evidence-revision that characterizes good science and good management. This activist evaluation culture will encourage innovative approaches at all levels. However, well-intentioned activism by itself is not enough, and may at times be risky, dangerous, and lead to detrimental consequences. In an evaluation culture, you won't act for action's sake; you'll always attempt to assess the effects of your actions.

This evaluation culture will be an accessible, *teaching-oriented* one that emphasizes the unity of formal evaluation and everyday thought. Most evaluations will be simple, informal, efficient, practical, low-cost, and easily carried out and understood by nontechnicians. Evaluations won't just be delegated to one person or department; everyone will be encouraged to become involved in evaluating what they and their organizations do. Where technical expertise is needed experts will be encouraged to also educate others about the technical side of what they do, trying to find ways to explain their techniques and methods adequately for non-technicians. Considerable resources will be devoted to teaching others about evaluation principles.

An evaluation culture will be *diverse, inclusive, participatory, responsive, and fundamentally non-hierarchical.* World problems cannot be solved by simple silver-bullet solutions. There is growing recognition in many arenas that the most fundamental problems are systemic, interconnected, and inextricably linked to social and economic issues and factors. Solutions will involve husbanding the resources, talents, and insights of a wide range of people. The formulation of problems and potential solutions needs to involve a broad range of constituencies. More than just research skills will be needed. Especially important will be skills in negotiation and consensus-building processes. Evaluators are familiar with arguments for greater diversity and inclusiveness; they've been talking about stakeholder, participative, multiple-constituency research for nearly two decades. No one that I know is seriously debating anymore whether there should be a move to more inclusive participatory approaches. The real question seems to be how such work might best be accomplished, and despite all the rhetoric about the importance of participatory methods, there is a long way to go in learning how to accomplish them effectively.

An evaluation culture will be a *humble, self-critical* one. Researchers will openly acknowledge limitations and recognize that what is learned from a single evaluation study, however well designed, will almost always be equivocal and tentative. In this regard, I believe cowardice in research is too often undervalued. I find it wholly appropriate that evaluators resist being drawn into making decisions for others, although certainly evaluation results should help inform the decision makers. A cowardly approach helps prevent the evaluator from being drawn into the political context, helping assure the impartiality needed for objective assessment, and it protects the evaluator from taking responsibility for making decisions that should be left to those who have been duly-authorized and who have to live with the consequences. Most program decisions, especially decisions about whether to continue a program or close it down, must include more input than an evaluation alone can ever provide. While evaluators can help elucidate what has happened in the past or might happen under certain circumstances, it is the responsibility of the organization and society as a whole to determine what ought to happen. The debate about the appropriate role of an evaluator in the decision-making process is an extremely intense one right now in evaluation circles, and my position advocating a cowardly reluctance of the evaluator to undertake a decision-making role may well be in the minority. This issue needs to be debated vigorously, especially for politically complex, international-evaluation contexts.

An evaluation culture will need to be an *interdisciplinary* one, doing more than just grafting one discipline onto another through constructing multidiscipline research teams. Such teams are needed, of course, but I mean to imply something deeper, more personally internalized; a need to move toward being nondisciplinary, consciously putting aside the blinders of peoples' respective specialties in an attempt to foster a more whole view of the phenomena being studied. As programs being evaluated, it will be important to speculate about a broad range of implementation factors or potential consequences. It should be possible to anticipate some of the organizational and systems-related features of these programs, the economic factors that might enhance or reduce implementation, their social and psychological dimensions, and especially whether the ultimate utilizers can understand or know how to utilize and be willing to utilize the results of evaluation work. It should also be possible to anticipate a broad spectrum of potential consequences: system-related, production-related, economic, nutritional, social, and environmental.

This evaluation culture will also be an honest, *truth-seeking* one that stresses accountability and scientific credibility. In many quarters in contemporary society, it appears that people have given up on the ideas of truth and validity. An evaluation culture needs to hold to the goal of getting at the truth while at the same time honestly acknowledging the revisability of all scientific knowledge. It is important to be critical of those who have given up on the goal of getting it right about reality, especially those among the humanities and social sciences who argue that truth is entirely relative to the knower, objectivity an impossibility, and reality nothing more than a construction or illusion that cannot be examined publicly. For them, the goal of seeking the truth is inappropriate and unacceptable, and science a tool of oppression rather than a road to greater enlightenment. Philosophers have, of course, debated such issues for thousands of years and will undoubtedly do so for thousands more. In the evaluation culture it will be important to check in on their thinking from time to time, but until they settle these debates, it is necessary to hold steadfastly to the goal of getting at the truth—the goal of getting it right about reality.

This evaluation culture will be prospective and *forward looking*, anticipating where evaluation feedback will be needed rather than just reacting to situations as they arise. Simple, low-cost evaluation and monitoring information systems will be constructed when new programs or technology are initiated; it will not do to wait until a program is complete or a technology is in the field before turning attention to its evaluation.

Finally, the evaluation culture I envision is one that will emphasize fair, open, *ethical, and democratic* processes. This will require moving away from private ownership of and exclusive access to data. The data from all evaluations needs to be accessible to all interested groups, allowing more extensive independent, secondary analyses and opportunities for replication or refutation of original results. Open commentary and debate regarding the results of specific evaluations should be encouraged. Especially when multiple parties have a stake in such results, it is important for reporting procedures to include formal opportunities for competitive review and response. An evaluation culture must continually strive for greater understanding of the ethical dilemmas posed by research. The desire for valid, scientific inference will at times cause conflicts with ethical principles. The situation is likely to be especially complex in international-evaluation contexts where evaluations may involve multiple cultures and countries that are at different stages of economic development and have different value systems and morals. It is important to be ready to deal with potential ethical and political issues posed by research methodologies in an open, direct, and democratic manner.

Do you agree with the values I'm describing here? What other characteristics might this evaluation culture have? You tell me. There are many more values and characteristics that ought to be considered. For now, the ones mentioned previously, and others in the literature, provide a starting point for the discussion. I hope you will add to the list, and I encourage each of you to criticize these tentative statements I've offered about the extraordinary potential of the evaluation culture that is in the process of evolving today.

Part

Part
2

Sampling

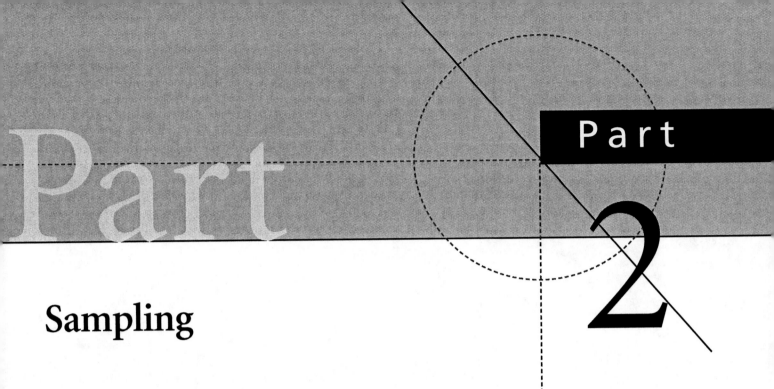

Chapter 2
Sampling

Sampling

Sampling is the process of selecting units (such as people and organizations) from a population of interest so that by studying the sample you can fairly generalize your results to the population from which the units were chosen. In this chapter, I begin by covering some of the key terms in sampling like population and sampling frame. Then, because some types of sampling rely on quantitative models, I'll talk about some of the statistical terms used in sampling. Finally, I'll discuss the major distinction between probability and nonprobability sampling methods and work through the major types in each.

Key Terms

area random sampling
bell curve
cluster random sampling
concept mapping
expert sampling
external validity
gradient of similarity
heterogeneity sampling
modal instance sampling
multi-stage sampling
nonprobability sampling
nonproportional quota
  sampling
population
population parameter
probability sampling
proportional quota sampling
Proximal Similarity Model
quota sampling
random selection
response
sample
sampling distribution
sampling error
sampling frame
sampling model
simple random sampling
snowball sampling
standard deviation
standard error
statistic
stratified random sampling
systematic random sample
validity

2-1 External Validity

To understand external validity, keep in mind that it is related to generalizing. Recall that validity refers to the approximate truth of propositions, inferences, or conclusions. So, *external validity* refers to the approximate truth of conclusions that involve generalizations. Put in more pedestrian terms, external validity is the degree to which the conclusions in your study would hold for other persons in other places and at other times.

Science approaches the providing of evidence for a generalization in two major ways. I'll call the first approach the *sampling model*. In the sampling model, you start by identifying the population you would like to generalize to (see Figure 2.1). Then, you draw a fair sample from that population and conduct your research with the sample. Finally, because the sample is representative of the population, you can automatically generalize your results back to the population. This approach has several problems. First, at the time of your study, you might not know what part of the population you will ultimately want to generalize to. Second, you may not be able to draw a fair or representative sample easily. Third, it's impossible to sample across all times that you might like to generalize to, such as next year.

Figure 2.1
The sampling model for external validity. The researcher draws a sample for a study from a defined population to generalize the results to the population.

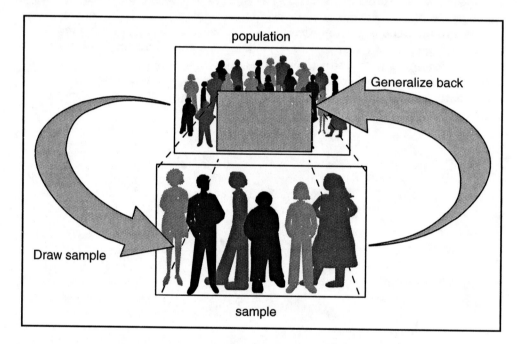

The second approach to generalizing is called the *Proximal Similarity Model* (see Figure 2.2). Proximal means nearby and similarity means. . . .well, it means similarity. The term proximal similarity was suggested by Donald T. Campbell as an appropriate relabeling of the term *external validity* (although he was the first to admit that it probably wouldn't catch on). With proximal similarity, you begin by thinking about different generalizability contexts and developing a theory about which contexts are more like your study and which are less so. For instance, you might imagine several settings that have people who are more similar to the people in your study or people who are less similar. This process also holds for times and places. When you place different contexts in terms of their relative similarities, you can call this implicit theoretical dimension a *gradient of similarity*. After you develop this proximal similarity framework, you can generalize. How? You can generalize the results of your study to other persons, places, or times that are more like (that is, more proximally similar to) your study. Notice that here, you can never generalize with certainty; these generalizations are always a question of more or less similar.

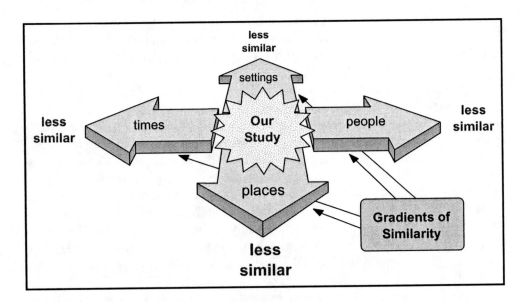

Figure 2.2
The proximal similarity
model for external validity.

A threat to *external validity* is an explanation of how you might be wrong in making a generalization. For instance, imagine that you conclude that the results of your study (which was done in a specific place, with certain types of people, and at a specific time) can be generalized to another context (for instance, another place, with slightly different people, at a slightly later time). In such a case, three major threats to external validity exist because there are three ways you could be wrong: people, places, and times. Your critics could, for example, argue that the results of your study were due to the unusual type of people who were in the study, or, they could claim that your results were obtained only because of the unusual place in which you performed the study. (Perhaps you did your educational study in a college town with lots of high-achieving, educationally oriented kids.) They might suggest that you did your study at a peculiar time. For instance, if you did your smoking-cessation study the week after the Surgeon General issued the well-publicized results of the latest smoking and cancer studies, you might get different results than if you had done it the week before.

2-1a Threats to External Validity

How can you improve external validity? One way, based on the sampling model, suggests that you do a good job of drawing a sample from a population. For instance, you should use random selection, if possible, rather than a nonrandom procedure. Additionally, once selected, you should try to assure that the respondents participate in your study and that you keep your dropout rates low. A second approach would be to use the theory of *proximal similarity* more effectively. How? Perhaps you could do a better job of describing the ways your contexts differ from others by providing data about the degree of similarity between various groups of people, places, and even times. You might even be able to map out the degree of proximal similarity among various contexts with a methodology like *concept mapping* as discussed in Chapter 1, "Foundations." Perhaps the best approach to criticisms of generalizations is simply to show critics that they're wrong—do your study in a variety of places, with different people, and at different times. That is, your external validity (ability to generalize) will be stronger the more you replicate your study.

2-1b Improving External Validity

2-2 Sampling Terminology

As with anything else in life you have to learn the language of an area if you're going to ever hope to use it. Here, I want to introduce several different terms for the major groups that are involved in a sampling process and the role that each group plays in the logic of sampling.

The major question that motivates sampling in the first place is: "Who do you want to generalize to?" (Or should it be: "To whom do you want to generalize?") In most social research, you are interested in more than just the people directly participating in your study. You would like to be able to talk in general terms and not be confined to only the people in your study. Now, at times you won't be concerned about generalizing. Maybe you're just evaluating a program in a local agency and don't care whether the program would work with other people in other places and at other times. In that case, sampling and generalizing might not be of interest. In other cases, you would really like to be able to generalize almost universally. When psychologists do research, they are often interested in developing theories that would hold for all humans; but in most applied social research, researchers are interested in generalizing to specific groups.

The group you wish to generalize to is called the **population** in your study (see Figure 2.3). This is the group you would like to sample from because this is the group you are interested in generalizing to. Let's imagine that you want to generalize to urban homeless males between the ages of 30 and 50 in the United States. If that is the population of interest, you are likely to have a hard time developing a reasonable sampling plan. You are probably not going to find an accurate listing of this population, and even if you did, you would almost certainly not be able to mount a national sample across hundreds of urban areas. So you probably should make a distinction between the population you would like to generalize to, and the population that is accessible to you. We'll call the former the *theoretical population* and the latter the *accessible population*. In this example, the accessible population might be homeless males between the ages of 30 and 50 in six selected urban areas across the United States.

Figure 2.3
The different groups in the sampling model.

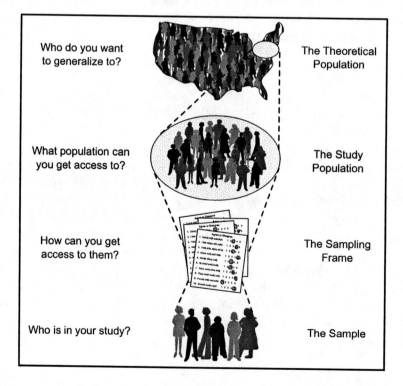

Who do you want to generalize to? — The Theoretical Population

What population can you get access to? — The Study Population

How can you get access to them? — The Sampling Frame

Who is in your study? — The Sample

After you identify the theoretical and accessible populations, you have to do one more thing before you can actually draw a sample: get a list of the members of the accessible population. (Or, you have to spell out in detail how you will contact them to assure representativeness.) The listing of the accessible population from which you'll draw your sample is called the ***sampling frame***. If you were doing a phone survey and selecting names from the telephone book, the phone book would be your sampling frame. That wouldn't be a great way to sample because significant subportions of the population either don't have a phone or have moved in or out of the area since the last phone book was printed. Notice that in this case, you might identify the area code and all three-digit prefixes within that area code and draw a sample simply by randomly dialing numbers (cleverly known as *random-digit-dialing*). In this case, the sampling frame is not a list *per se*, but is rather a procedure that you follow as the actual basis for sampling. Finally, you actually draw your sample (using one of the many sampling procedures described later in this chapter). The ***sample*** is the group of people you select to be in your study. Notice that I didn't say that the sample was the group of people who are actually *in* your study. You may not be able to contact or recruit all of the people you actually sample, or some could drop out over the course of the study. The group that actually completes your study is a subsample of the sample; it doesn't include nonrespondents or dropouts. (The problem of nonresponse and its effects on a study will be addressed in Chapter 6, "Design," when discussing mortality threats to internal validity.)

People often confuse the idea of random selection with the idea of random assignment. You should make sure that you understand the distinction between random selection and random assignment described in Chapter 7, "Experimental Design."

At this point, you should appreciate that sampling is a difficult multistep process and that you can go wrong in many places. In fact, as you move from each step to the next in identifying a sample, there is the possibility of introducing systematic error or *bias*. For instance, even if you are able to identify perfectly the population of interest, you may not have access to all of it. Even if you do, you may not have a complete and accurate enumeration or sampling frame from which to select. Even if you do, you may not draw the sample correctly or accurately. And, even if you do, your participants may not all come and they may not all stay. Depressed yet? Sampling is a difficult business indeed. At times like this I'm reminded of what one of my professors, Donald Campbell, used to say (I'll paraphrase here): "Cousins to the amoeba, it's amazing that we know anything at all!"

Let's begin by defining some simple terms that are relevant here. First, let's look at the results of sampling efforts. When you sample, the units that you sample—usually people—supply you with one or more responses. In this sense, a ***response*** is a specific measurement value that a sampling unit supplies. In Figure 2.4, the person responding to a survey instrument gives a response of '4'. When you look across the responses for your entire sample, you use a ***statistic***. There are a wide variety of statistics you can use: mean, median, mode, and so on. In this example, the mean or average for the sample is 3.72; but the reason you sample is to get an estimate for the population from which you sampled. If you could, you would probably prefer to measure the entire population. If you measure the entire population and calculate a value like a mean or average, this is not referred to as a statistic; it is a ***population parameter***.

2-3 Statistical Terms in Sampling

Figure 2.4
Statistical terms in sampling.

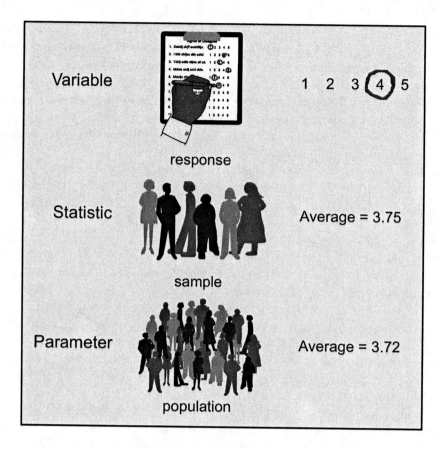

2-3a The Sampling Distribution

So how do you get from sample statistic to an estimate of the population parameter? A crucial midway concept you need to understand is the *sampling distribution*. To understand it, you have to be able and willing to do a thought experiment. Imagine that instead of just taking a single sample like you do in a typical study, you took three independent samples of the same population. Furthermore, imagine that for each of your three samples, you collected a single response and computed a single statistic, say, the mean of the response for each sample. This is depicted in the top part of Figure 2.5. Even though all three samples came from the same population, you wouldn't expect to get the exact same statistic from each. They would differ slightly due to the random luck of the draw or to the natural fluctuations or vagaries of drawing a sample. However, you would expect all three samples to yield a similar statistical estimate because they were drawn from the same population.

Now, for the leap of imagination! Imagine that you took an *infinite* number of samples from the same population and computed the average for each one. If you plotted the averages on a histogram or bar graph, you should find that most of them converge on the same central value and that you get fewer and fewer samples that have averages farther up or down from that central value. In other words, the bar graph would be well described by the *bell curve* shape that is an indication of a normal distribution in statistics. This is depicted in the bottom part of Figure 2.5. The distribution of an infinite number of samples of the same size as the sample in your study is known as the sampling distribution.

You don't ever actually construct a sampling distribution. Why not? You're not paying attention! Because to construct one, you would have to take an *infinite* number of samples and at least the last time I checked, on this planet infinite is not a number we know how to reach. So why do researchers even talk about a sampling distribution? Now that's a good question! Because you need to realize that your sample is just one of a potentially infinite number of samples that you could have taken. When you keep the sampling distribution in mind, you realize that while the statistic from your sample is probably near the center of the sampling distribution (because most of the samples would be there) you could have gotten one of the extreme samples just through the luck of the draw. If you take the average of the sampling distribution—the average of the averages of an infinite number of samples—you would be much closer to the true population average—the parameter of interest.

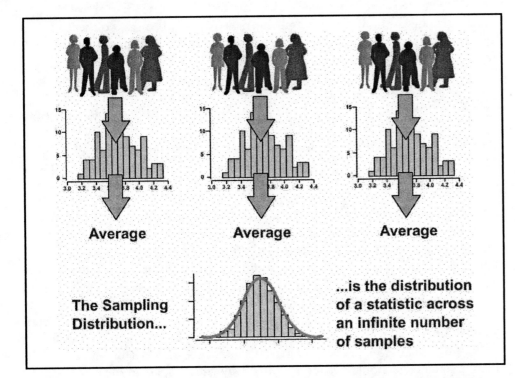

Figure 2.5
The sampling distribution.

So the average of the sampling distribution is essentially equivalent to the parameter. But what is the standard deviation of the sampling distribution? (Okay, don't remember what a standard deviation is? This is discussed in detail in the section "Descriptive Statistics" in Chapter 10, "Analysis.") The standard deviation of the sampling distribution tells us something about how different samples would be distributed. In statistics it is referred to as the **standard error** (so you can keep it separate in your minds from standard deviations. Getting confused? Go get a cup of coffee and come back in ten minutes. . . . Okay, let's try once more. . . .). A **standard deviation** is the spread of the scores around the average in a *single sample*. The standard error is the spread of the averages around the average of averages in a *sampling distribution*. Got it?

In sampling contexts, the standard error is called **sampling error**. Sampling error gives you some idea of the precision of your statistical estimate. A low sampling error means that you had relatively less variability or range in the sampling distribution. But here I go again; you never actually see the sampling distribution! So how do you calculate sampling error? You base your calculation *on the standard deviation of your sample*: the greater the sample's standard deviation, the greater the standard error (and the sampling error). The standard error is also related to the sample size: the greater your sample size, the *smaller* the standard error. Why? Because the greater the sample size, the closer your sample is to the actual popu-

2-3b Sampling Error

lation itself. If you take a *sample* that consists of the entire population, you actually have no sampling error because you don't have a sample; you have the entire population. In that case, the mean you estimate *is* the parameter.

2-3c The 65, 95, 99 Percent Rule

You've probably heard this one before, but it's so important that it's always worth repeating ... . There is a general rule that applies whenever you have a normal or bell-shaped distribution. Start with the average—the center of the distribution. If you go up and down (that is, left and right) one standard unit, you will include approximately 65 percent of the cases in the distribution (65 percent of the area under the curve). If you go up and down two standard units, you will include approximately 95 percent of the cases. If you go plus or minus three standard units, you will include 99 percent of the cases.

Notice that I didn't specify in the previous few sentences whether I was talking about standard *deviation* units or standard *error* units. That's because the same rule holds for both types of distributions (the raw data and sampling distributions). For instance, in Figure 2.6, the mean of the distribution is 3.75 and the standard unit is .25. (If this were a distribution of raw data, we would be talking in standard-deviation units. If it were a sampling distribution, we'd be talking in standard-error units.) If you go up and down one standard unit from the mean, you would be going up and down .25 from the mean of 3.75. Within this range— 3.5 to 4.0—you would expect to see approximately 65 percent of the cases. This section is marked in red on Figure 2.6. I leave it to you to figure out the other ranges. What does this all mean, you ask. If you are dealing with raw data and you know the mean and standard deviation of a sample, you can *predict* the intervals within which 65, 95, and 99 percent of your cases would be expected to fall. We call these intervals the—guess what—65, 95, and 99 percent confidence intervals.

Now, here's where everything should come together in one great aha! experience if you've been following along. If you have a *sampling distribution,* you should be able to predict the 65, 95, and 99 percent confidence intervals for where the population parameter should be; and isn't that why you sampled in the first place? So that you could predict where the population is on that variable? There's only one hitch. You don't actually have the sampling distribution. (I know this is the third time I've said this.) However, you do have the distribution for the sample itself; and from that distribution, you can estimate the standard error (the sampling error) because it is based on the standard deviation and you have that. Of course, you don't actually know the **population parameter** value; you're trying to find that out, but you can use your best estimate for that—the sample statistic. Now, if you have the mean of the sampling distribution (or set it to the mean from your sample) and you have an estimate of the standard error, which you calculate that from your sample, you have the two key ingredients that you need for your sampling distribution to estimate confidence intervals for the population parameter.

Perhaps an example will help. Let's assume you did a study and drew a single sample from the population. Furthermore, let's assume that the average for the sample was 3.75 and the standard deviation was .25. This is the raw data distribution depicted in Figure 2.7. What would the sampling distribution be in this case? Well, you don't actually construct it (because you would need to take an infinite number of samples) but you *can* estimate it. For starters, you must assume that the mean of the sampling distribution is the mean of the sample, which is 3.75. Then, you calculate the **standard error.** To do this, use the **standard deviation** for your sample and the sample size (in this case N=100), which gives you a standard error of .025 (just trust me on this). Now you have everything you need to estimate a confidence interval for the population parameter. You would estimate that the probability is 65 percent that the true parameter value falls between 3.725 and 3.775 (3.75 plus and minus .025); that the 95 percent confidence interval is 3.700 to 3.800; and that you can say with 99 percent confidence that the population value is between 3.675 and 3.825. Using your sample, you have just estimated the average for your population (that is, the mean of the sample which is 3.75) and you have given odds that the actual population mean falls within certain ranges.

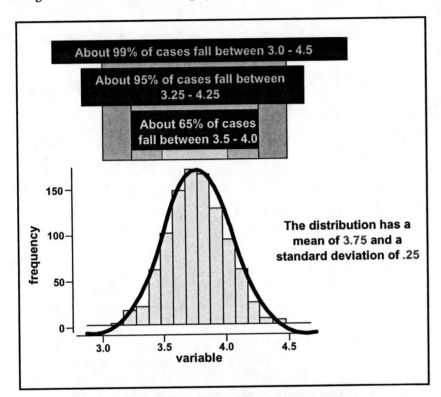

Figure 2.6
The 65, 95, 99 Percent Rule.

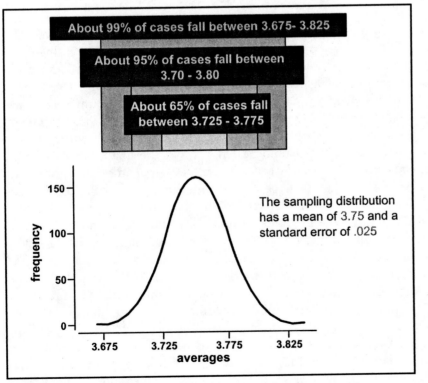

Figure 2.7
Estimating the population using a sampling distribution.

2-4 Probability Sampling

A *probability sampling* method is any method of sampling that utilizes some form of *random selection*. To have a random selection method, you must set up some process or procedure that assures that the different units in your population have equal probabilities of being chosen. Humans have long practiced various forms of random selection, such as picking a name out of a hat, or choosing the short straw. These days, we tend to use computers as the mechanism for generating random numbers as the basis for random selection.

2-4a Some Definitions

Before I can explain the various probability methods I have to define the following basic terms:

- **N** is the number of cases in the sampling frame.
- **n** is the number of cases in the sample.
- $_N C_n$ is the number of combinations (subsets) of n from N.
- **f = n/N** is the sampling fraction.

That's it. Now that you understand those terms, I can define the different probability sampling methods.

2-4b Simple Random Sampling

The simplest form of random sampling is called *simple random sampling*. Pretty tricky, huh? Here's the quick description of simple random sampling:

- **Objective:** To select *n* units out of *N* such that each $_N C_n$ has an equal chance of being selected.
- **Procedure:** Use a table of random numbers, a computer random-number generator, or a mechanical device to select the sample.

Let's see if I can make this somewhat stilted description a little more real. How do you select a simple random sample? Let's assume that you are doing some research with a small service agency to assess clients' views of quality of service over the past year. First, you have to get the *sampling frame* organized. To accomplish this, you go through agency records to identify every client over the past 12 months. If you're lucky, the agency has accurate computerized records and can quickly produce such a list (see Figure 2.8). Then, you have to draw the *sample* and decide on the number of clients you would like to have in the final sample. For the sake of the example, let's say you want to select 100 clients to survey and that there were 1000 clients over the past 12 months. Then, the sampling fraction is f = n/N = 100/1000 = .10 or 10 percent. To draw the sample, you have several options. You could print the list of 1000 clients, tear them into separate strips, put the strips in a hat, mix them up, close your eyes, and pull out the first 100. This mechanical procedure would be tedious and the quality of the sample would depend on how thoroughly you mixed up the paper strips and how randomly you reached into the hat. Perhaps a better procedure would be to use the kind of ball machine that is popular with many of the state lotteries. You would need three sets of balls numbered 0 to 9, one set for each of the digits from 000 to 999. (If you select 000 you call that 1000.) Number the list of names from 1 to 1000 and then use the ball machine to select the three digits that selects each person. The obvious disadvantage here is that you need to get the ball machines. (Where do they make those things, anyway? Is there a ball machine industry?)

Neither of these mechanical procedures is feasible and, with the development of inexpensive computers, there is a much easier way. Here's a simple procedure that's especially useful if you have the names of the clients already on the computer. Many computer programs can generate a series of random numbers. Let's assume you copy and paste the list of client names into a column in an Excel spreadsheet. Then, in the column right next to it paste the function =RAND( ), which is Excel's way of putting a random number between 0 and 1 in the cells. Then, sort both columns—the list of names and the random number—by the random numbers. This rearranges the list in random order from the lowest to the highest random number. Then, all you have to do is take the first hundred names in this sorted list. Pretty simple. You could probably accomplish the whole thing in under a minute.

Figure 2.8
Simple random sampling.

Simple random sampling is easy to accomplish and explain to others. Because simple random sampling is a fair way to select a sample, it is reasonable to generalize the results from the sample back to the population. Simple random sampling is not the most statistically efficient method of sampling and you may—just because of the luck of the draw—not get a good representation of subgroups in a population. To deal with these issues, you have to turn to other sampling methods.

2-4c Stratified Random Sampling

Stratified Random Sampling, also sometimes called *proportional* or *quota* random sampling, involves dividing your population into homogeneous subgroups and then taking a simple random sample in each subgroup. The following restates this in more formal terms:

Objective: Divide the population into nonoverlapping groups (*strata*) N_1, N_2, N_3, … N_i, such that $N_1 + N_2 + N_3 + … + N_i = N$. Then do a simple random sample of $f = n/N$ in each strata.

You might prefer stratified sampling over simple random sampling for several reasons. First, it assures that you will be able to represent not only the overall population, but also key subgroups of the population, especially small minority groups. If you want to be able to talk about subgroups, this may be the only way to ensure effectively you'll be able to do so. If the subgroup is extremely small, you can use different sampling fractions (f) within the different strata to randomly over-sample the small group. (Although you'll then have to weight the within-group estimates using the sampling fraction whenever you want overall population estimates.) When you use the same sampling fraction within strata you are conducting *proportionate* stratified random sampling. Using different sampling fractions in the strata is called *disproportionate* stratified random sampling. Second, stratified random sampling has more statistical precision than simple random sampling if the strata or groups are homogeneous. If they are, you should expect the variability within groups to be lower than the variability for the population as a whole. Stratified sampling capitalizes on that fact.

For example, let's say that the population of clients for your agency can be divided as shown in Figure 2.9 into three groups: Caucasian, African-American, and Hispanic-American. Furthermore, let's assume that both the African-Americans and Hispanic-Americans are relatively small minorities of the clientele (10 percent and 5 percent respectively). If you just did a simple random sample of n = 100 with a sampling fraction of 10 percent, you would expect by chance alone to get 10 and 5 persons from each of the two smaller groups. And, by chance, you could get even fewer than that! If you stratify, you can do better. First, you would determine how many people you want to have in each group. Let's say you still want to take a sample of 100 from the population of 1000 clients over the past year; but suppose you think that to say anything about subgroups, you will need at least 25 cases in each group. So, you sample 50 Caucasians, 25 African-Americans, and 25 Hispanic-Americans. You know that 10 percent of the population, or 100 clients, are African-American. If you randomly sample 25 of these, you have a within-stratum sampling fraction of 25/100 = 25%. Similarly, you know that 5 percent, or 50 clients, are Hispanic-American. So your within-stratum sampling fraction will be 25/50 = 50%. Finally, by subtraction you know there are 850 Caucasian clients. Your within-stratum sampling fraction for them is 50/850 = about 5.88%. Because the groups are more homogeneous within group than across the population as a whole, you can expect greater statistical precision (less variance), and, because you stratified, you know you will have enough cases from each group to make meaningful subgroup inferences.

Figure 2.9
Stratified random sampling.

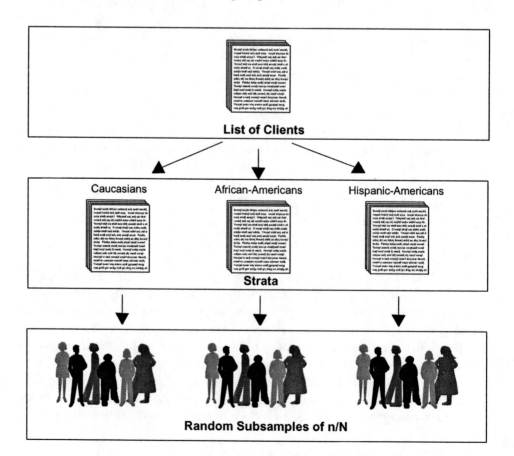

Systematic random sampling is a sampling method where you determine randomly where you want to start selecting in the *sampling frame* and then follow a rule to select every x^{th} element in the sampling frame list (where the ordering of the list is assumed to be random). To achieve a systematic random sample, follow these steps:

1. Number the units in the population from 1 to N.
2. Decide on the n (sample size) that you want or need.
3. Calculate k = N/n = the interval size.
4. Randomly select an integer between 1 and k.
5. Take every k^{th} unit.

All of this will be much clearer with an example. Let's assume, as shown in Figure 2.10, that you have a population that only has N = 100 people in it and that you want to take a sample of n = 20. To use systematic sampling, the population must be listed in a random order. The sampling fraction would be f = 20/100 = 20%. In this case, the interval size, k, is equal to N/n = 100/20 = 5. Now, select a random integer from 1 to 5. In this example, imagine that you chose 4. Now, to select the sample, start with the 4th unit in the list and take every k^{th} unit (every 5th, because k = 5). You would be sampling units 4, 9, 14, 19, and so on to 100 and you would wind up with 20 units in your sample.

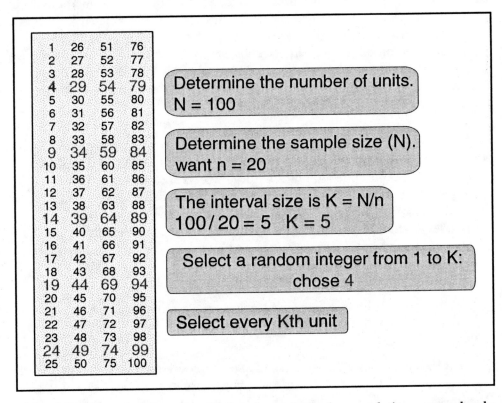

Figure 2.10
Systematic random sampling.

For this to work, it is essential that the units in the population are randomly ordered, at least with respect to the characteristics you are measuring. Why would you ever want to use systematic random sampling? For one thing, it is fairly easy to do. You only have to select a single random number to start things off. It may also be more precise than simple random sampling. Finally, in some situations there is simply no easier way to do random sampling. For instance, I once had to do a study that involved sampling a collection of books in the library. Once selected, I would have to go to the shelf, locate the book, and record when it last circulated. I knew that I had a fairly good sampling frame in the form of the shelf list (which is a card catalog where the entries are arranged in the order they occur on the shelf). To do a simple random sample, I could have estimated the total number of books and generated random numbers to draw the sample; but how would I find book #74,329 easily if that is the number I selected? I couldn't very well count the cards until I came to 74,329! Stratifying wouldn't solve that problem either. For instance, I could have stratified by card catalog drawer and drawn a simple random sample within each drawer. But I'd still be stuck counting cards. Instead, I did a systematic random sample. I estimated the number of books in the entire collection. Let's imagine it was 100,000. I decided that I wanted to take a sample of 1000 for a sampling fraction of 1000/100,000 = 1%. To get the sampling interval k, I divided N/n = 100,000/100 = 1000. Then I selected a random integer between 1 and 1000. Let's say I got 257. Next I did a little side study to determine how thick a thousand cards are in the card catalog (taking into account the varying ages of the cards). Let's say that on average I found that two cards that were separated by 1000 cards were about 2.75 inches apart in the catalog drawer. That information gave me everything I needed to draw the sample. I counted to the 257th by hand and recorded the book information. Then, I took a compass. (Remember those from your high-school math class? They're the funny little metal instruments with a sharp pin on one end and a pencil on the other that you used to draw circles in geometry class.) Then I set the compass at 2.75", stuck the pin end in at the 257th card and pointed with the pencil end to the next card (approximately 1000 books away). In this way, I approximated selecting the 257th, 1,257th, 2,257th, and so on. I was able to accomplish the entire selection procedure in very little time using this systematic random sampling approach. I'd probably still be there counting cards if I'd tried another random sampling method. (Okay, so I have no life. I got compensated nicely, I don't mind saying, for coming up with this scheme.)

2-4e Cluster (Area) Random Sampling

The problem with random sampling methods when you have to sample a population that's dispersed across a wide geographic region is that you will have to cover a lot of ground geographically to get to each of the units you sampled. Imagine taking a simple random sample of all the residents of New York State to conduct personal interviews. By the luck of the draw, you will wind up with respondents who come from all over the state. Your interviewers are going to have a lot of traveling to do. It is precisely to address this problem that *cluster or area random sampling* was invented.

In cluster sampling, you follow these steps:

1. Divide population into clusters (usually along geographic boundaries).
2. Randomly sample clusters.
3. Measure *all* units within sampled clusters.

For instance, Figure 2.11 shows a map of the counties in New York state. Let's say that you have to do a survey of town governments that requires you to go to the towns personally to interview key town officials. If you do a simple random sample of towns statewide, your sample is likely to come from all over the state and you will have to be prepared to cover the entire state geographically. Instead, you can do a cluster sampling of counties, let's say five counties in this example (shaded in the figure). Once these are selected, you go to *every* town government in the five county areas. Clearly this strategy will help you economize on mileage. Instead of having to travel all over the state, you can concentrate exclusively within the counties you selected. Cluster or area sampling is useful in situations like this, and is done primarily for efficiency of administration.

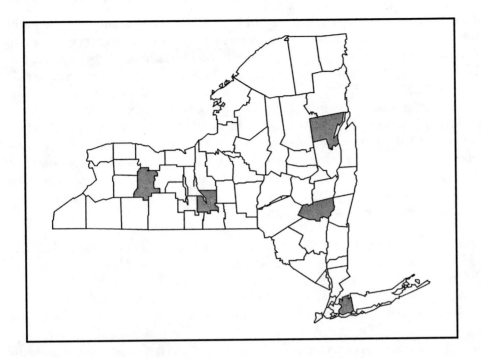

Figure 2.11
A county-level map of New York state used for cluster (area) random sampling.

2-4f Multi-Stage Sampling

The four methods covered so far—simple, stratified, systematic, and cluster—are the simplest random sampling strategies. In most real applied social research, you would use sampling methods that are considerably more complex than these simple variations. The most important principle here is that you can combine these simple methods in a variety of useful ways to help you address your sampling needs in the most efficient and effective manner possible. Combining sampling methods is called *multi-stage sampling.*

For example, consider the idea of sampling New York state residents for face-to-face interviews. Clearly you would want to do some type of *cluster sampling* as the first stage of the process. You might sample townships or census tracts throughout the state. In cluster sampling you would then measure everyone in the clusters you selected. Even if you are sampling census tracts, you may not be able to measure *everyone* who is in the census tract. So, you might set up a *systematic random sampling* process within the clusters. In this case, you would have a two-stage sampling process with stratified samples within cluster samples. Alternatively, consider the problem of sampling students in grade schools. You might begin with a national sample of school districts stratified by economics and educational level. Within selected districts, you might do a *simple random sample* of schools; within schools, you might do a simple random sample of classes or grades; and, within classes, you might even do a simple random sample of students. In this case, you have three or four stages in the sampling process and you use both stratified and simple random sampling. By combining different sampling methods, you can achieve a rich variety of probabilistic sampling methods to fit a wide range of social research contexts.

2-5 Nonprobability Sampling

The difference between nonprobability and *probability sampling* is that *nonprobability sampling* does not involve *random selection* and probability sampling does. Does that mean that nonprobability samples aren't representative of the population? Not necessarily; but it does mean nonprobability samples cannot depend upon the rationale of probability theory. At least with a probabilistic sample, you know the odds or probability that you have represented the population well. You can estimate confidence intervals for the statistic. With nonprobability samples, you may or may not represent the population well, and it will often be hard for you to know how well you've done so. In general, researchers prefer probabilistic or random sampling methods over nonprobabilistic ones and consider them to be more accurate and rigorous. However, in some circumstances in applied social research, it is not feasible, practical, or theoretically sensible to use random sampling. In the following paragraphs, I will present a variety of nonprobabilistic sampling alternatives to the probabilistic methods described earlier.

Nonprobability sampling methods are divided into two broad types: *accidental* or *purposive*. Most sampling methods are purposive in nature because the sampling problem is usually approached with a specific plan in mind. The most important distinctions among these types of sampling methods are between the different types of purposive sampling approaches.

2-5a Accidental, Haphazard, or Convenience Sampling

One of the most common methods of sampling goes under the various titles listed here: accidental, haphazard, or convenience. I would include in this category the traditional man-on-the-street (of course, now it's probably the person-on-the-street) interviews conducted frequently by television news programs to get a quick (although nonrepresentative) reading of public opinion. I would also argue that the typical use of college students in much psychological research is primarily a matter of convenience. (You don't really believe that psychologists use college students because they think they're representative of the population at large, do you?) In clinical practice, you might use clients available to you as your sample. In many research contexts, you sample by asking for volunteers. Clearly, the problem with all these types of samples is that you have no evidence that they are representative of the populations you're interested in generalizing to, and in many cases, you would suspect that they are not.

2-5b Purposive Sampling

In purposive sampling, you sample with a *purpose* in mind. Usually you would be seeking one or more specific predefined groups. For instance, have you ever run into people in a mall or on the street carrying clipboards and stopping various people and asking to interview them? Most likely, they are conducting a purposive sample (and most likely they are engaged in market research). They might be looking for Caucasian females between 30-40 years old. They size up the people passing by and stop people who look to be in that category and ask whether they will participate. One of the first things they're likely to do is verify that the respondent does in fact meet the criteria for being in the sample. Purposive sampling can be useful in situations where you need to reach a targeted sample quickly and where sampling for proportionality is not the primary concern. With a purposive sample, you are likely to get the opinions of your target population, but you are also likely to overweight subgroups in your population that are more readily accessible.

All of the methods that follow can be considered subcategories of purposive sampling methods. You might sample for specific groups or types of people as in modal instance, expert, or quota sampling. You might sample for diversity as in heterogeneity sampling; or you might capitalize on informal social networks to identify specific respondents who are hard to locate otherwise, as in snowball sampling. In all of these methods, you know what you want—you are sampling with a purpose.

Modal Instance Sampling

In statistics, the *mode* is the most frequently occurring value in a distribution. In sampling, when you do a **modal instance sample**, you are sampling the most frequent case, or the typical case. Many informal public opinion polls, for instance, interview a typical voter. This sampling approach has a number of problems: First, how do you know what the typical or modal case is? You could say that the modal voter is a person of average age, educational level, and income in the population; but, it's not clear that using the averages of these is the fairest (consider the skewed distribution of income, for instance). Additionally, how do you know that those three variables—age, education, income—are the ones most relevant for classifying the typical voter? What if religion or ethnicity is an important determinant of voting decisions? Clearly, modal instance sampling is only sensible for informal sampling contexts.

Expert Sampling

Expert sampling involves the assembling of a sample of persons with known or demonstrable experience and expertise in some area. Often, you convene such a sample under the auspices of a panel of experts. There are actually two reasons you might do expert sampling. First, it is the best way to elicit the views of persons who have specific expertise. In this case, expert sampling is essentially just a specific subcase of purposive sampling. The other reason you might use expert sampling is to provide evidence for the *validity* of another sampling approach you've chosen. For instance, let's say you do modal instance sampling and are concerned that the criteria you used for defining the modal instance is subject to criticism. You might convene an expert panel consisting of persons with acknowledged experience and insight into that field or topic and ask them to examine your modal definitions and comment on their appropriateness and validity. The advantage of doing this is that you aren't out on your own trying to defend your decisions; you have some acknowledged experts to back you. The disadvantage is that even the experts can be, and often are, wrong.

Quota Sampling

In *quota sampling*, you select people nonrandomly according to some fixed quota. The two types of quota sampling are proportional and nonproportional. In *proportional quota sampling*, you want to represent the major characteristics of the population by sampling a proportional amount of each. For instance, if you know the population has 40 percent women and 60 percent men, and that you want a total sample size of 100, you should continue sampling until you get those percentages and then stop. So, if you already have the 40 women for your sample, but not the 60 men, you would continue to sample men but even if legitimate women respondents come along, you would not sample them because you have already met your quota. The problem here (as in much purposive sampling) is that you have to decide the specific characteristics on which you will base the quota. Will it be by gender, age, education, race, or religion, etc.?

Nonproportional quota sampling is less restrictive. In this method, you specify the minimum number of sampled units you want in each category. Here, you're not concerned with having numbers that match the proportions in the population. Instead, you simply want to have enough to assure that you will be able to talk about even small groups in the population. This method is the nonprobabilistic analogue of stratified random sampling in that it is typically used to assure that smaller groups are adequately represented in your sample.

Heterogeneity Sampling

You sample for heterogeneity when you want to include all opinions or views, and you aren't concerned about representing these views proportionately. Another term for this is sampling for *diversity*. In many brainstorming or nominal group processes (including **concept mapping**), you would use some form of heterogeneity sampling because your primary interest is in getting a broad spectrum of ideas, not identifying the average or modal instance ones. In effect, what you would like to be sampling is not people, but ideas. You imagine that there is a universe of all possible ideas relevant to some topic and that you want to sample this population, not the population of people who have the ideas. Clearly, to get all of the ideas, and especially the outlier or unusual ones, you have to include a broad and diverse range of participants. **Heterogeneity sampling** is, in this sense, almost the opposite of modal instance sampling.

Snowball Sampling

In **snowball sampling**, you begin by identifying people who meet the criteria for inclusion in your study. You then ask them to recommend others they know who also meet the criteria. Although this method would hardly lead to representative samples, at times it may be the best method available. Snowball sampling is especially useful when you are trying to reach populations that are inaccessible or hard to find. For instance, if you are studying the homeless, you are not likely to be able to find good lists of homeless people within a specific geographical area. However, if you go to that area and identify one or two, you may find that they know who the other homeless people in their vicinity are and how you can find them.

SUMMARY

So, that's the basics of sampling methods. Quite a few options, aren't there? How about a table to summarize the choices and give you some idea of when they might be appropriate. Table 2.1 shows each sampling method, when it might best be used, and the major advantages and disadvantages of each.

Sampling is a critical component in virtually all social research. While I've presented a wide variety of sampling methods in this chapter, it's important that you keep them in perspective. The key is not which sampling method you use. The key is **external validity**—how valid the inferences from your sample are. You can have the best sampling method in the world and it won't guarantee that your generalizations are valid (although it does help!). Alternatively, you can use a relatively weak nonprobability sampling method and find that it is perfectly useful for your context. Ultimately whether your generalizations from your study to other persons, places, or times are valid is a judgment. Your critics, readers, friends, supporters, funders, and so on, will judge the quality of your generalizations, and they may not even agree with each other in their judgment. What might be convincing to one person or group may fail with another. Your job as a social researcher is to create a sampling strategy that is appropriate to the context and will assure that your generalizations are as convincing as possible to as many audiences as is feasible.

T A B L E **2.1 Summary of Sampling Methods**

Sampling Method	Use	Advantages	Disadvantages
Simple random sampling	Anytime.	Simple to implement; easy to explain to nontechnical audiences.	Requires a sample list (sampling frame) to select from.
Stratified random sampling	When concerned about underrepresenting smaller subgroups.	Allows you to over-sample minority groups to assure enough for subgroup analyses.	Requires a sample list (sampling frame) from which to select.
Systematic random sampling	When you want to sample every k^{th} element in an ordered set.	You don't have to count through all of the elements in the list to find the ones randomly selected.	If the order of elements is nonrandom, there could be systematic bias.
Cluster (area) random sampling	When organizing geographically makes sense.	More efficient than other methods when sampling across a geographically dispersed area.	Usually not used alone; coupled with other methods in a multi-stage approach.
Multi-stage random sampling	Anytime.	Combines sophistication with efficiency.	Can be complex and difficult to explain to nontechnical audiences.
Accidental, haphazard, or convenience nonprobability sampling	Anytime.	Very easy to do; almost like not sampling at all.	Very weak external validity; likely to be biased.
Modal instance purposive nonprobability sampling	When you only want to measure a typical respondent.	Easily understood by nontechnical audiences.	Results only limited to the modal case; little external validity.
Modal purposive nonprobability sampling	As an adjunct to other sampling strategies.	Experts can provide opinions to support research conclusions.	Likely to be biased; limited external validity.
Quota purposive nonprobability sampling	When you want to represent sub-groups.	Allows for over-sampling smaller subgroups.	Likely to be more biased than stratified random sampling; often depends on who comes along when.
Heterogeneity purposive non-probability sampling	When you want to sample for diversity or variety.	Easy to implement and explain; useful when you're interested in sampling for variety rather than representativeness.	Won't represent population views proportionately.
Snowball purposive nonprobability sampling	With hard to reach populations.	Can be used when there is no sampling frame.	Low external validity.

Measurement

Chapter 3
The Theory of Measurement

Chapter 4
Survey Research and Scaling

Chapter 5
Qualitative and Unobtrusive
 Measures

3

The Theory of Measurement

Measurement is the process of observing and recording the observations that are collected as part of a research effort. There are two major issues that will be considered here.

First, you have to understand the fundamental ideas or theory involved in measuring. In this chapter, I focus on how we think about and assess quality of measurement. In the section on construct validity, I present the theory of what constitutes a good measure. In the section on reliability of measurement, I consider the consistency or dependability of measurement, including consideration of true score theory and a variety of reliability estimators. In the section on levels of measurement, I explain the meaning of the four major levels of measurement: nominal, ordinal, interval, and ratio.

Key Terms

concept mapping
concurrent validity
construct validity
content validity
convergent validity
criterion-related validity
Cronbach's Alpha
discriminant validity
external validity
face validity
hypothesis
mono-method bias
mono-operation bias
nomological network
operationalization
pattern matching
predictive validity
reliability
standard deviation
translation validity
true score theory
validity

3-1 Construct Validity

onstruct validity refers to the degree to which inferences can legitimately be made from the *operationalizations* in your study to the theoretical constructs on which those operationalizations are based. Whoa! Can you believe that the term operationalization has eight syllables? That's a mouthful. What does it mean here? An operationalization is your translation of an idea or construct into something real and concrete. Let's say you have an idea for a treatment or program you would like to create. The operationalization is the program or treatment itself, as it exists after you create it. The construct validity issue is the degree to which the actual (operationalized) program reflects the ideal (the program as you conceptualized or envisioned it). Imagine that you want to measure the construct of self-esteem. You have an idea of what self-esteem means. You construct a 10-item paper-and-pencil instrument to measure self-esteem. The instrument is the operationalization; it's the translation of the idea of self-esteem into something concrete. The construct validity question here would be how well the 10-item instrument (the operationalization) reflects the idea you had of self-esteem. Well, I'll cover this in more detail later, but I didn't want to start the chapter with an eight-syllable word that will confuse you at the outset.

Like *external validity* (see the discussion in Chapter 2, "Sampling,") construct validity is related to generalizing. However, whereas external validity involves generalizing from your study context to other people, places, or times, construct validity involves generalizing from your program or measures to the *concept or idea* of your program or measures. You might think of construct validity as a labeling issue. When you implement a program that you call a Head Start program, is your label an accurate one? When you measure what you term self-esteem is that what you were really measuring?

I would like to address two major issues here. The first is the more straightforward one. I'll discuss several ways of thinking about the idea of construct validity, and several metaphors that might provide you with a foundation in the richness of this idea. Then, I'll discuss the major construct validity threats, the kinds of arguments your critics are likely to raise when you make a claim that your program or measure is valid.

In this text, as in most research methods texts, construct validity is presented in the section on measurement; it is typically presented as one of many different types of validity (for example face validity, predictive validity, or concurrent validity) that you might want to be sure your measures have. I don't see it that way at all. I see construct validity as the overarching quality of measurement with all of the other measurement validity labels falling beneath it. I don't see construct validity as limited only to measurement. As I've already implied, I think it is as much a part of the independent variable—the program or treatment—as it is the dependent variable. So, I'll try to make some sense of the various measurement validity types in this chapter and try to move you to think instead of the validity of *any* operationalization as falling within the general category of construct validity, with a variety of subcategories and subtypes.

To further demonstrate the concepts behind construct validity, I'd like to tell a story that is historical in nature. During World War II, the U.S. government involved hundreds (and perhaps thousands) of psychologists and psychology graduate students in the development of a wide array of measures that were relevant to the war effort. They needed personality screening tests for prospective fighter pilots, personnel measures that would enable sensible assignment of people to job skills, psychophysical measures to test reaction times, and so on. After the war, these psychologists needed to find gainful employment outside of the military, and it's not surprising that many of them moved into testing and measurement in a civilian context. During the early 1950s, the American Psychological Association became increasingly concerned with the quality or validity of all of the new measures that were being generated and decided to convene an effort to set standards for psychological measures. The first formal articulation of the idea of construct validity came from this effort and was couched under the somewhat grandiose term of the nomological network. (See the section on the nomological network later in this chapter.) The **nomological network** provided a theoretical basis for the idea of construct validity, but it didn't provide practicing researchers with a way to actually establish whether their measures had construct validity. In 1959, an attempt was made to develop a concrete, practical method for assessing construct validity using what is called a multitrait-multimethod matrix, or MTMM for short (more on this later in the chapter as well). To argue that your measures had construct validity under the MTMM approach, you had to demonstrate that there was *both convergent* and *discriminant* validity in your measures. You demonstrated construct validity when you showed that measures that are theoretically supposed to be highly interrelated are, in practice, highly interrelated. You showed discriminant validity when you demonstrated that measures that shouldn't be related to each other in fact were not.

While the MTMM did provide a methodology for assessing construct validity, it was a difficult one to implement well, especially in applied social research contexts and, in fact, has seldom been formally attempted. When the thinking about construct validity that underlies both the nomological network and the MTMM is examined carefully, one of the key themes that can be identified is in the idea of pattern. When you claim that your programs or measures have construct validity, you are essentially claiming that you, as a researcher, understand how your constructs or theories of the programs and measures operate in theory, and you are claiming that you can provide evidence that they behave in practice the way you think they should, that they follow the expected pattern.

The researcher essentially has a theory about how the programs and measures relate to each other (and other theoretical terms), a *theoretical pattern* if you will. The researcher provides evidence through observation that the programs or measures actually behave that way in reality, an *observed pattern*. When you claim construct validity, you're essentially claiming that your observed pattern—how things operate in reality—corresponds with your theoretical pattern—how you think the world works. I call this process pattern matching, and I believe that it is the heart of construct validity. It is clearly an underlying theme in both the nomological network and the MTMM ideas. Additionally, I think that, as researchers, we can develop concrete and feasible methods that enable practicing researchers to assess pattern matches to assess the construct validity of their research. The section on pattern matching later in this chapter lays out my idea of how you might use this approach to assess construct validity.

3-1a Measurement Validity Types

There's an awful lot of confusion in the methodological literature that stems from the wide variety of labels used to describe the validity of measures. I want to make two cases here. First, it's dumb to limit our scope only to the validity of measures. I really want to talk about the validity of any operationalization. That is, any time you translate a concept or construct into a functioning and operating reality (*the operationalization*), you need to be concerned about how well you performed the translation. This issue is as relevant when talking about treatments or programs as it is when talking about measures. (In fact, come to think of it, you could also think of sampling in this way.) The population of interest in your study is the construct and the sample is your operationalization. If you think of it this way, you are essentially talking about the construct validity of the sampling and construct validity merges with the idea of external validity as discussed in Chapter 2, "Sampling." The construct validity question, "How well does my sample represent the idea of the population?" merges with the ***external validity*** question, "How well can I generalize from my sample to the population?". Second, I want to use the term construct validity to refer to the general case of translating any construct into an operationalization. Let's use all of the other validity terms to reflect different ways you can demonstrate different aspects of construct validity.

With all that in mind, here's a list of the validity types that are typically mentioned in texts and research papers when talking about the quality of measurement and how I would organize and categorize them:

Construct validity
- **Translation validity**
  - Face validity
  - Content validity
- **Criterion-related validity**
  - Predictive validity
  - Concurrent validity
  - Convergent validity
  - Discriminant validity

I have to warn you here that I made this list up. I've never heard of translation validity before, but I needed a good name to summarize what both face and content validity are getting at, and that one seemed sensible. (See how easy it is to be a methodologist?) All of the other labels are commonly known, but the way I've organized them is different than I've seen elsewhere.

Let's see if I can make some sense out of this list. First, as mentioned previously, I would like to use the term *construct validity* to be the overarching category. Construct validity is the approximate truth of the conclusion that your operationalization accurately reflects its construct. All of the other validity types essentially address some aspect of this general issue (which is why I've subsumed them under the general category of construct validity). Second, I make a distinction between two broad types: translation validity and criterion-related validity. That's because I think these correspond to the two major ways you can assure/assess the validity of an operationalization.

In ***translation validity***, you focus on whether the operationalization is a good reflection of the construct. This approach is definitional in nature; it assumes you have a good, detailed definition of the construct and that you can check the operationalization against it. In ***criterion-related validity***, you examine whether the operationalization behaves the way it should given your theory of the construct. This type of validity is a more relational approach to construct validity. It assumes that your operationalization should function in predictable ways in relation to other operationalizations based upon your theory of the construct. (If all this seems a bit dense, hang in there until you've gone through the following discussion and then come back and reread this paragraph.) Let's go through the specific validity types.

Translation Validity

In essence, both of the translation validity types (face and content validity) attempt to assess the degree to which you accurately *translated* your construct into the operationalization, and hence the choice of name. Let's look at the two types of translation validity.

Face Validity

In *face validity*, you look at the operationalization and see whether *on its face* it seems like a good translation of the construct. This is probably the weakest way to try to demonstrate construct validity. For instance, you might look at a measure of math ability, read through the questions, and decide it seems like this is a good measure of math ability (the label *math ability* seems appropriate for this measure). Or, you might observe a teenage pregnancy-prevention program and conclude that it is indeed a teenage pregnancy-prevention program. Of course, if this is all you do to assess face validity, it would clearly be weak evidence because it is essentially a subjective judgment call. (Note that just because it is weak evidence doesn't mean that it is wrong. You need to rely on your subjective judgment throughout the research process. It's just that this form of judgment won't be especially convincing to others.) You can improve the quality of a face-validity assessment considerably by making it more systematic. For instance, if you are trying to assess the face validity of a math-ability measure, it would be more convincing if you sent the test to a carefully selected sample of experts on math-ability testing and they all reported back with the judgment that your measure appears to be a good measure of math ability.

Content Validity

In *content validity*, you essentially check the operationalization against the relevant content domain for the construct. This approach assumes that you have a good detailed description of the content domain, something that's not always true. For instance, you might lay out all of the criteria that should be met in a program that claims to be a teenage pregnancy-prevention program. You would probably include in this domain specification the definition of the target group, criteria for deciding whether the program is preventive in nature (as opposed to treatment-oriented), and criteria that spell out the content that should be included such as basic information on pregnancy, the use of abstinence, birth control methods, and so on. Then, armed with your criteria, you create a type of checklist when examining your program. Only programs that meet the checklist criteria can legitimately be defined as teenage pregnancy-prevention programs. This all sounds fairly straightforward, and for many operationalizations it will be. However for other constructs (such as self-esteem or intelligence), it will not be easy to decide which criteria constitute the content domain.

Criterion-Related Validity

In *criterion-related validity*, you check the performance of your operationalization against some criterion. How is this different from translation validity? In translation validity, the question is, How well did you translate the idea of the construct into its manifestation? No other measure comes into play. In criterion-related validity, you usually make a prediction about how the operationalization will *perform on some other measure* based on your theory of the construct. The differences among the criterion-related validity types is in the criteria they use as the standard for judgment.

For example, think again about measuring self-esteem. For content validity, you would try to describe all the things that self-esteem is in your mind and translate that into a measure. You might say that self-esteem involves how good you feel about yourself, that it includes things like your self-confidence and the degree to which you think positively about yourself. You could translate these notions into specific questions, a translation validity approach. On the other hand, you might reasonably expect that people with high self-esteem, as you construe it, would tend to act in certain ways. You might expect that you could distinguish them from people with low self-esteem. For instance, you might argue that high self-esteem people will volunteer for a task that requires self-confidence (such as speaking in public). Notice that in this case, you validate your self-esteem measure by demonstrating that it is correlated with some other independent indicator (raising hands to volunteer) that you theoretically expect high self-esteem people to evidence. This is the essential idea of criterion-related validity: validating a measure based on its relationship to another independent measure.

Predictive Validity

In **predictive validity**, you assess the operationalization's ability to predict something it should theoretically be able to predict. For instance, you might theorize that a measure of math ability should be able to predict how well a person will do in an engineering-based profession. You could give your measure to experienced engineers and see whether there is a high correlation between scores on the measure and their salaries as engineers. A high correlation would provide evidence for predictive validity; it would show that your measure can correctly predict something that you theoretically think it should be able to predict.

Concurrent Validity

In **concurrent validity**, you assess the operationalization's ability to distinguish between groups that it should theoretically be able to distinguish between. For example, if you come up with a way of assessing manic-depression, your measure should be able to distinguish between people who are diagnosed manic-depressive and those diagnosed paranoid schizophrenic. If you want to assess the concurrent validity of a new measure of empowerment, you might give the measure to both migrant farm workers and to the farm owners, theorizing that your measure should show that the farm owners are higher in empowerment. As in any discriminating test, the results are more powerful if you are able to show that you can discriminate between two similar groups.

Convergent Validity

In **convergent validity**, you examine the degree to which the operationalization is similar to (converges on) other operationalizations to which it theoretically should be similar. For instance, to show the convergent validity of a Head Start program, you might gather evidence that shows that the program is similar to other Head Start programs. To show the convergent validity of a test of arithmetic skills, you might correlate the scores on your test with scores on other tests that purport to measure basic math ability, where high correlations would be evidence of convergent validity.

Discriminant Validity

In **discriminant validity**, you examine the degree to which the operationalization is not similar to (diverges from) other operationalizations that it theoretically should be not be similar to. For instance, to show the discriminant validity of a Head Start program, you might gather evidence that shows that the program is *not* similar to other early childhood programs that don't label themselves as Head Start programs. To show the discriminant validity of a test of arithmetic skills, you might correlate the scores on your test with scores on tests of verbal ability, where *low* correlations would be evidence of discriminant validity.

Construct validity refers to the degree to which inferences can legitimately be made from the *operationalizations* in your study to the theoretical constructs on which those operationalizations were based. (I know I've said this before, but it never hurts to repeat something, especially when it sounds complicated.) I find that it helps me when thinking about construct validity to make a distinction between two broad territories that I call the *land of theory* and the *land of observation* as illustrated in Figure 3.1. The land of theory is what goes on inside your mind, and your attempt to explain or articulate this to others. It is all of the ideas, theories, hunches, and hypotheses you have about the world. In the land of theory, you think of the program or treatment as it should be. You find the idea or construct of the outcomes or measures you believe you are trying to affect. The land of observation consists of what you see happening in the world around you and the public manifestations of that world. In the land of observation, you find your actual program or treatment, and your actual measures or observational procedures. Presumably, you have constructed the land of observation based on your theories. You developed the program to reflect the kind of program you had in mind. You created the measures to get at what you wanted to get at.

3-1b Idea of Construct Validity

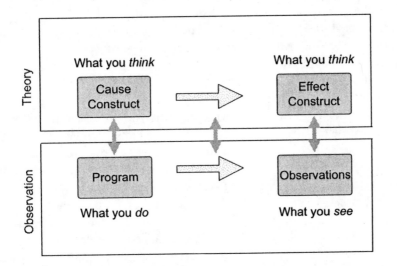

Figure 3.1
The idea of construct validity.

Construct validity is an assessment of how well your actual programs or measures reflect your ideas or theories, how well the bottom of Figure 3.1 reflects the top. Why is this important? Because when you think about the world or talk about it with others (land of theory), you are using words that represent concepts. If you tell parents that a special type of math tutoring will help their child do better in math, you are communicating at the level of concepts or constructs. You aren't describing in operational detail the specific things that the tutor will do with their child. You aren't describing the specific questions that will be on the math test on which their child will excel. You are talking in general terms, using constructs. If you based your recommendation on research that showed that the special type of tutoring improved children's math scores, you would want to be sure that the type of tutoring you are referring to is the same as what that study implemented and that the type of outcome you're saying should occur was the type the study measured. Otherwise, you would be mislabeling or misrepresenting the research. In this sense, construct validity can be viewed as a *truth in labeling* issue.

There really are two broad ways of looking at the idea of construct validity. I'll call the first the *definitionalist* perspective because it essentially holds that the way to assure construct validity is to define the construct so precisely that you can operationalize it in a straightforward manner. In a definitionalist view, you have either operationalized the construct correctly or you haven't; it's either/or type of thinking. Either this program is a "Type A Tutoring Program" or it isn't. Either you're measuring self-esteem or you aren't.

The other perspective I'd call *relationalist*. To a relationalist, things are not either/or or black-and-white; concepts are more or less related to each other. The meaning of terms or constructs differs relatively, not absolutely. The program in your study might be a "Type A Tutoring Program" in some ways, while in others it is not. It might be more that type of program than another program. Your measure might be capturing some of the construct of self-esteem, but it may not capture all of it. There may be another measure that is closer to the construct of self-esteem than yours is. Relationalism suggests that meaning changes gradually. It rejects the idea that you can rely on operational definitions as the basis for construct definition.

To get a clearer idea of this distinction, you might think about how the law approaches the construct of truth. Most of you have heard the standard oath that witnesses in a U.S. court are expected to swear. They are to tell "the truth, the whole truth and nothing but the truth." What does this mean? If witnesses had to swear only to tell the truth, they might choose to interpret that to mean that they should make sure what they say is true. However that wouldn't guarantee that they would tell *everything* they knew to be true. They might leave out some important things and still tell the truth. They just wouldn't be telling everything. On the other hand, they are asked to tell "nothing but the truth." This suggests that you can say simply that Statement X is true and Statement Y is not true.

Now, let's see how this oath translates into a measurement and construct validity context. For instance, you might want your measure to reflect the construct, the whole construct, and nothing but the construct. What does this mean? Let's assume, as shown in Figure 3.2, that you have five distinct constructs that are all conceptually related to each other: self-esteem, self-worth, self-disclosure, self-confidence, and openness. Most people would say that these concepts are similar, although they can be distinguished from each other. If you were trying to develop a measure of self-esteem, what would it mean to measure self-esteem, all of self-esteem, and nothing but self-esteem? If the concept of self-esteem overlaps with the others, how could you possibly measure all of it (that would presumably include the part that overlaps with others) *and* nothing but it? You couldn't! If you believe that meaning is relational in nature—that some concepts are closer in meaning than others—the legal model discussed here does not work well as a model for construct validity.

Figure 3.2
Distinguishing the construct of self-esteem from other similar constructs.

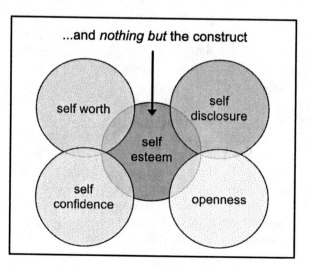

In fact, you will see that most social research methodologists have (whether they've thought about it or not) rejected the definitionalist perspective in favor of a relationalist one. To establish construct validity from a relationalist perspective you have to meet the following conditions:

- You have to set the construct you want to *operationalize* for example, self-esteem) within a *semantic net* (or net of meaning). This means that you have to tell what your construct is more or less similar to in meaning.

- You need to be able to provide direct evidence that you *control* the operationalization of the construct that your operationalizations look like what they should theoretically look like. If you are trying to measure self-esteem, you have to be able to explain why you operationalized the questions the way you did. If all your questions are addition problems, how can you argue that your measure reflects self-esteem and not adding ability?

- You have to provide evidence that your data supports your theoretical view of the relations among constructs. If you believe that self-esteem is closer in meaning to self-worth than it is to anxiety, you should be able to show that measures of self-esteem are more highly correlated with measures of self worth than with ones of anxiety.

3-1c Convergent and Discriminant Validity

Convergent and *discriminant validity* are both considered subcategories or subtypes of *construct validity*. The important thing to recognize is that they work together; if you can demonstrate that you have evidence for both convergent and discriminant validity, you have by definition demonstrated that you have evidence for construct validity. However, neither one alone is sufficient for establishing construct validity.

I find it easiest to think about convergent and discriminant validity as two interlocking propositions. In simple words, I would describe what they are doing as follows:

- Measures of constructs that theoretically *should* be related to each other are, in fact, observed to be related to each other (that is, you should be able to show a correspondence or *convergence* between similar constructs).

- Measures of constructs that theoretically should *not* be related to each other are, in fact, observed not to be related to each other (that is, you should be able to *discriminate* between dissimilar constructs).

To estimate the degree to which any two measures are related to each other you would typically use the correlation coefficient discussed in Chapter 10, "Analysis." That is, you look at the patterns of intercorrelations among the measures. Correlations between theoretically similar measures should be "high"; whereas correlations between theoretically dissimilar measures should be "low."

The main problem that I have with this convergent-discriminant idea has to do with my use of the quotations around the terms high and low in the previous sentence. The problem is simple: how high do correlations need to be to provide evidence for convergence and how low do they need to be to provide evidence for discrimination? The answer is that nobody knows! In general, convergent correlations should be as high as possible and discriminant ones should be as low as possible, but there is no hard and fast rule. Well, let's not let that stop us. One thing you can assume to be true is that the convergent correlations should always be *higher* than the discriminant ones. At least that helps a bit.

Before we get too deep into the idea of convergence and discrimination, let's take a look at each one using a simple example.

Convergent Validity

To establish convergent validity, you need to show that measures that should be related are in reality related. In Figure 3.3, you see four measures (each is an item on a scale) that all purport to reflect the construct of self-esteem. For instance, Item 1 might be the statement, "I feel good about myself," rated using a 1-to-5 scale. You theorize that all four items reflect the idea of self-esteem (which is why I labeled the top part of the figure *Theory*). On the bottom part of the figure (*Observation*), you see the intercorrelations of the four scale items. This might be based on giving your scale out to a sample of respondents. You should readily see that the item intercorrelations for all item pairings are extremely high. (Remember that correlations range from –1.00 to +1.00.) The correlations provide support for your theory that all four items are related to the same construct.

Figure 3.3
Convergent validity correlations.

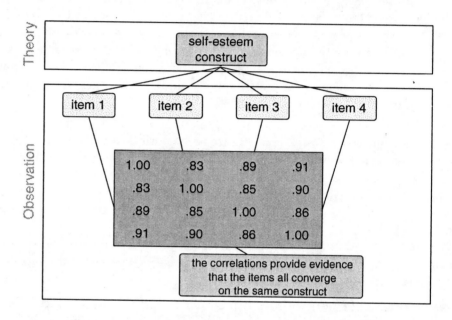

Notice, however, that whereas the high intercorrelations demonstrate the four items are probably related to the *same* construct, that doesn't automatically mean that the construct is *self-esteem*. Maybe there's some other construct to which all four items are related (more about this later). However, at least, you can assume from the pattern of correlations that the four items are converging on the same thing, whatever it might be called.

Discriminant Validity

To establish **discriminant validity,** you need to show that measures that should *not* be related are in reality *not* related. In Figure 3.4, you again see four measures (each is an item on a scale). Here, however, two of the items are thought to reflect the construct of self-esteem; whereas the other two are thought to reflect locus of control. The top part of the figure shows the theoretically expected relationships among the four items. If you have discriminant validity, the relationship between measures from different constructs should be low. (Again, nobody knows how low low should be, but I'll deal with that later.) There are four correlations between measures that reflect different constructs, and these are shown on the bottom of the figure (*Observation*). You should see immediately that these four cross-construct correlations are low (near zero) and certainly much lower than the convergent correlations in Figure 3.3.

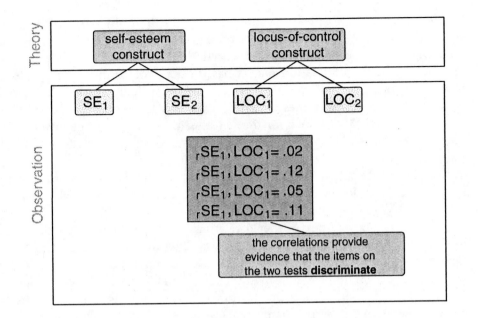

Figure 3.4
Discriminant validity
correlations.

As I mentioned previously, just because there is evidence that the two sets of two measures seem to be related to different constructs (because their intercorrelations are so low) doesn't mean that the constructs they're related to are self-esteem and locus of control. However the correlations do provide evidence that the two sets of measures are discriminated from each other.

Putting It All Together

Okay, so where does this leave us? I've shown how to provide evidence for convergent and discriminant validity separately; but as I said at the outset, to argue for **construct validity**, you really need to be able to show that both of these types of validity are supported. Given the previous discussions of convergent and discriminant validity, you should be able to see that you could put both principles together into a single analysis to examine both at the same time. This is illustrated in Figure 3.5.

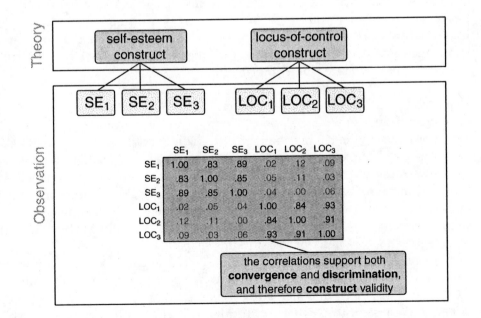

Figure 3.5
Convergent and discriminant validity correlations in a single table or correlation matrix.

Figure 3.5 shows six measures: three that are theoretically related to the construct of self-esteem and three that are thought to be related to locus of control. The top part of the figure shows this theoretical arrangement. The bottom of the figure shows what a correlation matrix based on a pilot sample might show. To understand this table, first you need to be able to identify the convergent correlations and the discriminant ones. The two sets or blocks of convergent coefficients appear in red: one 3 x 3 block for the self-esteem intercorrelations in the upper right of the table, and one 3 x 3 block for the locus-of-control correlations in the lower left. Additionally, two 3 x 3 blocks of discriminant coefficients appear in green, although if you're really sharp you'll recognize that they are the same values in mirror image. (Do you know why? You might want to read up on correlations in Chapter 10, "Analysis.")

How do you make sense of the correlations' patterns ? Remember that I said previously that there are no firm rules for how high or low the correlations need to be to provide evidence for either type of validity; but that the convergent correlations should always be higher than the discriminant ones. Take a good look at the table and you will see that in this example the convergent correlations are *always* higher than the discriminant ones. I would conclude from this that the correlation matrix provides evidence for both convergent and discriminant validity, all in one table!

It's true the pattern supports discriminant and convergent validity, but does it show that the three self-esteem measures actually measure self-esteem or that the three locus-of-control measures actually measure locus of control? Of course not. That would be much too easy.

So, what good is this analysis? It does show that, as you predicted, the three self-esteem measures seem to reflect the same construct (whatever that might be). The three locus-of-control measures also seem to reflect the same construct (again, whatever that is), and the two sets of measures seem to reflect two different constructs (whatever they are). That's not bad for one simple analysis.

Okay, so how do you get to the really interesting question? How do you show that your measures are actually measuring self-esteem or locus of control? I hate to disappoint you, but there is no simple answer to that. (I bet you knew that was coming.) You can do several things to address this question. First, you can use other ways to address construct validity to help provide further evidence that you're measuring what you say you're measuring. For instance, you might use a *face validity* or *content validity* approach to demonstrate that the measures reflect the constructs you say they are. (See the discussion of types of construct validity in this chapter for more information.)

One of the most powerful approaches is to include even more constructs and measures. The more complex your theoretical model (if you find confirmation of the correct pattern in the correlations), the more evidence you are providing that you know what you're talking about (theoretically speaking). Of course, it's also harder to get all the correlations to give you the exact right pattern as you add more measures. In many studies, you simply don't have the luxury of adding more and more measures because it's too costly or demanding. Despite the impracticality, if you can afford to do it, adding more constructs and measures enhances your ability to assess construct validity using approaches like the MTMM and the *nomological network* described later in this chapter.

Perhaps the most interesting approach to getting at construct validity involves the idea of pattern matching. Instead of viewing convergent and discriminant validity as differences of *kind*, **pattern matching** views them as differences in *degree*. Because of this, pattern matching seems a more reasonable idea when compared with the MTMM and the nomological network, and helps you avoid the problem of how high or low correlations need to be to say that you've established convergence or discrimination.

Before I launch into a discussion of the most common threats to construct validity, take a moment to recall what a threat to validity is. In a research study, you are likely to reach a conclusion that your program was a good *operationalization* of what you wanted and that your measures reflected what you wanted them to reflect. Would you be correct? How will you be criticized if you make these types of claims? How might you strengthen your claims? The kinds of questions and issues your critics will raise are what I mean by threats to construct validity.

I take the list of threats from the discussion in Cook and Campbell (Cook, T.D. and Campbell, D.T. 1979. *Quasi-Experimentation: Design and Analysis Issues for Field Settings.* Boston: Houghton Mifflin.) Although I love their discussion, I do find some of their terminology less than straightforward; much of what I'll do here is try to explain this stuff in terms that the rest of us might hope to understand.

Inadequate Preoperational Explication of Constructs

This section title isn't nearly as ponderous as it sounds. Here, *preoperational* means before translating constructs into measures or treatments, and *explication* means explanation; in other words, you didn't do a good enough job of *defining* (operationally) what you mean by the construct. How is this a threat? Imagine that your program consisted of a new type of approach to rehabilitation. A critic comes along and claims that, in fact, your program is neither *new* nor a true *rehabilitation* program. You are being accused of doing a poor job of thinking through your constructs. Here are some possible solutions:

- Think through your concepts better.
- Use methods (for example *concept mapping*) to articulate your concepts.
- Get experts to critique your operationalizations.

Mono-Operation Bias

Mono-operation bias pertains to the independent variable, cause, program, or treatment in your study: it does not pertain to measures or outcomes (see mono-method bias in the following section). If you only use a single version of a program in a single place at a single point in time, you may not be capturing the full breadth of the concept of the program. Every operationalization is flawed relative to the construct on which it is based. If you conclude that your program reflects the construct of the program, your critics are likely to argue that the results of your study reflect only the peculiar version of the program that you implemented, and not the actual construct you had in mind. Solution: try to implement multiple versions of your program.

Mono-Method Bias

Mono-method bias refers to your measures or observations, not to your programs or causes. Otherwise, it's essentially the same issue as mono-operation bias. With only a single version of a self-esteem measure, you can't provide much evidence that you're really measuring self-esteem. Your critics will suggest that you aren't measuring self-esteem, that you're only measuring part of it, for instance. Solution: try to implement multiple measures of key constructs and try to demonstrate (perhaps through a pilot or side study) that the measures you use behave as you theoretically expect them to behave.

Interaction of Different Treatments

You give a new program designed to encourage high-risk teenage girls to go to school and not become pregnant. The results of your study show that the girls in your treatment group have higher school attendance and lower birth rates. You're feeling pretty good about your program until your critics point out that the targeted at-risk treatment group in your study is also likely to be involved simultaneously in several other programs designed to have similar effects. Can you really claim that the program effect is a consequence of your program? The real program that the girls received may actually be the *combination* of the separate programs in which they participated. What can you do about this threat? One approach is to try to isolate the effects of your program from the effects of any other treatments. You could do this by creating a research design that uses a control group (This is discussed in detail in Chapter 6, "Design.") In this case, you could randomly assign some high-risk girls to receive your program and some to a no-program control group. Even if girls in both groups receive some other treatment or program, the only systematic difference between the groups is your program. If you observe differences between them on outcome measures, the differences must be due to the program. By using a control group that makes your program the only thing that differentiates the two groups, you control for the potential confound of multiple treatments.

Interaction of Testing and Treatment

Does testing or measurement itself make the groups more sensitive or receptive to the treatment? If it does, the testing is in effect a part of the treatment; it's inseparable from the effect of the treatment. This is a labeling issue (and, hence, a concern of **construct validity**) because you want to use the label *program* to refer to the program alone, but in fact it includes the testing. As in the previous threat, one way to control for this is through research design. If you are worried that a pretest makes your program participants more sensitive or receptive to the treatment, randomly assign your program participants into two groups, one of which gets the pretest and the other not. If there are differences on outcomes between these groups, you have evidence that there is an effect of the testing. If not, the testing doesn't matter. In fact, there is a research design known as the Solomon Four Group Design that was created explicitly to control for this. (This is discussed in the section "The Solomon Four-Group Design" in Chapter 7, "Experimental Design.")

Restricted Generalizability Across Constructs

This is what I like to refer to as the *unintended consequences* threat to construct validity. You do a study and conclude that Treatment X is effective. In fact, Treatment X does cause a reduction in symptoms, but what you failed to anticipate was the drastic negative consequences of the side effects of the treatment. When you say that Treatment X is effective, you have defined *effective* in regards to only the directly targeted symptom. But, in fact, significant unintended consequences might affect constructs you did not measure and cannot generalize to. This threat should remind you that you have to be careful about whether your observed effects (Treatment X is effective) would generalize to other potential outcomes. How can you deal with this threat? The critical issue here is to try to anticipate the unintended and measure any potential outcomes. For instance, the drug Viagra was not originally developed to help erectile dysfunction. It was created as a drug for hypertension. When that didn't pan out, it was tried as an anti-angina medicine. (The chemists had reason to think a drug designed for hypertension might work on angina.) It was only a chance observation, when the drug was being tested in Wales and men were reporting penile erections, that led the pharmaceutical company to investigate that potential outcome. This is an example of an unintended positive outcome (although there is more recent evidence on Viagra to suggest that the initial enthusiasm needs to be tempered by the potential for its own unanticipated negative side effects).

Confounding Constructs and Levels of Constructs

Imagine a study to test the effect of a new drug treatment for cancer. A fixed dose of the drug is given to a randomly assigned treatment group and a placebo to the other group. No treatment effects are detected, or perhaps the observed result is only true for a certain dosage level. Slight increases or decreases of the dosage may radically change the results. In this context, it is not fair for you to use the label for the drug as a description for your treatment because you only looked at a narrow range of dose. Like the other *construct validity* threats, this threat is essentially a labeling issue; your label is not a good description for what you implemented. What can you do about it? If you find a treatment effect at a specific dosage, be sure to conduct subsequent studies that explore the range of effective doses. Note that, although I use the term "dose" here, you shouldn't limit the idea to medical studies. If you find an educational program effective at a particular dose—say one hour of tutoring a week—conduct subsequent studies to see if dose responses change as you increase or decrease from there. Similarly, if you don't find an effect with an initial dose, don't automatically give up. It may be that at a higher dose the desired outcome will occur.

The Social Threats to Construct Validity

The remaining major threats to construct validity can be distinguished from the ones I discussed previously because they all stem from the social and human nature of the research endeavor. I cover these in the following sections.

Hypothesis Guessing

Most people don't just participate passively in a research project. They guess at what the real purpose of the study is. Therefore, they are likely to base their behavior on what they guess, not just on your treatment. In an educational study conducted in a classroom, students might guess that the key dependent variable has to do with class participation levels. If they increase their participation not because of your program but because they think that's what you're studying, you cannot label the outcome as an effect of the program. It is this labeling issue that makes this a construct validity threat. This is a difficult threat to eliminate. In some studies, researchers try to hide the real purpose of the study, but this may be unethical depending on the circumstances. In some instances, they eliminate the need for participants to guess by telling them the real purpose (although who's to say that participants will believe them). If this is a potentially serious threat, you may think about trying to control for it explicitly through your research design. For instance, you might have multiple program groups and give each one slightly different explanations about the nature of the study even though they all get exactly the same treatment or program. If they perform differently, it may be evidence that they were guessing differently and that this was influencing the results.

Evaluation Apprehension

Many people are anxious about being evaluated. Some are even phobic about testing and measurement situations. If their apprehension makes them perform poorly (and not your program conditions), you certainly can't label that as a treatment effect. Another form of evaluation apprehension concerns the human tendency to want to look good or look smart and so on. If, in their desire to look good, participants perform better (and not as a result of your program), you would be wrong to label this as a treatment effect. In both cases, the apprehension becomes confounded with the treatment itself and you have to be careful about how you label the outcomes. Researchers take a variety of steps to reduce apprehension. In any testing or measurement situation, it is probably a good idea to give participants some time to get comfortable and adjusted to their surroundings. You might ask a few warm-up questions knowing that you are not going to use the answers and trying to encourage the participant to get comfortable responding. (I guess this would be the social research equivalent to the mid-stream urine sample!) In many research projects, people misunderstand what you are measuring. If it is appropriate, you may want to tell them that there are no right or wrong answers and that they aren't being judged or evaluated based on what they say or do.

Experimenter Expectancies

These days, where we engage in lots of nonlaboratory applied social research, we generally don't use the term experimenter to describe the person in charge of the research. So, let's relabel this threat *researcher expectancies*. The researcher can bias the results of a study in countless ways, both consciously or unconsciously. Sometimes the researcher can communicate what the desired outcome for a study might be (and the participants' desire to look good leads them to react that way). For instance, the researcher might look pleased when participants give a desired answer. If researcher feedback causes the response, it would be wrong to label the response a treatment effect. As in many of the previous threats, probably the most effective way to address this threat is to control for it through your research design. For instance, if resources allow, you can have multiple experimenters who differ in their characteristics. Or, you can address the threat through measurement; you can measure expectations prior to the study and use this information in that analysis to attempt to adjust for expectations.

3-1e The Nomological Network

The nomological network (Figure 3.6) is an idea that was developed by Lee Cronbach and Paul Meehl in 1955 (Cronbach, L. and Meehl, P. "Construct Validity in Psychological Tests," *Psychological Bulletin*, 52, 4, (1955). 281-302.) as part of the American Psychological Association's efforts to develop standards for psychological testing. The term *nomological* is derived from Greek and means lawful, so the nomological network can be thought of as the lawful network. The nomological network was Cronbach and Meehl's view of **construct validity**. In short, to provide evidence that your measure has construct validity, Cronbach and Meehl argued that you had to develop a **nomological network** for your measure. This network would include the theoretical framework for what you are trying to measure, an empirical framework for how you are going to measure it, and specification of the linkages among and between these two frameworks.

According to Cronbach and Meehl, the nomological network is founded on the following principles that guide the researcher trying to establish construct validity:

- "Scientifically, to make clear what something is or means, so that laws can be set forth in which that something occurs.

- The laws in a nomological network may relate to:
    - Observable properties or quantities to each other
    - Different theoretical constructs to each other
    - Theoretical constructs to observables
- At least some of the laws in the network must involve observables.
- Learning more about a theoretical construct is a matter of elaborating the nomological network in which it occurs or of increasing the definiteness of its components.
- The basic rule for adding a new construct or relation to a theory is that it must generate laws (nomologicals) confirmed by observation or reduce the number of nomologicals required to predict some observables.
- Operations which are qualitatively different overlap or measure the same thing."

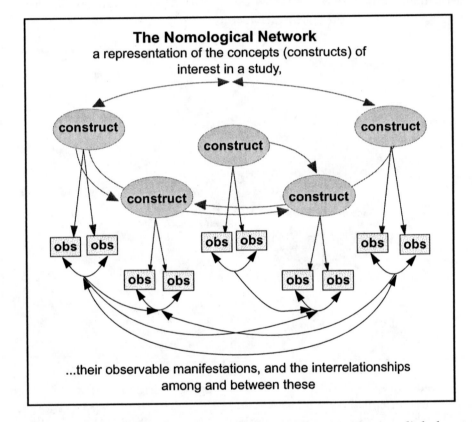

Figure 3.6
The nomological network.

What Cronbach and Meehl were trying to do with this idea is to link the conceptual/theoretical realm with the observable one because this is the central concern of construct validity. While the nomological network idea may be useful as a philosophical foundation for construct validity, it does not provide a practical and usable methodology for actually assessing construct validity. The next phase in the evolution of the idea of construct validity—the development of the MTMM—moved us a bit further toward a methodological approach to construct validity.

The *Multitrait-Multimethod Matrix* (hereafter labeled *MTMM*) is an approach to assessing the construct validity of a set of measures in a study. It was developed in 1959 by Campbell and Fiske (Campbell, D. and Fiske, D. "Convergent and Discriminant Validation by the Multitrait-Multimethod Matrix," *Psychological Bulletin*, 56, 2, 81-105. 1959.) in part as an attempt to provide a practical methodology that researchers could actually use (as opposed to the nomological network

3-1f The Multitrait-Multimethod Matrix

idea, which was theoretically useful but did not include a methodology). Along with the MTMM, Campbell and Fiske introduced two new types of validity: *convergent* and *discriminant*—as subcategories of construct validity. To recap, convergent validity is the degree to which concepts that should be related theoretically are interrelated in reality. ***Discriminant validity*** is the degree to which concepts that should *not* be related theoretically are, in fact, *not* interrelated in reality. You can assess both convergent and discriminant validity using the MTMM. To be able to claim that your measures have construct validity, you have to demonstrate both convergence and discrimination.

The MTMM (see Figure 3.7) is simply a matrix or table of correlations arranged to facilitate the assessment of construct validity. The MTMM assumes that you measure each of several concepts (called *traits* by Campbell and Fiske) by each of several methods (such as a paper-and-pencil test, a direct observation, or a performance measure). The MTMM is a restrictive methodology; ideally, you should measure *each* concept by *each* method.

Figure 3.7
The MTMM matrix.

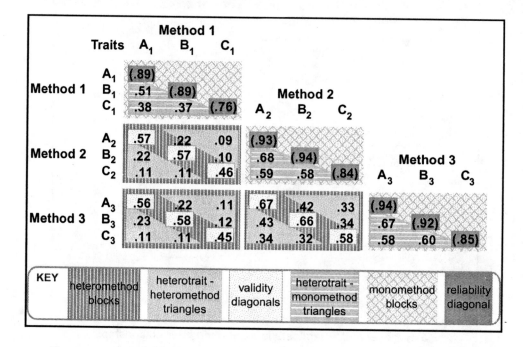

To construct an MTMM, you need to arrange the correlation matrix by methods within concepts. Figure 3.7 shows an MTMM for three concepts (traits 1, 2, and 3) each of which is measured with three different methods (A, B, and C) Note that you lay the matrix out in blocks by *method*. Essentially, the MTMM is just a correlation matrix between your measures, with one exception: instead of 1's along the diagonal (as in the typical correlation matrix) you substitute an estimate of the reliability of each measure as the diagonal (see the discussion on reliability later in this chapter).

Before you can interpret an MTMM, you have to understand how to identify the different parts of the matrix. First, you should note that the matrix consists of nothing but correlations. It is a square, symmetric matrix, so you only need to look at half of it. Figure 3.7 shows the lower triangle. Second, these correlations can be grouped into three kinds of shapes: diagonals, triangles, and blocks. The specific shapes are as follows:

- **The reliability diagonal (monotrait-monomethod).** These are estimates of the reliability of each measure in the matrix. You can estimate reliabilities in different ways (for example, test-retest or internal consistency). There are as many correlations in the reliability diagonal as there are measures; in this example there are nine measures and nine reliabilities. The first reliability in the example is the correlation of Trait A, Method 1 with Trait A, Method 1. (Hereafter, I'll abbreviate this relationship A1-A1). Notice that this is essentially the correlation of the measure with itself. In fact, such a correlation would always be perfect ($r = 1.0$). Instead, you substitute an estimate of reliability. You could also consider these values to be monotrait-monomethod correlations.

- **The validity diagonals (monotrait-heteromethod).** These are correlations between measures of the same trait measured using different methods. Since the MTMM is organized into method blocks, there is one validity diagonal in each method block. For example, look at the A1-A2 correlation of .57 in Figure 3.7. This is the correlation between two measures of the same trait (A) measured with two different measures (1 and 2). Because the two measures are of the same trait or concept, you would expect them to be strongly correlated. You could also consider these values to be monotrait-heteromethod correlations.

- **The heterotrait-monomethod triangles.** These are the correlations among measures that share the same method of measurement, for instance, A1 - B1 = .51 in the upper left heterotrait-monomethod triangle in Figure 3.7. Note that what these correlations share is method, not trait or concept. If these correlations are high, it is because measuring different things with the same method results in correlated measures. Or, in more straightforward terms, you have a strong methods factor.

- **Heterotrait-heteromethod triangles.** These are correlations that differ in both trait and method. For instance, A1-B2 is .22 in the example in Figure 3.7. Generally, because these correlations share neither trait nor method you expect them to be the lowest in the matrix.

- **The monomethod blocks.** These consist of all of the correlations that share the same method of measurement. There are as many blocks as there are methods of measurement.

- **The heteromethod blocks.** These consist of all correlations that do *not* share the same methods. There are $(K(K - 1))/2$ such blocks, where K = the number of methods. In the example in Figure 3.7, there are three methods and so there are $(3(3 - 1))/2 = (3(2))/2 = 6/2 = 3$ such blocks.

Principles of Interpretation

Now that you can identify the different parts of the MTMM, you can begin to understand the rules for interpreting it. You should realize that MTMM interpretation requires the researcher to use judgment. Even though some of the principles might be violated in a specific MTMM, you might still wind up concluding that you have fairly strong **construct validity**. In other words, you won't necessarily get *perfect* adherence to these principles in applied research settings, even when you do have evidence to support construct validity. To me, interpreting an MTMM is a lot like a physician's reading of an x-ray. A practiced eye can often spot things that the neophyte misses! A researcher who is experienced with MTMM can use it to identify weaknesses in measurement as well as to assess construct validity.

To help make the principles more concrete, let's make the example a bit more realistic. Imagine that you are going to conduct a study of sixth-grade students and you want to measure three traits or concepts: Self-Esteem (SE), Self-Disclosure

(SD), and Locus of Control (LC). Furthermore, you want to measure each of these traits three different ways: a Paper-and-Pencil (P&P) measure, a Teacher rating, and a Parent rating. The results are arrayed in the MTMM as shown in Figure 3.8. As the principles are presented, try to identify the appropriate coefficients in the MTMM and make a judgment yourself about the strength of construct validity claims.

Figure 3.8
An example of an MTMM matrix.

Traits	P&P			Teacher			Parent		
	SE_1	SD_1	LC_1	SE_2	SD_2	LC_2	SE_3	SD_3	LC_3
P&P									
SE_1	(.89)								
SD_1	.51	(.89)							
LC_1	.38	.37	(.76)						
Teacher									
SE_2	.57	.22	.09	(.93)					
SD_2	.22	.57	.10	.68	(.94)				
LC_2	.11	.11	.46	.59	.58	(.84)			
Parent									
SE_3	.56	.22	.11	.67	.42	.33	(.94)		
SD_3	.23	.58	.12	.43	.66	.34	.67	(.92)	
LC_3	.11	.11	.45	.34	.32	.58	.58	.60	(.85)

The following list contains the basic principles or rules for the MTMM. You use these rules to determine the strength of the construct validity:

- Coefficients in the reliability diagonal should consistently be the highest in the matrix. That is, a trait should be more highly correlated with itself than with anything else! This rule is uniformly true in the example in Figure 3.8.

- Coefficients in the validity diagonals should be significantly different from zero and high enough to warrant further investigation. This rule is essentially evidence of convergent validity. All of the correlations in Figure 3.8 meet this criterion.

  A validity coefficient should be higher than the values in its column and row in the same heterotrait-heteromethod triangle. In other words, (SE P&P) - (SE Teacher) should be greater than (SE P&P) - (SD Teacher), (SE P&P) - (LC Teacher), (SE Teacher) - (SD P&P) and (SE Teacher) - (LC P&P). This is true in all cases in Figure 3.8.

  A validity coefficient should be higher than all coefficients in the heterotrait-monomethod triangles. This rule essentially emphasizes that trait factors should be stronger than methods factors. Note that this is *not* true in all cases in the example in Figure 3.8. For instance, the (LC P&P) - (LC Teacher) correlation of .46 is less than (SE Teacher) - (SD Teacher), (SE Teacher) - (LC Teacher), and (SD Teacher) - (LC Teacher)—evidence that there might be a methods factor, especially on the Teacher observation method.

- The same *pattern* of trait interrelationship should be seen in all triangles. The example in Figure 3.8 clearly meets this criterion. Notice that in all triangles the SE-SD relationship is approximately twice as large as the relationships that involve LC.

Advantages and Disadvantages of MTMM

The MTMM idea provided an operational methodology for assessing construct validity. In the one matrix, it was possible to examine both convergent and discriminant validity simultaneously. By including methods on an equal footing with traits, Campbell and Fiske stressed the importance of looking for the effects of how we measure in addition to what we measure. Additionally, MTMM provided a rigorous framework for assessing construct validity.

Despite these advantages, MTMM has received little use since its introduction in 1959 for several reasons. First, in its purest form, MTMM requires a fully crossed measurement design; each of several traits is measured by each of several methods. Although Campbell and Fiske explicitly recognized that one could have an incomplete design, they stressed the importance of multiple replication of the same trait across methods. In some applied research contexts, it just isn't possible to measure all traits with all desired methods. (For example, what would you use to obtain multiple observations of weight?) In most applied social research, it isn't feasible to make methods an explicit part of the research design. Second, the judgmental nature of the MTMM may have worked against its wider adoption (although it should actually be perceived as a strength). Many researchers wanted a test for construct validity that would result in a single statistical coefficient that could be tested—the equivalent of a reliability coefficient. It was impossible with MTMM to quantify the *degree* of construct validity in a study. Finally, the judgmental nature of MTMM meant that different researchers could legitimately arrive at different conclusions.

A Modified MTMM —Leaving Out the Methods Factor

What if we try to obtain some of the benefits of the MTMM while minimizing some of the disadvantages that have limited its use? One of the major limiting aspects of the MTMM is the requirement that each construct be measured with multiple methods, a requirement that is just not practical in most applied social research. What if we eliminate that requirement? In this case, the MTMM becomes equivalent to a multitrait matrix and would look like the matrix shown earlier in Figure 3.5 when describing convergent and discriminant validity.

The important thing to notice about the matrix in Figure 3.5 is that *it does not include a methods factor* as a true MTMM would. The matrix does examine both convergent and discriminant validity (just like the MTMM) but it only explicitly looks at construct intra- and interrelationships. That is, it doesn't look at methods relationships like a full MTMM does.

You can see in Figure 3.9 that the MTMM idea really had two major themes. The first is the idea of looking simultaneously at the pattern of convergence and discrimination. This idea is similar in purpose to the notions implicit in the **nomological network** described earlier; you are looking at the *pattern* of interrelationships based upon your theory of the nomological net. The second idea in MTMM is the emphasis on methods as a potential confounding factor.

Although methods may confound the results, they won't necessarily do so in any given study; and, perhaps it is too much to ask of any single methodology that it simultaneously be able to assess construct validity and address the potential for methods factors in measurement. Perhaps if you split the two agendas, you will find that the feasibility of examining convergent and discriminant validity is greater; but what do you do about methods factors? One way to deal with them is to replicate research projects, rather than try to incorporate a methods test into a single research study. Thus, if you find a particular outcome in a study using several measures, you might see whether that same outcome is obtained when you replicate the study using *different methods of measurement* for the same constructs. The methods issue is considered more as an issue of generalizability (across measurement methods) rather than one of construct validity.

When viewed without the methods component, the idea of a MTMM is a much more realistic and practical approach for assessing convergent and discriminant validity, and hence construct validity. You will see that when you move away from the explicit consideration of methods and when you begin to see convergence and discrimination as differences of degree, you essentially have the foundation for the pattern matching approach to assessing construct validity as discussed in the following section.

Figure 3.9
MTMM emphasizes methods as confounding factors.

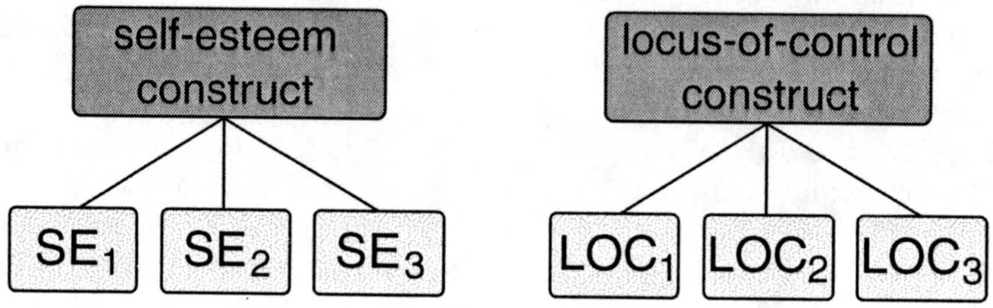

	SE$_1$	SE$_2$	SE$_3$	LOC$_1$	LOC$_2$	LOC$_3$
SE$_1$	1.00	.83	.89	.02	.12	.09
SE$_2$	.83	1.00	.85	.05	.11	.03
SE$_3$	.89	.85	1.00	.04	.00	.06
LOC$_1$	.02	.05	.04	1.00	.84	.93
LOC$_2$	.12	.11	.00	.84	1.00	.91
LOC$_3$	.09	.03	.06	.93	.91	1.00

3-1g Pattern Matching for Construct Validity

The idea of using pattern matching as a rubric for assessing **construct validity** is an area in which I have tried to make a contribution (Trochim, W. 1985. Pattern Matching, Validity, and Conceptualization in Program Evaluation. *Evaluation Review*, 9, 5:575-604 and Trochim, W. 1989. Outcome Pattern Matching and Program Theory. *Evaluation and Program Planning*, 12: 355-366.), although my work was clearly foreshadowed, especially in much of Donald T. Campbell's writings on the MTMM. Here, I'll try to explain what I mean by pattern matching with respect to construct validity.

The Theory of Pattern Matching

A pattern is any arrangement of objects or entities. The term arrangement is used here to indicate that a pattern is by definition nonrandom and at least potentially describable. All theories imply some pattern, but theories and patterns are not the same thing. In general, a theory postulates structural relationships between key constructs. The theory can be used as the basis for generating patterns of predictions. For instance, $E=MC^2$ can be considered a theoretical formulation. A pattern of expectations can be developed from this formula by generating predicted values for one of these variables given fixed values of the others. Not all theories are stated in mathematical form, especially in applied social research, but all theories provide information that enables the generation of patterns of predictions.

Pattern matching always involves an attempt to link two patterns where one is a theoretical pattern and the other is an observed or operational one. The top part of Figure 3.10 shows the realm of theory. The theory might originate from a formal tradition of theorizing, might be the investigator's ideas or hunches, or might arise from some combination of these. The conceptualization task involves the translation of these ideas into a specifiable theoretical pattern indicated by the top shape in the figure. The bottom part of the figure indicates the realm of observation. This is broadly meant to include direct observation in the form of impressions, field notes, and the like, as well as more formal objective measures. The collection or organization of relevant *operationalizations* (relevant to the theoretical pattern) is termed the observational pattern and is indicated by the lower shape in the figure. The inferential task involves the attempt to relate, link, or match these two patterns as indicated by the double arrows in the center of the figure. To the extent that the patterns match, one can conclude that the theory and any other theories might predict the same observed pattern.

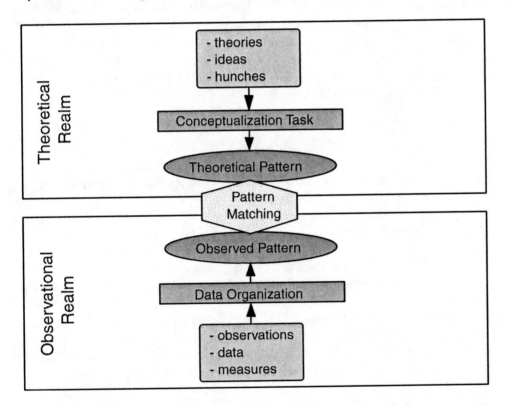

Figure 3.10
The idea of pattern matching.

It is important to demonstrate that no plausible alternative theories can account for the observed pattern and this task is made much easier when the theoretical pattern of interest is a unique one. In effect, a more complex theoretical pattern is like a unique fingerprint that one is seeking in the observed pattern. With more complex theoretical patterns, it is usually more difficult to construe sensible alternative patterns that would also predict the same result. To the extent that theoretical and observed patterns do not match, the theory may be incorrect or poorly formulated; the observations may be inappropriate or inaccurate, or some combination of both states may exist.

All research employs pattern-matching principles, although this is seldom done consciously. In the traditional two-group experimental context (see Chapter 7, "Experimental Design"), for instance, the typical theoretical outcome pattern is the hypothesis that there will be a significant difference between treated and untreated groups. The observed outcome pattern might consist of the averages for the two groups on one or more measures. The pattern match is accomplished by a test of significance such as the t-test or ANOVA. In survey research, pattern matching forms the basis of generalizations across different concepts or population subgroups. (This is covered in Chapter 4, "Survey Research and Scaling.") In qualitative research pattern matching lies at the heart of any attempt to conduct thematic analyses. (This is discussed in Chapter 5, "Qualitative and Unobtrusive Measures.")

While current research methods can be described in pattern-matching terms, the idea of pattern matching implies more and suggests how one might improve on these current methods. Specifically, pattern matching implies that *more complex patterns, if matched, yield greater validity for the theory.* Pattern matching does not differ fundamentally from traditional hypothesis testing and model building approaches. A theoretical pattern is an **hypothesis** about what is expected in the data. The observed pattern consists of the data used to examine the theoretical model. The major differences between pattern matching and more traditional hypothesis-testing approaches are that pattern matching encourages the use of more complex or detailed hypotheses and treats the observations from a multivariate rather than a univariate perspective.

Pattern Matching and Construct Validity

Although pattern matching can be used to address a variety of questions in social research, the emphasis here is on its use in assessing construct validity.

Figure 3.11 shows the pattern-matching structure for an example involving five measurement constructs: arithmetic, algebra, geometry, spelling, and reading. This example, uses **concept mapping** (see Chapter 2, "Sampling") to develop the theoretical pattern among these constructs. In concept mapping, you generate a large set of potential arithmetic, algebra, geometry, spelling, and reading questions. You sort them into piles of similar questions and develop a map that shows each question in relation to the others. On the map, questions that are more similar are closer to each other; those that are less similar are more distant. From the map, you can find the straight-line distances between all pair of points (all questions). This mapping is the matrix of inter-point distances. You might use the questions from the map when constructing your measurement instrument, or you might sample from these questions. On the observed side, you have one or more test instruments that contain a number of questions about arithmetic, algebra, geometry, spelling, and reading. You analyze the data and construct a matrix of inter-item correlations.

What you want to do is compare the matrix of inter-point distances from your concept map (the theoretical pattern) with the correlation matrix of the questions (the observed pattern). How do you achieve this? Let's assume that you had 100 prospective questions on your concept map, 20 for each construct. Correspondingly, you have 100 questions on your measurement instrument, 20 in each area. Thus, both matrices are 100 × 100 in size. Because both matrices are symmetric, you actually have $(N(N-1))/2 = (100(99))/2 = 9900/2 = 4{,}950$ unique pairs (excluding the diagonal). If you string out the values in each matrix, you can construct a vector or column of 4,950 numbers for each matrix. The first number is the value comparing pair (1,2); the next is (1,3) and so on to (N-1, N) or (99, 100). This procedure is illustrated in Figure 3.12. Now, you can compute the overall correlation between these two columns, which is the correlation between the theoretical and observed patterns (the pattern matching correlation). In this example, let's assume it is -.93. Why would it be a *negative* correlation? Because you are correlating *distances* on the map with the *similarities* in the correlations and you expect that *greater* distance on the map should be associated with *lower* correlation and *less* distance with *greater* correlation.

The pattern matching correlation is the overall estimate of the degree of construct validity in this example because it estimates the degree to which the operational measures reflect your theoretical expectations.

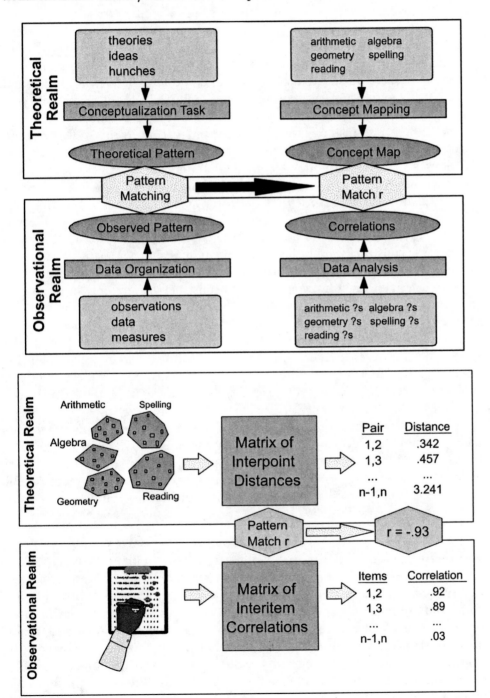

Figure 3.11
A pattern-matching example.

Figure 3.12
Linking expected relationships as measured through concept mapping to observed intercorrelations to achieve a pattern match for construct validity.

Advantages and Disadvantages of Pattern Matching

The pattern-matching approach to construct validity has several disadvantages. The most obvious is that pattern matching requires that you specify your theory of the constructs rather precisely. This is typically not done in applied social research, at least not to the level of specificity implied here; but perhaps it *should* be done. Perhaps the more restrictive assumption in pattern matching is that you are able to structure the theoretical and observed patterns the same way so that you can directly correlate them. This method requires you to quantify both patterns and, ultimately, describe them in matrices that have the same dimensions. In most research as it is currently done, it is relatively easy to construct a matrix of the inter-item correlations from the data. However researchers seldom currently use methods like concept mapping to estimate theoretical patterns that can be linked with the observed ones. Again, perhaps this ought to be done more frequently.

The pattern-matching approach has a number of advantages, especially relative to the **MTMM**. First, it is more *general* and *flexible* than MTMM. It does not require that you measure each construct with multiple methods. Second, it treats convergence and discrimination as a *continuum*. Concepts are more or less similar and so their interrelations would be more or less convergent or discriminant, which moves the convergent/discriminant distinction away from the simplistic dichotomous categorical notion to one that is more suitably post-positivist and continuous in nature. Third, the pattern-matching approach does make it possible to estimate the overall **construct validity** for a set of measures in a specific context—it is the correlation of the theoretical expectations with the observed relationships. Notice that you don't estimate construct validity for a single measure because construct validity, like discrimination, is always a relative metric. Just as you can only ask whether you have distinguished something if there is something to distinguish it from, you can assess construct validity only in terms of a theoretical semantic or nomological net, the conceptual context within which it resides. The pattern-matching correlation tells you, for your particular study, whether there is a demonstrable relationship between how you theoretically expect your measures to interrelate and how they interrelate in practice. Finally, because pattern matching requires a more specific theoretical pattern than you typically articulate, it *requires* you to specify what you think about the constructs. That's got to be a good thing.

Social research has long been criticized for conceptual sloppiness, for repackaging old constructs in new terminology and failing to develop an evolution of research around key theoretical constructs. Perhaps the emphasis on theory articulation in pattern matching will encourage researchers to be more careful about the conceptual underpinnings of their empirical work, and, after all, isn't that what construct validity is all about?

3-2 Reliability

Reliability has to do with the quality of measurement. In its everyday sense, reliability is the consistency or repeatability of your measures. Before I can define reliability precisely, I have to lay the groundwork. First, you have to learn about the foundation of reliability, the true score theory of measurement. Along with that, you need to understand the different types of measurement error because errors in measures play a key role in degrading reliability. With this foundation, you can consider the basic theory of reliability, including a precise definition of reliability. There you will find out that you cannot calculate reliability—you can only estimate it. Because of this, there are a variety of different types of reliability and multiple ways to estimate reliability for each type. In the end, it's important to integrate the idea of reliability with the other major criteria for the quality of measurement—validity—and develop an understanding of the relationships between reliability and validity in measurement.

True score theory is a theory about measurement. Like all theories, you need to recognize that it is not proven; it is postulated as a model of how the world operates. Like many powerful models, true score theory is a simple one. Essentially, *true score theory* maintains that every measurement is an additive composite of two components: true ability (or the true level) of the respondent on that measure; and random error. This is illustrated in Figure 3.13. You observe the measurement: a score on the test, the total for a self-esteem instrument, or the scale value for a person's weight. You don't observe what's on the right side of the equation. (Only God knows what those values are.) You assume that there are only the two components to the right side of the equal sign in the equation.

3-2a True Score Theory

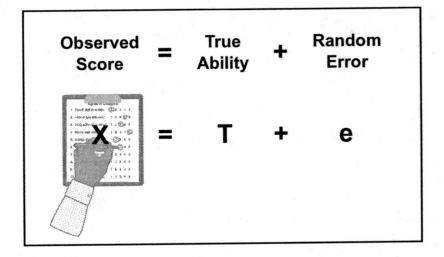

Figure 3.13
The basic equation of true score theory.

The simple equation of $X = T + e_X$ has a parallel equation at the level of the variance or variability of a measure. That is, across a set of scores, you can assume

$$\text{var}(X) = \text{var}(T) + \text{var}(e_X)$$

In more human terms, this means that the variability of your measure is the sum of the variability due to true score and the variability due to random error. This will have important implications when we consider some of the more advanced models for adjusting for errors in measurement later in the section "Nonequivalent Groups Analysis" in Chapter 11, "Analysis for Research Design."

Why is true score theory important? For one thing, it is a simple yet powerful model for measurement. It is a reminder that most measurement has an error component. Second, true score theory is the foundation of reliability theory, which will be discussed later in this chapter. A measure that has no random error (is all true score) is perfectly reliable; a measure that has no true score (is all random error) has zero reliability. Third, the true score theory can be used in computer simulations as the basis for generating observed scores with certain known properties.

You should know that the true score model is not the only measurement model available. Measurement theorists continue to come up with more and more complex models that they think represent reality even better. However these models are complicated enough that they lie outside the boundaries of this book. In any event, true score theory should give you an idea of why measurement models are important at all and how they can be used as the basis for defining key research ideas.

3-2b Measurement Error

True score theory is a good simple model for measurement, but it may not always be an accurate reflection of reality. In particular, it assumes that any observation is composed of the true value plus some random error value; but is that reasonable? What if all error is not random? Isn't it possible that some errors are systematic, that they hold across most or all of the members of a group? One way to deal with this notion is to revise the simple true score model by dividing the error component into two subcomponents, random error and systematic error. Figure 3.14 shows these two components of measurement error, what the difference between them is, and how they affect research.

Figure 3.14
Random and systematic errors in measurement.

$$X = T + e$$

$$X = T + e_r + e_s$$

What Is Random Error?

Random error is caused by any factors that randomly affect measurement of the variable across the sample. For instance, people's moods can inflate or deflate their performance on any occasion. In a particular testing, some children may be in a good mood and others may be depressed. If mood affects the children's performance on the measure, it might artificially inflate the observed scores for some children and artificially deflate them for others. The important thing about random error is that it does not have any consistent effects across the entire sample. Instead, it pushes observed scores up or down randomly. This means that if you could see all the random errors in a distribution they would have to sum to 0. There would be as many negative errors as positive ones. (Of course you can't see the random errors because all you see is the observed score X. God can see the random errors, of course, but she's not telling us what they are!) The important property of random error is that it adds variability to the data but does not affect average performance for the group (see Figure 3.15). Because of this, random error is sometimes considered *noise.*

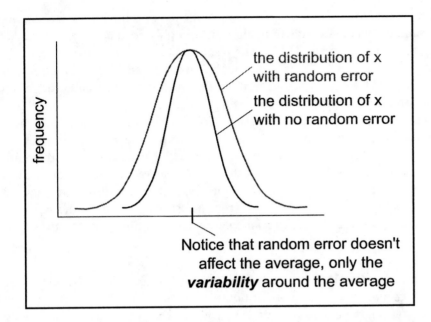

the distribution of x
with random error

the distribution of x
with no random error

Notice that random error doesn't
affect the average, only the
variability around the average

Figure 3.15
Random error adds variability to a distribution but does not affect central tendency (the average).

What Is Systematic Error?

Systematic error is caused by any factors that systematically affect measurement of the variable across the sample. For instance, if there is loud traffic going by just outside of a classroom where students are taking a test, this noise is liable to affect all of the children's scores—in this case, systematically lowering them. Unlike random error, systematic errors tend to be either positive or negative consistently; because of this, systematic error is sometimes considered to be *bias* in measurement (see Figure 3.16).

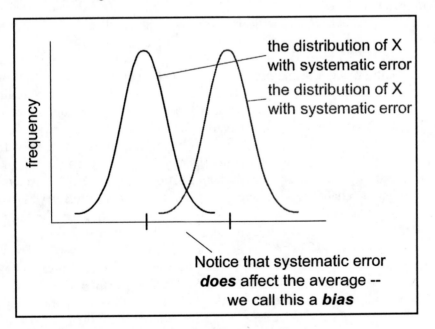

the distribution of X
with systematic error

the distribution of X
with systematic error

Notice that systematic error
does affect the average --
we call this a **bias**

Figure 3.16
Systematic error affects the central tendency of a distribution.

Reducing Measurement Error

So, how can you reduce measurement errors, random or systematic? One thing you can do is to pilot test your instruments to get feedback from your respondents regarding how easy or hard the measure was and information about how the testing environment affected their performance. Second, if you are gathering measures using people to collect the data (as interviewers or observers), you should make sure you train them thoroughly so that they aren't inadvertently introducing error. Third, when you collect the data for your study you should double-check the data thoroughly. All data entry for computer analysis should be double-punched and verified. This means that you enter the data twice, the second time having your data-entry machine check that you are typing the exact same data you typed the first time. Fourth, you can use statistical procedures to adjust for measurement error. These range from rather simple formulas you can apply directly to your data to complex modeling procedures for modeling the error and its effects. Finally, one of the best things you can do to deal with measurement errors, especially systematic errors, is to use multiple measures of the same construct. Especially if the different measures don't share the same systematic errors, you will be able to *triangulate* across the multiple measures and get a more accurate sense of what's happening.

3-2c Theory of Reliability

What is *reliability?* We hear the term used a lot in research contexts, but what does it really mean? If you think about how we use the word reliable in everyday language, you might get a hint. For instance, we often speak about a machine as reliable: "I have a reliable car." Or, news people talk about a "usually reliable source". In both cases, the word reliable usually means dependable or trustworthy. In research, the term reliable also means dependable in a general sense, but that's not a precise enough definition. What does it mean to have a dependable measure or observation in a research context? The reason dependable is not a good enough description is that it can be confused too easily with the idea of a valid measure (see the section, "Construct Validity," earlier in this chapter). Certainly, when researchers speak of a dependable measure, we mean one that is both reliable and valid. So we have to be a little more precise when we try to define reliability.

In research, the term reliability means repeatability or consistency. A measure is considered reliable if it would give you the same result over and over again (assuming that what you are measuring isn't changing).

Let's explore in more detail what it means to say that a measure is repeatable or consistent. I'll begin by defining a measure that I'll arbitrarily label X. It might be a person's score on a math achievement test or a measure of severity of illness. It is the value (numerical or otherwise) that you observe in your study. Now, to see how repeatable or consistent an observation is, you can measure it twice. You use subscripts to indicate the first and second observation of the same measure as shown in Figure 3.17. If you assume that what you're measuring doesn't change between the time of the first and second observation, you can begin to understand how you get at reliability. Although you observe a single score for what you're measuring, you usually think of that score as consisting of two parts: the true score or actual level for the person on that measure, and the error in measuring it (see the section "True Score Theory" earlier in this chapter).

It's important to keep in mind that you observe the **X** score; you never actually see the true (T) or error (e) scores. For instance, a student may get a score of 85 on a math achievement test. That's the score you observe, an X of 85. However the reality might be that the student is actually better at math than that score indicates. Let's say the student's true math ability is 89 (T=89). That means that the error for that student is -4. What does this mean? Well, while the student's true math ability may be 89, he/she may have had a bad day, may not have had breakfast, may have had an argument with someone, or may have been distracted while taking the test. Factors like these can contribute to errors in measurement that make the students' observed abilities appear lower than their true or actual abilities.

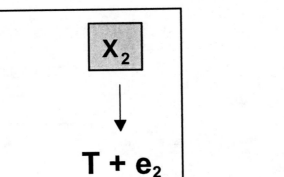

Figure 3.17
Reliability and true score
theory.

Okay, back to reliability. If your measure, X, is reliable, you should find that if you measure or observe it twice on the same persons, the scores should be pretty much the same, assuming that they aren't changing on the thing you're measuring between the two points in time. Why would they be the same? If you look at Figure 3.17, you should see that the only thing that the two observations have in common is their true scores, T. How do you know that? Because the error scores (e_1 and e_2) have different subscripts indicating that they are different values. (You are likely to have different errors on different occasions.) However the true score symbol (T) is the same for both observations. What does this mean? The two observed scores, X_1 and X_2, are related only to the degree that the observations share a true score. You should remember that the error score is assumed to be random (see the section "True Score Theory" earlier in this chapter). Sometimes errors will lead you to perform better on a test than your true ability (you had a good day guessing!) while other times they will lead you to score worse. The true score—your true ability on that measure—would be the same on both observations (assuming, of course, that your true ability didn't change between the two measurement occasions).

With this in mind, I can now define reliability more precisely. Reliability is a ratio or fraction. In layperson terms, you might define this ratio as shown in Figure 3.18.

$$\frac{\text{true level on the measure}}{\text{the entire measure}}$$

Figure 3.18
Reliability can be expressed
as a simple ratio.

You might think of reliability as the proportion of truth in your measure. Now, it makes no sense to speak of the reliability of a measure for an individual; reliability is a characteristic of a measure that's taken across individuals. So, to get closer to a more formal definition, I'll restate the definition of reliability in terms of a set of observations. The easiest way to do this is to speak of the variance of the scores. Remember that the variance is a measure of the spread or distribution of a *set* of scores. So, I can now state the definition as shown in Figure 3.19.

Figure 3.19
The reliability ratio can be expressed in terms of variances.

$$\frac{\text{the variance of the true score}}{\text{the variance of the measure}}$$

I might put this into slightly more technical terms by using the abbreviated name for the variance and our variable names (see Figure 3.20):

Figure 3.20
The reliability ratio expressed in terms of variances in abbreviated form.

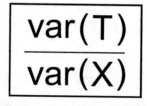

$$\frac{var(T)}{var(X)}$$

We're getting to the critical part now. If you look at the equation in Figure 3.20, you should recognize that you can easily determine or calculate the bottom part of the reliability ratio; it's just the variance of the set of observed scores. (You remember how to calculate the variance, don't you? It's the sum of the squared deviations of the scores from their mean, divided by the number of scores. If you're still not sure, see Chapter 10, "Analysis.") So how do you calculate the variance of the true scores? You can't see the true scores. (You only see X!) Only God knows the true score for a specific observation. Therefore, if you can't calculate the variance of the true scores, you can't compute the ratio, which means *you can't compute reliability!* Everybody got that? Here's the bottom line

You can't compute reliability because you can't calculate the variance of the true scores!

Great. So where does that leave you? If you can't compute reliability, perhaps the best you can do is to *estimate* it. Maybe you can get an estimate of the variability of the true scores. How do you do that? Remember your two observations, X_1 and X_2? You assume (using **true score theory** described earlier in this chapter) that these two observations would be related to each other to the degree that they share true scores. So, let's calculate the correlation between X_1 and X_2. Figure 3.21 shows a simple formula for the correlation:

Figure 3.21
The formula for estimating reliability.

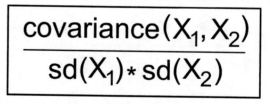

$$\frac{covariance(X_1, X_2)}{sd(X_1) * sd(X_2)}$$

In Figure 3.21, the *sd* stands for the **standard deviation** (which is the square root of the variance). If you look carefully at this equation, you can see that the covariance, which simply measures the shared variance between measures, must be an indicator of the variability of the true scores because the true scores in X_1 and X_2 are the only things the two observations share! So, the top part is essentially an estimate of *var(T)* in this context. Additionally, since the bottom part of the equation multiplies the standard deviation of one observation with the standard deviation of the same measure at another time, you would expect that these two values would be the same (it is the same measure we're taking) and that this is essentially the same thing as squaring the standard deviation for either observation. However, the square of the standard deviation is the same thing as the variance of the measure. So, the bottom part of the equation becomes the variance of the measure (or *var(X)*). If you read this paragraph carefully, you should see that the correlation between two observations of the same measure *is* an estimate of reliability. Got that? I've just shown that a simple and straightforward way to estimate the reliability of a measure is to compute the correlation of the measure administered twice!

It's time to reach some conclusions. You know from this discussion that you cannot calculate reliability because you cannot measure the true score component of an observation. You also know that you can *estimate* the true score component as the covariance between two observations of the same measure. With that in mind, you can estimate the reliability as the correlation between two observations of the same measure. It turns out that there are several ways to estimate this reliability correlation. These are discussed in the section "Types of Reliability" later in this chapter.

There's only one other issue I want to address here. How big is an estimate reliability? To figure this out, let's go back to the equation given earlier (see Figure 3.22).

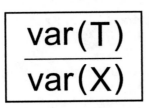

Figure 3.22
The reliability ratio expressed in terms of variances in abbreviated form.

Remember, because X = T + e, you can substitute in the bottom of the ratio as shown in Figure 3.23.

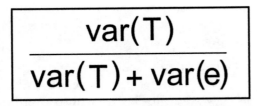

Figure 3.23
The reliability ratio expressed in terms of variances with the variance of the observed score subdivided according to true score theory.

With this slight change, you can easily determine the range of a reliability estimate. If a measure is *perfectly* reliable, there is no error in measurement; everything you observe is true score. Therefore, for a perfectly reliable measure, var(e) is zero and the equation would reduce to the equation shown in Figure 3.24.

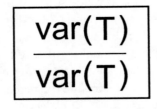

Figure 3.24
When there is no error in measurement you have perfect reliability and the reliability estimate is 1.0.

Therefore, reliability = 1. Now, if you have a perfectly unreliable measure, there is no true score; the measure is entirely error. In this case, the equation would reduce to the equation shown in Figure 3.25.

Figure 3.25
When there is only error in measurement, you have no reliability and the reliability estimate is 0.

$$\boxed{\dfrac{0}{\text{var}(e)}}$$

Therefore, the reliability = 0. From this you know that reliability will always range between 0 and 1.

The value of a reliability estimate tells you the proportion of variability in the measure attributable to the true score. A reliability of .5 means that about half of the variance of the observed score is attributable to truth and half is attributable to error. A reliability of .8 means the variability is about 80% true ability and 20% error, and so on.

3-2d Types of Reliability

You learned in the section "Theory of Reliability," earlier in this chapter, that it's not possible to calculate reliability exactly. Instead, you have to estimate reliability, and this is always an imperfect endeavor. Here, I want to introduce the major reliability estimators and talk about their strengths and weaknesses.

There are four *general classes of reliability estimates*, each of which estimates reliability in a different way:

- **Inter-rater or inter-observer reliability** is used to assess the degree to which different raters/observers give consistent estimates of the same phenomenon.
- **Test-retest reliability** is used to assess the consistency of a measure from one time to another.
- **Parallel-forms reliability** is used to assess the consistency of the results of two tests constructed in the same way from the same content domain.
- **Internal consistency reliability** is used to assess the consistency of results across items within a test.

I'll discuss each of these in turn.

Inter-Rater or Inter-Observer Reliability

Whenever you use humans as a part of your measurement procedure, you have to worry about whether the results you get are reliable or consistent. People are notorious for their inconsistency. We are easily distractible. We get tired of doing repetitive tasks. We daydream. We misinterpret.

So how do you determine whether two observers are being consistent in their observations? You probably should establish inter-rater reliability outside of the context of the measurement in your study. After all, if you use data from your study to establish reliability, and you find that reliability is low, you're kind of stuck. Probably it's best to do this as a side study or pilot study. If your study continues for a long time, you may want to reestablish inter-rater reliability from time to time to ensure that your raters aren't changing.

There are two major ways to actually estimate inter-rater **reliability**. If your measurement consists of categories—the raters are checking off which category each observation falls in—you can calculate the percent of agreement between the raters. For instance, let's say you had 100 observations that were being rated by two raters. For each observation, the rater could check one of three categories. Imagine that on 86 of the 100 observations the raters checked the same category.

In this case, the percent of agreement would be 86%. Okay, it's a crude measure, but it does give an idea of how much agreement exists, and it works no matter how many categories are used for each observation.

The other major way to estimate inter-rater reliability is appropriate when the measure is a continuous one. In such a case, all you need to do is calculate the correlation between the ratings of the two observers. For instance, they might be rating the overall level of activity in a classroom on a 1-to-7 scale. You could have them give their rating at regular time intervals (every 30 seconds). The correlation between these ratings would give you an estimate of the reliability or consistency between the raters (see Figure 3.26).

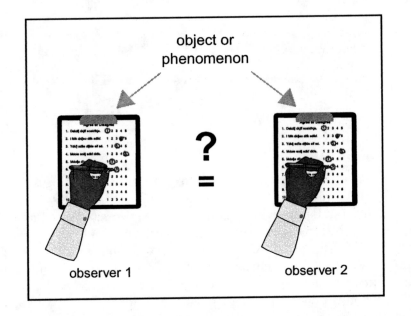

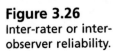
Figure 3.26
Inter-rater or inter-observer reliability.

You might think of this type of reliability as calibrating the observers. There are other things you could do to encourage reliability between observers, even if you don't estimate it. For instance, I used to work in a psychiatric unit where every morning a nurse had to do a ten-item rating of each patient on the unit. Of course, we couldn't count on the same nurse being present every day, so we had to find a way to ensure that all the nurses would give comparable ratings. The way we did it was to hold weekly calibration meetings where we would have all of the nurses' ratings for several patients and discuss why they chose the specific values they did. If there were disagreements, the nurses would discuss them and attempt to come up with rules for deciding when they would give a 3 or a 4 for a rating on a specific item. Although this was not an estimate of reliability, it probably went a long way toward improving the reliability between raters.

Test-Retest Reliability

You estimate test-retest *reliability* when you administer the same test to the same (or a similar) sample on two different occasions (see Figure 3.27). This approach assumes that there is no substantial change in the construct being measured between the two occasions. The amount of time allowed between measures is critical. You know that if you measure the same thing twice, the correlation between the two observations will depend in part on how much time elapses between the two measurement occasions. The shorter the time gap, the higher the correlation; the longer the time gap, the lower the correlation because the two observations are related over time; the closer in time you get, the more similar the factors that contribute to error. Since this correlation is the test-retest estimate of reliability, you can obtain considerably different estimates depending on the interval.

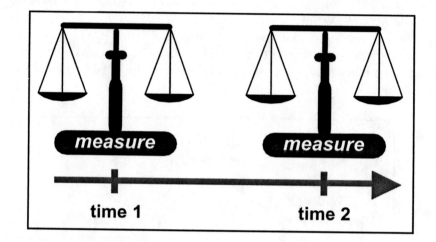

Parallel-Forms Reliability

In parallel-forms reliability, you first have to create two parallel forms. One way to accomplish this is to start with a large set of questions that address the same construct and then randomly divide the questions into two sets. You administer both instruments to the same sample of people. The correlation between the two parallel forms is the estimate of *reliability*. One major problem with this approach is that you have to be able to generate lots of items that reflect the same construct, which is often no easy feat. Furthermore, this approach makes the assumption that the randomly divided halves are parallel or equivalent. Even by chance, this will sometimes not be the case. The parallel-forms approach is similar to the split-half reliability described later. The major difference is that parallel forms are constructed so that the two forms can be used independently of each other and considered equivalent measures. For instance, you might be concerned about a testing threat to internal validity. If you use Form A for the pretest and Form B for the posttest, you minimize that problem. It would even be better if you randomly assign individuals to receive Form A or B on the pretest and then switch them on the posttest. With split-half reliability, you have an instrument to use as a single-measurement instrument and only develop randomly split halves for purposes of estimating *reliability* (see Figure 3.28).

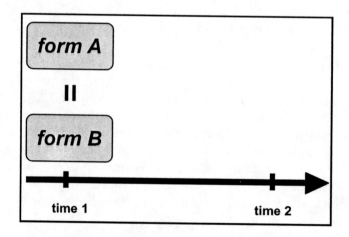

Internal Consistency Reliability

In internal-consistency reliability estimation, you use your single measurement instrument administered to a group of people on one occasion to estimate **reliability**. In effect, you judge the reliability of the instrument by estimating how well the items that reflect the same construct yield similar results. You are looking at how consistent the results are for different items for the same construct within the measure. There are a wide variety of internal-consistency measures you can use.

Average Inter-item Correlation

The average inter-item correlation uses all of the items on your instrument that are designed to measure the same construct. You first compute the correlation between each pair of items, as illustrated Figure 3.29. For example, if you have six items, you will have 15 different item pairings (15 correlations). The average inter-item correlation is simply the average or mean of all these correlations. In the example, you find an average inter-item correlation of .90 with the individual correlations ranging from .84 to .95.

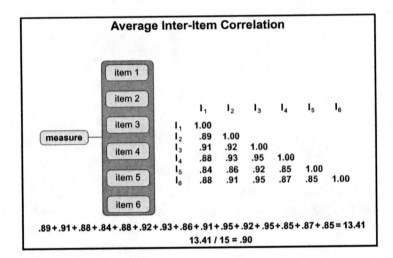

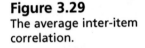

Figure 3.29
The average inter-item correlation.

Average Item-total Correlation

This approach also uses the inter-item correlations. In addition, you compute a total score for the six items and use that as a seventh variable in the analysis. Figure 3.30 shows the six item-to-total correlations at the bottom of the correlation matrix. They range from .82 to .88 in this sample analysis, with the average of these at .85.

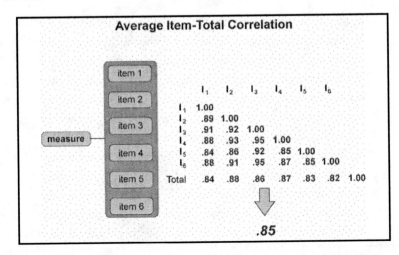

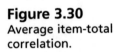

Figure 3.30
Average item-total correlation.

Split-Half Reliability

In split-half reliability, you randomly divide all items that purport to measure the same construct into two sets. You administer the entire instrument to a sample of people and calculate the total score for each randomly divided half. The split-half reliability estimate, as shown Figure 3.31, is simply the correlation between these two total scores. In the example, it is .87.

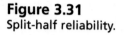

Figure 3.31
Split-half reliability.

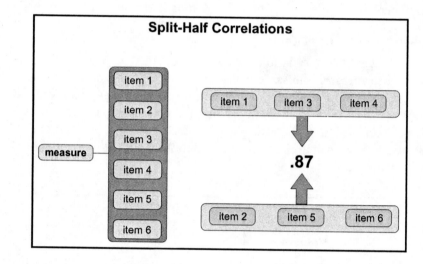

Cronbach's Alpha (α)

Imagine that you compute one split-half reliability and then randomly divide the items into another set of split halves and recompute, and keep doing this until you have computed all possible split-half estimates of **reliability. Cronbach's Alpha** is mathematically equivalent to the average of all possible split-half estimates (although that's not how it's typically computed). Notice that when I say you compute all possible split-half estimates, I don't mean that each time you measure a new sample! That would take forever. Instead, you calculate all split-half estimates from the same sample. Because you measured all your sample on each of the six items, all you have to do is have the computer analysis do the random subsets of items and compute the resulting correlations. Figure 3.32 shows several of the

Figure 3.32
Cronbach's alpha estimate of reliability.

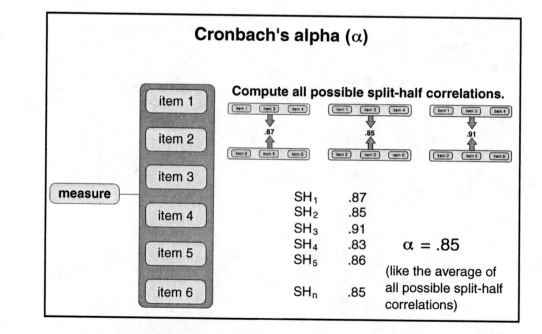

split-half estimates for our six-item example and lists them as SH with a subscript. Keep in mind that although Cronbach's Alpha is equivalent to the average of all possible split-half correlations, you would never actually calculate it that way. Some clever mathematician (Cronbach, I presume!) figured out a way to get the mathematical equivalent a lot more quickly.

Comparison of Reliability Estimators

Each of the reliability estimators has certain advantages and disadvantages. Inter-rater reliability is one of the best ways to estimate *reliability* when your measure is an observation. However, it requires multiple raters or observers. As an alternative, you could look at the correlation of ratings of the same single observer repeated on two different occasions. For example, let's say you collected videotapes of child-mother interactions and had a rater code the videos for how often the mother smiled at the child. To establish inter-rater reliability, you could take a sample of videos and have two raters code them independently. To estimate test-retest reliability, you could have a single rater code the same videos on two different occasions. You might use the inter-rater approach especially if you were interested in using a team of raters and you wanted to establish that they yielded consistent results. If you get a suitably high inter-rater reliability, you could then justify allowing them to work independently on coding different videos. You might use the test-retest approach when you only have a single rater and don't want to train any others. On the other hand, in some studies it is reasonable to do both to help establish the reliability of the raters or observers.

You use the parallel-forms estimator only in situations where you intend to use the two forms as alternate measures of the same thing. Both the parallel forms and all of the internal consistency estimators have one major constraint: you have to have lots of items designed to measure the same construct. This is relatively easy to achieve in certain contexts like achievement testing. (It's easy, for instance, to construct many similar addition problems for a math test.) However for more complex or subjective constructs, this can be a real challenge. With lots of items, Cronbach's Alpha tends to be the most frequently used estimate of internal consistency.

The test-retest estimator is especially feasible in most experimental and quasi-experimental designs that use a no-treatment control group. In these designs, you always have a control group that is measured on two occasions (pretest and posttest). The main problem with this approach is that you don't have any information about reliability until you collect the posttest and, if the reliability estimate is low, you're pretty much sunk.

Each of the reliability estimators gives a different value for reliability. In general, the test-retest and inter-rater reliability estimates will be lower in value than the parallel-forms and internal-consistency estimates because they involve measuring at different times or with different raters. Since reliability estimates are often used in statistical analyses of quasi-experimental designs (see the section "The Nonequivalent Groups Design" in Chapter 8, "Quasi-Experimental Design"), the fact that different estimates can differ considerably makes the analysis even more complex.

3-2e Reliability and Validity

We often think of *reliability* and *validity* as separate ideas but, in fact, they're related to each other. Here, I want to show you two ways you can think about their relationship.

Figure 3.33
The shooting-target metaphor for reliability and validity of measurement.

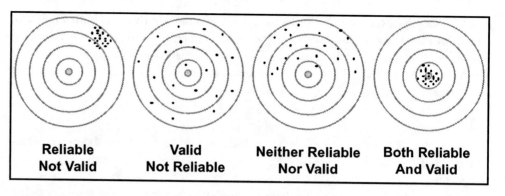

Reliable Not Valid   **Valid Not Reliable**   **Neither Reliable Nor Valid**   **Both Reliable And Valid**

One of my favorite metaphors for the relationship between reliability and validity is that of the target. Think of the center of the target as the concept you are trying to measure. Imagine that for each person you are measuring, you are taking a shot at the target. If you measure the concept perfectly for a person, you are hitting the center of the target. If you don't, you are missing the center. The more you are off for that person, the further you are from the center (see Figure 3.33).

Figure 3.33 shows four possible situations. In the first one, you are hitting the target consistently, but you are missing the center of the target. That is, you are consistently and systematically measuring the wrong value for all respondents. This measure is reliable, but not valid. (It's consistent but wrong.) The second shows hits that are randomly spread across the target. You seldom hit the center of the target but, on average, you are getting the right answer for the group (but not very well for individuals). In this case, you get a valid group estimate, but you are inconsistent. Here, you can clearly see that reliability is directly related to the variability of your measure. The third scenario shows a case where your hits are spread across the target and you are consistently missing the center. Your measure in this case is neither reliable nor valid. Finally, the figure shows the Robin Hood scenario; you consistently hit the center of the target. Your measure is both reliable and valid. (I bet you never thought of Robin Hood in those terms before.)

Another way to think about the relationship between reliability and validity is shown in Figure 3.34, which contains a 2 x 2 table. The columns of the table

Figure 3.34
Comparison of reliability and validity of measurement.

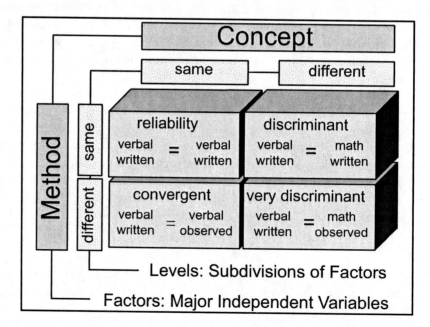

indicate whether you are trying to measure the same or different concepts. The rows show whether you are using the same or different methods of measurement. Imagine that you have two concepts you would like to measure: student verbal and math ability. Furthermore, imagine that you can measure each of these in two ways. First, you can use a written, paper-and-pencil exam (much like the SAT or GRE exams). Second, you can ask the students' classroom teachers to give you a rating of the students' ability based on their own classroom observation.

The first cell on the upper left shows the comparison of the verbal written test score with the verbal written test score; but how can you compare the same measure with itself? You could do this by estimating the reliability of the written test through a test-retest correlation, parallel forms, or an internal consistency measure (see the section "Types of Reliability" earlier in this chapter). What you are estimating in this cell is the reliability of the measure.

The cell on the lower left shows a comparison of the verbal written measure with the verbal teacher observation rating. Because you are trying to measure the same concept, you are looking at **convergent validity** (see "Measurement Validity Types," earlier in this chapter).

The cell on the upper left shows the comparison of the verbal written exam with the math written exam. Here, you are comparing two different concepts (verbal versus math) and so you would expect the relationship to be lower than a comparison of the same concept with itself (verbal versus verbal or math versus math). Thus, you are trying to discriminate between two concepts and this could be labeled **discriminant validity**.

Finally, you have the cell on the lower right. Here, you are comparing the verbal written exam with the math teacher observation rating. Like the cell on the upper right, you are also trying to compare two different concepts (verbal versus math) and so this is also a discriminant validity estimate. However, here you are also trying to compare two different methods of measurement (written exam versus teacher observation rating). So, I'll call this *very* discriminant to indicate that you would expect the relationship in this cell to be even lower than in the one above it.

The four cells incorporate the different values that you examine in the **MTMM** approach to estimating **construct validity** described earlier in this chapter.

When you look at reliability and validity in this way, you see that, rather than being distinct, they actually form a continuum. On one end is the situation where the concepts and methods of measurement are the same (reliability) and on the other is the situation where both concepts and methods of measurement are different (*very* discriminant validity).

3-3 Levels of Measurement

The level of measurement refers to the relationship among the values that are assigned to the attributes for a variable. What does that mean? Begin with the idea of the variable, for example party affiliation (see Figure 3.35). That variable has a number of attributes. Let's assume that in this particular election context, the only relevant attributes are republican, democrat, and independent. For purposes of analyzing the results of this variable, we arbitrarily assign the values 1, 2, and 3 to the three attributes. The *level of measurement* describes the relationship among these three values. In this case, the numbers function as shorter placeholders for the lengthier text terms. Don't assume that higher values mean more of something or lower numbers signify less. Don't assume the value of 2 means that democrats are twice something that republicans are or that republicans are in first place or have the highest priority just because they have the value of 1. In this case, the level of measurement can be described as nominal.

Figure 3.35
The level of measurement describes the relationship among the values associated with the attributes of a variable.

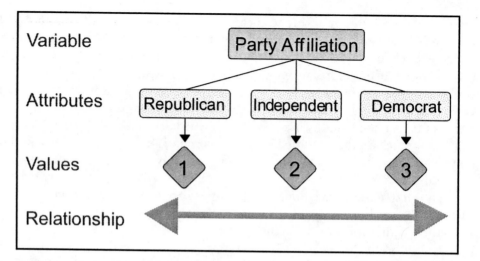

3-3a Why Is Level of Measurement Important?

First, knowing the level of measurement helps you decide how to interpret the data from that variable. When you know that a measure is nominal (like the one just described), you know that the numerical values are short codes for the longer names. Second, knowing the level of measurement helps you decide what statistical analysis is appropriate on the values that were assigned. If a measure is nominal, you know that you would never average the data values or do a t-test on the data.

There are typically four levels of measurement that are defined (see Figure 3.36):

- **Nominal**: In nominal measurement the numerical values simply name the attribute uniquely. No ordering of the cases is implied. For example, jersey numbers in basketball are measures at the nominal level. A player with number 30 is not more of anything than a player with number 15, and is certainly not twice whatever number 15 is.
- **Ordinal**: In ordinal measurement the attributes can be rank-ordered. Here, distances between attributes do not have any meaning. For example, on a survey you might code Educational Attainment as 0 = less than H.S.; 1 = some H.S.; 2 = H.S. degree; 3 = some college; 4 = college degree; 5 = post college. In this measure, higher numbers mean *more* education. Is distance from 0 to 1 the same as 3 to 4? Of course not. The interval between values is not interpretable in an ordinal measure.
- **Interval**: In interval measurement the distance between attributes *does* have meaning. For example, when we measure temperature (in Fahrenheit), the distance from 30-40 is same as distance from 70-80. The interval between values is interpretable. Because of this, it makes sense to compute an average of an interval variable, where it doesn't make sense to do so for ordinal scales. Note, however, that in interval measurement ratios don't make any sense; 80 degrees is not twice as hot as 40 degrees (although the attribute value is twice as large).
- **Ratio**: In ratio measurement there is always a meaningful absolute zero that is meaningful. This means that you can construct a meaningful fraction (or ratio) with a ratio variable. Weight is a ratio variable. In applied social research most *count* variables are ratio, for example, the number of clients in the past six months. Why? Because you can have zero clients and because it is meaningful to say, "We had twice as many clients in the past six months as we did in the previous six months."

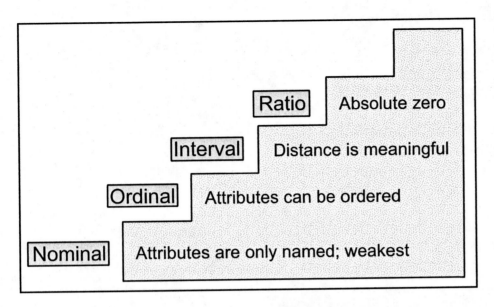

Figure 3.36
The hierarchy of measurement levels.

It's important to recognize that there is a hierarchy implied in the level of measurement idea. At lower levels of measurement, assumptions tend to be less restrictive and data analyses tend to be less sensitive. At each level up the hierarchy, the current level includes all of the qualities of the one below it and adds something new. In general, it is desirable to have a higher level of measurement (such as interval or ratio) rather than a lower one (such as nominal or ordinal).

SUMMARY

This chapter laid the foundation for the idea of measurement. Three broad topics were considered. First, **construct validity** refers to the degree to which you are measuring what you intended to measure. Construct validity is divided into translation validity (the degree to which you translated the construct well) and criterion-related validity (the degree to which your measure relates to or predicts other criteria as theoretically predicted). There is a long tradition of methods that attempt to assess construct validity that goes back to the original articulation of the **nomological network**, through the **MTMM** matrix and on to **pattern-matching** approaches. Second, **reliability** refers to the consistency or dependability of your measurement. Reliability is based upon **true score theory**, which holds that any observation can be divided into two—a true score and error component. Reliability is defined as the ratio of the true score variance to the observed variance in a measure. Third, the level of a measure describes the relationship implicit among that measure's values and determines the type of statistical manipulations that are sensible. With these three ideas—construct validity, reliability, and level of measurement—as a foundation, you can now move on to some of the more practical and useful aspects of measurement in the next few chapters.

Chapter

4

Survey Research and Scaling

Survey research is one of the most important areas of measurement in applied social research. This chapter covers the different types of surveys that are possible. These are roughly divided into two broad areas: questionnaires and interviews. Next, I'll explain how you select the survey method best for your situation. After you select the survey method, you have to construct the survey itself. I'll discuss a number of issues, including the different types of questions; decisions about question content; decisions about question wording; decisions about response format; and question placement and sequence in your instrument. I'll turn next to some of the special issues involved in administering a personal interview. Finally, I'll consider some of the advantages and disadvantages of survey methods.

In the second part of this chapter, I'll move on to discuss scaling, which evolved from the need to measure abstract concepts that seem to be unmeasurable, such as self-esteem. First, I discuss general issues in scaling, which cover the distinction between the scale and the response format. I also explain the difference between multidimensional and unidimensional scaling. Finally I look in depth at three types of unidimensional scales: Thurstone, Likert, and Guttman. From these discussions, you should not only learn how to use the various scales, but you should also learn when each scale type is most appropriate.

Key Terms

concept mapping
cumulative or Guttman scale
dichotomous question
filter or contingency question
interval level response
Likert scale
median
multioption variable
nominal response format
ordinal response format
projective question
response brackets
response format
response scale
sample
sampling
sampling frame
scaling
semantic differential
single-option variable
structured response formats
unstructured response formats

4-1 Survey Research

4-1a Types of Surveys

The broad area of survey research encompasses any measurement procedures that involve asking questions of respondents. A survey can be anything from a short paper-and-pencil feedback form to an intensive one-on-one, in-depth interview.

Surveys can be divided into two broad categories: the questionnaire and the interview. Questionnaires are usually paper-and-pencil instruments that the respondent completes. Interviews are completed by the interviewer based on what the respondent says. Sometimes, it's hard to tell the difference between a questionnaire and an interview. For instance, some people think that questionnaires always ask short closed-ended questions while interviews always ask broad open-ended ones; but you will see questionnaires with open-ended questions (although they do tend to be shorter than interview questions) and there will often be a series of closed-ended questions asked in an interview.

Survey research has changed dramatically in the last ten years. Automated telephone surveys use random dialing methods. Computerized kiosks in public places allow people to ask for input. A new variation of group interview has evolved as focus group methodology. Increasingly, survey research is tightly integrated with the delivery of service. Your hotel room has a survey on the desk. Your waiter presents a short customer satisfaction survey with your check. You get a call for an interview several days after your last call to a computer company for technical assistance, and are asked to complete a short survey when you visit a Web site. Here, I'll describe the major types of questionnaires and interviews, keeping in mind that technology is leading to rapid evolution of methods. I'll discuss the relative advantages and disadvantages of these different survey types in the section "Advantages and Disadvantages of Survey Methods," later in this chapter.

Questionnaires

When most people think of questionnaires, they think of the *mail survey*. All of us have, at some time, received a questionnaire in the mail. Mail surveys have many advantages. They are relatively inexpensive to administer. You can send the exact same instrument to a wide number of people. They allow the respondent to fill it out at their own convenience. However, there are some disadvantages as well. Response rates from mail surveys are often low, and, mail questionnaires are not the best vehicles for asking for detailed written responses.

A second type is the *group-administered questionnaire*. A sample of respondents is brought together and asked to respond to a structured sequence of questions. Traditionally, questionnaires have been administered in group settings for convenience. The researcher can give the questionnaire to those who are present and be fairly sure that there will be a high response rate. If the respondents don't understand the meaning of a question, they can ask for clarification. Additionally, in many organizational settings, it is relatively easy to assemble the group (in a company or business, for instance).

What's the difference between a group-administered questionnaire and a group interview or focus group? In the group-administered questionnaire, each respondent is *handed an instrument* and asked to complete it while in the room. Each respondent completes an instrument. In the group interview or focus group, the interviewer facilitates the session. People work as a group, listening to each other's comments and answering the questions. Someone takes notes for the entire group; people don't complete an interview individually.

A less familiar type of questionnaire is the *household drop-off* survey. In this approach, a researcher goes to the respondent's home or business and hands the respondent the instrument. In some cases, the respondent is asked to mail it back; in others, the interviewer returns to pick it up. This approach attempts to blend the advantages of the mail survey and the group-administered questionnaire. Like the mail survey, the respondent can work on the instrument in private, when it's convenient. Like the group-administered questionnaire, the interviewers make personal contact with the respondent; they don't just send an impersonal survey instrument. Additionally, the respondents can ask questions about the study and get clarification on what they are being asked to do. Generally, this increases the percentage of people willing to respond.

Interviews

Interviews are a far more personal form of research than questionnaires. In the *personal interview*, the interviewer works directly with the respondent. In contrast to mail surveys, the interviewer has the opportunity to probe or ask follow-up questions, and interviews are generally easier for the respondent, especially if you are seeking opinions or impressions. Interviews can be time consuming and they are resource intensive. The interviewer is considered a part of the measurement instrument and interviewers have to be well trained to respond to any contingency.

Almost everyone is familiar with the *telephone interview*. Telephone interviews enable a researcher to gather information rapidly. Most of the major public opinion polls that are reported are based on telephone interviews. Like personal interviews, they allow for some personal contact between the interviewer and the respondent. They also allow the interviewer to ask follow-up questions; but they have some major disadvantages. Many people don't have publicly listed telephone numbers; some don't have telephones; people often don't like the intrusion of a call to their homes; and telephone interviews have to be relatively short or people will feel imposed upon.

Selecting the type of survey you are going to use is one of the most critical decisions in many social research contexts. A few simple rules will help you make the decision; you have to use your judgment to balance the advantages and disadvantages of different survey types. Here, all I want to do is give you a number of questions you might ask to guide your decision.

4-1b Selecting the Survey Method

Population Issues

The first set of considerations has to do with the population and its accessibility.

- **Can the population be enumerated?** For some populations, you have a complete listing of the units to be sampled. For others, such a list is difficult or impossible to compile. For instance, there are complete listings of registered voters or person with active drivers licenses; but no one keeps a complete list of homeless people. If you are doing a study that requires input from homeless persons, it's likely that you'll need to go and find the respondents personally. In such contexts, you can pretty much rule out the idea of mail surveys or telephone interviews.
- **Is the population literate?** Questionnaires require that your respondents read. While this might seem initially like a reasonable assumption for most adult populations, recent research suggests that the instance of adult illiteracy is alarmingly high. Even if your respondents can read to some degree, your questionnaire might contain difficult or technical vocabulary. Clearly, you would expect some populations to be illiterate. Young children would not be good targets for questionnaires.

- **Are there language issues?** We live in a multilingual world. Virtually every society has members who speak a language other than the predominant language. Some countries (like Canada) are officially multilingual, and our increasingly global economy requires us to do research that spans countries and language groups. Can you produce multiple versions of your questionnaire? For mail instruments, can you know in advance which language your respondent speaks, or do you send multiple translations of your instrument? Can you be confident that important connotations in your instrument are not culturally specific? Could some of the important nuances get lost in the process of translating your questions?

- **Will the population cooperate?** People who do research on illegal immigration have a difficult methodological problem. They often need to speak with illegal immigrants or people who may be able to identify others who are. Why would those respondents cooperate? Although the researcher may mean no harm, the respondents are at considerable risk legally if information they divulge should get into the hands of the authorities. The same can be said for any target group that is engaging in illegal or unpopular activities.

- **What are the geographic restrictions?** Is your population of interest dispersed over too broad a geographic range for you to study feasibly with a personal interview? It may be possible for you to send a mail instrument to a nationwide sample. You may be able to conduct phone interviews with them; but it will almost certainly be less feasible to do research that requires interviewers to visit directly with respondents if they are widely dispersed.

Sampling Issues

The *sample* is the actual group you will have to contact in some way. When doing survey research you need to consider several important sampling issues.

- **What data is available?** What information do you have about your sample? Do you have current addresses? Current phone numbers? Are your contact lists up to date?

- **Can respondents be found?** Can your respondents be located? Some people are very busy. Some travel a lot. Some work the night shift. Even if you have an accurate phone or address, you may not be able to locate or make contact with your sample.

- **Who is the respondent?** Who is the respondent in your study? Let's say you draw a sample of households in a small city. A household is not a respondent. Do you want to interview a specific individual? Do you want to talk only to the head of household (and how is that person defined)? Are you willing to talk to any member of the household? Do you state that you will speak to the first adult member of the household who opens the door? What if that person is unwilling to be interviewed but someone else in the house is willing? How do you deal with multifamily households? Similar problems arise when you sample groups, agencies, or companies. Can you survey any member of the organization? Or, do you only want to speak to the Director of Human Resources? What if the person you would like to interview is unwilling or unable to participate? Do you use another member of the organization?

- **Can all members of the population be sampled?** If you have an incomplete list of the population (*sampling frame*) you may not be able to sample every member of the population. Lists of various groups are extremely hard to keep up to date. People move or change their names. Even though they are on your sampling frame listing, you may not be able to get to them. It's also possible they are not even on the list.

- **Are response rates likely to be a problem?** Even if you are able to solve all of the other population and sampling problems, you still have to deal with the issue of response rates. Some members of your sample will simply refuse to respond. Others have the best of intentions, but can't seem to find the time to send in your questionnaire by the due date. Still others misplace the instrument or forget about the appointment for an interview. Low response rates are among the most difficult of problems in survey research. They can ruin an otherwise well-designed survey effort.

Question Issues

Sometimes the nature of what you want to ask respondents determines the type of survey you select.

- **What types of questions can you ask?** Are you going to be asking personal questions? Are you going to need to get lots of detail in the responses? Can you anticipate the most frequent or important types of responses and develop reasonable closed-ended questions?

- **How complex will the questions be?** Sometimes you are dealing with a complex subject or topic. The questions you want to ask are going to have multiple parts. You may need to branch to subquestions.

- **Will screening questions be needed?** A screening question may be needed to determine whether the respondent is qualified to answer your question of interest. For instance, you wouldn't want to ask for respondents' opinions about a specific computer program without first screening to find out whether they have any experience using the program. Sometimes you have to screen on several variables (for example, age, gender, and experience). The more complicated the screening, the less likely it is that you can rely on paper-and-pencil instruments without confusing the respondent.

- **Can question sequence be controlled?** Is your survey one in which you can construct a reasonable sequence of questions in advance? Or, are you doing an initial exploratory study in which you may need to ask follow-up questions that you can't easily anticipate?

- **Will lengthy questions be asked?** If your subject matter is complicated, you may need to give the respondent some detailed background for a question. Can you reasonably expect your respondent to sit still long enough in a phone interview to ask your question?

- **Will long response scales be used?** If you are asking people about the different computer equipment they use, you may have to have a lengthy response list (CD-ROM drive, floppy drive, mouse, touch pad, modem, network connection, external speakers, and so on). Clearly, it may be difficult to ask about each of these in a short phone interview.

Content Issues

The content of your study can also pose challenges for the different survey types you might utilize.

- **Can the respondents be expected to know about the issue?** If respondents do not keep up with the news (for example by reading the newspaper, watching television news, or talking with others), they may not even know of the news issue you want to ask them about. Or, if you want to do a study of family finances and you are talking to the spouse who doesn't pay the bills on a regular basis, he or she may not have the information to answer your questions.

- **Will respondent need to consult records?** Even if the respondents understand what you're asking about, you may need to allow them to consult their records to get an accurate answer. For instance, if you ask them how much money they spent on food in the past month, they may need to look up their personal check and credit card records. In this case, you don't want to be involved in an interview where they would have to go look things up while they keep you waiting. (They wouldn't be comfortable with that.)

Bias Issues

People come to the research endeavor with their own sets of biases and prejudices. Sometimes, these biases will be less of a problem with certain types of survey approaches.

- **Can social desirability be avoided?** Respondents generally want to look good in the eyes of others. None of us likes to look like we don't know an answer. We don't want to say anything that would be embarrassing. If you ask people about information that may put them in this kind of position, they may not tell you the truth, or they may spin the response so that it makes them look better. This may be more of a problem in a face-to face interview situation or a phone interview.

- **Can interviewer distortion and subversion be controlled?** Interviewers may distort an interview as well. They may not ask difficult questions or ones that make them uncomfortable. They may not listen carefully to respondents on topics for which they have strong opinions. They may make the judgment that they already know what the respondent would say to a question based on their prior responses, even though that may not be true.

- **Can false respondents be avoided?** With mail surveys, it may be difficult to know who actually responded. Did the head of household complete the survey or someone else? Did the CEO actually give the responses or instead pass the task off to a subordinate? Are the people you're speaking with on the phone actually who they say they are? At least with personal interviews, you have a reasonable chance of knowing to whom you are speaking. In mail surveys or phone interviews, this may not be the case.

Administrative Issues

Last, but certainly not least, you have to consider the feasibility of the survey method for your study.

- **Costs:** Cost is often the major determining factor in selecting survey type. You might prefer to do personal interviews, but can't justify the high cost of training and paying for the interviewers. You may prefer to send out an extensive mailing but can't afford the postage to do so.

- **Facilities:** Do you have the facilities (or access to them) to process and manage your study? In phone interviews, do you have well-equipped phone surveying facilities? For focus groups, do you have a comfortable and accessible room to host the group? Do you have the equipment needed to record and transcribe responses?
- **Time:** Some types of surveys take longer than others. Do you need responses immediately (as in an overnight public opinion poll)? Have you budgeted enough time for your study to send out mail surveys and follow-up reminders, and to get the responses back by mail? Have you allowed for enough time to get enough personal interviews to justify that approach?
- **Personnel:** Different types of surveys make different demands of personnel. Interviews require well-trained and motivated interviewers. Group administered surveys require people who are trained in group facilitation. Some studies may be in a technical area that requires some degree of expertise in the interviewer.

Clearly, there are lots of issues to consider when you are selecting which type of survey to use in your study, and there is no clear and easy way to make this decision in many contexts because it might be that no one approach is clearly the best. You may have to make tradeoffs and weigh advantages and disadvantages as discussed later in this chapter. There is judgment involved. Two expert researchers might, for the same problem or issue, select entirely different survey methods; but, if you select a method that isn't appropriate or doesn't fit the context, you can doom a study before you even begin designing the instruments or questions themselves.

4-1c Constructing the Survey

Constructing a survey instrument is an art in itself. You must make numerous small decisions—about content, wording, format, and placement—that can have important consequences for your entire study. Although there's no one perfect way to accomplish this job, I do have advice to offer that might increase your chances of developing a better final product.

Now that you know about the two major types of surveys—questionnaires and interviews—you need to learn how to write survey questions. There are three areas involved in writing a question:

- Determining the question content, scope, and purpose
- Choosing the response format that you use for collecting information from the respondent
- Figuring out how to word the question to get at the issue of interest

Finally, after you have your questions written, there is the issue of how best to place them in your survey.

You'll see that although many aspects of survey construction are just common sense, if you are not careful, you can make critical errors that have dramatic effects on your results.

Types of Questions

Survey questions can be divided into two broad types: *structured* and *unstructured*. From an instrument design point of view, the structured questions pose the greater difficulties (see the section "Response Format" later in this chapter). From a content perspective, it may actually be more difficult to write good unstructured questions. Here, I'll discuss the variety of structured questions you can consider for your survey. (I discuss unstructured questioning more in the section "Interviews" later in this chapter.)

Dichotomous Response Formats

When a question has two possible responses, it is considered **dichotomous**. Surveys often use dichotomous questions that ask for a Yes/No, True/False, or Agree/Disagree response (see Figure 4.1). There are a variety of ways to lay these questions out on a questionnaire:

Figure 4.1
Dichotomous response formats for a survey question.

> Do you believe that the death penalty is ever justified?
>
> ____Yes
>
> ____No
>
> Please enter your gender:
>
> ☐ Male   ☐ Female

Questions Based on Level of Measurement

We can also classify questions in terms of the level of measurement used in the question's response format. (This is covered in Chapter 3, "The Theory of Measurement.") For instance, you might measure occupation using a nominal response format as in Figure 4.2. In a **nominal response format**, the number next to each response has no meaning except as a placeholder for that response; The choices are a 2 for a lawyer and a 1 for a truck driver. From the numbering system used you can't infer that a lawyer is twice something that a truck driver is.

Figure 4.2
A nominal-level response format for a survey question.

> Occupational Class:
> 1 = truck driver
> 2 = lawyer
> 3 = etc.

You might ask respondents to rank order their preferences for presidential candidates using an **ordinal response format** as in Figure 4.3.

Figure 4.3
An ordinal-level response format for a survey question.

> Rank the candidates in order of preference from best to worst...
>
> ____Bob Dole
>
> ____Bill Clinton
>
> ____Newt Gingrich
>
> ____Al Gore

In this example, you want the respondent to put a 1, 2, 3, or 4 next to the candidate, where 1 is the respondent's first choice. Note that this could get confusing. The respondents might check their favorite candidate, or assign higher numbers to candidates they prefer more instead of understanding that you want rank ordering. You might want to state the prompt more explicitly so the respondent knows you want a number from 1 to 4.

You can also construct survey questions that attempt to measure using an *interval level response* format. One of the most common of these types is the traditional 1-to-5 rating (or 1-to-7, or 1-to-9, and so on). This is sometimes referred to as a *Likert scale* (see "Likert Scaling," later in this chapter). In Figure 4.4, you see how you might ask an opinion question using a 1-to-5 bipolar scale. (It's called bipolar because there is a neutral point and the two ends of the scale are at opposite positions of the opinion.)

The death penalty is justifiable under some circumstances.				
1	2	3	4	5
strongly disagree	disagree	neutral	agree	strongly agree

Figure 4.4
An interval-level response format for a survey question.

Another interval response format uses an approach called the *semantic differential* as shown in Figure 4.5. Here, an object is assessed by the respondent on a set of bipolar adjective pairs (using a 5-point rating scale).

Please state your opinions on national health insurance on the scale below

	very much	some-what	neither	some-what	very much	
interesting	☐	☐	☐	☐	☐	boring
simple	☐	☐	☐	☐	☐	complex
uncaring	☐	☐	☐	☐	☐	caring
useful	☐	☐	☐	☐	☐	useless

Figure 4.5
A semantic differential response format for a survey question.

Finally, you can also get at interval measures by using what is called a *cumulative or Guttman scale* (see "Guttman Scaling," later in this chapter) response format. Here, the respondents check each item with which they agree. The items themselves are constructed so that they are cumulative; if you agree with one item, you probably agree with all of the ones above it in the list (see Figure 4.6).

Figure 4.6
A cumulative response format for a survey question.

> Please check each statement that you agree with:
> __Are you willing to permit immigrants to live in your country?
> __Are you willing to permit immigrants to live in your community?
> __Are you willing to permit immigrants to live in your neighborhood?
> __Would you be willing to have an immigrant live next door to you?
> __Would you let your child marry an immigrant?

Filter or Contingency Questions

Sometimes you have to ask the respondents one question to determine whether they are qualified or experienced enough to answer a subsequent one. This requires using a **filter or contingency question.** For instance, you may want to ask one question if the respondent has ever smoked marijuana and a different question if he or she has not. In this case, you would have to construct a filter question to determine first whether the respondent has ever smoked marijuana (see Figure 4.7).

Figure 4.7
A filter or contingency question.

> Have you ever smoked marijuana?
>
> ☐ Yes
>
> ☐ No
>
> If yes, about how many times have you smoked marijuana?
>
> ☐ Once
>
> ☐ 2 to 5 times
>
> ☐ 6 to 10 times
>
> ☐ 11 to 20 times
>
> ☐ more than 20 times

Filter questions can be complex. Sometimes, you have to have multiple filter questions to direct your respondents to the correct subsequent questions. You should keep the following conventions in mind when using filters:

- **Try to avoid having more than three levels (two jumps) for any question.** Too many jumps will confuse respondents and may discourage them from continuing with the survey.
- **If only two levels, use graphic to jump (for example an arrow and box).** The example in Figure 4.7 shows how you can make effective use of an arrow and box to help direct the respondent to the correct subsequent question.
- **If possible, jump to a new page.** If you can't fit the response to a filter on a single page, it's probably best to be able to say something like, *If YES, please turn to page 4,* rather than *If YES, please go to Question 38,* because

the respondent will generally have an easier time finding a page than a specific question.

Question Content

For each question in your survey, you should ask yourself how well it addresses the content you are trying to get at. The following sections cover some content-related questions you can ask about your survey questions.

Is the Question Necessary/Useful?

Examine each question to determine whether you need to ask it at all and whether you need to ask it at the level of detail you currently have, as in the following examples:

- Do you need the age of *each* child or just the *number of children under 16?*
- Do you need to *ask income* or can you *estimate?*

Are Several Questions Needed?

This is the classic problem of the *double-barreled question.* You should think about splitting each of the following questions into two separate ones. You can often spot these kinds of problems by looking for the conjunction *and* in your question as in the following examples:

- What are your feelings towards African-Americans *and* Hispanic-Americans?
- What do you think of proposed changes in benefits *and* hours?

Another reason you might need more than one question is that the question you ask does not cover all possibilities. For instance, if you ask about earnings, the respondent might not mention all income (such as dividends or gifts). If you ask the respondents if they're in favor of public TV, they might not understand that you're asking generally. They may not be in favor of public TV for themselves (they never watch it), but might favor it for their children (who watch *Sesame Street* regularly). You might be better off asking two questions: one about their own viewing and one about the viewing habits of other members of their households.

Sometimes you need to ask additional questions because your question does not provide you with enough context to interpret the answer. For instance, if you ask about attitudes towards Catholics, can you interpret this without finding out about your respondents' attitudes towards religion in general or other religious groups?

At times, you need to ask additional questions because your question does not determine the intensity of the respondent's attitude or belief. For example, if respondents say they support public TV, you probably should also ask whether they ever watch it or if they would be willing to have their tax dollars spent on it. It's one thing for respondents to tell you they support something; but the intensity of that response is greater if they are willing to back their sentiment of support with their behavior.

Do Respondents Have the Needed Information?

Look at each question in your survey to see whether the respondent is likely to have the necessary information to be able to answer the question. For example, let's say you want to ask the following question:

Do you think Dean Rusk acted correctly in the Bay of Pigs crisis?

The respondents won't be able to answer this question if they have no idea who Dean Rusk was or what the Bay of Pigs crisis was. In surveys of television viewing, you cannot expect the respondent to answer questions about shows they have never watched. You should ask a filter question first (such as, Have you ever watched the show *ER?*) before asking for opinions about it.

Does the Question Need to Be More Specific?

Sometimes researchers ask their questions too generally and the information they obtain is difficult to interpret. For example, let's say you want to find out respondent's opinions about a specific book. You could ask the following question:

How well did you like the book?

and offer some scale ranging from Not At All to Extremely Well; but what would the response mean? What does it mean to say you liked a book extremely well? Instead, you might ask questions designed to be more specific:

Did you recommend the book to others?
or
Did you look for other books by that author?

Is the Question Sufficiently General?

You can err in the other direction as well by being too specific. For instance, if you ask people to list the television programs they liked best in the past week, you could get a different answer than if you asked them which show they've enjoyed most over the past year. Perhaps a show they don't usually like had a great episode in the past week, or their favorite show was preempted by another program.

Is the Question Biased or Loaded?

One danger in question writing is that your own biases and blind spots may affect the wording (see the section "Question Wording" in this chapter). For instance, you might generally be in favor of tax cuts. If you ask the following question:

What do you see as the benefits of a tax cut?

you're only asking about one side of the issue. You might get a different picture of the respondents' positions if you also asked about the disadvantages of tax cuts. The same thing could occur if you are in favor of public welfare and you ask

What do you see as the disadvantages of eliminating welfare?

without also asking about the potential benefits.

Will the Respondent Answer Truthfully?

For each question on your survey, ask yourself whether respondents will have any difficulty answering the question truthfully. If there is some reason why they may not, consider rewording the question. For instance, some people are sensitive about answering questions about their exact age or income. In this case, you might give them **response brackets** to choose from (such as between 30 and 40 years old, or between $50,000 and $100,000 annual income). Sometimes even bracketed responses won't be enough. Some people do not like to share how much money they give to charitable causes. (They may be afraid of opening themselves up to even more solicitations.) No matter how you word the question, they would not be likely to tell you their contribution rate. Sometimes you can work around such problems by posing the question in terms of *a hypothetical projective respondent* (a little bit like a projective test). In this case, you might get reasonable estimates if you ask the respondent how much money "people you know" typically give in a year to charitable causes. Finally, you can sometimes dispense with asking a question at all if you can obtain the answer unobtrusively. (This is covered in Chapter 5, "Qualitative and Unobtrusive Measures.") If you are interested in finding out which magazines the respondents read, you might instead tell them you are collecting magazines for a recycling drive and ask if they have any old ones to donate. (Of course, you have to consider the ethical implications of such deception!)

Response Format

The *response format* is how you collect the answer from the respondent. Let's start with a simple distinction between what I call *unstructured response formats* and *structured response formats.*

Structured Response Formats

Structured response formats help the respondent to respond more easily and help the researcher accumulate and summarize responses more efficiently; but, they can also constrain the respondent and limit the researcher's ability to understand what the respondent really means. There are many different structured response formats, each with its own strengths and weaknesses. We'll review the major ones here.

Fill-in-the-Blank. One of the simplest response formats is a blank line. A blank line can be used for a number of different response types as shown in Figure 4.8.

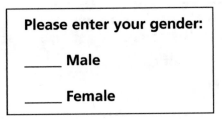

Figure 4.8
The fill-in-the-blank response format.

Here, the respondent would probably put a check mark or an X next to the response. This is also an example of a *dichotomous* response because it only has two possible values. Other common dichotomous responses are True/False and Yes/No. Here's another common use of a fill-in-the-blank response format, as shown in Figure 4.9:

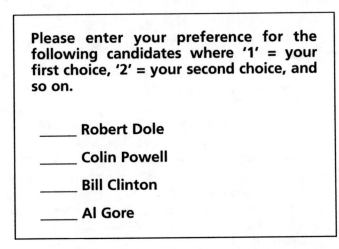

Figure 4.9
Another type of fill-in-the-blank response format.

In this example, the respondent writes a number in each blank. Notice that here, you expect the respondent to place a number on every blank, whereas in the previous example, you expect the respondent to choose only one. Then, of course, there's the classic shown in Figure 4.10.

Figure 4.10
Who hasn't seen this fill-in-the-blank?

Name: ____________________

And there's always the classic fill-in-the-blank test item (see Figure 4.11):

Figure 4.11
The fill-in-the-blank test item.

One of President Lincoln's most famous speeches, the __________ Address, only lasted a few minutes when delivered.

Check the Answer. The respondent places a check next to the response(s). The simplest form would be the example given previously that asks the respondents to indicate their gender. Sometimes, you supply a box that the person can fill in with an X, which is sort of a variation on the check mark. Figure 4.12 shows a check-box format:

Figure 4.12
The check-box format is useful when you want respondents to select more than one item.

Please check if you have the following item on the computer you use most:

- ☐ modem
- ☐ printer
- ☐ CD-ROM drive
- ☐ joystick
- ☐ scanner

Notice that in this example, it is possible to check more than one response. By convention, you usually use the check-mark format when you want to allow the respondent to select multiple items.

This type of question is sometimes referred to as a ***multioption variable.*** You have to be careful when you analyze data from a multioption variable. Because the respondent can select any of the options, you have to treat this type of variable in your analysis *as though each option is a separate variable.* For instance, for each option you would normally enter either a 0 if the respondent did not check it or a 1 if the respondent did check it. For the previous example, if the respondent had only a modem and CD-ROM drive, you would enter the sequence 1, 0, 1, 0, 0 in five separate variables. There is an important reason why you should code this variable as either 0 or 1 when you enter the data. If you do, and you want to determine what percent of your sample that has a modem, all you have to do is compute the average of the 0's and 1's for the modem variable. For instance, if you have 10 respondents and only 3 have a modem, the average would be 3/10 = .30 or 30%, which is the percent who checked that item.

The previous example is also a good example of a check-list item. Whenever you use a checklist, you want to be sure that you ask the following questions:

- Are all of the alternatives covered?
- Is the list of reasonable length (not too long)?
- Is the wording impartial?
- Is the form of the response easy, uniform?

Sometimes you may not be sure that you have covered all of the possible responses in a checklist. If that is the case, you should probably allow the respondent to write in any other options that apply.

Circle the Answer. Sometimes respondents are asked to circle an item to indicate their response. Usually you are asking them to circle a number. For instance, you might have the example shown in Figure 4.13.

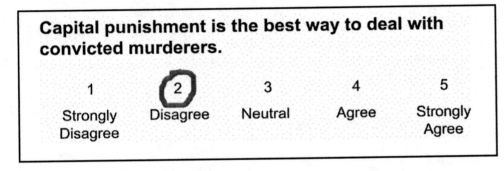

> **Capital punishment is the best way to deal with convicted murderers.**
>
> 1　　2　　3　　4　　5
>
> Strongly　Disagree　Neutral　Agree　Strongly
> Disagree　　　　　　　　　　Agree

Figure 4.13
A circle-the-answer response format.

In computer contexts, it's not feasible to have respondents circle a response. In this case, you tend to use an option button as shown in Figure 4.14.

> Capital punishment is the best way to deal with convicted murderers.
>
> ○　　○　　○　　○　　○
>
> Strongly　Disagree　Neutral　Agree　Strongly
> Disagree　　　　　　　　　　Agree

Figure 4.14
An option button response format on the Web.

Only one option at a time can be checked. The rule of thumb is that you ask people to circle an item or click a button when you only want them to be able to select one of the options. In contrast to the ***multioption variable*** described previously, this type of item is referred to as a ***single-option variable***; even though the respondents have multiple *choices,* they can only select one of them. You would analyze this as a single variable that can take the integer values from 1 to 5.

Unstructured Response Formats

A wide variety of structured response formats exist; however, there are relatively few unstructured ones. What is an ***unstructured response format?*** Generally, it's written text. If the respondent (or interviewer) writes down text as the response, you have an unstructured response format. These can vary from short comment boxes to the transcript of an interview.

In almost every short questionnaire, there's one or more short text field questions. One of the most frequent is shown in Figure 4.15.

Figure 4.15
The most common unstructured response format allows the respondent to add comments.

```
┌─────────────────────────────────────────────────┐
│                                                   │
│  Please add any other comments:                   │
│                                                   │
│  _____  │
│                                                   │
│  _____  │
│                                                   │
│  _____  │
│                                                   │
└─────────────────────────────────────────────────┘
```

Actually, there's really not much more to text-based response formats of this type than writing the prompt and allowing enough space for a reasonable response.

Transcripts are an entirely different matter. In those cases, the transcriber has to decide whether to transcribe every word or only record major ideas, thoughts, quotes, and so on. In detailed transcriptions, you may also need to distinguish different speakers (such as the interviewer and respondent) and have a standard convention for indicating comments about what's going on in the interview, including nonconversational events that take place and thoughts of the interviewer.

Question Wording

One of the major difficulties in writing good survey questions is getting the wording right. Even slight wording differences can confuse the respondent or lead to incorrect interpretations of the question. Here, I outline some questions you can ask about how you worded each of your survey questions.

Can the Question Be Misunderstood?

The survey author always has to be on the lookout for questions that could be misunderstood or confusing. For instance, if you ask a person for his or her nationality, it might not be clear what you want. (Do you want someone from Malaysia to say Malaysian, Asian, or Pacific Islander?) Or, if you ask for marital status, do you want people to say simply that they are either married or not married? Or, do you want more detail (like divorced, widow/widower, and so on)?

Some terms are too vague to be useful. For instance, if you ask a question about the mass media, what do you mean? The newspapers? Radio? Television?

Here's one of my favorites. Let's say you want to know the following:

What kind of headache remedy do you use?

Do you want to know what brand name medicine respondents take? Do you want to know about home remedies? Are you asking whether they prefer a pill, capsule, or caplet?

What Assumptions Does the Question Make?

Sometimes you don't stop to consider how a question will appear from the respondent's point of view. You don't think about the assumptions behind the questions. For instance, if you ask what social class someone's in, you assume that they know what social class is and that they think of themselves as being in one. In this kind of case, you may need to use a filter question first to determine whether either of these assumptions is true.

Is the Time Frame Specified?

Whenever you use the words will, could, might, or may in a question, you might suspect that the question asks a time-related question. Be sure that, if it does, you have specified the time frame precisely. For instance, you might ask:

Do you think Congress will cut taxes?

or something like

Do you think Congress could successfully resist tax cuts?

Neither of these questions specifies a time frame.

How Personal Is the Wording?

By changing just a few words, a question can go from being relatively impersonal to probing into private perspectives. Consider the following three questions, each of which asks about the respondent's satisfaction with working conditions:

- Are working conditions satisfactory or not satisfactory in the plant where you work?
- Do you feel that working conditions are satisfactory or not satisfactory in the plant where you work?
- Are you personally satisfied with working conditions in the plant where you work?

The first question is stated from a fairly detached, objective viewpoint. The second asks how you feel. The last asks whether you are personally satisfied. Be sure the questions in your survey are at an appropriate level for your context. Be sure there is consistency in this across questions in your survey.

Is the Wording too Direct?

At times, asking a question too directly may be threatening or disturbing for respondents. For instance, consider a study in which you want to discuss battlefield experiences with former soldiers who experienced trauma. Examine the following three question options:

- How did you feel about being in the war?
- How well did the equipment hold up in the field?
- How well were new recruits trained?

The first question may be too direct. For this population, it may elicit powerful negative emotions based on individual recollections. The second question is a less direct one. It asks about equipment in the field; but, for this population, it may also lead the discussion toward more difficult issues to discuss directly. The last question is probably the least direct and least threatening. Bashing the new recruits is standard protocol in almost any social context. The question is likely to get the respondent talking and recounting anecdotes, without eliciting much stress. Of course, all of this may simply be begging the question. If you are doing a study where the respondents might experience high levels of stress because of the questions you ask, you should reconsider the ethics of doing the study.

Other Wording Issues

The nuances of language guarantee that the task of the question writer is endlessly complex. Without trying to generate an exhaustive list, here are a few other guidelines to keep in mind:

- Questions should not contain difficult or unclear terminology.
- Questions should make each alternative explicit.

- Question wording should not be objectionable.
- Question wording should not be loaded or slanted.

Question Placement

One of the most difficult tasks facing the survey designer involves the ordering of questions. Which topics should be introduced early in the survey, and which later? If you leave your most important questions until the end, you may find that your respondents are too tired to give them the kind of attention you would like. If you introduce them too early, they may not yet be ready to address the topic, especially if it is a difficult or disturbing one. There are no easy answers to these problems; you have to use your judgment. Whenever you think about question placement, consider the following potential issues:

- The answer may be influenced by prior questions.
- The question may come too early or too late to arouse interest.
- The question may not receive sufficient attention.

The Opening Questions

Just as in other aspects of life, first impressions are important in survey work. The first few questions you ask will determine the tone for the survey and can help put your respondent at ease. With that in mind, the opening few questions should, in general, be easy to answer. You might start with some simple descriptive questions that will get the respondent rolling. You should never begin your survey with sensitive or threatening questions.

Sensitive Questions

In much of your social research, you will have to ask respondents about difficult or uncomfortable subjects. Before asking such questions, you should attempt to develop some trust or rapport with the respondent. Often, preceding the sensitive questions with some easier warm-up ones will help; but, you have to make sure that the sensitive material does not come up abruptly or appear unconnected to the rest of the survey. It is often helpful to have a transition sentence between sections of your instrument to give the respondent some idea of the kinds of questions that are coming. For instance, you might lead into a section on personal material with the following transition: "In this next section of the survey, we'd like to ask you about your personal relationships. Remember, we do not want you to answer any questions if you are uncomfortable doing so."

A Checklist of Considerations

The survey-design business has lots of conventions or rules of thumb. You can use the following checklist to review your instrument:

- Start with easy, nonthreatening questions.
- Put more difficult, threatening questions near the end.
- Never start a mail survey with an open-ended question.
- For historical demographics, follow chronological order.
- Ask about one topic at a time.
- When switching topics, use a transition.
- Reduce response set (the tendency of respondent to just keep checking the same response).
- For filter or contingency questions, make a flowchart.

You are imposing in the life of your respondents. You are asking for their time, their attention, their trust, and often, for personal information. Therefore, you should always keep in mind the golden rule of survey research (and, I hope, for the rest of your life as well!):

> *Do unto your respondents as you would have them do unto you!*

To put this in more practical terms, you should keep the following in mind:

- Thank the respondent at the beginning for allowing you to conduct your study.
- Keep your survey as short as possible—only include what is absolutely necessary.
- Be sensitive to the needs of the respondent.
- Be alert for any sign that the respondent is uncomfortable.
- Thank the respondent at the end for participating.
- Assure the respondent that you will send a copy of the final results.

Interviews are among the most challenging and rewarding forms of measurement. They require a personal sensitivity and adaptability as well as the ability to stay within the bounds of the designed protocol. Here, I describe the preparation you need to do for an interview study and the process of conducting the interview itself.

The Role of the Interviewer

The interviewer is really the jack-of-all-trades in survey research. The interviewer's role is complex and multifaceted. It includes the following tasks:

- **Locate and enlist cooperation of respondents:** The interviewer has to find the respondent. In door-to-door surveys, this means being able to locate specific addresses. Often, the interviewer has to work at the least desirable times (like immediately after dinner or on weekends) because that's when respondents are most readily available.
- **Motivate respondents to do good job:** If the interviewer does not take the work seriously, why would the respondent? The interviewer has to be motivated and has to be able to communicate that motivation to the respondent. Often, this means that the interviewer has to be convinced of the importance of the research.
- **Clarify any confusion/concerns:** Interviewers have to be able to think on their feet. Respondents may raise objections or concerns that were not anticipated. The interviewer has to be able to respond candidly and informatively.
- **Observe quality of responses:** Whether the interview is personal or over the phone, the interviewer is in the best position to judge the quality of the information that is being received. Even a verbatim transcript will not adequately convey how seriously the respondent took the task, or any gestures or body language that were observed.
- **Conduct a good interview:** Last, and certainly not least, the interviewer has to conduct a good interview! Every interview has a life of its own. Some respondents are motivated and attentive; others are distracted or disinterested. The interviewer also has good or bad days. Assuring a consistently high-quality interview is a challenge that requires constant effort.

Training the Interviewers

One of the most important aspects of any interview study is the training of the interviewers themselves. In many ways, the interviewers are your measures, and the quality of the results is totally in their hands. Even in small studies involving only a single researcher-interviewer, it is important to organize in detail and rehearse the interviewing process before beginning the formal study.

Here are some of the major topics that you should consider during interviewer training:

- **Describe the entire study:** Interviewers need to know more than simply how to conduct the interview itself. They should learn about the background for the study, previous work that has been done, and why the study is important.

- **State who is sponsor of research:** Interviewers need to know who they are working for. They—and their respondents—have a right to know not only what agency or company is conducting the research, but also who is paying for the research.

- **Teach enough about survey research:** While you seldom have the time to teach a full course on survey-research methods, the interviewers need to know enough that they respect the survey method and are motivated. Sometimes it may not be apparent why a question or set of questions was asked in a particular way. The interviewers will need to understand the rationale behind the way you constructed the instrument.

- **Explain the sampling logic and process:** Naive interviewers may not understand why *sampling* is so important. They may wonder why you go through the difficulty of selecting the sample so carefully. You will have to explain that sampling is the basis for the conclusions that will be reached and for the degree to which your study will be useful.

- **Explain interviewer bias:** Interviewers need to know the many ways they can inadvertently bias the results. They also need to understand why it is important that they not bias the study. This is especially a problem when you are investigating political or moral issues on which people have strongly held convictions. While the interviewers may think they are doing good for society by slanting results in favor of what they believe, they need to recognize that doing so could jeopardize the entire study in the eyes of others.

- **Walk through the interview:** When you first introduce the interview, it's a good idea to walk through the entire protocol so the interviewers can get an idea of the various parts or phases and how they interrelate.

- **Explain respondent selection procedures, including the following:**
  - **Reading maps:** It's astonishing how many adults don't know how to follow directions on a map. In personal interviews, interviewers may need to locate respondents spread over a wide geographic area. They often have to navigate by night (respondents tend to be most available in evening hours) in neighborhoods they're not familiar with. Teaching basic map reading skills and confirming that the interviewers can follow maps is essential.
  - **Identifying households:** In many studies, it is impossible in advance to say whether every sample household meets the sampling requirements for the study. In your study, you may want to interview only people who live in single-family homes. It may be impossible to distinguish townhouses and apartment buildings in your

sampling frame. The interviewer must know how to identify the appropriate target household.

- **Identifying respondents:** Just as with households, many studies require respondents who meet specific criteria. For instance, your study may require that you speak with a male head-of-household between the ages of 30 and 40 who has children under 18 living in the same household. It may be impossible to obtain statistics in advance to target such respondents. The interviewer may have to ask a series of filtering questions before determining whether the respondent meets the sampling needs.

- **Rehearse the interview:** You should probably have several rehearsal sessions with the interview team. You might even videotape rehearsal interviews to discuss how the trainees responded in difficult situations. The interviewers should be familiar with the entire interview before ever facing a respondent.

- **Explain supervision:** In most interview studies, the interviewers will work under the direction of a supervisor. In some contexts, the supervisors may be faculty advisors; in others, they may be the bosses. To assure the quality of the responses, the supervisor may have to observe a subsample of interviews, listen in on phone interviews, or conduct follow-up assessments of interviews with the respondents. This practice can be threatening to the interviewers. You need to develop an atmosphere in which everyone on the research team—interviewers and supervisors—feel like they're working together towards a common end.

- **Explain scheduling:** The interviewers have to understand the demands being made on their schedules and why these are important to the study. In some studies, it will be imperative to conduct the entire set of interviews within a certain time period. In most studies, it's important to have the interviewers available when it's convenient for the respondents, not necessarily the interviewer.

The Interviewer's Kit

It's important that interviewers have all of the materials they need to do a professional job. Usually, you will want to assemble an interviewer kit that can be easily carried and that includes all of the important materials such as following:

- A professional-looking 3-ring notebook (this might even have the logo of the company or organization conducting the interviews)
- Maps
- Sufficient copies of the survey instrument
- Official identification (preferable a picture ID)
- A cover letter from the principal investigator or sponsor
- A phone number the respondent can call to verify the interviewer's authenticity

Conducting the Interview

So all the preparation is complete, the interviewers, with their kits in hand, are ready to proceed. It's finally time to do an actual interview. Each interview is unique, like a small work of art (and sometimes the art may not be very good). Each interview has its own ebb and flow—its own pace. To the outsider, an interview looks like a fairly standard, simple, prosaic effort; but to the interviewer, it can be filled with special nuances and interpretations that aren't often immediately apparent. Every interview includes some common components. There's the opening, where the interviewer gains entry and establishes the rapport and tone for what follows. There's the middle game, the heart of the process, which consists of the protocol of questions and the improvisations of the probe. Finally, there's the endgame, the wrap-up, during which the interviewer and respondent establish a sense of closure. Whether it's a two-minute phone interview or a personal interview that spans hours, the interview is a bit of theater, a mini-drama that involves real lives in real time.

Opening Remarks

In many ways, the interviewer has the same initial problem that a salesperson has. The interviewers have to get the respondents' attention initially for a long enough period that they can sell them on the idea of participating in the study. Many of the remarks here assume an interview that is being conducted at a respondent's residence; but the analogies to other interview contexts should be straightforward.

- **Gaining entry:** The first thing the interviewer must do is gain entry. Several factors can enhance the prospects. Probably the most important factor is initial appearance. The interviewer needs to dress professionally and in a manner that will be comfortable to the respondent. In some contexts, a business suit and briefcase may be appropriate; in others, it may intimidate. The way the interviewers appear initially to the respondent has to communicate some simple messages; that they're trustworthy, honest, and nonthreatening. Cultivating a manner of professional confidence, the sense that the respondent has nothing to worry about because the interviewers know what they're doing is a difficult skill to teach interviewers and an indispensable skill for achieving initial entry.

- **Doorstep technique:** If the interviewer is standing on the doorstep and someone has opened the door, even if only halfway, the interviewer needs to smile and briefly state why he or she is there. Have your interviewers suggest what they would like the respondent to do. Not ask. Suggest. Instead of saying, "May I come in to do an interview," have them try a more imperative approach like, "I'd like to take a few minutes of your time to interview you for a very important study."

- **Introduction:** If interviewers get this far without having doors slammed in their faces, chances are they will be able to get an interview. Without waiting for the respondent to ask questions, they should introduce themselves. Be sure your interviewers have this part of the process memorized so they can deliver the essential information in 20-30 seconds at most. They should state their name and the name of the organization they represent as well as show their identification badge and the letter that introduces them. You want them to have as legitimate an appearance as possible. If they have a three-ring binder or clipboard with the logo of your organization, they should have it out and visible. They should assume that the respondent will be interested in participating in your important study—assume that they will be doing an interview there.

- **Explaining the study:** At this point, the interviewers have been invited to come in. (After all, they're standing there in the cold, holding an assortment of materials, clearly displaying their credentials, and offering the respondent the chance to participate in an interview; to many respondents, it's a rare and exciting event. They are seldom asked their views about anything, and yet they know that important decisions are made all the time based on input from others.) When the respondent has continued to listen long enough, the interviewer needs to explain the study. There are three rules to this critical explanation: 1) Keep it short; 2) Keep it short; and 3) Keep it short! The respondent doesn't have to or want to know all of the nuances of this study, how it came about, how you convinced your thesis committee to buy into it, and so on. Provide the interviewers with a one- or two-sentence description of the study and have them memorize it. No big words. No jargon. No detail. There will be more than enough time for that later. (Interviewers should bring some written materials to leave at the end for that purpose.) Provide a 25-words-or-less description. What the interviewers *should* spend some time on is assuring the respondent that they are interviewing them confidentially, and that their participation is voluntary.

Asking the Questions

The interviewer has gotten in and established an initial rapport with the respondent. It may be that the respondent was in the middle of doing something when the interviewer arrived and needs a few minutes to finish the phone call or send the kids off to do homework. Then it's time to begin the interview itself. Here are some hints you can give your interviewers:

- **Use questionnaire carefully, but informally:** The questionnaire is the interviewer's friend. It was developed with a lot of care and thoughtfulness. While interviewers have to be ready to adapt to the needs of the setting, their first instinct should always be to trust the instrument that was designed; but they also need to establish a rapport with the respondent. If they bury their faces in the instrument and read the questions, they'll appear unprofessional and disinterested. Reassure them that even though they may be nervous, the respondent is probably even more nervous. Encourage interviewers to memorize the first few questions, so they need refer to the instrument only occasionally, using eye contact and a confident manner to set the tone for the interview and help the respondent get comfortable.
- **Ask questions exactly as written:** Sometimes interviewers will think that they could improve on the tone of a question by altering a few words to make it simpler or more friendly. Urge them not to. They should ask the questions as they are on the instrument. During the training and rehearsals, allow the interviewers to raise any issues they have with the questions. It is important that the interview be as standardized as possible across respondents. (This is true except in certain types of exploratory or interpretivist research where the explicit goal is to avoid any standardizing.)
- **Follow the order given:** When interviewers know an interview well, they may see a respondent bring up a topic that they know will come up later in the interview. They may be tempted to jump to that section. Urge them not to. This can cause them to lose their place or omit questions that build a foundation for later questions.
- **Ask every question:** Sometimes interviewers will be tempted to omit a question because they thought they already heard what the respondent will say. Urge them not to assume. For example, let's say you were conducting an interview with college-age women about the topic of date rape. In an

earlier question, the respondent mentioned that she knew of a woman on her dormitory floor who had been raped on a date within the past year. A few questions later, the interviewer is supposed to ask, "Do you know of anyone personally who was raped on a date?" Interviewers might figure they already know that the answer is yes and decide to skip the question. Encourage them to say something like, "I know you may have already mentioned this, but do you know of anyone personally who was raped on a date?" At this point, the respondent may say, "Well, in addition to the woman who lived down the hall in my dorm, I know of a friend from high school who experienced date rape." If the interviewer hadn't asked the question, this detail would remain undiscovered.

- **Don't finish sentences:** Silence is one of the most effective devices for encouraging respondents to talk. If interviewers finish their sentences for them, they imply that what they had to say is transparent or obvious, or that they don't want to give them the time to express themselves in their own language.

Obtaining Adequate Responses—The Probe

When the respondent gives a brief, cursory answer, your interviewer needs to elicit a more thoughtful, thorough response. Teach the following probing techniques:

- **The silent probe:** The most effective way to encourage someone to elaborate is to do nothing at all—just pause and wait. This is referred to as the silent probe. It works (at least in certain cultures) because the respondent is uncomfortable with pauses or silence. It suggests to the respondents that the interviewer is waiting, listening for what they will say next.
- **Overt encouragement:** At times, interviewers can encourage the respondent directly. They should try to do so in a way that does not imply approval or disapproval of what the respondent said (that could bias their subsequent results). Overt encouragement could be as simple as saying uh-huh or okay after the respondent completes a thought.
- **Elaboration:** Interviewers can encourage more information by asking for elaboration. For instance, it is appropriate to ask questions like "Would you like to elaborate on that?" or "Is there anything else you would like to add?"
- **Ask for clarification:** Sometimes, interviewers can elicit greater detail by asking the respondent to clarify something that was said earlier by saying something like, "A minute ago you were talking about the experience you had in high school. Could you tell me more about that?"
- **Repetition:** This is the old psychotherapist trick. You say something without really saying anything new. For instance, the respondent just described a traumatic childhood experience. The interviewer might say "What I'm hearing you say is that you found that experience very traumatic" and then pause. The respondent is likely to say something like, "Well, yes, and it affected the rest of my family as well. In fact, my younger sister…."

Recording the Response

Although we have the capability to record a respondent in audio and/or video, most interview methodologists don't think it's a good idea. Respondents are often uncomfortable when they know their remarks will be recorded word-for-word. They may strain to say things only in a socially acceptable way. Although you would get a more detailed and accurate record, it is likely to be distorted by the process of obtaining it. This may be more of a problem in some situations than in others. It is increasingly common to be told that your conversation may be recorded during a phone interview; and most focus-group methodologies use unobtrusive recording equipment to capture what's being said. However, in general, personal interviews are still best when recorded by the interviewer using pen and paper. Here, I assume the paper-and-pencil approach.

- **Record responses immediately:** The interviewers should record responses as they are being stated. This conveys the idea that they are interested enough in what the respondent is saying to write it down. The interviewers don't have to write down every single word; but you may want them to record certain key phrases or quotes verbatim. Implement a system for distinguishing what the respondent says verbatim from what interviewers are characterizing (how about quotations, for instance).
- **Include all probes:** Have your interviewers indicate every single probe that you use. Develop a shorthand for different standard probes. Use a clear form for writing them in (for example, place probes in the left margin). Use abbreviations where possible; abbreviations will help interviewers capture more of the discussion. Develop a standardized system (R=respondent; DK=don't know). If interviewers create an abbreviation on the fly, have them indicate its origin. For instance, if your interviewer decides to abbreviate Spouse with an S, have them make a notation in the right margin saying S=Spouse.

Concluding the Interview

To bring the interview to closure, have your interviewers remember the following:

- **Thank the respondent:** Don't forget to do this. Even if the respondents were troublesome or uninformative, it is important to be polite and thank them for their time
- **Tell them when you expect to send results:** You owe it to your respondents to show them what you learned. Now, they may not want your entire 300-page dissertation. It's common practice to prepare a short, readable, jargon-free summary of interviews to send to the respondents.
- **Don't be brusque or hasty:** Interviewers need to allow for a few minutes of winding-down conversation. The respondent may be interested in how the results will be used. While the interviewers are putting away their materials and packing up to go, have them engage the respondent. Some respondents may want to keep on talking long after the interview is over. Provide your interviewers with a way to cut off the conversation politely and make their exit. For instance, you might have your interviewers say, "I would love to stay to discuss this more with you but, unfortunately, I have another interview appointment I must keep."
- **Immediately after leaving have the interviewer write down any notes about how the interview went:** Sometimes interviewers will have observations about the interview that they didn't want to write down while they were with the respondent. (Perhaps they noticed the respondent become upset by a question, or detected hostility in a response.) Immediately after the interview have them go over their notes and make any other comments and observations; but to be sure to distinguish these from the notes made during the interview (by using a different color pen, for instance).

4-1f Advantages and Disadvantages of Survey Methods

It's hard to compare the advantages and disadvantages of the major different survey types. Even though each type has some general advantages and disadvantages, there are exceptions to almost every rule. Table 4.1 shows my general assessment.

TABLE 4.1   Advantages and disadvantages of different survey methods.

Issue	Questionnaire			Interview	
	Group	Mail	Drop-Off	Personal	Phone
Are visual presentations possible?	Yes	Yes	Yes	Yes	No
Are long response categories possible?	Yes	Yes	Yes	???	No
Is privacy a feature?	No	Yes	No	Yes	???
Is the method flexible?	No	No	No	Yes	Yes
Are open-ended questions feasible?	No	No	No	Yes	Yes
Are reading and writing needed?	???	Yes	Yes	No	No
Can you judge quality of response?	Yes	No	???	Yes	???
Are high response rates likely?	Yes	No	Yes	Yes	No
Can you explain study in person?	Yes	No	Yes	Yes	???
Is it low cost?	Yes	Yes	No	No	No
Are staff and facilities needs low?	Yes	Yes	No	No	No
Does it give access to dispersed samples?	No	Yes	No	No	No
Does respondent have time to formulate answers?	No	Yes	Yes	No	No
Is there personal contact?	Yes	No	Yes	Yes	No
Is a long survey feasible?	No	No	No	Yes	No
Is there quick turnaround?	No	Yes	No	No	Yes

4-2 Scaling

Scaling is the branch of measurement that involves the construction of an instrument that associates qualitative constructs with quantitative metric units. Scaling evolved out of efforts in psychology and education to measure unmeasurable constructs such as authoritarianism and self-esteem. In many ways, scaling remains one of the most arcane and misunderstood aspects of social research measurement. It attempts to do one of the most difficult of research tasks—measure abstract concepts.

Most people don't even understand what scaling is. The basic idea of scaling is described in the following section, "General Issues in Scaling." The discussion includes the important distinction between a scale and a response format. Scales are generally divided into two broad categories: unidimensional and multidimensional. The unidimensional scaling methods were developed in the first half of the twentieth century and are generally named after their inventors. We'll look at three types of unidimensional scaling methods here:

- Thurstone or Equal-Appearing Interval Scaling
- Likert or Summative Scaling
- Guttman or Cumulative Scaling

In the late 1950s and early 1960s, measurement theorists developed advanced techniques for creating multidimensional scales. Although these techniques are not considered here, you may want to look at the method of **concept mapping** that relies on that approach to see the power of these multivariate methods (covered in Chapter 1, "Foundations").

S.S. Stevens came up with what I think is the simplest and most straightforward definition of scaling. He said, "Scaling is the assignment of objects to numbers according to a rule."

What does that mean? In most scaling, the objects are text statements, usually statements of attitude or belief. In Figure 4.16, three statements describe attitudes towards immigration. To scale these statements, you have to assign numbers to them. Usually, you would like the result to be on at least an interval scale (see "Levels of Measurement" in Chapter 3, "The Theory of Measurement"), as indicated by the ruler in the figure. What does "according to a rule" mean? If you look at the statements, you can see that as you read down, the attitude towards immigration becomes more restrictive; if a people agree with a statement on the list, it's likely that they will also agree with all of the statements higher on the list. In this case, the rule is a *cumulative* one. So what is scaling? It's how you get numbers that can be meaningfully assigned to objects; it's a set of procedures. The following paragraphs introduce several approaches to scaling.

4-3 General Issues in Scaling

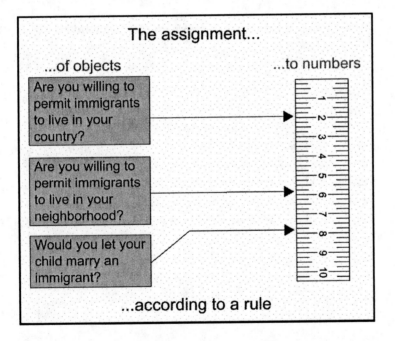

Figure 4.16
Scaling as the assignment of numbers according to a rule.

First, I have to clear up one of my pet peeves. People often confuse the idea of a scale and a response scale. A **response scale** is the way you collect responses from people on an instrument. You might use a **dichotomous response** scale like Agree/Disagree, True/False, or Yes/No; or, you might use an **interval response scale** like a 1-to-5 or 1-to-7 rating. However, if all you are doing is attaching a response scale to an object or statement, you can't call that scaling. As you will see, scaling involves procedures that you perform independently of the respondent so that you can come up with a numerical value for the object. In true scaling research, you use a scaling procedure to develop your instrument (scale) and a response scale to collect the responses from participants. Simply assigning a 1-to-5 response scale for an item is *not* scaling! The differences are illustrated in Table 4.2.

T A B L E **4.2**   **Differences between scaling and response scales.**

Scale	Response Scale
Results from a process	Used to collect the response for an item
Each item on a scale has a scale value	Item not associated with a scale value
Refers to a set of items	Used for a single item

4-3a Purposes of Scaling

Why do scaling? Why not just create text statements or questions and use response formats to collect the answers? First, sometimes you do scaling to test a hypothesis. You might want to know whether the construct or concept is a single dimensional or multidimensional one (more about dimensionality later). Sometimes, you do scaling as part of exploratory research. You want to know what dimensions underlie a set of ratings. For instance, if you create a set of questions, you can use scaling to determine how well they hang together and whether they measure one concept or multiple concepts; but probably the most common reason for doing scaling is for scoring purposes. When a participant gives responses to a set of items, you often want to assign a single number that represents that person's overall attitude or belief. In Figure 4.16, we would like to be able to give a single number that describes a person's attitudes towards immigration, for example.

4-3b Dimensionality

A scale can have any number of dimensions in it. Most scales that researchers develop have only a few dimensions. What's a dimension? Think of a dimension as a number line as illustrated in Figure 4.17. If you want to measure a construct, you have to decide whether the construct can be measured well with one number line or whether it may need more. For instance, height is a concept that is unidimensional or one-dimensional. You can measure the concept of height well with only a single number line (a ruler). Weight is also unidimensional; you can mea-sure it with a scale. Thirst might also be considered a unidimensional concept; you are either more or less thirsty at any given time. It's easy to see that height and weight are unidimensional; but what about a concept like self-esteem? If you think you can measure a person's self-esteem well with a single ruler that goes from low to high, you probably have a unidimensional construct.

Figure 4.17
Unidimensional scales.

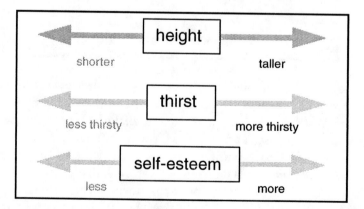

What would a two-dimensional concept be? Many models of intelligence or achievement postulate two major dimensions: mathematical and verbal ability. In this type of two-dimensional model, a person can be said to possess two types of achievement, as illustrated in Figure 4.18. Some people will be high in verbal skills and lower in math. For others, it will be the reverse. If a concept is truly two-dimensional, it is not possible to depict a person's level on it using only a single number line. In other words, to describe achievement you would need to locate a person as a point in two dimensional (x,y) space as shown in Figure 4.18.

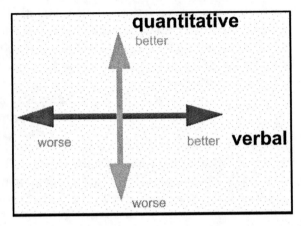

Figure 4.18
A two-dimensional scale.

Okay, let's push this one step further: how about a three-dimensional concept? Psychologists who study the idea of meaning theorized that the meaning of a term could be well described in three dimensions. Put in other terms, any objects can be distinguished or differentiated from each other along three dimensions. They labeled these three dimensions *activity*, *evaluation*, and *potency*. They called this general theory of meaning the **semantic differential**. Their theory essentially states that you can rate any object along those three dimensions. For instance, think of the idea of ballet. If you like the ballet, you would probably rate it high on activity, favorable on evaluation, and powerful on potency. On the other hand, think about the concept of a book like a novel. You might rate it low on activity (it's passive), favorable on evaluation (assuming you like it), and about average on potency. Now, think of the idea of going to the dentist. Most people would rate it low on activity (it's a passive activity), unfavorable on evaluation, and powerless on potency. (Few routine activities make you feel as powerless!) The theorists who came up with the idea of the semantic differential thought that the meaning of any concepts could be described well by rating the concept on these three dimensions. In other words, to describe the meaning of an object you have to locate it as a dot somewhere within the cube (three-dimensional space), as shown in Figure 4.19.

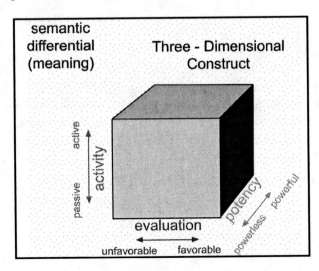

Figure 4.19
A three-dimensional scale.

4-3c Unidimensional or Multidimensional?

What are the advantages of using a unidimensional model? Unidimensional concepts are generally easier to understand. You have either more or less of it, and that's all. You're either taller or shorter, heavier or lighter. It's also important to understand what a unidimensional scale is as a foundation for comprehending the more complex multidimensional concepts; but the best reason to use unidimensional scaling is because you believe the concept you are measuring is unidimensional in reality. As you've seen, many familiar concepts (height, weight, temperature) are actually unidimensional. However, if the concept you are studying is in fact multidimensional in nature, a unidimensional scale or number line won't describe it well. If you try to measure academic achievement on a single dimension, you would place every person on a single line ranging from low to high achievers. How would you score someone who is a high math achiever and terrible verbally, or vice versa? A unidimensional scale can't capture that type of achievement.

4-3d The Major Unidimensional Scale Types

There are three major types of unidimensional scaling methods. They are similar in that they each measure the concept of interest on a number line. However, they differ considerably in how they arrive at scale values for different items. The three methods are Thurstone or Equal-Appearing Interval Scaling, Likert or Summative Scaling, and Guttman or Cumulative Scaling. Each of these approaches is described in the following sections.

4-4 Thurstone Scaling

Thurstone was one of the first and most productive scaling theorists. He actually invented three different methods for developing a unidimensional scale: the *method of equal-appearing intervals,* the *method of successive intervals,* and the *method of paired comparisons.* The three methods differed in how the scale values for items were constructed, but in all three cases, the resulting scale was rated the same way by respondents. To illustrate Thurstone's approach, I'll show you the easiest method of the three to implement, the method of equal-appearing intervals.

4-4a The Method of Equal-Appearing Intervals

Developing the Focus: The Method of Equal-Appearing Intervals starts like almost every other scaling method—with a large set of statements. Oops! I did it again! You can't start with the set of statements; you have to first define the focus for the scale you're trying to develop. Let this be a warning to all of you: methodologists like me often start our descriptions with the first objective, methodological step (in this case, developing a set of statements) and forget to mention critical foundational issues like the development of the focus for a project. So, let's try this again....

The Method of Equal-Appearing Intervals starts like almost every other scaling method—with the development of the focus for the scaling project. Because this is a unidimensional scaling method, you assume that the concept you are trying to scale is reasonably thought of as one-dimensional. The description of this concept should be as clear as possible so that the person(s) that will create the statements have a clear idea of what you are trying to measure. I like to state the focus for a scaling project in the form of an open-ended statement to give to the people who will create the draft or candidate statements. For instance, you might start with the following focus statement:

One specific attitude that people might have towards the Greek System of fraternities and sororities is...

You want to be sure that everyone who is generating statements has some idea of what you are after in this focus command. You especially want to be sure that technical language and acronyms are spelled out and understood.

Generating Potential Scale Items: In this phase, you're ready to create statements. You want a large set of candidate statements (80-100) because you are going to select your final scale items from this pool. You also want to be sure that all of the statements are worded similarly—that they don't differ in grammar or structure. For instance, you might want them each to be worded as a statement with which respondents agree or disagree. You don't want some of them to be statements while others are questions.

For our example focus on developing the Greek system, we might generate statements like the following examples, which came from a class exercise I did in my undergrad class:

1. They build lasting friendships.
2. They are not minority friendly.
3. If you can't make friends, buy 'em!
4. They make it easier to get laid.
5. Black pants and tight shirts hide what's really there…
6. They employ members of the Ithaca community: housecleaners, cooks, repairmen, plumbers.
7. They pump money into the economy.
8. You can meet people of different backgrounds with similar ideologies.
9. Being part of the system enhances the college experience.
10. They all look alike (Northface, JCrew rollneck sweater, jeans…)
11. It's a way to meet people.
12. It's an organization full of drunk white people.
13. Fakes sisterhood relationships.
14. You will make the greatest connections for the future.
15. The girls are airheads.
16. They have beautiful houses for the most part.
17. They encourage demeaning attitudes towards women.
18. They make people think they are cool to give themselves higher and undeserved self-esteem.
19. They discourage people from being unique.
20. They help you meet people, people just like you.
21. Ambivalence.
22. Conflicting values.
23. They provide alternate housing.
24. They are a necessary evil.
25. They cost too much money.
26. They encourage drinking.
27. They encourage dating, drugs, and sex.
28. They are the cause of many accidents, deaths, and injuries.
29. They help very different types of people to live with one another and learn to get along and work together.
30. They foster leadership among members.
31. They help students fit in to a university.
32. They are a big time commitment but worth it.
33. They help students fit in at large universities.
34. They help establish friendships between the freshmen and upperclassmen.

35. Frats are elitist.
36. They promote the ideals/beliefs of their specific house.
37. They are a great source of alcohol and drugs.
38. They alienate students who are not involved.
39. They provide a social support system.
40. They help people adjust and make it through college.
41. They provide an outlet for stress.
42. They encourage underage drinking.
43. Membership does have its privileges.
44. Some of their goals are admirable.
45. Some people take it way too seriously.
46. They make alcohol easily available.
47. They are very important freshman year, but not after that.
48. They promote violence (paddling and beatings) and foster an atmosphere that encourages binge drinking.
49. It won't get better than this!
50. They allow those lacking a sense of self to feel included in a social interaction.
51. They are one big SUPERFICIAL realm.
52. They give people something to believe in.
53. They give people a chance to give back to something.
54. They are only for certain types of people.
55. They take up too much of students' time and cause students to do poorly academically.
56. They promote sisterhood and brotherhood.
57. They help students find their niche at college.
58. They discourage creativity and individual differences.
59. They make people become extremely shallow.
60. They encourage people to discriminate against others.
61. They provide strong friendships that cannot be found anywhere else on a campus.
62. Pledging takes away from study time.
63. They provide an alternative to on-campus housing.
64. They are extremely time consuming.
65. They promote negative views of women.
66. They provide future job opportunities.
67. They provide most of the donations after they graduate.
68. They engage in community service and philanthropy to support causes.
69. They act as a family away from home.
70. They teach caring for others.
71. Being affiliated often reduces the identity of those who conform.
72. They promote confidence.
73. They distract from academics.
74. The desire to fit in is more important than real desires/opinions of the participants.
75. There is too much hazing.
76. They make finding a place to live really easy.
77. They promote interaction through intramurals and sports.
78. They are too big a part of college life.
79. They're only there for social purposes.

80. They pressure individuals to go with decisions made by the group.
81. They get rid of small fish/big pond feeling.
82. They promote inclusion.
83. They promote interaction within the university as well as in the community.
84. They help you make friends for a lifetime.
85. They encourage exclusion.
86. All sorority girls wear black pants.
87. They provide funding for the university.
88. They create a sense of a family at school.
89. They promote community service.
90. They create a social-support network.
91. They induce group interaction and social gatherings.
92. They promote illegal behaviors.
93. They really can limit your scope of friends.
94. They induce group behavior contrary to the individual's beliefs.
95. People join just as an excuse to party.
96. They are fake and pointless.
97. They develop leadership abilities.
98. People do it because they need somewhere to belong.
99. People join just for the parties.
100. It is a really shallow system.

Rating the Scale Items: So now you have a set of statements. The next step is to have your participants (judges) rate each statement on a 1-to-11 scale in terms of how much each statement indicates a *favorable* attitude towards the Greek system. Pay close attention here! You *don't* want the participants to tell you what their attitudes towards the Greek system are, or whether they would agree with the statements. You want them to rate the favorableness of each statement in terms of an attitude towards the Greek system, where 1 = extremely unfavorable attitude towards the Greek system and 11 = extremely favorable attitude towards the Greek system. (Note that I could just as easily had the judges rate how much each statement represents a negative attitude towards the Greek system. If I did, the scale I developed would have higher scale values for people with more negative attitudes.) One easy way to actually accomplish this is to type each statement on a separate index card and have each judge rate them by sorting them into eleven piles as shown in Figure 4.20.

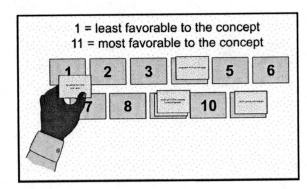

Figure 4.20
Rating the candidate statements on a 1-to-11 scale by sorting them manually.

Computing Scale Score Values for Each Item: The next step is to analyze the rating data. For each statement, you need to compute the median and the interquartile range. The *median* is the value above and below which 50% of the ratings fall. The first quartile (Q1) is the value below which 25% of the cases fall and above which 75% of the cases fall—in other words, the 25th percentile. The median is the 50th percentile. The third quartile, Q3, is the 75th percentile. The Interquartile Range is the difference between third and first quartile, or Q3 - Q1. Figure 4.21 shows a histogram for a single item and indicates the median and Interquartile Range.

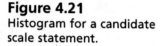

Figure 4.21
Histogram for a candidate scale statement.

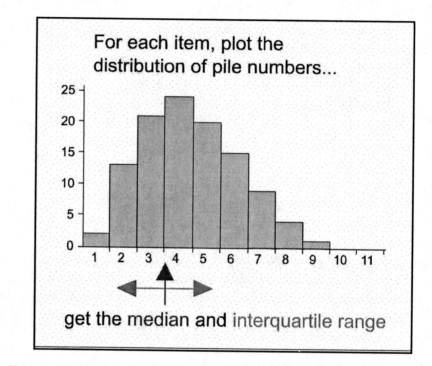

You can compute these values easily with any introductory statistics program or with most spreadsheet programs. To facilitate the final selection of items for your scale, you might want to sort the table of medians and interquartile range in ascending order by median and, within that, in descending order by interquartile range. For the items in the Greek System example, you would get a table like Table 4.3.

TABLE **4.3** **The median, first and third quartile, and interquartile range for the Greek System data.**

Median	25%	75%	IQR	Statement
2	2	3	1	3. If you can't make friends, buy 'em!
2	2	3	1	13. They fake sisterhood relationships.
2	2	3	1	15. The girls are airheads.
2	1	3	2	12. They are an organization full of drunk white people.
2	1	3	2	28. They are the cause of many accidents, deaths, and injuries.
2	1	3	2	48. They promote violence (paddling and beatings) and foster an atmosphere that encourages binge drinking.

Median	25%	75%	IQR	Statement
2	1	3	2	51. They are one big SUPERFICIAL realm.
2	2	4	2	59. They make people become extremely shallow.
2	1	3	2	60. They encourage people to discriminate against others.
2	1	3	2	96. They are fake and pointless.
2	1	3	2	100. It is a really shallow system.
3	3	4	1	35. Frats are elitist.
3	3	4	1	58. They discourage creativity and individual differences.
3	3	4	1	71. Being affiliated often reduces the identity of those who conform.
3	3	4	1	94. They induce group behavior contrary to the individual's beliefs.
3	2	4	2	2. They are not minority friendly.
3	2	4	2	17. They encourage demeaning attitudes towards women.
3	2	4	2	19. They discourage people from being unique.
3	2	4	2	38. They alienate students who are not involved.
3	2	4	2	65. They promote negative views of women.
3	2	4	2	75. There is too much hazing.
3	2	4	2	85. They encourage exclusion.
3	2	4	2	92. They promote illegal behaviors.
4	3	4	1	55. They take up too much of students' time and cause students to do poorly academically.
4	3	4	1	80. They pressure individuals to go with decisions made by the group.
4	3	5	2	5. Black pants and tight shirts hide what's really there…
4	3	5	2	10. They all look alike (Northface, JCrew rollneck sweater, jeans…)
4	3	5	2	62. Pledging takes away from study time.
4	3	5	2	73. They distract from academics.
4	3	5	2	74. The desire to fit in is more important than real desires/opinions of the participants.
4	3	5	2	93. They really can limit your scope of friends.
4	3	5	2	95. People join just as an excuse to party.
4	2	5	3	18. They make people think they are cool and give them higher and undeserved self-esteem.
4	3	6	3	26. They encourage drinking.
4	2	5	3	42. They encourage underage drinking.
4	2.25	6	3.75	24. They are a necessary evil.
4	2	6	4	27. They encourage dating, drugs, and sex.
4	2	6	4	37. They are a great source of alcohol and drugs.

continues →

T A B L E **4.3** **continued**

Median	25%	75%	IQR	Statement
4.5	3	6	3	99. People join just for the parties.
5	4	5	1	64. They are extremely time consuming
5	4	5	1	78. They are too big a part of college life.
5	4	6	2	22. Conflicting values.
5	3	5	2	25. They cost too much money.
5	4	6	2	45. Some people take it way too seriously.
5	4	6	2	46. They make alcohol easily available.
5	4	6	2	54. They are only for certain types of people.
5	4	6	2	79. They're only there for social purposes.
5	4	6	2	98. People do it because they need somewhere to belong.
5	3	6	3	86. All sorority girls wear black pants.
6	6	6	0	21. Ambivalence.
6	5	7	2	36. They promote the ideals/beliefs of their specific house.
6	4	6	2	47. They are very important freshman year, but not after that.
6	4	8	4	4. They make it easier to get laid.
7	7	8	1	43. Membership does have its privileges.
7	7	8	1	76. They make finding a place to live really easy.
7	6	8	2	6. They employ members of the Ithaca community: housecleaners, cooks, repairmen, plumbers.
7	6	8	2	7. They pump money into the economy.
7	6	8	2	20. They help you meet people, people just like you.
7	6	8	2	23. Alternate housing.
7	6	8	2	52. They give people something to believe in.
7	6	8	2	63. They provide an alternative to on-campus housing.
7	6	8	2	82. They promote inclusion.
7	6	10	4	49. It won't get better than this!
7	4	8	4	50. They allow those lacking a sense of self to feel included in a social interaction.
8	8	9	1	33. They help students fit in at large universities.
8	8	9	1	34. They help establish friendships between the freshmen and upperclassmen.
8	8	9	1	40. They help people to adjust and to make it through college.
8	8	9	1	57. They help students find their niche at college.
8	8	9	1	72. They promote confidence.

Median	25%	75%	IQR	Statement
8	8	9	1	83.They promote interaction within the university as well as in the community.
8	8	9	1	91. They induce group interaction and social gatherings.
8	7	9	2	31. They help students fit in to a university.
8	7	9	2	32. They are a big time commitment but worth it.
8	7	9	2	41. They provide an outlet for stress.
8	7	9	2	44. Some of their goals are admirable.
8	7	9	2	53. They give people a chance to give back to something.
8	7	9	2	67. They provide most of the donations after they graduate.
8	7	9	2	77. They promote interaction through intramurals and sports.
8	7	9	2	81. They get rid of small fish/big pond feeling.
8	7	9	2	87. They provides large funding for the university.
8	6	9	3	16. They have beautiful houses for the most part.
9	9	10	1	30. They foster leadership among members.
9	8	9	1	39. They provide a social-support system.
9	7	9	2	8.You can meet people of different backgrounds with similar ideologies.
9	8	10	2	9. Being part of the system enhances the college experience.
9	8	10	2	14. You will make the greatest connections for the future.
9	8	10	2	29. They help very different types of people live with one another and learn to get along and work together.
9	8	10	2	56. They promote sisterhood and brotherhood.
9	8	10	2	66. They provide future job opportunities.
9	8	10	2	68. They engage in community service and philanthropy to support causes.
9	8	10	2	69. They act as a family away from home.
9	8	10	2	70. They teach caring for others.
9	8	10	2	88. They create a sense of a family at school.
9	8	10	2	89. They promote community service.
9	8	10	2	90. They create a social-support network.
9	8	10	2	97. They develop leadership abilities.
9	7	10	3	11. It's a way to meet people.
10	9	10.75	1.75	1. They build lasting friendships
10	9	11	2	84. You make friends for a lifetime.
10	8	11	3	61. They provide strong friendships that cannot be found anywhere else on a campus

Selecting the Final Scale Items: Now you have to select the final statements for your scale. You should select statements that are at equal intervals across the range of medians. Ideally, one statement would be selected for each of the eleven median values. Within each value, you should try to select the statement that has the smallest interquartile range (the statement with the least amount of variability across judges). You don't want the statistical analysis to be the only deciding factor here. Look over the candidate statements at each level and select the statement that makes the most sense. If you find that the best statistical choice is a confusing statement, select the next best choice.

When my class went through its statements, we came up with the following set of items for our scale:

- They induce group behavior contrary to the individual's beliefs. (94-3)
- They make finding a place to live really easy. (76-7)
- They are too big a part of college life. (78-5)
- They provide a social support system. (39-9)
- They build lasting friendships. (1-10)
- They are the cause of many accidents, deaths, and injuries. (28-2)
- They distract from academics. (73-4)
- They help students find their niche at college. (57-8)
- They promote the ideals/beliefs of their specific house. (36-6)

The first value in parentheses after each statement is the statement number and the second is its scale value. Items with higher scale values should, in general, indicate a more favorable attitude towards fraternities and sororities. Notice that the order of the statements with respect to scale values is randomly scrambled. Also, notice that no item in the scale has a value of 1 or 11.

Administering the Scale: You now have a scale—a yardstick you can use for measuring attitudes towards the Greek system. You can give it to participants and ask them to agree or disagree with each statement. To get that person's total scale score, you average the scale scores of all the items that person agreed with. For instance, let's say a respondent who is an avid fan of the Greek system—perhaps even a fraternity or sorority member—completed the scale as shown in Table 4.4.

TABLE   **4.4   An example Greek System scale response form for a hypothetical respondent who is very favorable towards the Greek System.**

___Agree _X_Disagree	They induce group behavior contrary to the individual's beliefs. (94-3)
_X_Agree ___Disagree	They make finding a place to live really easy. (76-7)
___Agree _X_ Disagree	They are too big a part of college life. (78-5)
_X_Agree ___ Disagree	They provide a social support system. (39-9)
_X_ Agree ___ Disagree	They build lasting friendships. (1-10)
___ Agree _X_ Disagree	They are the cause of many accidents, deaths, and injuries. (28-2)
___ Agree _X_ Disagree	They distract from academics. (73-4)
_X_ Agree ___ Disagree	They help students find their niche at college. (57-8)
_X_ Agree ___ Disagree	They promote the ideals/beliefs of their specific house. (36-6)

If you're following along with the example, you should see that the respondent checked five items as Agree. When you take the average scale values for these five items, you get a final value for this respondent of 8. This is where this particular respondent would fall on your yardstick that measures attitudes towards the Greek system. Now, let's look at the responses for a hypothetical person who simply hates the Greek system and everything it represents, as shown in Table 4.5.

T A B L E **4.5**   **An example Greek System scale response form for a hypothetical respondent who is very negative towards the Greek System.**

_X_ Agree ___ Disagree	They induce group behavior contrary to the individual's beliefs. (94-3)
___ Agree _X_ Disagree	They make finding a place to live really easy. (76-7)
_X_ Agree ___ Disagree	They are too big a part of college life. (78-5)
___ Agree _X_ Disagree	They provide a social support system. (39-9)
___ Agree _X_ Disagree	They build lasting friendships. (1-10)
_X_ Agree ___ Disagree	They are the cause of many accidents, deaths, and injuries. (28-2)
_X_ Agree ___ Disagree	They distract from academics. (73-4)
___ Agree _X_ Disagree	They help students find their niche at college. (57-8)
___ Agree _X_ Disagree	They promote the ideals/beliefs of their specific house. (36-6)

In this example, the respondent only checked four items, all of which are on the negative end of the scale. When you average the scale items for the statements with which the respondent agreed, you get an average score of 3.5, considerably lower or more negative in attitude than the first respondent.

4-4b The Other Thurstone Methods

The other Thurstone scaling methods are similar to the Method of Equal-Appearing Intervals. All of them begin by focusing on a concept that is assumed to be unidimensional and involve generating a large set of potential scale items. All of them result in a scale consisting of relatively few items that the respondent rates on Agree/Disagree basis. The major differences are in how the data from the judges is collected. For instance, the method of paired comparisons requires each judge to make a judgment about each pair of statements. With lots of statements, this can become time consuming.

4-5 Likert Scaling

Like Thurstone or Guttman Scaling, *Likert Scaling* is a unidimensional scaling method. Here, I'll explain the basic steps in developing a Likert or Summative scale.

Defining the Focus: As in all scaling methods, the first step is to define what it is you are trying to measure. Because this is a unidimensional scaling method, it is assumed that the concept you want to measure is one-dimensional in nature. You might operationalize the definition as an instruction to the people who are going to create or generate the initial set of candidate items for your scale.

Generating the Items: Next, you have to create the set of potential scale items. These should be items that can be rated on a 1-to-5 or 1-to-7 Disagree-Agree response scale. Sometimes you can create the items by yourself based on your intimate understanding of the subject matter. More often than not though, it's helpful to engage a number of people in the item creation step. For instance, you might use some form of brainstorming to create the items. It's desirable to have as large a set of potential items as possible at this stage; about 80-100 would be best.

Rating the Items: The next step is to have a group of judges rate the items. Usually you would use a 1-to-5 rating scale where:

1 = Strongly unfavorable to the concept
2 = Somewhat unfavorable to the concept
3 = Undecided
4 = Somewhat favorable to the concept
5 = Strongly favorable to the concept

Notice that, as in other scaling methods, the judges are not telling you what they believe; they are judging how favorable each item is with respect to the construct of interest.

Selecting the Items: The next step is to compute the intercorrelations between all pairs of items, based on the ratings of the judges. In making judgments about which items to retain for the final scale there are several analyses you can perform:

- Throw out any items that have a low correlation with the total (summed) score across all items. In most statistics packages, it is relatively easy to compute this type of Item-Total correlation. First, you create a new variable that is the sum of all of the individual items for each respondent. Then, you include this variable in the correlation-matrix computation. (If you include it as the last variable in the list, the resulting Item-Total correlations will all be the last line of the correlation matrix and will be easy to spot.) How low should the correlation be for you to throw out the item? There is no fixed rule here; you might eliminate all items that have a correlation with the total score less than .6, for example. (This is covered in the discussion on correlation in Chapter 10, "Analysis.")

- For each item, get the average rating for the top quarter of judges and the bottom quarter. Then, do a t-test of the differences between the mean value for the item for the top and bottom quarter judges. (An in-depth discussion of t-tests appears in Chapter 10, "Analysis.") Higher t-values mean that there is a greater difference between the highest and lowest judges. In more practical terms, items with higher t-values are better discriminators, so you want to keep these items. In the end, you will have to use your judgment about which items are most sensibly retained. You want a relatively small number of items on your final scale (from 10-15) and you want them to have high Item-Total correlations and high discrimination (that is high t-values).

Administering the Scale: You're now ready to use your Likert scale. Each respondent is asked to rate each item on some response scale. For instance, respondents could rate each item on a 1-to-5 response scale where:

1 = Strongly disagree
2 = Disagree
3 = Undecided
4 = Agree
5 = Strongly agree

There are a variety of possible response scales (1-to-7, 1-to-9, 0-to-4). All of these odd-numbered scales have a middle value, which is often labeled Neutral or

Undecided. It is also possible to use a forced-choice response scale with an even number of responses and no middle neutral or undecided choice. In this situation, respondents are forced to decide whether they lean more towards the agree- or disagree-end of the scale for each item.

The final score for the respondent on the scale is the sum of his or her ratings for all of the items. (This is why this is sometimes called a summated scale.) On some scales, you will have items that are reversed in meaning from the overall direction of the scale. These are called *reversal items*. You will need to reverse the response value for each of these items before summing for the total. That is, if the respondent gave a 1, you make it a 5; if a respondent gave a 2, you make it a 4; 3 = 3; 4 = 2; and, 5 = 1.

Table 4.6 shows an example of a ten-item Likert scale that attempts to estimate the level of self-esteem a person has on the job. Notice that this instrument has no center or neutral point in the response scale; the respondent has to declare whether he/she is in agreement or disagreement with the item.

4-5a Example: The Employment Self-Esteem Scale

TABLE 4.6   The Employment Self-Esteem Likert Scale.

Strongly Disagree	Somewhat Disagree	Somewhat Agree	Strongly Agree	1. I feel good about my work on the job.
Strongly Disagree	Somewhat Disagree	Somewhat Agree	Strongly Agree	2. On the whole, I get along well with others at work.
Strongly Disagree	Somewhat Disagree	Somewhat Agree	Strongly Agree	3. I am proud of my ability to cope with difficulties at work.
Strongly Disagree	Somewhat Disagree	Somewhat Agree	Strongly Agree	4. When I feel uncomfortable at work, I know how to handle it.
Strongly Disagree	Somewhat Disagree	Somewhat Agree	Strongly Agree	5. I can tell that other people at work are glad to have me there.
Strongly Disagree	Somewhat Disagree	Somewhat Agree	Strongly Agree	6. I know I'll be able to cope with work for as long as I want.
Strongly Disagree	Somewhat Disagree	Somewhat Agree	Strongly Agree	7. I am proud of my relationship with my supervisor at work.
Strongly Disagree	Somewhat Disagree	Somewhat Agree	Strongly Agree	8. I am confident that I can handle my job without constant assistance.
Strongly Disagree	Somewhat Disagree	Somewhat Agree	Strongly Agree	9. I feel like I make a useful contribution at work.
Strongly Disagree	Somewhat Disagree	Somewhat Agree	Strongly Agree	10. I can tell that my coworkers respect me.

4-6 Guttman Scaling

Guttman scaling is also sometimes known as *cumulative scaling* or *scalogram analysis*. The purpose of Guttman scaling is to establish a one-dimensional continuum for a concept you want to measure. What does that mean? Essentially, you would like a set of items or statements so that a respondent who agrees with any specific question in the list will also agree with all previous questions. Put more formally, you would like to be able to predict item responses perfectly knowing only the total score for the respondent. For example, imagine a ten-item cumulative scale. If the respondent scores a four, it should mean that he/she agreed with the first four statements. If the respondent scores an eight, it should mean he/she agreed with the first eight. The object is to find a set of items that perfectly matches this pattern. In practice, you would seldom expect to find this cumulative pattern perfectly. So, you use scalogram analysis to examine how closely a set of items corresponds with this idea of cumulativeness. Here, I'll explain how you develop a Guttman scale.

Define the Focus: As in all of the scaling methods, you begin by defining the focus for your scale. Let's imagine that you want to develop a cumulative scale that measures U.S. citizen attitudes towards immigration. You would want to be sure to specify in your definition whether you are talking about any type of immigration (legal and illegal) from anywhere (Europe, Asia, Latin and South America, Africa).

Develop the Items: Next, as in all scaling methods, you would develop a large set of items that reflect the concept. You might do this yourself or you might engage a knowledgeable group to help. Let's say you came up with the following statements:

- I would permit a child of mine to marry an immigrant.
- I believe that this country should allow more immigrants in.
- I would be comfortable if a new immigrant moved next door to me.
- I would be comfortable with new immigrants moving into my community.
- It would be fine with me if new immigrants moved onto my block.
- I would be comfortable if my child dated a new immigrant.

Of course, you would want to come up with many more statements (about 80-100 is desirable).

Rate the Items: Next, you would want to have a group of judges rate the statements or items in terms of how favorable they are to the concept of immigration. They would give a Yes if the item is favorable toward immigration and a No if it is not. Notice that you are not asking the judges whether they personally agree with the statement. Instead, you're asking them to make a judgment about how the statement is related to the construct of interest.

Develop the Cumulative Scale: The key to Guttman scaling is in the analysis. You construct a matrix or table that shows the responses of all the respondents on all of the items. You then sort this matrix so that respondents who agree with more statements are listed at the top and those who agree with fewer are at the bottom. For respondents with the same number of agreements, sort the statements from left to right from those that most agreed to, to those that fewest agreed to. You might get a table something like the one in Figure 4.22. Notice that the scale is nearly cumulative when you read from left to right across the columns (items). Specifically a person who agreed with Item 7 always agreed with Item 2. Someone who agreed with Item 5 always agreed with Items 7 and 2. The matrix shows that the cumulativeness of the scale is not perfect, however. While in general, a person agreeing with Item 3 tended to also agree with 5, 7, and 2, there are several exceptions to that rule.

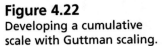
Figure 4.22
Developing a cumulative
scale with Guttman scaling.

Respondent	When sorted by row and column it will show whether there is a cumulative scale					
	Item 2	Item 7	Item 5	Item 3	Item 8	Item ...
7	Y	Y	Y	Y	Y	Y
15	Y	Y	Y	-	(Y)	-
3	Y	Y	Y	Y	-	-
29	Y	Y	Y	Y	-	-
19	Y	Y	Y	-	-	-
32	Y	Y	-	(Y)	-	-
41	Y	Y	-	-	-	-
6	Y	Y	-	-	-	-
14	Y	-	-	(Y)	-	-
33	-	-	-	-	-	-

exceptions

Although you can examine the matrix if there are only a few items in it, if there are many items you need to use a data analysis called *scalogram analysis* to determine the subsets of items from the pool that best approximate the cumulative property. Then, you review these items and select your final scale elements. There are several statistical techniques for examining the table to find a cumulative scale. Because there is seldom a perfectly cumulative scale, you usually have to test how good it is. These statistics also estimate a scale score value for each item. This scale score is used in the final calculation of a respondent's score.

Administering the Scale: After you've selected the final scale items, it's relatively simple to administer the scale. You simply present the items and ask respondents to check items with which they agree. For our hypothetical immigration scale, the items might be listed in cumulative order as follows:

- I believe that this country should allow more immigrants in.
- I would be comfortable with new immigrants moving into my community.
- It would be fine with me if new immigrants moved onto my block.
- I would be comfortable if a new immigrant moved next door to me.
- I would be comfortable if my child dated a new immigrant.
- I would permit a child of mine to marry an immigrant.

Of course, when you give the items to the respondent, you would probably want to mix up the order. The final scale might look the one in Table 4.7.

TABLE **4.7   Response form for a Guttman scale on attitudes about immigration.**

INSTRUCTIONS: Place a check next to each statement you agree with.

_____ I would permit a child of mine to marry an immigrant.

_____ I believe that this country should allow more immigrants in.

_____ I would be comfortable if a new immigrant moved next door to me.

_____ I would be comfortable with new immigrants moving into my community.

_____ It would be fine with me if new immigrants moved onto my block.

_____ I would be comfortable if my child dated a new immigrant.

Each scale item has a scale value associated with it (obtained from the scalogram analysis). To compute a respondent's scale score you simply sum the scale values of every item the respondent agrees with. In this example, the final value should be an indication of the respondent's attitude towards immigration.

SUMMARY

A lot of territory was covered in this chapter. You've learned about the different types of surveys: questionnaires and interviews and how to choose between them. You learned how to construct a questionnaire and address issues of question content, response formats, and question wording and placement. You learned how to train interviewers and the basic steps involved in conducting an interview. And, I showed you what a scale is and described the basic univariate scale types: Thurstone, Likert, and Guttman. You saw that scales can be used as stand-alone instruments, but they can also be integrated into a larger survey. Based on this chapter, you should feel pretty confident taking a crack at developing your own survey instrument. The next chapter introduces you to several forms of measurement—qualitative and unobtrusive—that are distinct from survey research but equally important in social research.

Chapter

5

Qualitative and Unobtrusive Measures

This chapter presents two broad areas of measurement—qualitative measurement and unobtrusive measurement. Each of them is distinct from traditional survey and scaling methods described in Chapter 4, "Survey Research and Scaling." Qualitative measurement comes from a long tradition of field research, originally in anthropology and then subsequently in psychology, sociology, and the other social sciences. This tradition is extremely complex and varied, and there's probably as much variation and dispute within the tradition as there is in more quantitative traditions. Even the simple notion that qualitative means nonquantitative has begun to break down as we recognize the intimate interconnectedness between the two. This chapter introduces the qualitative tradition and gives you the flavor of some of the qualitative/quantitative disputes of the past few decades. Then I discuss qualitative data, the different approaches to collecting it, the broader qualitative methods, and the standards for judging the validity of qualitative measurement.

Unobtrusive measures are ones that are collected without interfering in the lives of the respondents. They also represent a broad tradition of measurement in social research. They range from traditional content analysis of text documents and secondary analysis of data to some of the most clever and indirect methods of measurement you'll see.

Key Terms

case study
coding
construct validity
content analysis
direct observation
epistemological assumptions
ethnography
exception dictionary
external validity
field research
grounded theory
hypothesis
indirect measure
median
memoing
ontological assumptions
open coding
participant observation
phenomenology
post-positivism
qualitative data
qualitative measures
quantitative
reliability
sample
sampling
secondary analysis
selective coding
true score theory
unobtrusive measures
unstructured interviewing
validity

5-1 Qualitative Measures

Qualitative research is a vast and complex area of methodology that can easily take up whole textbooks on its own. The purpose of this section is to introduce you to the idea of qualitative research (and how it is related to quantitative research) and introduce you to the major types of qualitative research data, approaches, and methods.

So what is qualitative research and what are qualitative measures? **Qualitative measures** are any measures where the data is not recorded in numerical form. (I know, it's a pain to define something by telling you what it is not, but this really is the most accurate way to look at the breadth of qualitative measures.) Qualitative measures include short written responses on surveys; interviews; anthropological field research; video and audio data recording; and many other approaches, all of which are characterized by a non-numerical format. Qualitative research is any research that relies primarily or exclusively on qualitative measures.

You should consider four important questions before you undertake qualitative research:

- Do you want to generate new theories or hypotheses?
- Do you need to achieve a deep understanding of the issues?
- Are you willing to trade detail for generalizability?
- Is funding available for this research?

These questions are addressed in the following sections.

Do You Want to Generate New Theories or Hypotheses?

One of the major reasons for doing qualitative research is to become more experienced with the phenomenon in which you're interested. Too often in applied social research (especially in economics and psychology) graduate students jump from doing a literature review of a topic of interest to writing a research proposal complete with theories and **hypotheses** based on current thinking. What they miss is the direct experience of the phenomenon. Before mounting a study, all students should probably be required to spend some time living with the phenomenon they are studying. For example, before looking at the effects of a new psychotropic drug for the mentally ill, go spend some time visiting mental health treatment contexts to observe what occurs. If you do, you are likely to approach the existing literature on the topic with a fresh perspective born of your direct experience as well as formulate your own ideas about what causes what to happen. This is where most of the more interesting and valuable new theories and hypotheses originate, and good qualitative research can play a major role in this theory development.

Do You Need to Achieve a Deep Understanding of the Issues?

I believe that qualitative research has special value for investigating complex and sensitive issues. For example, if you are interested in how people view topics like God and religion, human sexuality, the death penalty, gun control, and so on, my guess is that you would be hard pressed to develop a **quantitative** methodology that would do anything more than summarize a few key positions on these issues. While this does have its place (and its done all the time), if you really want to try to achieve a deep understanding of how people think about these topics, some type of in-depth interviewing is probably required.

Are You Willing to Trade Detail for Generalizability?

Qualitative research certainly excels at generating detailed information. Of course, some quantitative studies are detailed also in that they involve collecting extensive numeric data; but in detailed quantitative research, the data itself tends to both shape and limit the analysis. For example, if you collect a simple interval-level quantitative measure, the analyses you are likely to do with it are fairly delimited (such as descriptive statistics, use in correlation, regression, or multivariate models, and so on). Generalizing tends to be a straightforward endeavor in most quantitative research. After all, when you collect the same variable from everyone in your sample, all you need to do to generalize to the *sample* as a whole is to compute some aggregate statistic like a mean or *median.*

Things are not so simple in most qualitative research. The data is rawer and seldom pre-categorized. Consequently, you need to be prepared to organize all of that raw detail. Additionally there are almost an infinite number of ways to accomplish this. Even generalizing across a sample of interviews or written documents becomes a complex endeavor.

The detail in most qualitative research is both a blessing and a curse. On the positive side, it enables you to describe the phenomena of interest with great richness, in the original language of the research participants. In fact, some of the best qualitative research is often published in book form, often in a style that almost approaches a narrative story. One of my favorite writers (and, I daresay, one of the finest qualitative researchers) is Studs Terkel. He has written intriguing accounts of the Great Depression (*Hard Times*), World War II (*The Good War*), and socioeconomic divisions in America (*The Great Divide*) among others. In each book, he follows a similar qualitative methodology, identifying informants who directly experienced the phenomenon in question, interviewing them at length, and then editing the interviews heavily so that they tell a story that is different from what any individual interviewee might tell but addresses the question of interest. On the negative side, when you have that kind of detail, it's hard to determine what the generalizable themes are. In fact, many qualitative researchers don't even care about generalizing; they're content to generate rich descriptions of their phenomena.

That's why there is so much value in mixing qualitative and quantitative research. Quantitative research excels at summarizing large amounts of data and reaching generalizations based on statistical projections. Qualitative research excels at telling the story from the participant's viewpoint, providing the rich descriptive detail that sets quantitative results into their human context.

Is Funding Available for This Research?

I hate to be crass, but in most social research, you do have to worry about how it will be paid for. There is little point in proposing research that would be unlikely to be carried out for lack of funds. For qualitative research, this is an often especially challenging issue. Because much qualitative research takes an enormous amount of time, is labor intensive, and yields results that may not be generalizable for policy making or decision making, many funding sources view it as a frill or as simply too expensive.

There's a lot that you should (and shouldn't) do when proposing qualitative research to enhance its fundability. My pet peeve with qualitative research proposals is when the author says something along these lines. (Of course, I'm paraphrasing here. No good qualitative researcher would come out and say something like this directly.)

> *This study uses an emergent, exploratory, inductive qualitative approach. Because the basis of such an approach is that one does not predetermine or delimit the directions the investigation might take, there is no way to propose specific budgetary or time estimates.*

Of course, this is silly! There is always a way to estimate (or at least make an educated guess!) about budgets and time limits. As an alternative that doesn't hem you in or constrain the methodology, you might reword the same passage in the following manner:

> *This study uses an emergent, exploratory, inductive qualitative approach. Because the basis of such an approach is that one does not predetermine or delimit the directions the investigation might take, it is especially important to detail the specific stages that this research will follow in addressing the research questions. [Inset detailed description of data collection, coding, analysis, etc. Especially note where there may be iterations of the phases.] Because of the complexities involved in this type of research, the proposal is divided into several broad stages with funding and time estimates provided for each. [Provide detail.]*

Notice that the first approach is almost an insult to the reviewer. In the second, the author acknowledges the unpredictability of qualitative research but does as reasonable a job as possible to anticipate the course of the study, its costs, and milestones. It is certainly more fundable.

5-1a The Qualitative/Quantitative Debate

Probably more energy has been expended on debating the differences between and relative advantages of qualitative and quantitative methods than almost any other methodological topic in social research. The qualitative/quantitative debate is one of those hot-button issues that almost invariably triggers an intense encounter in the hotel bar at any social research convention. I've seen friends and colleagues degenerate into academic enemies faster than you can say last call.

After years of being involved in such verbal brawling, as an observer and direct participant, the only conclusion I've been able to reach is that this debate is much ado about nothing. To say that one or the other approach is better is, in my view, simply trivializing a far complex topic than a dichotomous choice can truly settle. Both quantitative and qualitative research rest on rich and varied traditions that come from multiple disciplines and both have been employed to address almost any research topic you can think of. In fact, in almost every applied social research project, I believe there is value in consciously combining qualitative and quantitative methods in what is referred to as a mixed-methods approach.

I find it useful when thinking about this debate to distinguish between the general *assumptions* involved in undertaking a research project (qualitative, quantitative, or mixed) and the *data* that is collected. At the data level, I believe that there is little difference between the qualitative and the quantitative. However, at the level in which assumptions are made, the differences can be profound and irreconcilable, which is why the fighting rages on.

Qualitative and Quantitative Data

It may seem odd that I would argue that there is little difference between qualitative and quantitative *data*. After all, qualitative data typically consists of words whereas quantitative data consists of numbers. Aren't these fundamentally different? I don't think so, for the following reasons:

- All qualitative data can be coded quantitatively.
- All quantitative data is based on qualitative judgment.

I'll consider each of these reasons in turn.

All Qualitative Data Can Be Coded Quantitatively

What I mean here is simple. Anything that is qualitative can be assigned meaningful numerical values. These values can then be manipulated numerically or quantitatively to help you achieve greater insight into the meaning of the data so you can examine specific hypotheses. Consider a simple example. Many surveys have one or more short, open-ended questions that ask the respondent to supply text responses. The simplest case is probably the sentence that is often tacked onto a short survey, "Please add any additional comments." The immediate responses are text-based and qualitative; but you can always (and usually will) perform some type of simple classification of the text responses. You might sort the responses into simple categories, for instance. Often, you'll give each category a short label that represents the theme in the response. What you don't often recognize is that even the simple act of categorizing can be viewed as a quantitative one. For instance, let's say that you develop five themes that the respondents express in their open-ended response. Assume that you have ten respondents. You could easily set up a simple coding table like the one in Table 5.1 to represent the coding of the ten responses into the five themes.

TABLE **5.1.**   **Coding of qualitative data into five themes for ten respondents.**

Person	Theme 1	Theme 2	Theme 3	Theme 4	Theme 5
1	✓	✓		✓	
2	✓		✓		
3	✓	✓		✓	
4		✓		✓	
5		✓		✓	✓
6	✓	✓			✓
7			✓	✓	✓
8		✓		✓	
9			✓		✓
10				✓	✓

This is a simple qualitative thematic coding analysis. But, you can represent exactly the same information quantitatively as in Table 5.2.

TABLE **5.2.**   **Quantitative coding of the data in Table 5.1.**

Person	Theme 1	Theme 2	Theme 3	Theme 4	Theme 5	Totals
1	1	1	0	1	0	3
2	1	0	1	0	0	2
3	1	1	0	1	0	3
4	0	1	0	1	0	2
5	0	1	0	1	1	3
6	1	1	0	0	1	3
7	0	0	1	1	1	3
8	0	1	0	1	0	2
9	0	0	1	0	1	2
10	0	0	0	1	1	2
Totals	4	6	3	7	5	

Notice that this is exactly the same data. The first table (Table 5.1) would probably be called a qualitative coding while the second (Table 5.2) is clearly quantitative. The quantitative coding gives you additional useful information and makes it possible to do analyses that you couldn't do with the qualitative coding. For instance, simply by adding down the columns in Table 5.2, you can say that Theme 4 was the most frequently mentioned and, by adding across the rows, you can say that all respondents touched on two or three of the five themes. However, you can do even more. For instance, you could look at the similarities among the themes based on which respondents addressed them. How? Table 5.3 shows a simple correlation matrix for the data in Table 5.2.

T A B L E **5.3 Correlations between the five themes in Table 5.2.**

	Theme 1	Theme 2	Theme 3	Theme 4
Theme 2	0.250			
Theme 3	-0.089	-0.802		
Theme 4	-0.356	0.356	-0.524	
Theme 5	-0.408	-0.408	0.218	-0.218

The analysis shows that Themes 2 and 3 are strongly negatively correlated: People who said Theme 2 seldom said Theme 3 and vice versa. (Check it for yourself.) You can also look at the similarity among respondents as shown in Table 5.4.

T A B L E **5.4 Correlations between the ten respondents in Table 5.2.**

	P1	P2	P3	P4	P5	P6	P7	P8	P9
P2	-0.167								
P3	1.000	-0.167							
P4	0.667	-0.667	0.667						
P5	0.167	-1.000	0.167	0.667					
P6	0.167	-0.167	0.167	-0.167	0.167				
P7	-0.667	-0.167	-0.667	-0.167	0.167	-0.667			
P8	0.667	-0.667	0.667	1.000	0.667	-0.167	-0.167		
P9	-1.000	0.167	-1.000	-0.667	-0.167	-0.167	0.667	-0.667	
P10	-0.167	-0.667	-0.167	0.167	0.667	-0.167	0.667	0.167	0.167

You can see immediately that Persons 1 and 3 are perfectly correlated (r = +1.0) as are Persons 4 and 8. There are also a few perfect opposites (r = -1.0) — P1 and P9, P2 and P5, and P3 and P9.

You could do much more. If you had more respondents (and you often would with a survey), you could do some simple multivariate analyses. For instance, you could draw a similarity map of respondents based on their intercorrelations. The map would have one dot per respondent and respondents with more similar responses would cluster closer together.

The point is that the line between qualitative and quantitative is less distinct than we sometimes imagine. All qualitative data can be quantitatively coded in an almost infinite variety of ways. This doesn't detract from the qualitative information. You can still do any judgmental syntheses or analyses you want; but recognizing the similarities between qualitative and quantitative information opens up new possibilities for interpretation that might otherwise go unutilized. Now to the other side of the coin....

All Quantitative Data Is Based on Qualitative Judgment

Numbers in and of themselves can't be interpreted without understanding the assumptions that underlie them. Take, for example, a simple 1-to-5 rating variable, shown in Figure 5.1.

Capital punishment is the best way to deal with convicted murderers.

1	2	3	4	5
Strongly Disagree	Disagree	Neutral	Agree	Strongly Agree

Figure 5.1
A rating illustrates that quantitative data is based on qualitative judgments.

Here, the respondent answered 2=Disagree. What does this mean? How do you interpret the value 2 here? You can't really understand this quantitative value unless you dig into some of the judgments and assumptions that underlie it:

- Did the respondent understand the term capital punishment?
- Did the respondent understand that 2 means that he or she is disagreeing with the statement?
- Does the respondent have any idea about alternatives to capital punishment (otherwise how can he or she judge what's best)?
- Did the respondent read carefully enough to determine that the statement was limited only to convicted murderers (for instance, rapists were not included)?
- Does the respondent care or was he or she just circling anything arbitrarily?
- How was this question presented in the context of the survey (for example, did the questions immediately before this one bias the response in any way)?
- Was the respondent mentally alert (especially if this is late in a long survey or the respondent had other things going on earlier in the day)?
- What was the setting for the survey (lighting, noise, and other distractions)?
- Was the survey anonymous? Was it confidential?
- In the respondent's mind, is the difference between a 1 and a 2 the same as between a 2 and a 3 (meaning, is this an interval scale)?

I could go on and on, but my point should be clear. All numerical information involves numerous judgments about what the number means. The bottom line here is that quantitative and qualitative data are, at some level, virtually inseparable. Neither exists in a vacuum; nor can either be considered totally apart from the other. To ask which is better or more valid or has greater verisimilitude or whatever ignores the intimate connection between them. To do good research, you need to use both the *qualitative* and the *quantitative* measurements.

Qualitative and Quantitative Assumptions

To say that qualitative and quantitative data is similar only tells half the story. After all, the intense academic wrangling of the qualitative-quantitative debate must have some basis in reality. My sense is that there are some fundamental differences, but that they lie primarily at the level of assumptions about research (epistemological and ontological assumptions) rather than at the level of the data.

First, let's do away with the most common myths about the differences between qualitative and quantitative research. Many people believe the following:

* Quantitative research is confirmatory and deductive in nature.
* Qualitative research is exploratory and inductive in nature.

I think that while there's a shred of truth in these statements, they are not exactly correct. In general, a lot of quantitative research tends to be confirmatory and deductive. However lots of quantitative research can be classified as exploratory as well; and while much qualitative research does tend to be exploratory, it can also be used to confirm specific deductive hypotheses. The problem I have with these kinds of statements is that they don't acknowledge the richness of both traditions. They don't recognize that both qualitative and quantitative research can be used to address almost any kind of research question.

So, if the difference between qualitative and quantitative is not along the exploratory-confirmatory or inductive-deductive dimensions, where is it?

My belief is that the heart of the quantitative-qualitative debate is philosophical, not methodological. Many qualitative researchers operate under different *epistemological assumptions* from those that quantitative researchers follow. For instance, many qualitative researchers believe that the best way to understand any phenomenon is to view it in its context. They see all quantification as limited in nature, looking only at one small portion of a reality that cannot be split or unitized without losing the importance of the whole phenomenon. For some qualitative researchers, the best way to understand what's going on is to become immersed in it. Move into the culture or organization you are studying and experience what it is like to be a part of it. Be flexible in your inquiry of people in context. Rather than approach measurement with the idea of constructing a fixed instrument or set of questions, allow the questions to emerge and change as you become familiar with what you are studying.

Many qualitative researchers also operate under different *ontological assumptions* about the world. They don't assume that there is a single unitary reality apart from our perceptions. Since each of us experiences reality from our own point of view, each of us experiences a different reality. Conducting research without taking this into account violates the fundamental view of the individual. Consequently, qualitative researchers may be opposed to methods that attempt to aggregate across individuals on the grounds that each individual is unique. They also argue that the researcher is a unique individual and that all research is essentially influenced or biased by each researcher's individual perceptions.

In the end, people who consider themselves primarily qualitative or primarily quantitative tend to be almost as diverse as those from the opposing camps. Some qualitative researchers fit comfortably into the post-positivist tradition of *post-positivism* common to much contemporary quantitative research. Some quantitative researchers (albeit, probably fewer) use quantitative information as the basis for exploration, recognizing the inherent limitations and complex assumptions beneath all numbers. In either camp, you'll find intense and fundamental disagreement about both philosophical assumptions and the nature of data. Increasingly, researchers are interested in blending the two traditions, attempting to take advantage of each.

Qualitative data is extremely varied in nature. It includes virtually any information that can be captured that is not numerical in nature. Here are some of the major categories or types of qualitative data:

- **In-depth interviews**—These include both individual interviews (one-on-one) as well as group interviews (including focus groups). The data can be recorded in numerous ways including stenography, audio recording, video recording, and written notes. In-depth interviews differ from direct observation primarily in the nature of the interaction. In interviews, it is assumed that there is a questioner and one or more interviewees. The purpose of the interview is to probe the ideas of the interviewees about the phenomenon of interest.
- **Direct observation**—I use the term *direct observation* broadly here. It differs from interviewing in that the observer does not actively query the respondent. It can include everything from *field research* where one lives in another context or culture for a period of time to photographs that illustrate some aspect of the phenomenon. The data can be recorded in many of the same ways as interviews (stenography, audio, and video) and through pictures (photos or drawings). (For example, courtroom drawings of witnesses are a form of direct observation.)
- **Written documents**—Usually this refers to existing documents (as opposed to transcripts of interviews conducted for the research). It can include newspapers, magazines, books, Web sites, memos, transcripts of conversations, annual reports, and so on. Usually written documents are analyzed with some form of content analysis (see the discussion on content analysis later in this chapter.)

5-1b Qualitative Data

A qualitative approach is a general way of thinking about conducting qualitative research. It describes, either explicitly or implicitly, the purpose of the qualitative research, the role of the researcher(s), the stages of research, and the method of data analysis. Here, four of the major qualitative approaches are introduced: ethnography, phenomenology, field research, and grounded theory.

5-1c Qualitative Approaches

Ethnography

The ethnographic approach to qualitative research comes largely from the field of anthropology. The emphasis in *ethnography* is on studying an entire culture. Originally, the idea of a culture was tied to the notion of ethnicity and geographic location (such as the culture of the Trobriand Islands), but it has been broadened to include virtually any group or organization. That is, you can study the culture of a business or defined group, such as a Rotary club.

Ethnography is an extremely broad area with a great variety of practitioners and methods. However, the most common ethnographic approach is *participant observation* as a part of field research. The ethnographer becomes immersed in the culture as an active participant and records extensive field notes. As in grounded theory, there is no preset limiting of what will be observed and no real ending point in an ethnographic study.

Phenomenology

Phenomenology is sometimes considered a philosophical perspective as well as an approach to qualitative methodology. It has a long history in several social research disciplines including psychology, sociology, and social work. Phenomenology is a school of thought that emphasizes a focus on people's subjective experiences and interpretations of the world. That is, the phenomenologist wants to understand how the world appears to others.

Field Research

Field research can also be considered either a broad approach to qualitative research or a method of gathering *qualitative data*. The essential idea is that the researcher goes into the field to observe the phenomenon in its natural state or in situ. As such, it is probably most related to the method of *participant observation*. The field researcher typically takes extensive field notes that are subsequently coded and analyzed.

Grounded Theory

Grounded theory is a qualitative research approach that was originally developed by Glaser and Strauss in the 1960s. The self-defined purpose of grounded theory is to develop theory about phenomena of interest; but they are not talking about abstract theorizing. Instead the *theory* needs to be *grounded* or rooted in observation; hence the term.

Grounded theory is a complex *iterative* process. The research begins with the raising of *generative questions* that help guide the research but are not intended to be either static or confining. As the researcher begins to gather data, *core theoretical concept(s)* are identified. Tentative *linkages* are developed between the theoretical core concepts and the data. This early phase of the research tends to be open and can take months. Later on, the researcher is more engaged in verification and summary. The effort tends to evolve toward one *core category* that is central. Grounded theory includes the following key analytic strategies:

- *Coding* is a process for categorizing qualitative data and describing the implications and details of these categories. Initially you use **open coding,** considering the data in minute detail while developing some initial categories. Later, you move to more **selective coding** where you systematically code with respect to a core concept.
- *Memoing* is a process for recording your thoughts and ideas as they evolve throughout the study. You might think of memoing as extensive marginal notes and comments. Again, early in the process these memos tend to be open; whereas later on they tend to increasingly focus in on the core concept.
- **Integrative diagrams and sessions** are used to pull all of the detail together to help make sense of the data with respect to the emerging theory. The diagrams can be any form of graphic that is useful at that point in theory development. They might be concept maps, directed graphs, or even simple cartoons that can act as summarizing devices. This integrative work is best done in group sessions where different members of the research team can interact and share ideas to increase insight.

Eventually you approach a *conceptually dense theory* as each new observation leads to new linkages that lead to revisions in the theory and more data collection. The core concept or category is identified and fleshed out in detail.

When does the grounded theory process end? One answer is never. Clearly, the process described here could continue indefinitely. Grounded theory doesn't have a clearly demarcated point for ending a study. Essentially, the project ends when the researcher decides to quit.

What do you have when you're finished? Presumably you have an extremely well-considered explanation for some phenomenon of interest—the grounded theory. This theory can be explained in words and is usually presented with much of the contextually relevant detail collected.

A variety of methods are common in qualitative measurement. In fact, the methods are largely limited by the imagination of the researcher. Here I discuss a few of the more common methods.

5-1d Qualitative Methods

Participant Observation

One of the most common methods for *qualitative data* collection, *participant observation*, is also one of the most demanding. It requires that the researcher become a participant in the culture or context being observed. The literature on participant observation discusses how to enter the context, the role of the researcher as a participant, the collection and storage of field notes, and the analysis of field data. Participant observation often requires months or years of intensive work because the researcher needs to become accepted as a natural part of the culture to ensure that the observations are of the natural phenomenon.

Direct Observation

Direct observation is distinguished from participant observation in a number of ways. First, a direct observer doesn't typically try to become a participant in the context. However, the direct observer does strive to be as unobtrusive as possible so as not to bias the observations. Second, direct observation suggests a more detached perspective. The researcher is watching rather than taking part. Consequently, technology can be a useful part of direct observation. For instance, you can videotape the phenomenon or observe from behind one-way mirrors. Third, direct observation tends to be more focused than participant observation. The researcher is observing certain sampled situations or people rather than trying to become immersed in the entire context. Finally, direct observation tends not to take as long as participant observation. For instance, one might observe child-mother interactions under specific circumstances in a laboratory setting from behind a one-way mirror, looking especially for the nonverbal cues being used.

Unstructured Interviewing

Unstructured interviewing involves direct interaction between the researcher and a respondent or group. It differs from traditional structured interviewing in several important ways. First, although the researcher may have some initial guiding questions or core concepts to ask about, there is no formal structured instrument or protocol. Second, the interviewer is free to move the conversation in any direction of interest that may come up. Consequently, unstructured interviewing is particularly useful for exploring a topic broadly. However, there is a price for this lack of structure. Because each interview tends to be unique with no predetermined set of questions asked of all respondents, it is usually more difficult to analyze unstructured interview data, especially when synthesizing across respondents.

Unstructured interviewing may very well be the most common form of data collection of all. You could say it is the method being used whenever anyone asks someone else a question! It is especially useful when conducting site visits or casual focus groups designed to explore a context or situation.

Case Studies

A *case study* is an intensive study of a specific individual or specific context. For instance, Freud developed case studies of several individuals as the basis for the theory of psychoanalysis and Piaget did case studies of children to study developmental phases. There is no single way to conduct a case study, and a combination of methods (such as **unstructured interviewing** and **direct observation**) can be used.

5-1e Qualitative Validity

Depending on their philosophical perspectives, some qualitative researchers reject the framework of **validity** that is commonly accepted in more quantitative research in the social sciences. They reject the basic realist assumption that there is a reality external to our perception of it. Consequently, it doesn't make sense to be concerned with the truth or falsity of an observation with respect to an external reality (which is a primary concern of validity). These qualitative researchers argue for different standards of judging the quality of research.

For instance, Guba and Lincoln proposed four criteria for judging the soundness of qualitative research and explicitly offered these as an alternative to more traditional quantitatively oriented criteria. They felt that their four criteria better reflected the underlying assumptions involved in much qualitative research. Their proposed criteria and the analogous quantitative criteria are listed in Table 5.5.

T A B L E **5.5** **Criteria for judging research quality from a more qualitative perspective.**

Traditional Criteria for Judging Quantitative Research	Alternative Criteria for Judging Qualitative Research
Internal validity	Credibility
External validity	Transferability
Reliability	Dependability
Objectivity	Confirmability

Credibility

The credibility criteria involves establishing that the results of qualitative research are credible or believable from the perspective of the participant in the research. Since from this perspective the purpose of qualitative research is to describe or understand the phenomena of interest from the participant's eyes, the participants are the only ones who can legitimately judge the credibility of the results.

Transferability

Transferability refers to the degree to which the results of qualitative research can be generalized or transferred to other contexts or settings. From a qualitative perspective, transferability is primarily the responsibility of the one doing the generalizing. The qualitative researcher can enhance transferability by doing a thorough job of describing the research context and the assumptions that were central to the research. The person who wishes to transfer the results to a different context is then responsible for making the judgment of how sensible the transfer is.

Dependability

The traditional quantitative view of reliability is based on the assumption of replicability or repeatability (see **reliability** in Chapter 3, "The Theory of Measurement"). Essentially, it is concerned with whether you would obtain the same results if you could observe the same thing twice. However, you can't actually measure the same thing twice; by definition if you are measuring twice, you are measuring two different things. To estimate reliability, quantitative researchers construct various hypothetical notions (for example, **true score theory** as described in Chapter 3) to try to get around this fact.

The idea of dependability, on the other hand, emphasizes the need for the researcher to account for the ever-changing context within which research occurs. The researcher is responsible for describing the changes that occur in the setting and how these changes affect the way the researcher approached the study.

Confirmability

Qualitative research tends to assume that each researcher brings a unique perspective to the study. Confirmability refers to the degree to which the results could be confirmed or corroborated by others. There are a number of strategies for enhancing confirmability. The researcher can document the procedures for checking and rechecking the data throughout the study. Another researcher can take a devil's advocate role with respect to the results, and this process can be documented. The researcher can actively search for and describe *negative instances* that contradict prior observations. After the study, a researcher can conduct a *data audit* that examines the data collection and analysis procedures and makes judgments about the potential for bias or distortion.

There has been considerable debate among methodologists about the value and legitimacy of this alternative set of standards for judging qualitative research. On the one hand, many quantitative researchers see the alternative criteria as just a relabeling of the already successful *quantitative* criteria to accrue greater legitimacy for qualitative research. They suggest that a correct reading of the quantitative criteria would show that they are not limited to quantitative research alone and can be applied equally well to qualitative data. They argue that the alternative criteria represent a different philosophical perspective that is subjectivist rather than realist. They claim that research inherently assumes that some reality is being observed and can be observed with greater or less accuracy or validity. If you don't make this assumption, they would contend, you simply are not engaged in research (although that doesn't mean that what you are doing is not valuable or useful).

Perhaps there is some legitimacy to this counter argument. Certainly a broad reading of the traditional quantitative criteria might make their standards of validity appropriate to the qualitative realm as well. Historically, however, the traditional quantitative criteria have been described almost exclusively in terms of quantitative research. No one has yet done a thorough job of translating how the same criteria might apply in qualitative research contexts. For instance, the discussions of *external validity* have been dominated by the idea of statistical *sampling* as the basis for generalizing. Additionally, considerations of *reliability* have traditionally been inextricably linked to the notion of **true score theory**.

However, qualitative researchers do have a point about the irrelevance of traditional quantitative criteria. How could we judge the external validity of a qualitative study that does not use formalized sampling methods? How can we judge the reliability of *qualitative data* when there is no mechanism for estimating the true score? No one has adequately explained how the operational procedures used to assess validity and reliability in quantitative research can be translated into legitimate corresponding operations for qualitative research.

Alternative criteria may not be necessary (and I personally hope that more work is done on broadening the traditional criteria so that they legitimately apply across the entire spectrum of research approaches). Additionally alternative criteria can be confusing for students and newcomers to this discussion. However, these alternatives do serve to remind us that qualitative research cannot be considered merely an extension of the quantitative paradigm into the realm of non-numeric data.

5-2 Unobtrusive Measures

Unobtrusive measures are measures that don't require the researcher to intrude in the research context. **Direct observation** and **participant observation** require the researcher to be physically present. This can lead the respondents to alter their behavior to look good in the eyes of the researcher. A questionnaire is an interruption in the natural stream of behavior. Respondents tire of filling out a survey or become resentful of the questions asked.

Unobtrusive measurement presumably reduces the biases that result from the intrusion of the researcher or measurement instrument. However, unobtrusive measures depend on the context and, in many situations, are simply not available or feasible. For some constructs, there may not be any sensible way to develop unobtrusive measures.

Three types of unobtrusive measurement are discussed here: indirect measures, content analysis, and secondary analysis of data.

5-2a Indirect Measures

An **indirect measure** is an unobtrusive measure that occurs naturally in a research context. The researcher is able to collect the data without introducing any formal measurement procedure.

The types of indirect measures that may be available are limited only by the researcher's imagination and inventiveness. For instance, let's say you would like to measure the popularity of various exhibits in a museum. It may be possible to set up some type of mechanical measurement system that is invisible to the museum patrons. In one study, the system was simple. The museum installed new floor tiles in front of each exhibit it wanted a measurement on and, after a period of time, researchers measured the wear-and-tear on the tiles as an indirect measure of patron traffic and interest. You might be able to improve on this approach considerably using electronic measures. For instance, you might construct an electrical device that senses movement in front of an exhibit, or place hidden cameras and code patron interest based on videotaped evidence.

One of my favorite indirect measures occurred in a study of radio station listening preferences. Rather than conducting an obtrusive, costly, and time-consuming survey or interview about favorite radio stations, the researchers went to local auto dealers and garages and checked all cars that were being serviced to see what station the radios were currently tuned to. In a similar manner, if you want to know magazine preferences, you might rummage through the trash of your *sample* or even stage a door-to-door magazine recycling effort, noting which magazines you collect.

These examples illustrate one of the most important points about indirect measures; you have to be careful about ethics when using this type of measurement. In an indirect measure you are, by definition, collecting information without the respondents' knowledge. In doing so, you may be violating their right to privacy and you are certainly not using informed consent. Of course, some types of information may be public and therefore do not involve an invasion of privacy, but you should also be especially careful to review the ethical implications of the use of indirect measures.

There may be times when an indirect measure is appropriate, readily available, and ethical. Just as with all measurement, however, you should be sure to attempt to estimate the *reliability* and *validity* of the measures. For instance, collecting radio station preferences at two different time periods and correlating the results might be useful for assessing test-retest reliability; or, you can include the indirect measure along with other direct measures of the same construct (perhaps in a pilot study) to help establish *construct validity*.

Content analysis is the analysis of text documents. The analysis can be quantitative, qualitative, or both. Typically, the major purpose of content analysis is to identify patterns in text. Content analysis is an extremely broad area of research. It includes the following types of analysis:

5-2b Content Analysis

- **Thematic analysis of text**—The identification of themes or major ideas in a document or set of documents. The documents can be any kind of text including field notes, newspaper articles, technical papers, or organizational memos.
- **Indexing**—A variety of automated methods for rapidly indexing text documents exists. For instance, Key Words in Context (KWIC) analysis is a computer analysis of text data. A computer program scans the text and indexes all key words. A key word is any term in the text that is not included in an exception dictionary. Typically you would set up an *exception dictionary* that includes all nonessential words like is, and, and of. All key words are alphabetized and listed with the text that precedes and follows it, so the researcher can see the word in the context in which it occurred in the text. In an analysis of interview text, for instance, you could easily identify all uses of the term abuse and the context in which they were used.
- **Quantitative descriptive analysis**—Here the purpose is to describe features of the text quantitatively. For instance, you might want to find out which words or phrases were used most frequently in the text. Again, this type of analysis is most often done directly with computer programs.

Content analysis has several problems you should keep in mind. First, you are limited to the types of information available in text form. If you are studying the way a news story is being handled by the news media, you probably would have a ready population of news stories from which you could sample. However, if you are interested in studying people's views on capital punishment, you are less likely to find an archive of text documents that would be appropriate. Second, you have to be especially careful with *sampling* to avoid bias. For instance, a study of current research on methods of treatment for cancer might use the published literature as the population. This would leave out both the writing on cancer that did not get published for one reason or another as well as the most recent work that has not yet been published. Finally, you have to be careful about interpreting results of automated context analyses. A computer program cannot determine what someone meant by a term or phrase. It is relatively easy in a large analysis to misinterpret a result because you did not take into account the subtleties of meaning.

However, content analysis has the advantage of being unobtrusive and, depending on whether automated methods exist, can be a relatively rapid method for analyzing large amounts of text.

5-2c Secondary Analysis of Data

Secondary analysis, like content analysis, makes use of already existing data sources. However, secondary analysis typically refers to the re-analysis of quantitative data rather than text.

In our modern world, an unbelievable mass of data is routinely collected by governments, businesses, schools, and other organizations. Much of this information is stored in electronic databases that can be accessed and analyzed. In addition, many research projects store raw data in electronic form in computer archives so that others can also analyze the data. The following list shows some of the data available for secondary analysis:

- Census bureau data
- Crime records
- Standardized testing data
- Economic data
- Consumer data

Secondary analysis often involves combining information from multiple databases to examine research questions. For example, you might join crime data with census information to assess patterns in criminal behavior by geographic location and group.

Secondary analysis has several advantages. First, it is efficient. It makes use of data that was already collected by someone else. It is the research equivalent of recycling. Second, it often allows you to extend the scope of your study considerably. In many small research projects, it is impossible to consider taking a national sample because of the costs involved. Many archived databases are already national in scope and, by using them, you can leverage a relatively small budget into a much broader study than if you collected the data yourself.

However, secondary analysis is not without difficulties. Frequently it is no trivial matter to access and link data from large complex databases. Often you have to make assumptions about which data to combine and which variables are appropriately aggregated into indexes. Perhaps more importantly, when you use data collected by others, you often don't know what problems occurred in the original data collection. Large, well-financed national studies are usually documented thoroughly; but even detailed documentation of procedures is often no substitute for direct experience collecting data.

One of the most important and least utilized purposes of secondary analysis is to replicate prior research findings. In any original data analysis, there is the potential for errors. In addition, data analysts tend to approach the analysis from their own perspective using the analytic tools with which they are familiar. In most research, the data is analyzed only once by the original research team. It seems an awful waste. Data that might have taken months or years to collect is only examined once in a relatively brief way and from one analyst's perspective. In social research, we generally do a terrible job of documenting and archiving the data from individual studies and making it available in electronic form for others to reanalyze; and, we tend to give little professional credit to studies that are reanalyzed. Nevertheless, in the hard sciences, the tradition of replicability of results is a critical one and we in the applied social sciences could benefit by directing more of our efforts to secondary analysis of existing data.

SUMMARY

This chapter began by comparing *qualitative* and *quantitative data*. I made the point that each type of data has its strengths and weaknesses and are often best when used together. Qualitative data can always be quantitized and quantitative data is often based on qualitative input.

Qualitative data can be collected through *in-depth interviews, direct observation,* and written documents. Qualitative *validity* cannot be established with the same rules that apply to validity of quantitative data. Guba and Lincoln proposed four criteria for judging the validity of qualitative data: credibility, transferability, dependability, and confirmability.

Unobtrusive measures are ways of collecting data that don't require researcher interaction with the population of interest. *Indirect measures* require the researcher to set up conditions so that those being studied are unaware that they are being studies. Other types of unobtrusive measures are the use of *content analysis* and the *secondary analysis of data*.

Part

Part

Design

Chapter 6
Design

Chapter 7
Experimental Design

Chapter 8
Quasi-Experimental Design

Chapter 9
Advanced Design Topics

Design

Research design provides the glue that holds the research project together. A design is used to structure the research, to show how all of the major parts of the research project—the samples or groups, measures, treatments or programs, and methods of assignment—work together to address the central research questions. In this chapter, after a brief introduction to research design, I'll show you how to classify the major types of designs. You'll see that a major distinction is between the experimental designs that use random assignment to groups or programs and the quasi-experimental designs that don't use random assignment. (People often confuse random selection with the idea of random assignment. You should make sure that you understand the distinction between random selection and random assignment as described in Chapter 7, "Experimental Design.") Understanding the relationships among designs is important when you need to make design choices, which involves thinking about the strengths and weaknesses of different designs.

Key Terms

causal
causal relationship
compensatory equalization of
  treatment
compensatory program
compensatory rivalry
construct validity
control group
diffusion or imitation of
  treatment
external validity
history threat
instrumentation threat
internal validity
maturation threat
mortality threat
multiple-group threat
null case
posttest-only nonexperimental
  design
posttest-only randomized
  experiment
pre-post nonequivalent groups
  quasi-experiment
quasi-experimental designs
random selection
regression artifact
regression threat
regression to the mean
resentful demoralization
sample
selection bias
selection-history threat
selection-instrumentation
selection-maturation threat
selection-mortality
selection-regression
selection-testing threat
single-group threat
social threats to internal validity
temporal precedence
testing threat
variables

6-1 Internal Validity

Internal validity is the approximate truth about inferences regarding cause-effect or *causal* relationships. Thus, internal validity is only relevant in studies that try to establish a causal relationship. It's not relevant in most observational or descriptive studies, for instance. However, for studies that assess the effects of social programs or interventions, internal validity is perhaps the primary consideration. In those contexts, you want to be able to conclude that your program or treatment made a difference—it improved test scores or reduced symptomology, as shown in Figure 6.1. However, there may be reasons, other than your program, that explain why test scores improve or symptoms reduce. The key question of internal validity is whether observed changes can be attributed to your program or intervention (the cause) and not to other possible causes (sometimes described as alternative explanations for the outcome).

Figure 6.1
A schematic view of the conceptual context for internal validity.

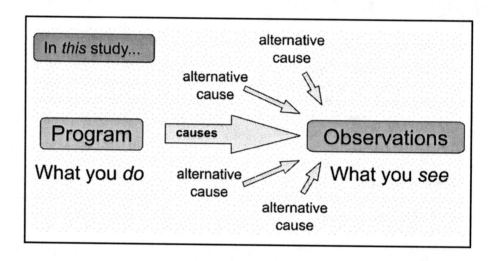

One of the things that's most difficult to grasp about internal validity is that it is only relevant to the specific study in question. That is, you can think of internal validity as a zero-generalizability concern. All that internal validity means is that you have evidence that what you did in the study (for example, the program) caused what you observed (the outcome) to happen. It doesn't tell you whether what you did for the program was what you wanted to do or whether what you observed was what you wanted to observe; those are **construct validity** concerns (see Chapter 3, "The Theory of Measurement"). It is possible to have internal validity in a study and not have construct validity. For instance, imagine a study in which you are looking at the effects of a new computerized tutoring program on math performance in first-grade students. Imagine that the tutoring is unique in that it has a heavy computer-game component and you think that will really improve math performance. Finally, imagine that you were wrong. (Hard, isn't it?) It turns out that math performance did improve, and that it was because of something you did, but that it had nothing to do with the computer program. What caused the improvement was the individual attention that the adult tutor gave to the child; the computer program didn't make any difference. This study would have internal validity because something you did affected something that you observed. (You did cause *something* to happen.) The study would not have construct validity because the label "computer-math program" does not accurately describe the actual cause. A more accurate label might be "personal adult attention."

Since the key issue in internal validity is the causal one, I'll begin by discussing the conditions that need to be met to establish a causal relationship in a research project. Then I'll discuss the different threats to internal validity—the kinds of criticisms your critics will raise when you try to conclude that your program caused the outcome. For convenience, I divide the threats to validity into three categories. The first involves the *single-group threats*—criticisms that apply when you are only studying a single group that receives your program. The second consists of the *multiple-group threats*—criticisms that are likely to be raised when you have several groups in your study (such as a program and a comparison group). Finally, I'll discuss what I call the *social threats to internal validity*—threats that arise because social research is conducted in real-world human contexts where people will react to not only what affects them, but also to what is happening to others around them.

How do you establish a cause-effect (causal) relationship? What criteria do you have to meet? Generally, you must meet three criteria before you can say that you have evidence for a *causal relationship:*

- Temporal precedence
- Covariation of the cause and effect
- No plausible alternative explanations

Temporal Precedence

To establish *temporal precedence*, you have to show that your cause happened *before* your effect. Sounds easy, huh? Of course my cause has to happen before the effect. Did you ever hear of an effect happening before its cause? Before you get lost in the logic here, consider a classic example from economics: does inflation cause unemployment? It certainly seems plausible that as inflation increases, more employers find that to meet costs they have to lay off employees. So it seems that inflation could, at least partially, be a cause for unemployment. However, both inflation and employment rates are occurring together on an ongoing basis. Is it possible that fluctuations in employment can affect inflation? If employment in the work force increases (lower unemployment) there is likely to be more demand for goods, which would tend to drive up the prices (that is, inflate them) at least until supply can catch up. So which is the cause and which the effect, inflation or unemployment? It turns out that this kind of cyclical situation involves ongoing processes that interact and that both may cause and, in turn, be affected by the other (see Figure 6.2). It is hard to establish a causal relationship in this situation.

6-1a Establishing Cause and Effect

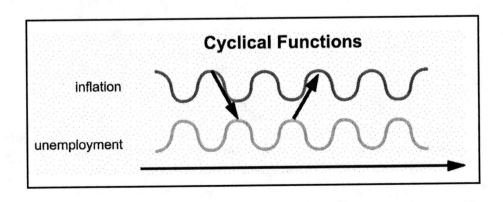

Figure 6.2
The difficulty in establishing temporal precedence in a causal relationship.

Covariation of the Cause and Effect

What does this mean? Before you can show that you have a *causal* relationship you have to show that you have some type of relationship. For instance, consider the syllogism:

If X then Y
If not X then not Y.

If you observe that whenever X is present, Y is also present, and whenever X is absent, Y is too, you have demonstrated that there is a relationship between X and Y. I don't know about you, but sometimes I find it's not easy to think about X's and Y's. Let's put this same syllogism in program evaluation terms:

If program then outcome
If not program then not outcome.

Or, in colloquial terms: whenever you give the program you observe the outcome but when you don't give the program you don't observe the outcome. This provides evidence that the program and outcome are related. Notice, however, that this syllogism doesn't provide evidence that the program caused the outcome; perhaps some other factor present with the program caused the outcome rather than the program. The relationships described so far are simple binary relationships. Sometimes you want to know whether different amounts of the program lead to different amounts of the outcome—a continuous relationship:

If more of the program then more of the outcome
If less of the program then less of the outcome.

No Plausible Alternative Explanations

Just because you show there's a relationship doesn't mean it's a causal one. It's possible that some other variable or factor is causing the outcome. This is sometimes referred to as the third-variable or missing-variable problem and it's at the heart of the *internal-validity* issue. What are some of the possible plausible alternative explanations? Later in this chapter, when I discuss the threats to internal validity (see single-group threats, multiple-group threats, or social threats), you'll see that each threat describes a type of alternative explanation.

To argue that you have demonstrated internal validity—that you have shown there's a causal relationship—you have to rule out the plausible alternative explanations. How do you do that? One of the major ways is with your research design. Let's consider a simple single-group threat to internal validity, a *history threat*. Let's assume you measure your program group before you begin the program (to establish a baseline), you give the group the program, and then you measure the member's performance afterwards in a posttest. You see a marked improvement in the group's performance, which you would like to infer is caused by your program. One of the plausible alternative explanations is that you have a history threat; it's not your program that caused the gain but some other specific historical event. For instance, your anti-smoking campaign did not cause the reduction in smoking; but rather the Surgeon General's latest report was issued between the time you gave your pretest and posttest. How do you rule this out with your research design? One of the simplest ways would be to incorporate the use of a *control group*—a group, comparable to your program group, that didn't receive the program. However, the group did experience the Surgeon General's latest report. If you find that it didn't show a reduction in smoking even though it experienced the same Surgeon General's report, you have effectively ruled out the Surgeon General's report as a plausible alternative explanation, in this example a history threat.

In most applied social research that involves evaluating programs, ***temporal precedence*** is not a difficult criterion to meet because you administer the program before you measure effects. Establishing covariation is relatively simple because you have some control over the program and can set things up so you have some people who get it and some who don't (if X and if not X). Typically the most difficult criterion to meet is the third—ruling out alternative explanations for the observed effect. That is why research design is such an important issue and why it is intimately linked to the idea of internal validity.

What is meant by a ***single-group threat?*** Let's consider two single-group designs and then consider the threats that are most relevant with respect to internal validity. The top design in the Figure 6.3 shows a posttest-only single-group design. Here, a group of people receives your program and afterwards is given a posttest. In the bottom part of the figure, you see a pretest-posttest, single-group design. In this case, the participants receive a pretest or baseline measure, the program or treatment, and then a posttest.

6-1b Single-Group Threats

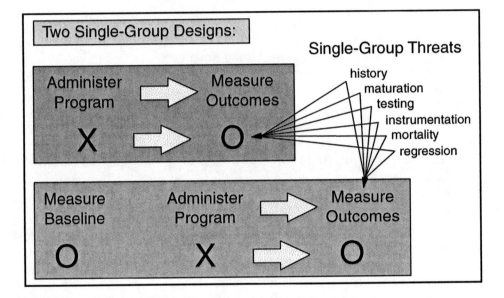

Figure 6.3
Single-group threats to internal validity.

To help make this a bit more concrete, let's imagine that you are studying the effects of a compensatory education program in mathematics for first-grade students on a measure of math performance, such as a standardized math-achievement test. In the post-only design, you would give the first graders the program and then give a math-achievement posttest. You might choose not to give them a baseline measure because you have reason to believe they have no prior knowledge of the math skills you are teaching. It wouldn't make sense to pretest them if you expect them all to get a score of zero. In the pre-post design, you are not willing to assume that your group members have no prior knowledge. You measure the baseline to determine where the students start out in math achievement. You might hypothesize that the change or gain from pretest to posttest is due to your special math-tutoring program. This is a ***compensatory program*** because it is only given to students who are identified as potentially low in math ability on the basis of some screening mechanism.

With either of these scenarios in mind, consider what would happen if you observe a certain level of posttest math achievement or a change or gain from pretest to posttest. You want to conclude that the observed outcome is due to your math program. How could you be wrong? Here are some of the threats to *interval validity* that your critics might raise, some of the plausible alternative explanations for your observed effect:

- **History threat**—It's not your math program that caused the outcome; it's something else, some historical event that occurred. For instance, lots of first graders watch the public TV program *Sesame Street,* and every *Sesame Street* show presents some elementary math concepts. Perhaps these shows caused the outcome and not your math program.

- **Maturation threat**—The children would have had the exact same outcome even if they had never had your special math-training program. All you are doing is measuring normal maturation or growth in the understanding that occurs as part of growing up; your math program has no effect. How is this maturation explanation different from a history threat? In general, if a specific event or chain of events could cause the outcome, it is a history threat, whereas a *maturation threat* consists of all the events that typically transpire in your life that could cause the outcome (without being specific as to which ones are the active causal agents).

- **Testing threat**—This threat only occurs in the pre-post design. What if taking the pretest made some of the children more aware of that kind of math problem; it primed them for the program so that when you began the math training they were ready for it in a way that they wouldn't have been without the pretest. This is what is meant by a *testing threat;* taking the pretest, not getting your program affects how participants do on the posttest.

- **Instrumentation threat**—Like the testing threat, the *instrumentation threat* operates only in the pretest-posttest situation. What if the change from pretest to posttest is due not to your math program but rather to a change in the test that was used? In many schools when repeated testing is administered, the exact same test is not used (in part because teachers are worried about a testing threat) but rather alternate forms of the same tests are given out. These alternate forms were designed to be equivalent in the types of questions and level of difficulty, but what if they aren't? Perhaps part or all of any pre-post gain is attributable to the change in instrument, not to your program. Instrumentation threats are especially likely when the instrument is a human observer. The observers may get tired over time or bored with the observations. Conversely, they might get better at making the observations as they practice more. In either event, the change in instrumentation, not the program, leads to the outcome.

- **Mortality threat**—Mortality doesn't mean that people in your study are dying (although if they are, it would be considered a *mortality threat*). Mortality is used metaphorically here. It means that people are dying with respect to your study. Usually, it means that they are dropping out of the study. What's wrong with that? Let's assume that in your compensatory math-tutoring program you have a nontrivial drop-out rate between pretest and posttest. Assume also that the kids who are dropping out had the low pretest math-achievement test scores. If you look at the average gain from pretest to posttest using all of the scores available to you on each occasion, you would include these low-pretest subsequent dropouts in the pretest and not in the posttest. You'd be dropping out the potential low scorers from the posttest, or you'd be artificially inflating the posttest average over what it would have been if no students had dropped out. You won't necessarily solve this problem by comparing pre-post averages for only those kids who stayed in the study. This subsample would certainly not be representative even of the original entire sample. Furthermore, you know that because of regression threats (see the following section) these students may appear to actually do worse on the posttest, simply as an artifact of the nonrandom dropout or mortality in your study. When mortality is a threat, the researcher can often gauge the degree of the threat by comparing the drop-out group against the nondrop-out group on *pretest* measures. If there are no major differences, it may be more reasonable to assume that mortality was happening across the entire sample and is not biasing results greatly. However, if the pretest differences are large, you must be concerned about the potential biasing effects of mortality.

- **Regression threat**—A *regression threat*, also known as a *regression artifact* or *regression to the mean*, is a statistical phenomenon that occurs whenever you have a nonrandom *sample* from a population and two measures that are imperfectly correlated. Okay, I know that's gibberish. Let me try again. Assume that your two measures are a pretest and posttest (and you can certainly bet these aren't perfectly correlated with each other). Furthermore, assume that your sample consists of low pretest scorers. The regression threat means that the pretest average for the group in your study will appear to increase or improve (relative to the overall population) even if you don't do anything to them, even if you never give them a treatment. Regression is a confusing threat to understand at first. I like to think about it as the *you can only go up (or down) from here* phenomenon. If you include in your program only the kids who constituted the lowest ten percent of the class on the pretest, what are the chances that they would constitute exactly the lowest ten percent on the posttest? Not likely. Most of them would score low on the posttest, but they aren't likely to be the lowest ten percent twice. For instance, maybe a few kids made a few lucky guesses and scored at the eleventh percentile on the pretest; they might not be so lucky on the posttest. Now if you choose the lowest ten percent on the pretest, they can't get any lower than being the lowest; they can only go up from there, relative to the larger population from which they were selected. This purely statistical phenomenon is what we mean by a regression threat. You can see a more detailed discussion of why regression threats occur and how to estimate them in the following section on regression to the mean.

How do you deal with these single-group threats to internal validity? Although you can rule out threats in several ways, one of the most common approaches to ruling those discussed previously is through your research design. For instance, instead of doing a single-group study, you could incorporate a **control group**. In this scenario, you would have two groups: one receives your program and the other one doesn't. In fact, the only difference between these groups should be the program. If that's true, the control group would experience all the same history and maturation threats, have the same testing and instrumentation issues, and have similar rates of mortality and regression to the mean. In other words, a good control group is one of the most effective ways to rule out the single-group threats to internal validity. Of course, when you add a control group, you no longer have a single-group design, and you still have to deal with two major types of threats to internal validity: the **multiple-group threats** to internal validity and the **social threats to internal validity** (see the respective sections later in this chapter).

Regression to the Mean

A *regression threat*, also known as a *regression artifact* or *regression to the mean,* is a statistical phenomenon that occurs whenever you have a nonrandom sample from a population and two measures that are imperfectly correlated.

Figure 6.4 shows the regression to the mean phenomenon. The top part of the figure shows the pretest distribution for a population. Pretest scores are distributed normally; the frequency distribution looks like a bell-shaped curve. Assume that the sample for your study was selected exclusively from the low pretest scorers. You can see on the top part of the figure where their pretest mean is; clearly, it is considerably below the population average. What would you predict the posttest to look like? First, assume that your program or treatment doesn't work at all (the *null case*). A naive assumption would be that your *sample* would score as badly on the posttest as on the pretest; but they don't! The bottom of the figure shows where the sample's posttest mean would have been without regression and where it actually is. In actuality, the sample's posttest mean wound up closer to the posttest population mean than the pretest mean was to the pretest population mean. In other words, the sample's mean appears to *regress toward the mean* of the population from pretest to posttest.

Figure 6.4
Regression to the mean.

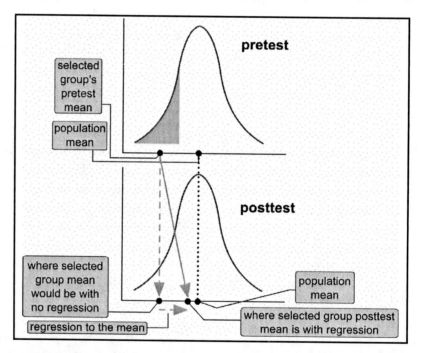

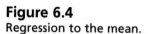

Why Does Regression to the Mean Happen?

To see why regression to the mean happens, consider a concrete case. In your study, you select the lowest 10 percent of the population based on pretest scores. What are the chances that on the posttest that exact group will once again constitute the lowest 10 percent of the population? Slim to none. Most of them will probably be in the lowest ten percent on the posttest, but if even only a few are not, the group's mean will have to be closer to the population's posttest than it was to the pretest. The same thing is true on the other end. If you select as your sample the highest 10 percent pretest scorers, they aren't likely to be the highest ten percent on the posttest (even though most of them may be in the top 10 percent). If even a few score below the top 10 percent on the posttest, the group's posttest mean will have to be closer to the population posttest mean than to its pretest mean.

Regression to the mean can be very hard to grasp. It even causes experienced researchers difficulty in its more advanced variations. To help you understand what regression to the mean is, and how it can be described, I've listed a few statements you should memorize about the regression to the mean phenomenon (and I provide a short explanation for each):

- **Regression to the mean is a *statistical* phenomenon.** Regression to the mean occurs for two reasons. First, it results because you asymmetrically sampled from the population. If you randomly sample from the population, you would observe (subject to random error) that the population and your sample have the same pretest average. Because the sample is already at the population mean on the pretest, it is impossible for it to regress towards the mean of the population any more.
- **Regression to the mean is a *group* phenomenon.** You cannot tell which way an individual's score will move based on the regression to the mean phenomenon. Even though the group's average will move toward the population's, some individuals in the group are likely to move in the other direction.
- **Regression to the mean happens between *any two variables*.** Here's a common research mistake. You run a program and don't find any overall group effect. So, you decide to look at those who did best on the posttest (your success stories) and see how much they gained over the pretest. You are selecting a group that is extremely high on the posttest. The group members are unlikely to be the best on the pretest as well (although many of them will be). So, the group's pretest mean *has* to be closer to the population mean than its posttest one. You describe this nice gain and are almost ready to write up your results when someone suggests you look at your failure cases (the people who scored worst on your posttest). When you check on how they scored on the pretest, you find that they weren't the worst scorers there. If they had been the worst scorers both times, you would have simply said that your program didn't have any effect on them. But now it looks worse than that; it looks like your program actually made them worse relative to the population! What will you do? How will you ever get your grant renewed? Or your paper published? Or, heaven help you, how will you ever get tenured?

  What you have to realize is that the pattern of results I just described happens any time you measure two measures. It happens forwards in time (from pretest to posttest). It happens backwards in time (from posttest to pretest). It happens across measures collected at the same time (height and weight)! It will happen even if you don't give your program or treatment.
- **Regression to the mean is a *relative* phenomenon.** Regression to the mean has nothing to do with overall maturational trends. Notice in Figure 6.4 I didn't bother labeling the x-axis in either the pretest or posttest distribution. It could be that everyone in the population gains 20 points (on average) between the pretest and the posttest; but regression to the mean would still be operating, even in that case. That is, the low scorers would, on average, gain more than the population gain of 20 points (and thus their mean would be closer to the population's).
- **You can have regression up or down.** If your sample consists of below-population-mean scorers, the regression to the mean will make it appear that they move *up* on the other measure. However, if your sample consists of high scorers, the mean will appear to move *down* relative to the popula-

tion. (Note that even if the mean increases, the group could lose ground to the population. So, if a high-pretest-scoring sample gains five points on the posttest while the overall sample gains 15, you could suspect regression to the mean as an alternative explanation (to our program) for that relatively low change.)

- **The more extreme the sample group, the greater the regression to the mean.** If your sample differs from the population by only a little bit on the first measure, there won't be much regression to the mean because there isn't much room for regression; the group is already near the population mean. So, if you have a sample, even a nonrandom one, that is a good subsample of the population, regression to the mean will be inconsequential (although it will be present). However, if your sample is extreme relative to the population (for example, the lowest or highest 10 percent), the group's mean is further from the population's and has more room to regress.

- **The less correlated the two variables, the greater the regression to the mean.** The other major factor that affects the amount of regression to the mean is the correlation between the two *variables*. If the two variables are *perfectly* correlated, the highest scorer on one is the highest on the other, next highest on one is next highest on the other, and so on. No regression to the mean occurs. However, this is unlikely to ever happen in practice. Measurement theory demonstrates that there is no such thing as perfect measurement; all measurement is assumed (under the true score model, as discussed in Chapter 3, "The Theory of Measurement,") to have some random error in measurement. It is only when the measure has no random error—is perfectly reliable—that you can expect it to correlate perfectly. Since that doesn't happen in the real world, you have to assume that measures have some degree of unreliability, that relationships between measures will not be perfect, and that there will appear to be regression to the mean between these two measures, given asymmetrically sampled subgroups.

The Formula for the Percent of Regression to the Mean

You can estimate exactly the percent of **regression to the mean** in any given situation with the following formula:

$$Prm = 100(1 - r)$$

where:

Prm = the percent of regression to the mean
r = the correlation between the two measures

Consider the following four cases:

- If $r = 1$, there is no (0%) regression to the mean.
- If $r = .5$, there is 50% regression to the mean.
- If $r = .2$, there is 80% regression to the mean.
- If $r = 0$, there is 100% regression to the mean.

In the first case, the two variables are perfectly correlated and there is no regression to the mean. With a correlation of .5, the sampled group moves *fifty percent* of the distance from the no-regression point to the mean of the population. If the correlation is a small .20, the sample will regress 80 percent of the distance. If no correlation exists between the measures, the sample regresses all the way back to the population mean! It's worth thinking about what this last case means. With zero correlation, knowing a score on one measure gives you absolutely no information about the likely score for that person on the other measure.

In that case, your best guess for how any person would perform on the second mea-sure will be the mean of that second measure.

Estimating and Correcting Regression to the Mean

Given the percentage formula, for any given situation you can estimate the regression to the mean. All you need to know is the mean of the sample on the first measure, the population mean on both measures, and the correlation between measures. Consider a simple example as shown in Figure 6.5. Here, assume that the pretest population mean is 50 and that you selected a low-pretest scoring sample that has a mean of 30. To begin with, also assume that you do not give any program or treatment (the **null case**) and that the population is not changing over time on the characteristic being measured (steady-state). Given this, you would predict that the population mean would be 50 and that the sample would get a posttest score of 30 *if there was no regression to the mean*. Now, assume that the correlation is .50 between the pretest and posttest for the population. Given the formula, you would expect the sampled group to regress 50 percent of the distance from the no-regression point to the population mean, or 50 percent of the way from 30 to 50. In this case, you would observe a score of 40 for the sampled group, which would constitute a 10-point pseudo-effect or regression artifact.

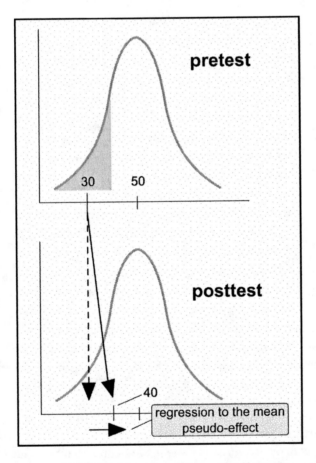

Figure 6.5
An example of regression to the mean when the correlation between measures is .5.

Now, relax some of the initial assumptions. For instance, as illustrated in Figure 6.6, assume that between the pretest and posttest the population gained 15 points on average (and that this gain was uniform across the entire distribution, that is, the variance of the population stayed the same across the two measurement occasions). In this case, a sample that had a pretest mean of 30 would be expected to reach a posttest mean of 45 (30+15) if there is no regression to the mean (r=1). But here, the correlation between pretest and posttest is .5, so you would expect to see regression to the mean that covers 50 percent of the distance from the mean of 45 to the population posttest mean of 65. That is, you would observe a posttest average of 55 for your sample, again a pseudo-effect of 10 points.

Figure 6.6
An example of regression to the mean when there is also growth over time.

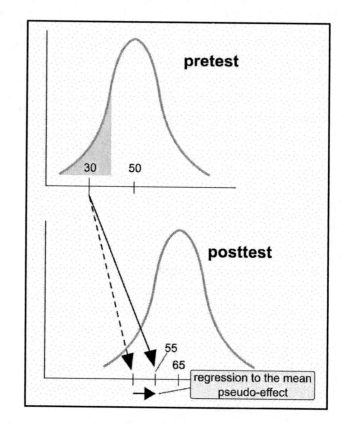

Regression to the mean is one of the trickiest threats to validity. It is subtle in its effects, and even excellent researchers sometimes fail to catch a potential regression artifact. You might want to learn more about the regression to the mean phenomenon. One good way to do that would be to simulate the phenomenon. If you already understand the basic idea of simulation, you can do a manual (dice rolling) simulation of regression artifacts or a computerized simulation of regression artifacts.

6-1c Multiple-Group Threats

A multiple-group design typically involves at least two groups and before-after measurements. Most often, one group receives the program or treatment while the other does not and constitutes the control or comparison group. However, sometimes one group gets the program and the other gets either the standard program or another program you would like to compare. In this case, you would be comparing two programs for their relative outcomes. Typically, you would construct a multiple-group design so that you could compare the groups directly. In such designs, the key *internal validity* issue is the degree to which the groups are comparable before the study. If they are comparable, and the only difference between them is the program, posttest differences can be attributed to the program; but that's a big *if*. If the groups aren't comparable to begin with, you won't know how much of the outcome to attribute to your program or to the initial differences between groups.

There really is only one *multiple group threat* to internal validity: that the groups were not comparable before the study. This threat is called a *selection bias* or *selection threat*. A selection threat is *any* factor other than the program that leads to posttest differences between groups. Whenever you suspect that outcomes differ between groups not because of your program but because of prior group differences, you are suspecting a selection bias. Although the term selection bias is used as the general category for all prior differences, when you know specifically what the group difference is, you usually hyphenate it with the selection term. The multiple-group selection threats directly parallel the single-group threats. For instance, whereas history is a single-group threat, selection-history is its multiple-group analogue.

As with the single-group threats to internal validity, I'll provide simple examples involving a new compensatory mathematics-tutoring program for first graders. The design is a pretest-posttest design that divides the first graders into two groups: one receiving the new tutoring program and the other not receiving it. Here are the major multiple-group threats to internal validity for this case:

- **Selection-History threat**—A *selection-history threat* is any other event that occurs between pretest and posttest that the groups experience differently. Because this is a selection threat, the groups differ in some way. Because it's a history threat, the way the groups differ is with respect to their reactions to history events. For example, what if the television-viewing habits of the children in one group differ from those in the other group? Perhaps the program-group children watch *Sesame Street* more frequently than those in the control group do. Since *Sesame Street* is a children's show that presents simple mathematical concepts in interesting ways, it may be that a higher average posttest math score for the program group doesn't indicate the effect of your math tutoring; it's really an effect of the two groups experiencing a relevant event differentially—in this case *Sesame Street*—between the pretest and posttest.

- **Selection-Maturation threat**—A *selection-maturation threat* results from differential rates of normal growth between pretest and posttest for the groups. In this case, the two groups are different in their different rates of maturation with respect to math concepts. It's important to distinguish between history and maturation threats. In general, history refers to a discrete event or series of events whereas maturation implies the normal, ongoing developmental process that takes place. In any case, if the groups are maturing at different rates with respect to the outcome, you cannot assume that posttest differences are due to your program; they may be selection-maturation effects.

- **Selection-Testing threat**—A *selection-testing threat* occurs when a *differential* effect of taking the pretest exists between groups on the posttest. Perhaps the test primed the children in each group differently or they may have learned differentially from the pretest. In these cases, an observed posttest difference can't be attributed to the program. It could be the result of selection testing.

- **Selection-Instrumentation threat**—*Selection-instrumentation* refers to any differential change in the test used for each group from pretest to posttest. In other words, the test changes differently for the two groups. Perhaps the test consists of observers, who rate the class performance of the children. What if the program group observers, for example, become better at doing the observations while, over time, the comparison group observers become fatigued and bored. Differences on the posttest could easily be due to this differential instrumentation—selection-instrumentation—and not to the program.

- **Selection-Mortality threat**—*Selection-mortality* arises when there is differential nonrandom dropout between pretest and posttest. In our example, different types of children might drop out of each group, or more may drop out of one than the other. Posttest differences might then be due to the different types of dropouts—the selection-mortality—and not to the program.

- **Selection-Regression threat**—Finally, *selection-regression* occurs when there are different rates of *regression to the mean* in the two groups. This might happen if one group is more extreme on the pretest than the other. In the context of our example, it may be that the program group is getting a disproportionate number of low math ability children because teachers think they need the math tutoring more (and the teachers don't understand the need for comparable program and comparison groups). Because the tutoring group has the lower scorers, its mean regresses a greater distance toward the overall population mean and its group members appear to gain more than their comparison-group counterparts. This is not a real program gain; it's a selection-regression artifact.

When you move from a single group to a multiple group study, what do you gain from the rather significant investment in a second group? If the second group is a **control group** and is comparable to the program group, you can rule out the **single-group threats** to **internal validity** because those threats will all be reflected in the comparison group and cannot explain why posttest group differences would occur. But the key is that the groups must be comparable. How can you possibly hope to create two groups that are truly comparable? The best way to do that is to randomly assign persons in your sample into the two groups—you conduct a randomized or true experiment (see the discussion of experimental designs in Chapter 7, "Experimental Design").

However, in many applied research settings you can't randomly assign, either because of logistical or ethical factors. In those cases, you typically try to assign two groups nonrandomly so that they are as equivalent as you can make them. You might, for instance, have one classroom of first graders assigned to the math-tutoring program whereas the other class is the comparison group. In this case, you would hope the two are equivalent, and you may even have reasons to believe that they are. Nonetheless, they may not be equivalent, and because you did not use a procedure like random assignment to at least ensure that they are probabilistically equivalent, you have to take extra care to look for pre-existing differences and adjust for them in the analysis. If you measure the groups on a pretest, you can examine whether they appear to be similar on key measures before the study begins and make some judgment about the plausibility that a **selection bias** exists. There are also ways to adjust statistically for pre-existing differences between groups if they are present, although these procedures are notoriously assumption-laden and fairly complex. Research designs that look like randomized or true experiments (they have multiple groups and pre-post measurement) but use nonrandom assignment to choose the groups are called **quasi-experimental designs** (see the discussion of quasi-experimental designs in Chapter 8, "Quasi-Experimental Design").

Even if you move to a multiple-group design and have confidence that your groups are comparable, you cannot assume that you have strong **internal** *validity*. A number of social threats to internal validity arise from the human interaction in applied social research and you will need to address them.

Applied social research is a human activity. The results of such research are affected by the human interactions involved. The ***social threats to internal validity*** refer to the social pressures in the research context that can lead to posttest differences not directly caused by the treatment itself. Most of these threats occur because the various groups (for example, program and comparison), or key people involved in carrying out the research (such as managers, administrators, teachers, and principals), are aware of each other's existence and of the role they play in the research project or are in contact with one another. Many of these threats can be minimized by *isolating the two groups from each other*, but this leads to other problems. For example, it's hard to randomly assign and then isolate; this is likely to reduce generalizability or ***external validity*** (see external validity in Chapter 2, "Sampling"). Here are the major social interaction threats to internal validity:

6-1d Social Interaction Threats

- **Diffusion or imitation of treatment**—*Diffusion or imitation of treatment* occurs when a comparison group learns about the program either directly or indirectly from program group participants. In a school context, children from different groups within the same school might share experiences during lunch hour. Or, comparison group students, seeing what the program group is getting, might set up their own experience to try to imitate that of the program group. In either case, if the diffusion or imitation affects the posttest performance of the comparison group, it can jeopardize your ability to assess whether your program is causing the outcome. Notice that this threat to validity tends to equalize the outcomes between groups, minimizing the chance of seeing a program effect even if there is one.
- **Compensatory rivalry**—In the *compensatory rivalry* case, the comparison group knows what the program group is getting and develops a competitive attitude with the program group. The students in the comparison group might see the special math-tutoring program the other group is getting and feel jealous. This could lead them to compete with the program group "just to show " how well they can do. Sometimes, in contexts like these, the participants are even encouraged by well-meaning teachers or administrators to compete with each other. (Although this might make educational sense as a motivation for the students in both groups to work harder, it works against the ability of researchers to see the effects of their program.) If the rivalry between groups affects posttest performance, it could make it more difficult to detect the effects of the program. As with diffusion and imitation, this threat generally equalizes the posttest performance across groups, increasing the chance that you won't see a program effect, even if the program is effective.
- **Resentful demoralization**—*Resentful demoralization* is almost the opposite of compensatory rivalry. Here, students in the comparison group know what the program group is getting and instead of developing a rivalry, the group members become discouraged or angry and give up (sometimes referred to informally as the screw-you effect). Or, if the program group is assigned to an especially difficult or uncomfortable condition, they can rebel in the form of resentful demoralization. Unlike the previous two threats, this one is likely to exaggerate posttest differences between groups, making your program look even more effective than it actually is.

- **Compensatory equalization of treatment**—*Compensatory equalization of treatment* is the only threat of the four that primarily involves the people who help manage the research context rather than the participants themselves. When program and comparison-group participants are aware of each other's conditions, they might wish they were in the other group (depending on the perceived desirability of the program, it could work either way). In our education example, they or their parents or teachers might pressure the administrators to have them reassigned to the other group. The administrators may begin to feel that the allocation of goods to the groups is not fair and may compensate one group for the perceived advantage of the other. If the special math-tutoring program were being done with state-of-the-art computers, you can bet that the parents of the children assigned to the traditional noncomputerized comparison group will pressure the principal to equalize the situation. Perhaps the principal will give the comparison group some other good, or grant access to the computers for other subjects. If these compensating programs equalize the groups on posttest performance, they will tend to work against your detecting an effective program even when it does work. For instance, a compensatory program might improve the self-esteem of the comparison group and eliminate your chances of discovering whether the math program would cause changes in self-esteem relative to traditional math training.

As long as people engage in applied social research, you have to deal with the realities of human interaction and its effect on the research process. The threats described here can often be minimized by constructing multiple groups that are unaware of each other (for example, a program group from one school and a comparison group from another) or by training administrators in the importance of preserving group membership and not instituting equalizing programs. However, researchers will never be able to eliminate entirely the possibility that human interactions are making it more difficult to assess cause-effect relationships.

6-2 Introduction to Design

Research design can be thought of as the *structure* of research; the research design tells you how all the elements in a research project fit together. Researchers often use concise notations to describe a design, which enables them to summarize a complex design structure efficiently. A design includes the following elements:

- **Observations or measures**—These are symbolized by an O in design notation. An O can refer to a single measure (a measure of body weight), a single instrument with multiple items (a 10-item, self-esteem scale), a complex multipart instrument (a survey), or a whole battery of tests or measures given out on one occasion. If you need to distinguish among specific measures, you can use subscripts with the O, as in O_1, O_2, and so on.
- **Treatments or programs**—These are symbolized with an X in design notation. The X can refer to a simple intervention (such as a one-time surgical technique) or to a complex hodgepodge program (such as an employment-training program). Usually, a no-treatment control or comparison group has no symbol for the treatment. (Although some researchers use X+ and X- to indicate the treatment and control respec-

tively.) As with observations, you can use subscripts to distinguish different programs or program variations.

- **Groups**—Each group in a design is given its own line in the design structure. For instance, if the design notation has three lines, the design contains three groups.
- **Assignment to group**—Assignment to group is designated by a letter at the beginning of each line (or group) that describes how the group was assigned. The major types of assignment are:
  - R = random assignment
  - N = nonequivalent groups
  - C = assignment by cutoff

Don't worry at this point if you don't know what some of these are; each of these assignment strategies characterizes a different type of design and will be described later when discussing that design type.

- **Time**—Time moves from left to right. Elements that are listed on the left occur before elements that are listed on the right.

It's always easier to explain design notation through examples than it is to describe it in words. Figure 6.7 shows the design notation for a pretest-posttest (or before-after) treatment versus comparison-group randomized experimental design. Let's go through each of the parts of the design. There are two lines in the notation, so you should realize that the study has two groups. There are four Os in the notation: two on each line and two for each group. When the Os are stacked vertically on top of each other, it means they are collected at the same time. In the notation, the two Os taken before (to the left of) the treatment are the pretest. The two Os taken after the treatment is given are the posttest. The R at the beginning of each line signifies that the two groups are randomly assigned (making it an experimental design as described in Chapter 7, "Experimental Design").

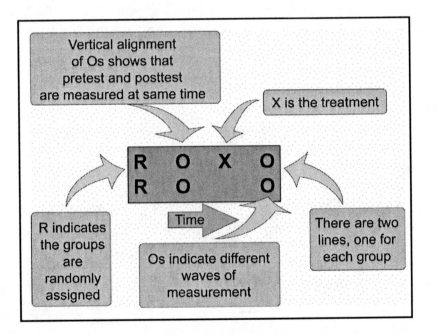

Figure 6.7
A detailed example of design notation.

The design is a treatment-versus-comparison-group one, because the top line (treatment group) has an X, whereas the bottom line (*control group*) does not. You should be able to see why many of my students call this type of notation the tic-tac-toe method of design notation; there are lots of Xs and Os! Sometimes you have to use more than simply the Os or Xs. Figure 6.8 shows the identical research design with some subscripting of the Os. What does this mean? Because all of the Os have a subscript of 1, some measure or set of measures was collected for both groups on both occasions. But the design also has two Os with a subscript of 2, both taken at the posttest. This means that some measure or set of measures was collected *only* at the posttest.

Figure 6.8
An example of a design notation that includes subscripts.

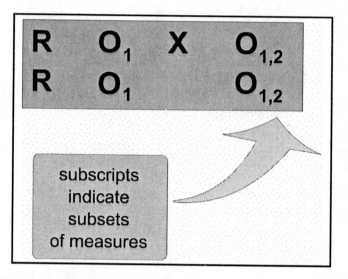

With this simple set of rules for describing a research design in notational form, you can concisely explain even complex design structures. Additionally, using a notation helps to show common design substructures across different designs that you might not recognize as easily without the notation.

6-3 Types of Designs

What are the different major types of research designs? You can classify designs into a simple threefold classification by asking some key questions as shown in Figure 6.9.

Figure 6.9
Basic questions that distinguish the major types of designs.

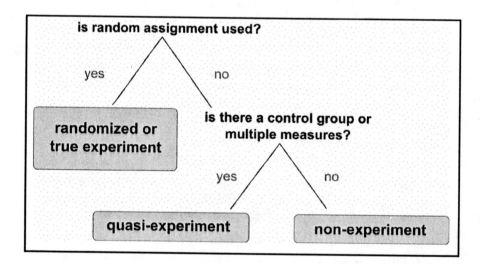

First, does the design use random assignment to groups? (Don't forget that random *assignment* is not the same thing as **random selection** of a sample from a population!) If random assignment is used, the design is a randomized experiment or *true* experiment. If random assignment is not used, ask a second question:

Does the design use *either* multiple groups or multiple waves of measurement? If the answer is yes, label it a **quasi-experimental design**. If no, call it a nonexperimental design.

This threefold classification is especially useful for describing the design with respect to **internal validity**. A randomized experiment generally is the strongest of the three designs when your interest is in establishing a cause-effect relationship. A nonexperiment is generally the weakest in this respect. I have to hasten to add here that I don't mean that a nonexperiment is the weakest of the three designs *overall*, but only with respect to internal validity or causal assessment. In fact, the simplest form of nonexperiment is a one-shot survey design that consists of nothing but a single observation O. This is probably one of the most common forms of research and, for some research questions—especially descriptive ones—is clearly a strong design. When I say that the nonexperiment is the weakest with respect to internal validity, all I mean is that it isn't a particularly good method for assessing the cause-effect relationships that you think might exist between a program and its outcomes.

To illustrate the different types of designs, consider one of each in design notation as shown in Figure 6.10. The first design is a **posttest-only randomized experiment**. You can tell it's a randomized experiment because it has an R at the beginning of each line, indicating random assignment. The second design is a **pre-post nonequivalent groups quasi-experiment**. You know it's not a randomized experiment because random assignment wasn't used. Additionally you know it's not a nonexperiment because both multiple groups and multiple waves of measurement exist. That means it must be a quasi-experiment. You add the label *nonequivalent* because in this design you do not explicitly control the assignment and the groups may be nonequivalent or not similar to each other (see nonequivalent group designs, Chapter 9, "Advanced Design Topics"). Finally, you see a **posttest-only nonexperimental design**. You might use this design if you want to study the effects of a natural disaster like a flood or tornado and you want to do so by interviewing survivors. Notice that in this design, you don't have a comparison group (for example, you didn't interview in a town down the road that didn't have the tornado to see what differences the tornado caused) and you don't have multiple waves of measurement (a pre-tornado level of how people in the ravaged town were doing before the disaster). Does it make sense to do the nonexperimental study? Of course! You could gain valuable information by well-conducted post-disaster interviews. However, you may have a hard time establishing which of the things you observed are due to the disaster rather than to other factors like the peculiarities of the town or pre-disaster characteristics.

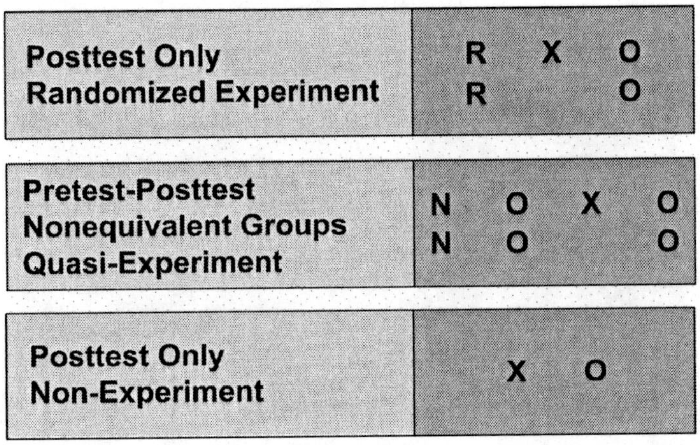

| Posttest Only Randomized Experiment | R | X | O |
| | R | | O |

| Pretest-Posttest Nonequivalent Groups Quasi-Experiment | N | O | X | O |
| | N | O | | O |

| Posttest Only Non-Experiment | | X | O |

Figure 6.10
Notational for examples of each of the three major classes of research design.

SUMMARY

Research design helps you to put together all of the disparate pieces of your research project: the participants or *sample*, the measures, and the data analysis. This chapter showed that research design is intimately connected with the topic of *internal validity* because the type of research design you construct determines whether you can address *causal* questions, such as whether your treatment or program made a difference on outcome measures. There are three major types of problems—threats to validity—that occur when trying to assure internal validity. *Single-group threats* occur when you have only a single program group in your study. Researchers typically try to avoid single-group threats by using a comparison group, but this leads to *multiple-group threats* or *selection threats* when the groups are not comparable. Since all social research involves human interaction, you must also be concerned about *social threats to internal validity* that can make your groups perform differently but are unrelated to the treatment or program. Research designs can get somewhat complicated. To keep them straight and describe them succinctly researchers use design notation that describes the design in abstract form.

Experimental Design

Experimental designs are often touted as the most rigorous of all research designs, or as the gold standard against which all other designs are judged. In one sense, they probably are. If you can implement an experimental design well (and that is a big *if* indeed), the experiment is probably the strongest design with respect to internal validity (see Chapter 6, "Design").

This chapter introduces the idea of an experimental design and describes why it is strong in *internal validity*. I show that the key distinguishing feature of experimental design—random assignment to group—depends on the idea of probabilistic equivalence and explain what that means. I then try to head off one of the biggest sources of confusion to most students—the distinction between *random selection* and *random assignment*. Then I get into the heart of the chapter, describing how to classify the different experimental designs, presenting each type in turn.

Key Terms

ANCOVA (Analysis of
 Covariance)
ANOVA (Analysis of Variance)
causal
control group
covariates
external validity
factor
factorial designs
fully-crossed factorial design
incomplete factorial design
interaction effect
internal validity
level
main effect
multiple-group threats
null case
probabilistic equivalence
random assignment
random selection
Randomized Block design
sampling
selection-instrumentation
 threats
selection mortality
selection-testing
single-group threats to internal
 validity
social threats to internal validity
Solomon Four-Group design
stratified random sampling
Switching-Replications design
testing threat to internal validity
true-score theory
two-group posttest-only
 randomized experiment
variability

7-1 Introduction to Experimental Design

7-1a Experimental Designs and Internal Validity

As mentioned earlier, experimental designs are usually considered the strongest of all designs in internal validity (see the discussion on internal validity in Chapter 6, "Design"). Why? Recall that internal validity is at the center of all **causal** or cause-effect inferences. When you want to determine whether some program or treatment *causes* some outcome or outcomes to occur, you are interested in having strong internal validity. Essentially, you want to assess the proposition:

If X, then Y.

Or, in more colloquial terms:

If the program is given, then the outcome occurs.

Unfortunately, it's not enough to show that when the program or treatment occurs, the expected outcome also happens because many reasons, other than the program, might account for why you observed the outcome. To show that there is a causal relationship, you have to simultaneously address the two propositions:

If X, then Y

and

If not X, then not Y.

Or, once again more colloquially:

If the program is given, then the outcome occurs
and
If the program is **not** given, then the outcome does **not** occur.

If you are able to provide evidence for both of these propositions, you've in effect isolated the program from all of the other potential causes of the outcome. You've shown that when the program is present, the outcome occurs and when it's not present, the outcome doesn't occur. That points to the causal effectiveness of the program.

Think of all this like a fork in the road. Down one path, you implement the program and observe the outcome. Down the other path, you don't implement the program and the outcome doesn't occur. But, can you take *both* paths in the road in the same study? How can you be in two places at once? Ideally, what you want is to have the same conditions—the same people, context, time, and so on—and see whether when the program is given you get the outcome and when the program is not given you don't. Obviously, you can never achieve this hypothetical situation. If you give the program to a group of people, you can't simultaneously not give it! So, how do you get out of this apparent dilemma?

Perhaps you just need to think about the problem a little differently. What if you could create two groups or contexts that are as similar as you can possibly make them? If you could be confident that the two situations are comparable, you could administer your program in one (and see whether the outcome occurs) and not give the program in the other (and see whether the outcome doesn't occur). If the two contexts are comparable, this is like taking both forks in the road simultaneously. You can have your cake and eat it too, so to speak.

That's exactly what an experimental design tries to achieve. In the simplest type of experiment, you create two groups that are equivalent to each other. One group (the program or treatment group) gets the program and the other group (the comparison or **control group**) does not. In all other respects, the groups are treated the same. They have similar people, live in similar contexts, have similar backgrounds, and so on. Now, if you observe differences in outcomes between these two groups, the differences must be due to the only thing that differs between them—that one received the program and the other didn't.

Okay, so how do you create two equivalent groups? The approach used in experimental design is to assign people randomly from a common pool of people into the two groups. The experiment relies on this idea of *random assignment* to groups as the basis for obtaining two similar groups. Then, you give one the program or treatment and you don't give it to the other. You observe the same outcomes in both groups.

The key to the success of the experiment is in the random assignment. In fact, even with random assignment, you never expect the groups you create to be exactly the same. How could they be, when they are made up of different people? You rely on the idea of probability and assume that the two groups are *probabilistically equivalent* or equivalent within known probabilistic ranges.

If you randomly assign people to two groups, and you have enough people in your study to achieve the desired probabilistic equivalence, you can consider the experiment strong in *internal validity* and you probably have a good shot at assessing whether the program causes the outcome(s). (See the discussion of statistical power and sample size in Chapter 9, "Advanced Design Topics.")

However, many things can go wrong. You may not have a large enough sample. Some people might refuse to participate in your study or drop out part way through. You might be challenged successfully on ethical grounds. (After all, to use this approach you have to deny the program to some people who might be equally deserving of it as others.) You might meet resistance from the staff members in your study who would like some of their favorite people to get the program.

The bottom line here is that experimental design is intrusive and difficult to carry out in most real-world contexts, and because an experiment is often an intrusion, you are setting up an artificial situation so that you can assess your causal relationship with high internal validity. As a result, you are limiting the degree to which you can generalize your results to real contexts where you haven't set up an experiment. That is, you have reduced your external validity to achieve greater internal validity.

In the end, there is no simple answer (no matter what anyone tells you). If the situation is right, an experiment is a strong design, but it isn't automatically so. I would estimate that randomized experiments are probably appropriate in no more than 10 percent of the social research studies that attempt to assess causal relationships.

Experimental design is a complex subject in its own right. I've been discussing the simplest of experimental designs—a two-group program versus comparison-group design; but there are many experimental design variations that attempt to accomplish different things or solve different problems. In this chapter, you'll explore the basic experimental design, look at the major variations, and learn the principles that underlie all experimental-design strategies.

7-1b Two-Group Experimental Designs

The simplest of all experimental designs is the *two-group, posttest-only, randomized experiment* (see Figure 7.1). In design notation, it has two lines—one for each group—with an R at the beginning of each line to indicate that the groups were randomly assigned.

One group gets the treatment or program (the X) and the other group is the comparison group and doesn't get the program. (Note that you could alternatively have the comparison group receive the standard or typical treatment, in which case this study would be a relative comparison.)

Figure 7.1
Notation for the basic
two-group posttest-only,
randomized experimental
design.

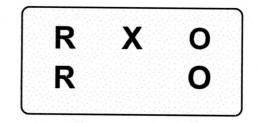

Notice that a pretest is not required for this design. Usually you include a pretest to determine whether groups are comparable prior to the program. However, because this design uses *random assignment,* you can assume that the two groups are *probabilistically equivalent* to begin with and the pretest is not required (although you'll see with covariance designs later in this chapter that a pretest may still be desirable in this context).

In this design, you are most interested in determining whether the two groups are different after the program. Typically, you measure the groups on one or more measures (the Os in the notation) and you compare them by testing for the differences between the means using a t-test or one way *Analysis of Variance (ANOVA),* which is covered in Chapter 9, "Advanced Design Topics."

The posttest-only randomized experiment is the strongest of all research designs with respect to the threats to internal validity as shown in Figure 7.2. The figure indicates (with a check mark) that it is strong against all the *single-group threats to internal validity* because it's not a single group design! (Tricky, huh?) It's also strong against the *multiple-group threats* except for *selection mortality.* For instance, it's strong against the *selection-testing* and *selection-instrumentation threats* because it doesn't use repeated measurement. The selection-mortality threat can be a problem if there are differential rates of dropouts in the two groups. This could result if the treatment or program is a noxious or negative one (such as a painful medical procedure like chemotherapy) or if the control group condition is painful or intolerable. This design is susceptible to all of the *social threats to internal validity.* Because the design requires random assignment in some institutional settings such as schools, it is more likely to utilize persons who would be aware of each other and of the conditions to which you have assigned them.

Figure 7.2
Threats to internal validity
for the posttest-only,
randomized experimental
design.

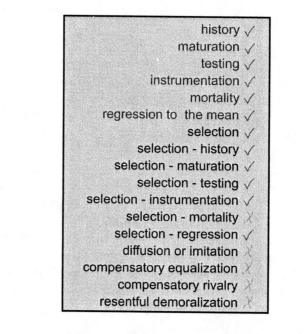

The posttest-only, randomized experimental design is, despite its simple structure, one of the best research designs for assessing cause-effect relationships. It is relatively easy to execute and because it uses only a posttest, is relatively inexpensive. However, there are many variations on this simple experimental design. You can begin to explore these by looking at how you classify the various experimental designs (see the section "Classifying Experimental Designs," later in this chapter).

What do I mean by the term *probabilistic equivalence* and why is it important to experimental design? Well, to begin with, I certainly *don't* mean that two groups are equal to each other. When you deal with human beings, it is impossible to ever say that any two individuals or groups are equal or equivalent. Clearly the important term in the phrase is probabilistic. This means that the type of equivalence you have is based on the notion of probabilities. In more concrete terms, probabilistic equivalence means that you know *perfectly* the odds of finding a difference between two groups. Notice, it doesn't mean that the means of the two groups will be equal. It just means that you know the odds that they won't be equal. Figure 7.3 shows two groups, one with a mean of 49 and the other with a mean of 51. Could these two groups be probabilistically equivalent even though their averages are different? Certainly!

7-1c Probabilistic Equivalence

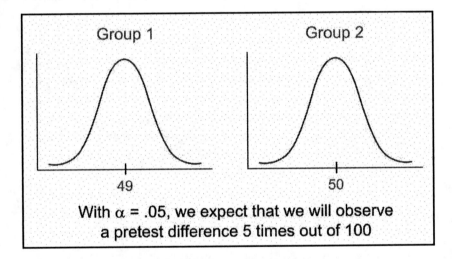

Figure 7.3
Probabilistic equivalence does not mean that two randomly selected groups will obtain the exact same average score.

You achieve probabilistic equivalence through the mechanism of random assignment to groups. When you randomly assign to groups, you can calculate the chance that the two groups will differ just because of the random assignment (that is by chance alone). Let's say you are assigning a group of first-grade students to two groups. Further, let's assume that the average test scores for these children for a standardized test with a population mean of 50 were 49 and 51 respectively. You might conduct a t-test to see whether the means of the two randomly assigned groups are statistically different. Through random assignment and the law of large numbers, the chance that they will be different is 5 out of 100 when you set the significance level to .05 (that is, $\alpha = .05$). In other words, 5 times out of every 100, when you randomly assign two groups, you can expect to get a significant difference at the .05 level of significance.

When you assign randomly, groups can only differ due to chance assignment because their assignment is entirely based on the randomness of assignment. If, by chance, the groups differ on one variable, you have no reason to believe that they will automatically be different on any other. Even if you find that the groups differ on a pretest, you have no reason to suspect that they will differ on a posttest. Why? Because their pretest difference had to be a chance one. So, when you randomly assign, you are able to assume that the groups do have a form of equivalence. You don't expect them to be equal; but you can expect them to be probabilistically equal.

7-1d Random Selection and Assignment

Random selection is how you draw the sample of people for your study from a population. *Random assignment* is how you assign the sample that you draw to different groups or treatments in your study.

It is possible to have *both* random selection and assignment in a study. Let's say you drew a random sample of 100 clients from a population list of 1000 current clients of your organization. That is random sampling. Now, let's say you randomly assign 50 of these clients to get some new additional treatment and the other 50 to be controls. That's random assignment.

It is also possible to have *only one of these* (random selection or random assignment) but not the other in a study. For instance, if you do not randomly draw the 100 cases from your list of 1000 but instead just take the first 100 on the list, you do not have random selection. You could, however, still randomly assign this nonrandom sample to treatment versus control. Or, you could randomly select 100 from your list of 1000 and then nonrandomly (haphazardly) assign them to treatment or control groups.

It's also possible to have *neither* random selection nor random assignment. In a typical nonequivalent-groups design (see Chapter 8, "Quasi-Experimental Design") in education you might nonrandomly choose two fifth-grade classes to be in your study. This is nonrandom selection. Then, you could arbitrarily assign one group to get the new educational program and the other to be the control group. This is nonrandom (or nonequivalent) assignment.

Random selection is related to **sampling** (see Chapter 2, "Sampling"). Therefore it is most closely related to the **external validity** (or generalizability) of your results. After all, researchers randomly sample so that their research participants better represent the larger group from which they're drawn. Random assignment is most closely related to design. In fact, when you randomly assign participants to treatments you have, by definition, an experimental design. Therefore, random assignment is most related to **internal validity** (see Chapter 6, "Design"). After all, researchers randomly assign to help ensure that their treatment groups are similar to each other (equivalent) prior to the treatment.

7-2 Classifying Experimental Designs

Although many experimental design variations exist, you can classify and organize them using a simple signal-to-noise ratio metaphor. In this metaphor, assume that what you observe or see in a research study can be divided into two components: the signal and the noise. (By the way, this is directly analogous to the discussion of signal and noise in the **true -score theory** of measurement discussed in Chapter 3, "The Theory of Measurement.") Figure 7.4 shows a time series with a slightly downward slope. However, because there is so much **variability** or noise in the series, it is difficult even to detect the downward slope. When you divide the series into its two components, you can clearly see the slope.

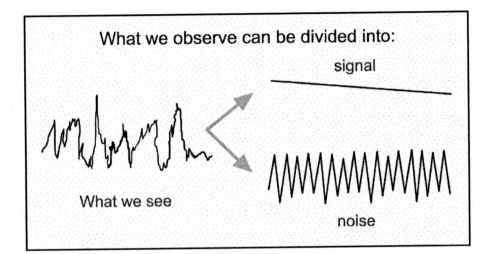

Figure 7.4
How an observed time
series can be decomposed
into its signal and noise.

In most research, the signal is related to the key variable of interest—the construct you're trying to measure, or the program or treatment that's being implemented. The noise consists of all of the random factors in the situation that make it harder to see the signal: the lighting in the room, local distractions, how people felt that day, and so on. You can construct a ratio of these two by dividing the signal by the noise (see Figure 7.5). In research, you want the signal to be high relative to the noise. For instance, if you have a powerful treatment or program (meaning a strong signal) and good measurement (that is, low noise) you have a better chance of seeing the effect of the program than if you have either a strong program and weak measurement or a weak program and strong measurement.

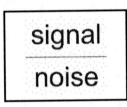

Figure 7.5
The signal-to-noise ratio is
simply a fraction where
signal is divided by noise.

You can further classify the experimental designs into two categories: signal enhancers or noise reducers. Doing either of these things—enhancing signal or reducing noise—improves the quality of the research. The *signal-enhancing experimental designs* are called the **factorial designs**. In these designs, the focus is almost entirely on the setup of the program or treatment, its components, and its major dimensions. In a typical factorial design, you would examine several different variations of a treatment. Factorial designs are discussed in the next section of this chapter.

The two major types of *noise-reducing experimental designs* are covariance designs and blocking designs. In these designs, you typically use information about the makeup of the sample or about pre-program variables to remove some of the noise in your study. Covariance and blocking designs are discussed in the following the section on factorial design.

Factorial designs focus on the signal in your research by directly manipulating your program or features of your program or treatment. Factorial designs are especially efficient because they enable you to examine which features or combinations of features of your program or treatment have an effect. I'll start with the

7-3 Factorial Designs

simplest factorial design, show you why it is such an efficient approach, explain how to interpret the results, and then move on to more advanced variations.

7-3a The Basic 2 x 2 Factorial Design

Probably the easiest way to begin understanding factorial designs is by looking at an example (see Figure 7.6). Imagine a design where you have an educational program in which you would like to look at a variety of program variations to see which works best. For instance, you would like to vary the amount of time the children receive instruction, with one group getting one hour of instruction per week and another getting four hours per week. Additionally, you'd like to vary the setting so that one group gets the instruction in class (probably pulled off into a corner of the classroom) and the other group is pulled out of the classroom for instruction in another room. You could think about having four separate studies to do this; but when you vary the amount of time in instruction, which setting would you use: in class or pull out? And, when you study setting, what amount of instruction time would you use: one hour, four hours, or something else?

Figure 7.6
An example of a basic 2 x 2 factorial design.

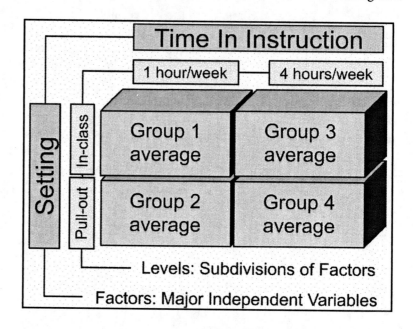

With factorial designs, you don't have to compromise when answering these questions. You can have it both ways if you cross each of your two times in instruction conditions with each of your two settings. Let's begin by doing some defining of terms. In factorial designs, a *factor* is a major independent variable. This example has two factors: time in instruction and setting. A *level* is a subdivision of a factor. In this example, time in instruction has two levels and setting has two levels.

Sometimes you depict a factorial design with a numbering notation. In this example, you can say that you have a 2 x 2 (spoken two-by-two) factorial design. In this notation, the *number of numbers* tells you how many factors there are and the *number values* tell you how many levels. A 3 x 4 factorial design has 2 factors where one factor has 3 levels and the other has 4. The order of the numbers makes no difference and you could just as easily term this a 4 x 3 factorial design. You can easily determine the number of different treatment groups that you have in any factorial design by multiplying through the number notation. For instance, the school study example has 2 x 2 = 4 groups. A 3 x 4 factorial design requires 3 x 4 = 12 groups.

You can also depict a factorial design in design notation. Because of the treatment-level combinations, it is useful to use subscripts on the treatment (X) symbol. Figure 7.7 shows that there are four groups, one for each combination of levels of factors. It also shows that the groups were randomly assigned and that this is a posttest-only design.

$$
\begin{aligned}
&R \quad X_{11} \quad O\\
&R \quad X_{12} \quad O\\
&R \quad X_{21} \quad O\\
&R \quad X_{22} \quad O
\end{aligned}
$$

Figure 7.7
Design notation for a 2 × 2 factorial design.

Now, let's look at a variety of different results you might get from this simple 2 × 2 factorial design. Each of the following figures describes a different possible outcome. Each outcome is shown in table form (the 2 × 2 table with the row and column averages) and in graphic form (with each factor taking a turn on the horizontal axis). Take the time to understand how and why the information in the tables agrees with the information in both of the graphs. Also study the graphs and figures to verify that the pair of graphs in each figure show the exact same information graphed in two different ways. The lines in the graphs are technically not necessary; they are a visual aid that enables you to track where the averages for a single level go across *levels* of another factor. Keep in mind that the values in the tables and graphs are group averages on the outcome variable of interest. In this example, the outcome might be a test of achievement in the subject being taught. Assume that scores on this test range from 1 to 10 with higher values indicating greater achievement. You should study carefully the outcomes in each figure to understand the differences between these cases.

The Null Outcome

The *null case* is a situation in which the treatments have no effect. Figure 7.8a assumes that even if you didn't give the training, you would expect students to score a 5 on average on the outcome test. You can see in this hypothetical case that all four groups score an average of 5 and therefore the row and column averages must be 5. You can't see the lines for both levels in the graphs because one line falls right on top of the other.

The Main Effects

A *main effect* is an outcome that is a consistent difference between levels of a factor. For instance, you would say there's a main effect for setting if you find a statistical difference between the averages for the in-class and pull-out groups, *at all levels* of time in instruction. Figure 7.8b depicts a main effect of time. For all settings, the four-hour/week condition worked better than the one-hour/week condition. It is also possible to have a main effect for setting (and none for time).

In the second main effect graph, shown in Figure 7.8c, you see that in-class training was better than pull-out training for all amounts of time.

Finally, it is possible to have a main effect on both variables simultaneously, as depicted in the third main effect (see Figure 7.8d). In this instance, four hours/week always works better than one hour/week and in-class setting always works better than the pull-out setting.

Interaction Effects

If you could look at only main effects, factorial designs would be useful. But, because of the way you combine levels in factorial designs, they also enable you to examine the *interaction effects* that exist between factors. An interaction effect exists when differences on one factor depend on which level you are on in another factor. It's important to recognize that an interaction is between factors, not levels. You wouldn't say there's an interaction between four hours/week and in-class treatment. Instead, you would say that there's an interaction between time and setting, and then you would describe the specific levels involved.

How do you know whether there is an interaction in a factorial design? There are three ways you can determine whether an interaction exists. First, when you run the statistical analysis, the statistical table will report on all main effects and interactions. Second, you know there's an interaction when you can't talk about effect on one factor without mentioning the other factor. If you can say at the end of your study that time in instruction makes a difference, you know that you have a main effect and not an interaction (because you did not have to mention the setting factor when describing the results for time). On the other hand, when you have an interaction, it is impossible to describe your results accurately without mentioning both factors. Finally, you can always spot an interaction in the graphs of group means; whenever lines are not parallel, an interaction is present! If you check out the main effect graphs in Figure 7.8c, you will notice that all of the lines within a graph are parallel. In contrast, for all of the interaction graphs, you will see that the lines are not parallel.

In the first interaction effect graph (see Figure 7.8e), one combination of levels—four hours/week and in-class setting—shows better results than the other three.

The second interaction (see Figure 7.8f) shows more complex cross-over interaction. Here, at one hour/week the pull-out group does better than the in-class group whereas at four hours/week the reverse is true. Furthermore, both of these combinations of levels do equally well.

Factorial design has several important features. First, it gives you great flexibility for exploring or enhancing the signal (treatment) in your studies. Whenever you are interested in examining treatment variations, factorial designs should be strong candidates as the designs of choice. Second, factorial designs are efficient. Instead of conducting a series of independent studies, you are effectively able to combine these studies into one. Finally, factorial designs are the only effective way to examine interaction effects.

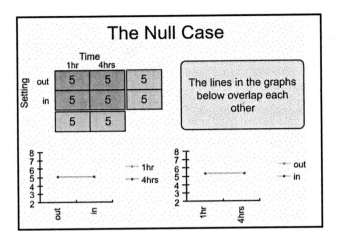

Figure 7.8a
The null effects case in a 2 × 2 factorial design.

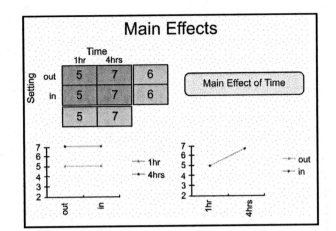

Figure 7.8b
A main effect of time in instruction in a 2 × 2 factorial design.

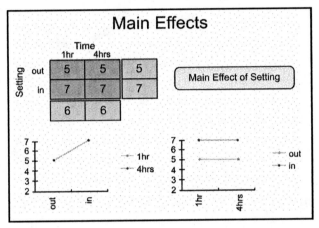

Figure 7.8c
A main effect of setting in a 2 × 2 factorial design.

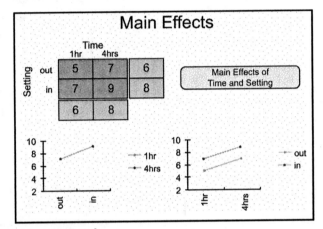

Figure 7.8d
Main effects of both time and setting in a 2 × 2 factorial design.

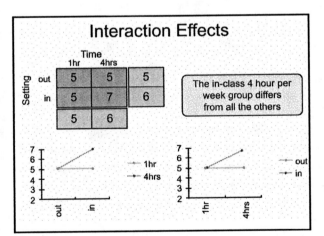

Figure 7.8e
An interaction in a 2 × 2 factorial design.

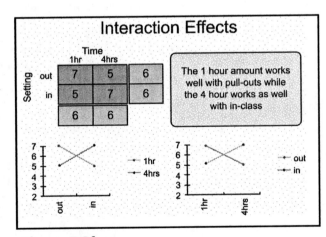

Figure 7.8f
A cross-over interaction in a 2 × 2 factorial design.

So far, you have only looked at a simple 2 × 2 factorial design structure. You may want to look at some factorial design variations in the following section to get a deeper understanding of how these designs work. You may also want to examine how to approach the statistical analysis of factorial experimental designs (see Chapter 9, "Advanced Design Topics").

7-3b Factorial Design Variations

This section discusses a number of different factorial designs. I'll begin with a two-factor design where one of the factors has more than two levels. Then I'll introduce the three-factor design. Finally, I'll present the idea of the incomplete factorial design.

A 2 × 3 Example

For these examples, I'll construct an example designed to study of the effect of different treatment combinations for cocaine abuse. Here, the dependent measure is a severity-of-illness rating performed by the treatment staff. The outcome ranges from 1 to 10, where higher scores indicate more severe illness: in this case, more severe cocaine addiction. Furthermore, assume that the levels of treatment are as follows:

- Factor 1: Treatment
  - Psychotherapy
  - Behavior modification
- Factor 2: Setting
  - Inpatient
  - Day treatment
  - Outpatient

Note that the setting factor in this example has three levels.

Figure 7.9a shows what an effect for the setting outcome might look like. You have to be careful when interpreting these results because higher scores mean the patient is doing *worse*. It's clear that inpatient treatment works best, day treatment is next best, and outpatient treatment is worst of the three. It's also clear that there is no difference between the two treatment levels (psychotherapy and behavior modification). Even though both graphs in the figure depict the exact same data, it's easier to see the main effect for setting in the graph on the lower left where setting is depicted with different lines on the graph rather than at different points along the horizontal axis.

Figure 7.9b shows a *main effect* for treatment with psychotherapy performing better (remember the direction of the outcome variable) in all settings than behavior modification. The effect is clearer in the graph on the lower right where treatment levels are used for the lines. Note that in both this and Figure 7.9a, the lines in all graphs are parallel, indicating that there are no *interaction effects*.

Figure 7.9c shows one possible interaction effect; day treatment is never the best condition. Furthermore, you see that psychotherapy works best with inpatient care, and behavior modification works best with outpatient care.

The other interaction effect shown in Figure 7.9d is a bit more complicated. Although there may be some main effects mixed in with the interaction, what's important here is that there is a unique combination of levels of factors that stands out as superior: psychotherapy done in the inpatient setting. After you identify a best combination like this, the main effects are virtually irrelevant.

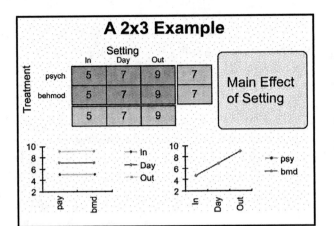

Figure 7.9a
Main effect of setting in a 2 x 3 factorial design.

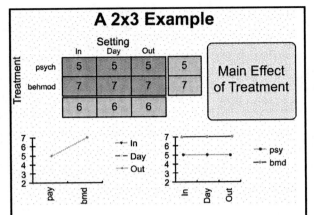

Figure 7.9b
Main effect of treatment in a 2 x 3 factorial design.

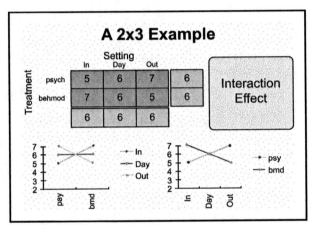

Figure 7.9c
An interaction effect in a 2 x 3 factorial design.

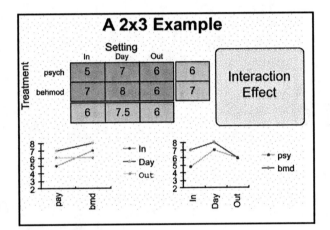
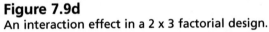

Figure 7.9d
An interaction effect in a 2 x 3 factorial design.

A Three-Factor Example

Now let's examine what a three-factor study might look like. I'll use the same factors as in the previous example for the first two factors; but here I'll include a new factor for dosage that has two levels. The factor structure in this 2 × 2 × 3 factorial experiment is as follows:

- Factor 1: Dosage
    - 100 mg.
    - 300 mg.
- Factor 2: Treatment
    - Psychotherapy
    - Behavior modification
- Factor 3: Setting
    - Inpatient
    - Day treatment
    - Outpatient

Notice that in this design you have 2 x 2 x 3 = 12 groups (see Figure 7.10). Although it's tempting in factorial studies to add more factors, the number of groups always increases multiplicatively (is that a real word?). Notice also that to show the tables of means, you have to have two tables that each show a two-factor relationship. It's also difficult to graph the results in a study like this because there will be many different possible graphs. In the statistical analysis, you can look at the main effects for each of your three factors, the three two-way interactions (for example, treatment vs. dosage, treatment vs. setting, and setting vs. dosage) and at the one three-way interaction. Whatever else may be happening, it is clear that one combination of three levels works best: 300 mg. and psychotherapy in an inpatient setting. Thus, this study has a three-way interaction. If you were an administrator having to make a choice among the different treatment combinations, you would be best advised to select that one (assuming your patients and setting are comparable to the ones in this study).

Figure 7.10
Example of a 2 x 2 x 3 factorial design.

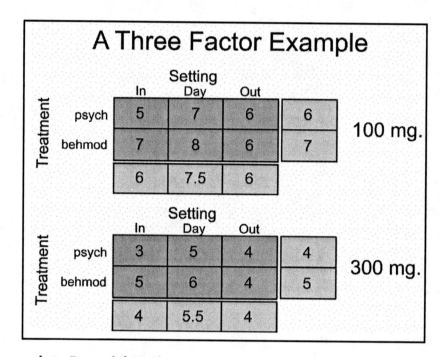

Incomplete Factorial Design

It's clear that factorial designs can become cumbersome and have too many groups even with only a few factors. In much research, you won't be interested in a *fully-crossed factorial design* like the ones shown previously that pair every combination of levels of factors. Some of the combinations may not make sense from a policy or administrative perspective, or you simply may not have the funds to implement all combinations. In this case, you may decide to implement an incomplete factorial design. In this variation, some of the cells are intentionally left empty; you don't assign people to get those combinations of factors.

One of the most common uses of **incomplete factorial design** is to allow for a control or placebo group that receives no treatment. In this case, it is actually impossible to implement a group that simultaneously has several levels of treatment factors and receives no treatment at all. So, you consider the control group to be its own cell in an incomplete factorial rubric, which allows you to conduct both relative and absolute treatment comparisons within a single study and to get a fairly precise look at different treatment combinations (see Figure 7.11).

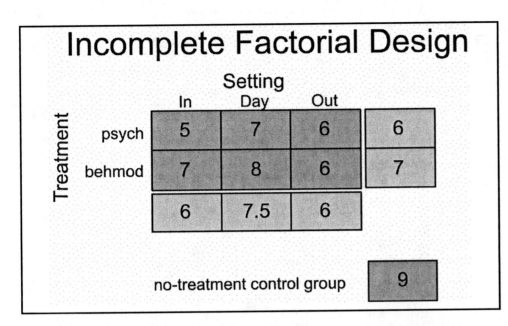

Figure 7.11
An incomplete factorial
design.

The ***Randomized Block design*** is research design's equivalent to ***stratified random sampling*** (see Chapter 2, "Sampling"). Like stratified sampling, randomized block designs are constructed to reduce noise or variance in the data (see the section, "Classifying Experimental Designs," earlier in this chapter). How do they do it? They require you to divide the sample into relatively homogeneous subgroups or blocks (analogous to strata in stratified sampling). Then, the experimental design you want to apply is implemented within each block or homogeneous subgroup. The key idea is that the ***variability*** within each block is less than the variability of the entire sample. Thus each estimate of the treatment effect within a block is more efficient than estimates across the entire sample. When you pool these more efficient estimates across blocks, you should get a more efficient estimate overall than you would without blocking.

Figure 7.12 shows a simple example. Let's assume that you originally intended to conduct a simple posttest-only randomized experimental design; but you recognized that your sample has several intact or homogeneous subgroups. For instance, in a study of college students, you might expect that students are relatively homogeneous with respect to class or year. So, you decide to block the sample into four groups: freshman, sophomore, junior, and senior. If your hunch is correct—that the variability within class is less than the variability for the entire *sample*—you will probably get more powerful estimates of the treatment effect within each block (see the discussion on statistical power in Chapter 9, "Advanced Design Topics"). Within each of your four blocks, you would implement the simple post-only randomized experiment.

Notice a couple of things about this strategy. First, to an external observer, it may not be apparent that you are blocking. You implement the same design in each block, and there is no reason that the people in different blocks need to be segregated or separated physically from each other. In other words, blocking doesn't necessarily affect anything that you do with the research participants. Instead, blocking is a strategy for grouping people in your data analysis to reduce noise; it is an *analysis* strategy. Second, you will only benefit from a blocking design if you are correct in your hunch that the blocks are more homogeneous than the entire sample is. If you are wrong—if different college-level classes aren't relatively homogeneous with respect to your measures—you will actually be hurt

7-4 Randomized Block Designs

by blocking. (You'll get a less powerful estimate of the treatment effect.) How do you know whether blocking is a good idea? You need to consider carefully whether the groups are relatively homogeneous. If you are measuring political attitudes, for instance, is it reasonable to believe that freshmen are more like each other than they are like sophomores or juniors? Would they be more homogeneous with respect to measures related to drug abuse? Ultimately the decision to block involves judgment on the part of the researcher.

Figure 7.12.
The basic randomized block design.

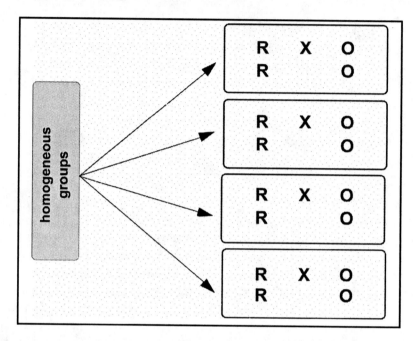

7-4a How Blocking Reduces Noise

So how does blocking work to reduce noise in the data? To see how it works, you have to begin by thinking about the nonblocked study. Figure 7.13a shows the pretest-posttest distribution for a hypothetical pre-post randomized experimental design. The X symbol indicates a program group case and the O symbol signifies comparison-group members. You can see that for any specific pretest value, the program group tends to outscore the comparison group by about 10 points on the posttest (meaning, there is about a 10-point posttest mean difference).

Figure 7.13a
Pre-post distribution for a randomized experimental design without blocking.

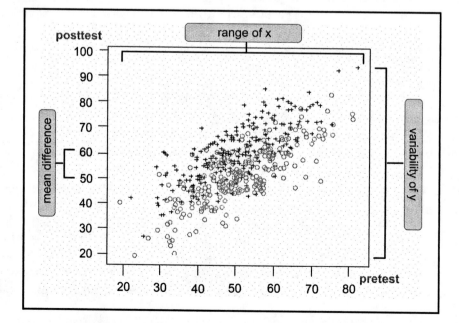

Figure 7.13b
Pre-post distribution for a randomized block design.

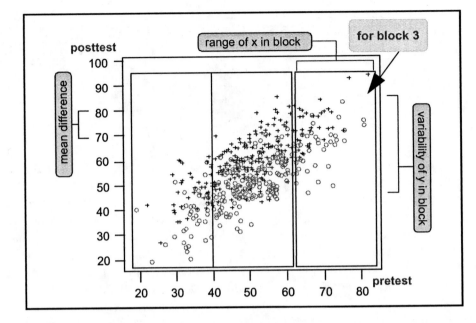

Now, let's consider an example that divides the sample into three relatively homogeneous blocks. To see what happens graphically, you'll use the pretest measure to block. This ensures that the groups are homogeneous. Let's look at what is happening within the third block (see Figure 7.13a). Notice that the mean difference is still the same as it was for the entire sample—about 10 points within each block. Also notice that the variability of the posttest is much less within the block than it is for the entire sample. Remember that the treatment effect estimate is a signal-to-noise ratio. The signal in this case is the mean difference. The noise is the variability. Figures 7.13a and 7.13b show that you haven't changed the signal by moving to blocking; there is still about a 10-point posttest difference. However, you have changed the noise; the **variability** on the posttest is much smaller within each block than it is for the entire **sample**. So, the treatment effect will have less noise for the same signal.

It should be clear from the graphs that the blocking design in this case yields the stronger treatment effect. However, this is true only because the blocks were homogeneous. If the blocks weren't homogeneous—their variability was as large as the entire sample's—you would actually get worse estimates than in the simple randomized experimental case. You'll see how to analyze data from a **Randomized Block design** in the section, "Randomized Block Analysis" in Chapter 11, "Analysis for Research Design."

7-5 Covariance Designs

The basic **Analysis of Covariance Design** (**ANCOVA** or **ANACOVA**) is a pretest-posttest randomized experimental design. The notation shown in Figure 7.14 suggests that the pre-program measure is the same one as the post-program measure (otherwise you would use subscripts to distinguish the two), and so you would call this a pretest. Note however that the pre-program measure doesn't have to be a pretest; it can be any variable measured prior to the program intervention. It is also possible for a study to have more than one covariate.

The pre-program measure or pretest is sometimes also called a covariate because of the way it's used in the data analysis; you co-vary it with the outcome variable or posttest to remove variability or noise. Thus, the ANCOVA design falls in the class of a noise-reduction experimental design (see "Classifying Experimental Designs" earlier in this chapter).

Figure 7.14
Notation for the basic analysis of covariance design.

In social research, you frequently hear about statistical adjustments that attempt to control for important factors in your study. For instance, you might read that an analysis examined posttest performance after *adjusting for* the income and educational level of the participants. In this case, *income* and *education level* are covariates. *Covariates* are the variables you *adjust for* in your study. Sometimes the language that will be used is that of *removing the effects* of one variable from another. For instance, you might read that an analysis examined posttest performance after *removing the effect of* income and educational level of the participants.

7-5a How Does a Covariate Reduce Noise?

One of the most important ideas in social research is how you make a statistical adjustment—adjust one variable based on its covariance with another variable. If you understand this idea, you'll be well on your way to mastering social research. What I want to do here is show you a series of graphs that illustrate pictorially what it means to adjust for a covariate.

Let's begin with data from a simple ANCOVA design as described previously. Figure 7.15a shows the pre-post bivariate distribution. Each dot on the graph represents the pretest and posttest score for an individual. The X signifies a program or treated case and O describes a control or comparison case. You should be able to see a few things immediately. First, you should be able to see a whopping treatment effect! It's so obvious that you don't even need statistical analysis to tell you whether there's an effect (although you may want to use statistics to estimate its size and probability). How do I know there's an effect? Look at any pretest value (value on the horizontal axis). Now, look up from that value; you are looking up the posttest scale from lower to higher posttest scores. Do you see any pattern with respect to the groups? It should be obvious to you that the program cases (the Xs) tend to score higher on the posttest at any given pretest value. Second, you should see that the posttest variability has a range of about 70 points.

Figure 7.15b shows the graph with straight lines fitted to the data. The lines on the graph are regression lines that describe the pre-post relationship for each of the groups. The regression line shows the expected posttest score for any pretest score. The treatment effect is even clearer with the regression lines. You should see that the line for the treated group is about 10 points higher than the line for the comparison group at any pretest value.

What you want to do is remove some of the variability in the posttest while preserving the difference between the groups. In other terms, you want to *adjust* the posttest scores for pretest variability. In effect, you want to *subtract out* the pretest. You might think of this as subtracting the line from each group from the data for each group. How do you do that? Well, why don't you actually subtract? Find the posttest difference between the line for a group and each actual value (see Figure 7.15c). Each of these differences is called a *residual;* it's what's left over when you subtract a line from the data.

Now, here comes the tricky part. What does the data look like when you subtract out a line? You might think of it almost like turning the graph in Figure 7.15c clockwise until the regression lines are horizontal. Figures 7.15d and 7.15e show this in two steps. First, you construct an x-y axis system where the x dimension is parallel to the regression lines.

Then, you actually turn the graph clockwise so that the regression lines are flat horizontally (see Figure 7.15e). Notice how big the posttest variability or range is in Figure 7.15e (as indicated by the double arrow). You should see that the range is considerably smaller than the 70 points with which you started. You should also see that the difference between the lines is the same as it was before. So, you have in effect reduced posttest variability while maintaining the group difference. You've lowered the noise while keeping the signal at its original strength. The statistical adjustment procedure will result in a more efficient and more powerful estimate of the treatment effect.

You should also note the shape of the pre-post relationship. Essentially, the plot now looks like a zero correlation between the pretest and posttest and, in fact, it is. How do I know it's a zero correlation? Because any line that can fit through the data well would be horizontal. There's no slope or relationship, and there shouldn't be. This graph shows the pre-post relationship *after you've removed the pretest!* If you've removed the pretest from the posttest there will be no pre-post correlation left.

Finally, redraw the axes to indicate that the pretest has been removed. Figure 7.15f shows the posttest values as the original posttest values minus the line (the predicted posttest values). That's why you see that the new posttest axis has 0 at its center. Negative values on the posttest indicate that the original point fell below the regression line on the original axis. Here, the posttest range is about 50 points instead of the original 70, even though the difference between the regression lines is the same. You've lowered the noise while retaining the signal.

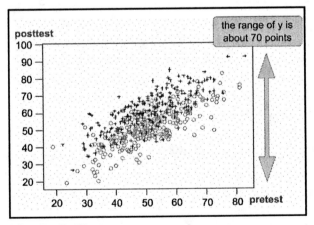

Figure 7.15a
A pre-post distribution for a covariance design.

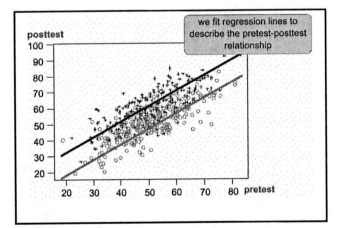

Figure 7.15b
Pre-post distribution for a covariance design with regression lines fitted.

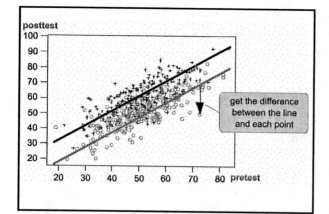

Figure 7.15c
Subtract the posttest value from the predicted posttest value to obtain the residual for a single participant (point).

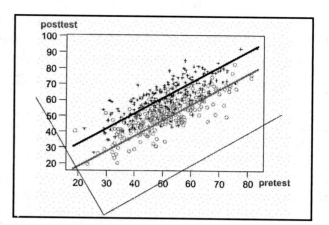

Figure 7.15d
Construct x-y axes with respect to the regression lines.

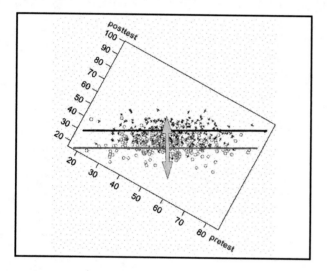

Figure 7.15e
The rotated view of Figure 7.15d with the pre-post relationship removed.

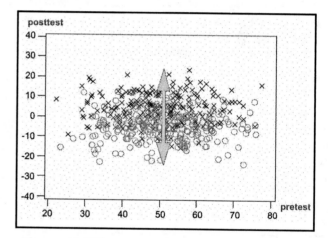

Figure 7.15f
The pre-post distribution when the pre-post relationship has been adjusted out.

*Disclaimer: Okay, I know some statistical hotshot out there is fuming about the inaccuracy in my previous description. My picture rotation is not exactly what you do when you adjust for a **covariate**. My description suggests that you drop perpendicular lines from the regression line to each point to obtain the subtracted difference. In fact, you drop lines that are perpendicular to the horizontal axis, not the regression line itself (in Least Squares regression you are minimizing the sum of squares of the residuals on the dependent variable, not jointly on the independent and dependent variable as suggested here). In any event, although my explanation may not be perfectly accurate from a statistical point of view, it's not far off, and it conveys clearly the idea of subtracting out a relationship. I thought I'd just put this disclaimer in to let you know I'm not dumb enough to believe that my description is perfectly accurate.*

The adjustment for a covariate in the *ANCOVA* design is accomplished with the statistical analysis, not through rotation of graphs. See the section "Analysis of Covariance" in Chapter 11, "Analysis for Reseach Design" for details.

Here are some thoughts to conclude this topic: The *ANCOVA* design is a noise-reducing experimental design. It *adjusts* posttest scores for variability on the covariate (pretest); this is what it means to *adjust* for the effects of one variable on another in social research. You can use *any* continuous variable as a covariate, but the pretest is usually best. Why? Because the pretest is usually the variable that is most highly correlated with the posttest. (A variable should correlate highly with itself, shouldn't it?) Because it's so highly correlated, when you subtract it out or remove it, you're removing extraneous variability from the posttest. The rule in selecting covariates is to select the measure(s) that correlate most highly with the outcome and, for multiple covariates, have little intercorrelation. (Otherwise, you're simply adding redundant covariates and you actually lose precision by doing that.) For example, you probably wouldn't want to use both gross and net income as two covariates in the same analysis because they are highly related and therefore redundant as adjustment variables.

7-6 Hybrid Experimental Designs

Hybrid experimental designs are just what the name implies—new strains that are formed by combining features of more established designs. Many variations can be constructed from standard design features. Here, I'm going to introduce two hybrid designs. I'm featuring these because they illustrate especially well how a design can be constructed to address specific threats to internal validity.

7-6a The Solomon Four-Group Design

The *Solomon Four-Group design* is designed to deal with a potential *testing threat to internal validity* discussed in Chapter 6, "Design." Recall that a testing threat occurs when the act of taking a test affects how people score on a retest or posttest. The design notation is shown in Figure 7.16. It's probably not a big surprise that this design has four groups. Note that two of the groups receive the treatment and two do not. Furthermore, two of the groups receive a pretest and two do not. One way to view this is as a 2 x 2 (Treatment Group X Measurement Group) *factorial design*. Within each treatment condition, one group is pretested and one is not. By explicitly including testing as a factor in the design, you can assess experimentally whether a testing threat is operating.

Figure 7.16
Design notation for the Solomon Four-Group Design.

Let's look at a couple of possible outcomes from this design. The first outcome graph (see Figure 7.17) shows what the data might look like if there is a treatment or program effect and no testing threat. You need to be careful when interpreting this graph to note that there are six dots: one to represent the average for each O in the design notation. To help you visually see the connection between the pretest and posttest average for the same group, a line connects the dots. The two dots that are not connected by a line represent the two post-only groups. Look first at the two pretest means. They are close to each other because the groups were randomly assigned. On the posttest, both treatment groups outscored both controls. Now, look at the posttest values. There appears to be no difference between the treatment groups, even though one got a pretest and the other did not. Similarly, the two control groups scored about the same on the posttest. Thus, the pretest did not appear to affect the outcome. However, both treatment groups clearly outscored both controls. There is a main effect for the treatment.

Figure 7.17
Solomon Four-Group design with a treatment effect and no testing threat.

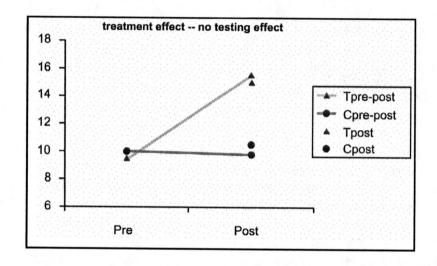

Now, look at a result with evidence of a testing threat (see Figure 7.18). In this outcome, the pretests are again equivalent (because the groups were randomly assigned). Each treatment group outscored its comparable *control group*. The pre-post treatment outscored the pre-post control; and the post-only treatment outscored the post-only control. These results indicate that there is a treatment effect. However, here both groups that had the pretest outscored their comparable non-pretest group. That's evidence of a testing threat.

Figure 7.18
Solomon Four-Group design with both a treatment effect and a testing threat.

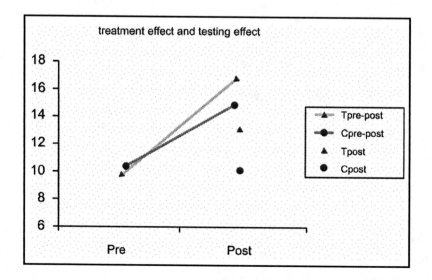

The *Switching-Replications design* is one of the strongest of the experimental designs. When the circumstances are right for this design, it addresses one of the major problems in experimental designs: the need to deny the program to some participants through random assignment. The design notation (see Figure 7.19) indicates that this is a two-group design with three waves of measurement. You might think of this as two pre-post, treatment-control designs grafted together. That is, the implementation of the treatment is repeated or *replicated*. In the repetition of the treatment, the two groups *switch* roles; the original control group becomes the treatment group in phase 2; whereas the original treatment acts as the control. By the end of the study, all participants have received the treatment.

The Switching-Replications design is most feasible in organizational contexts where programs are repeated at regular intervals. For instance, it works especially well in schools that are on a semester system. All students are pretested at the beginning of the school year. During the first semester, Group 1 receives the treatment, and during the second semester, Group 2 gets it. The design also enhances organizational efficiency in resource allocation. Schools need to allocate only enough resources to give the program to half of the students at a time.

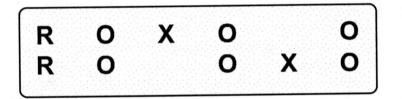

Let's look at two possible outcomes. In the first example, the program is given to the first group, and the recipients do better than the controls (see Figure 7.20). In the second phase, when the program is given to the original controls, they catch up to the original program group. Thus, you have a converge-diverge-reconverge outcome pattern. You might expect a result like this when the program covers specific content that the students master in the short term and where you don't expect them to continue improving as a result.

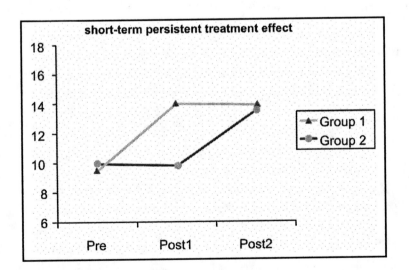

Figure 7.19
Notation for the Switching-Replications, randomized experimental design.

Figure 7.20
Switching Replications design with a short-term persistent treatment effect.

Now, look at the other example result (see Figure 7.21). During the first phase, you see the same result as before; the program group improves while the control group does not. As before, during the second phase, the original control group, in this case the program group, improved as much as the first program group did.

This time, however, during phase two the original program group continued to increase even after it no longer received the program. Why would this happen? It could happen in circumstances where the program has continuing effects. For instance, if the program focused on learning skills, students might continue to improve even after the formal program period because they continue to apply the skills and improve in them.

Figure 7.21
Switching Replications design with a long term continuing treatment effect.

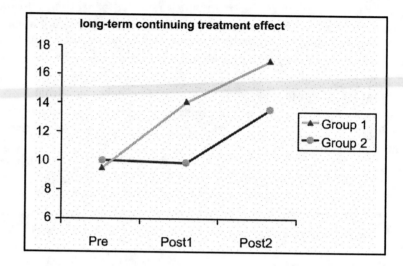

I said earlier that both the **Solomon Four-Group** and the **Switching-Replications** designs addressed specific threats to **internal validity**. It's obvious that the Solomon design addressed a testing threat. But what does the Switching-Replications design address? Remember that in randomized experiments, especially when the groups are aware of each other, there is the potential for **social threats to internal validity;** compensatory rivalry, compensatory equalization, and resentful demoralization are all likely to be present in educational contexts where programs are given to some students and not to others. The Switching-Replications design helps mitigate these threats because it ensures that everyone will eventually get the program. Additionally, it allocates who gets the program first in the fairest possible manner, through the lottery of **random assignment.**

SUMMARY

This chapter introduced experimental designs. The basic idea of a **randomized experiment** was presented along with consideration of how it addresses **internal validity**, the key concepts of **probabilistic equivalence**, and the distinction between **random selection** and **random assignment**. Experimental designs can be classified as signal enhancers or noise reducers. **Factorial designs** were presented as signal enhancers that emphasize studying different combinations of treatment (signal) features. Two types of noise reducing strategies—**randomized blocks** and **covariance** designs—were presented along with descriptions of how each acts to reduce noise in the data. Finally, two hybrid experimental designs—the **Solomon Four-Groups** and **Switching-Replications designs**—were presented to illustrate the versatility of experimental designs and the ability to tailor designs that address specific threats to internal validity.

Chapter 8

Quasi-Experimental Design

A *quasi-experimental design* is one that looks a bit like an experimental design but lacks the key ingredient—*random assignment*. My mentor, Don Campbell, often referred to these designs as queasy experiments because they give the experimental purists a queasy feeling. With respect to *internal validity*, they often appear to be inferior to randomized experiments. However there is something compelling about these designs; taken as a group, they are more frequently implemented than their randomized cousins.

I'm not going to try to cover the quasi-experimental designs comprehensively. Instead, I'll present two of the classic quasi-experimental designs in some detail. Probably the most commonly used quasi-experimental design (and it may be the most commonly used of all designs) is the nonequivalent-groups design (NEGD). In its simplest form, it requires a pretest and posttest for a treated and comparison group. It's identical to the Analysis of Covariance (*ANCOVA*) randomized experimental design (see Chapter 7, "Experimental Design,") except that the groups are not created through random assignment. You will see that the lack of random assignment and the potential nonequivalence between the groups complicates the statistical analysis of the nonequivalent groups design (as covered in the discussion of analysis in Chapter 10, "Analysis").

The second design I'll focus on is the regression-discontinuity design. I'm not including it just because I did my dissertation on it and wrote a book about it (although those were certainly factors weighing in its favor). I include it because I believe it is an important (and often misunderstood) alternative to randomized experiments because its distinguishing characteristic—assignment to treatment using a cutoff score on a pretreatment variable—allows you to assign to the program those who need or deserve it most. At first glance, the regression-discontinuity design strikes most people as biased because of regression to the mean (discussed in Chapter 6, "Design"). After all, you're assigning low scorers to one group and high scorers to the other. In the discussion of the statistical analysis of the regression discontinuity design (see Chapter 10), I'll show you why this isn't the case.

Finally, I'll briefly present an assortment of other quasi-experiments that have specific applicability or noteworthy features, including the Proxy-Pretest design, Double-Pretest design, Nonequivalent Dependent-Variables design, Pattern-Matching design, and the Regression Point Displacement design.

Key Terms

ANCOVA
causal
construct validity
control group
Double-Pretest design
internal validity
Nonequivalent Dependent
 Variables (NEDV) design
Nonequivalent-Groups design
 (NEGD)
null case
pattern-matching
Pattern-Matching NEDV design
Proxy-Pretest design
quantitative
quasi-experimental design
random assignment
Regression-Discontinuity (RD)
regression line
Regression Point Displacement
 (RPD)
regression to the mean
selection bias
selection instrumentation
selection regression
selection testing
selection threats
selection-history threat
selection-maturation threat
selection-mortality
Separate Pre-Post Samples
statistics
Switching-Replications design
threats to internal validity
variables

215

8-1 The Nonequivalent-Groups Design

The *Nonequivalent-Groups Design (NEGD)* is probably the most frequently used design in social research. Why? Because it is one of the most intuitively sensible designs around. If you want to study the effects of your program, you probably recognize the need to have a group of people receive the program. That's your program group, and, you probably see that it would be sensible to measure that group before and after the program so you can see how much the program improved or changed them. That's the pre-post measurement. Once you understand the basic problem of *internal validity* (see Chapter 6, "Design") you will readily admit that it would be nice to have a comparable group that differs from your program group in only one respect—it doesn't get the program. That's your *control group*. Put all of these elements together and you have the basic NEGD. Although the design is intuitively straightforward, it is not without its difficulties or challenges. The major challenge stems from the term nonequivalent in its title. If your comparison group is really similar to the program group in all respects—except for receiving the program—this design is an excellent one. But how do you assure that the groups are equivalent? And, what do you do if they are not? That's the central challenge for this design and I'll take some time here to address this issue.

8-1a The Basic Design

The NEGD is structured like a pretest-posttest randomized experiment, but it lacks the key feature of the randomized designs—*random assignment*. The design notation for the basic NEGD is shown in Figure 8.1.

Figure 8.1
Notation for the Nonequivalent-Groups Design (NEGD).

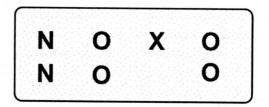

In the NEGD, you most often use intact groups that you think are similar as the treatment and control groups. In education, you might pick two comparable classrooms or schools. In community-based research, you might use two similar communities. You try to select groups that are as similar as possible, so you can fairly compare the treated one with the comparison one; but you can never be sure the groups are comparable. Put another way, it's unlikely that the two groups would be as similar as they would if you assigned them through a random lottery. Because it's often likely that the groups are not equivalent, this design was named the Nonequivalent-Groups design to remind us of that. The design notation (refer to Figure 8.1) uses the letter N to indicate that the groups are nonequivalent.

So, what does the term nonequivalent mean? In one sense, it means that assignment to group was not random. In other words, the researcher did not control the assignment to groups through the mechanism of random assignment. As a result, the groups may be different prior to the study. That is, the NEGD is especially susceptible to the internal validity threat of selection (see Chapter 6). Any prior differences between the groups may affect the outcome of the study. Under the worst circumstances, this can lead you to conclude that your program didn't make a difference when in fact it did, or that it did make a difference when in fact it didn't.

Let's begin our exploration of the NEGD by looking at some hypothetical results. Figure 8.2a shows a bivariate distribution in the simple pre-post, two-group study. The *treated cases* are indicated with *X*s and the *comparison cases* are indicated with *O*s. A couple of things should be obvious from the graph. To begin, you don't even need **statistics** to see that there is a whopping treatment effect. (Although statistics would help you estimate the size of that effect more precisely.) The program cases (*X*s) consistently score better on the posttest than the comparison cases (*O*s) do. If positive scores on the posttest are better, you can conclude that the program improved things. Second, in the **NEGD** the biggest threat to **internal validity** is selection—that the groups differed before the program. Does that appear to be the case here? Although it may be harder to see, the program group does appear to be a little further to the right on average. This suggests that program group participants did have an initial advantage on the pretest and that the positive results may be due in whole or in part to this initial difference.

You can see the initial difference, the **selection bias**, when you look at the graph in Figure 8.2b. It shows that the program group scored about five points higher than the comparison group on the pretest. The comparison group had a pretest average of about 50, whereas the program group averaged about 55. It also shows that the program group scored about fifteen points higher than the comparison group on the posttest. That is, the comparison group posttest score was again about 55, whereas this time the program group scored around 65. These observations suggest that there is a potential selection threat, although the initial five-point difference doesn't explain why you observe a fifteen-point difference on the posttest. It may be that there is still a legitimate treatment effect here, even given the initial advantage of the program group.

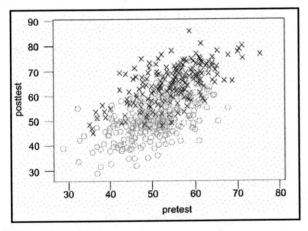

Figure 8.2a
Bivariate distribution for a hypothetical example of a Nonequivalent-Groups Design.

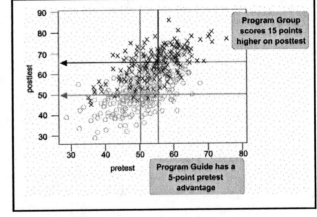

Figure 8.2b
Nonequivalent-Groups Design with pretest and posttest averages marked for each group.

Possible Outcome 1[1]

Let's take a look at several different possible outcomes from a NEGD to see how they might be interpreted. The important point here is that each of these outcomes has a different storyline. Some are more susceptible to threats to **internal**

---

[1] The discussion of the five possible outcomes is based on the discussion in Cook, T.D. and Campbell, D.T. (1979). *Quasi-Experimentation: Design & Analysis Issues for Field Settings.* Houghton Mifflin, Boston, pps. 103-112.

validity than others. Before you read each of the descriptions, take a good look at the associated graph and try to figure out how you would explain the results. If you were a critic, what kinds of problems would you be looking for? Then, read the synopsis and see if it agrees with your perception.

Sometimes it's useful to look at the means for the two groups. Figure 8.3 shows the means for the distribution in with the pre-post means of the program group joined with a blue line and the pre-post means of the comparison group joined with a green one. This first outcome shows the situation in the two bivariate plots. Here, you can see much more clearly both the original pretest difference of five points and the larger fifteen-point posttest difference.

Figure 8.3
Plot of pretest and posttest means for possible outcome 1.

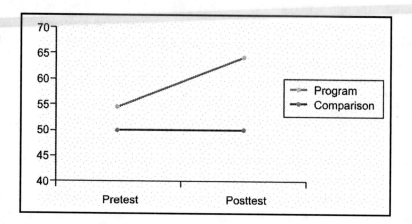

How might you interpret these results? To begin, you need to recall that with the NEGD you are usually most concerned about *selection threats*. Which selection threats might be operating here? The key to understanding this outcome is that the comparison group did not change between the pretest and the posttest. Therefore, it would be hard to argue that that the outcome is due to a *selection-maturation threat*. Why? Remember that a selection-maturation threat means that the groups are maturing at different rates and that this creates the illusion of a program effect when there is not one. However, because the comparison group didn't mature (change) at all, it's hard to argue that differential maturation produced the outcome. What could have produced the outcome? A *selection-history threat* certainly seems plausible. Perhaps some event occurred (other than the program) that the program group reacted to and the comparison group didn't. Maybe a local event occurred for the program group but not for the comparison group. Notice how much more likely it is that outcome pattern 1 is caused by such a history threat than by a maturation difference. What about the possibility of *selection regression?* This one actually works a lot like the selection-maturation threat. If the jump in the program group is due to *regression to the mean*, it would have to be because the program group was below the overall population pretest average and consequently regressed upwards on the posttest. However, if that's true, it should be even more the case for the comparison group who started with an even lower pretest average. The fact that it doesn't appear to regress at all helps rule out the possibility that outcome 1 is the result of regression to the mean.

Possible Outcome 2

The second hypothetical outcome (see Figure 8.4) presents a different picture. Here, both the program and comparison groups gain from pre to post, with the program group gaining at a slightly faster rate. This is almost the definition of a selection-maturation threat. The fact that the two groups differed to begin with suggests that they may already be maturing at different rates. The posttest scores don't do anything to help rule out that possibility. This outcome might also arise from a selection-history threat. If the two groups, because of their initial differences, react differently to some historical event, you might obtain the outcome pattern shown. Both *selection testing* and *selection instrumentation* are also possibilities, depending on the nature of the measures used. This pattern could indicate a *selection-mortality* problem if there are more low-scoring program cases that drop out between testings. What about selection-regression? It doesn't seem likely, for much the same reasoning as for outcome 1. If there were an upwards regression to the mean from pre to post, you would expect that regression to be greater for the comparison group because it has the lower pretest score.

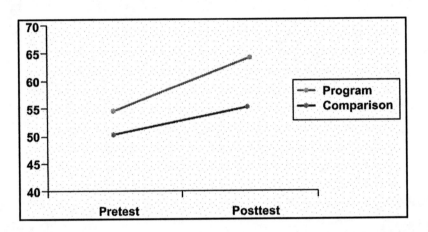

Figure 8.4
Plot of pretest and posttest means for possible outcome 2.

Possible Outcome 3

This third possible outcome (see Figure 8.5) cries out selection-regression! Or, at least it would if it could cry out. The regression scenario is that the program group was selected so that it was extremely high (relative to the population) on the pretest. The fact that the group scored lower, approaching the comparison group on the posttest, may simply be due to its regressing toward the population mean. You might observe an outcome like this when you study the effects of giving a scholarship or an award for academic performance. You give the award because students did well (in this case, on the pretest). When you observe the group's posttest performance, relative to an average group of students, it appears to perform worse. Pure regression! Notice how this outcome doesn't suggest a selection-maturation threat. What kind of maturation process would have to occur for the highly advantaged program group to decline while a comparison group evidences no change?

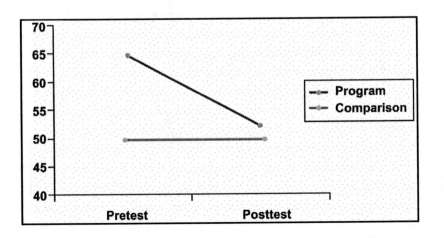

Figure 8.5
Plot of pretest and posttest means for possible outcome 3.

Possible Outcome 4

The fourth possible outcome also suggests a selection-regression threat (see Figure 8.6). Here, the program group is disadvantaged to begin with. The fact that it appears to pull closer to the comparison group on the posttest may be due to regression. This outcome pattern may be suspected in studies of compensatory programs—programs designed to help address some problem or deficiency. For instance, compensatory education programs are designed to help children who are doing poorly in some subject. They are likely to have lower pretest performance than more average comparison children. Consequently, they are likely to regress to the mean in a pattern similar to the one shown in outcome 4.

Figure 8.6
Plot of pretest and posttest means for possible outcome 4.

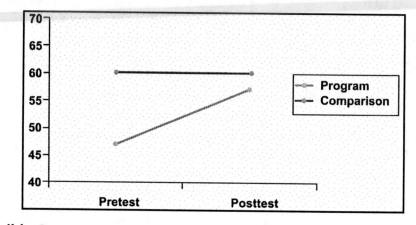

Possible Outcome 5

This last hypothetical outcome (see Figure 8.7) is sometimes referred to as a cross-over pattern. Here, the comparison group doesn't appear to change from pre to post; but the program group does, starting out lower than the comparison group and ending up above it. This is the clearest pattern of evidence for the effectiveness of the program of all five of the hypothetical outcomes. It's hard to come up with a threat to internal validity that would be plausible here. Certainly, there is no evidence for selection maturation here unless you postulate that the two groups are involved in maturational processes that tend to start and stop and just coincidentally you caught the program group maturing while the comparison group had gone dormant. However, if that were the case, why did the program group actually cross over the comparison group? Why didn't it approach the comparison group and stop maturing? How likely is this outcome as a description of normal maturation? Not very. Similarly, this isn't a selection-regression result. Regression might explain why a low-scoring program group approaches the comparison group posttest score (as in outcome 4), but it doesn't explain why it crosses over.

Figure 8.7
Plot of pretest and posttest means for possible outcome 5.

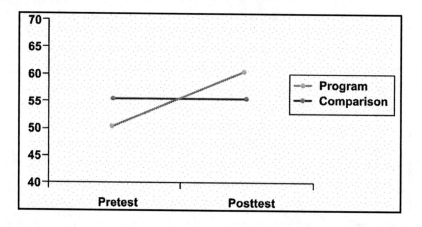

Although this fifth outcome is the strongest evidence for a program effect, you can't very well construct your study expecting to find this kind of pattern. It would be a little bit like giving your program to the toughest cases and seeing whether you can improve them so much that they not only become like average cases, but actually outperform them. That's an awfully big expectation with which to saddle any program. Typically, you wouldn't want to subject your program to that kind of expectation. If you do happen to find that kind of result, you really have a program effect that beats the odds.

8-2 The Regression-Discontinuity Design

What a terrible name! In everyday language, both parts of the term, Regression-Discontinuity, have primarily negative connotations. To most people regression implies a reversion backwards or a return to some earlier, more primitive state; whereas discontinuity suggests an unnatural jump or shift in what might otherwise be a smoother, more continuous process. To a research methodologist, however, the term regression-discontinuity carries no such negative meaning. Instead, the *Regression-Discontinuity (RD)* design is seen as a useful method for determining whether a program or treatment is effective.

The label RD design actually refers to a set of design variations. In its simplest most traditional form, the RD design is a pretest-posttest program-comparison group strategy. The unique characteristic that sets RD designs apart from other pre-post group designs is the method by which research participants are assigned to conditions. In RD designs, participants are assigned to program or comparison groups solely on the basis of a cutoff score on a pre-program measure. Thus the RD design is distinguished from randomized experiments (or randomized clinical trials) and from other quasi-experimental strategies by its unique method of assignment. This cutoff criterion implies the major advantage of RD designs; they are appropriate when you want to target a program or treatment to those who most need or deserve it. Thus, unlike its randomized or quasi-experimental alternatives, the RD design does not require you to assign potentially needy individuals to a no-program comparison group to evaluate the effectiveness of a program.

The RD design has not been used frequently in social research. The most common implementation has been in compensatory education evaluation where school children who obtain scores that fall below some predetermined cutoff value on an achievement test are assigned to remedial training designed to improve their performance. The low frequency of use may be attributable to several factors. Certainly, the design is a relative latecomer. Its first major field tests did not occur until the mid-1970s when it was incorporated into the nationwide evaluation system for compensatory education programs funded under Title I of the Elementary and Secondary Education Act (ESEA) of 1965. In many situations, the design has not been used because one or more key criteria were absent. For instance, RD designs force administrators to assign participants to conditions solely on the basis of *quantitative* indicators, thereby often unpalatably restricting the degree to which judgment, discretion, or favoritism can be used. Perhaps the most telling reason for the lack of wider adoption of the RD design is that at first glance the design doesn't seem to make sense. In most research, you want to have comparison groups that are equivalent to program groups on pre-program indicators, so that post-program differences can be attributed to the program itself. However, because of the cutoff criterion in RD designs, program and comparison groups are deliberately and maximally different on pre-program characteristics, an apparently insensible anomaly. An understanding of how the design actually works depends on at least a conceptual familiarity with regression analysis, thereby making the strategy a difficult one to convey to nonstatistical audiences.

Despite its lack of use, the RD design has great potential for evaluation and social research. From a methodological point of view, inferences drawn from a well-implemented RD design are comparable in *internal validity* to conclusions from randomized experiments. Thus, the RD design is a strong competitor to randomized designs when *causal* hypotheses are being investigated. From an ethical perspective, RD designs are compatible with the goal of getting the program to those most in need. It is not necessary to deny the program from potentially deserving recipients simply for the sake of a scientific test. From an administrative viewpoint, the RD design is often directly usable with existing measurement efforts, such as the regularly collected statistical information typical of most management-information systems. The advantages of the RD design warrant greater educational efforts on the part of the methodological community to encourage its use where appropriate.

8-2a The Basic RD Design

The basic RD design is a pretest-posttest two-group design. The term pretest-posttest implies that the same measure (or perhaps alternate forms of the same measure) is administered before and after some program or treatment. (In fact, the RD design does not require that the pre and post measures be the same.) The term pretest implies that the same measure is given twice; whereas the term pre-program measure implies more broadly that before and after measures may be the same or different. It is assumed that a cutoff value on the pretest or pre-program measure is being used to assign persons or other units to the program. Two-group versions of the RD design might imply either that some treatment or program is being contrasted with a no-program condition or that two alternative programs are being compared. The description of the basic design as a two-group design implies that a single pretest-cutoff score is used to assign participants to either the program, or comparison group. The term *participants* refers to the units assigned. In many cases, participants are individuals, but they could be any definable units such as hospital wards, hospitals, counties, and so on. The term program is used in this discussion of the RD design to refer to any program, treatment, or manipulation whose effects you want to examine. In notational form, the basic RD design might be depicted as shown Figure 8.8:

- *C* indicates that groups are assigned by means of a cutoff score.
- An *O* stands for the administration of a measure to a group.
- An *X* depicts the implementation of a program.
- Each group is described on a single line (for example program group on top and control group on the bottom).

Figure 8.8
Notation for the Regression-Discontinuity (RD) design.

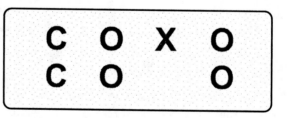

To make this initial presentation more concrete, imagine a hypothetical study examining the effect of a new treatment protocol for inpatients with a particular diagnosis. For simplicity, assume that you want to try the new protocol on patients who are considered most ill and that for each patient you have a continuous quantitative indicator of health that is a composite rating that takes values from 1 to

100, where high scores indicate greater health. Furthermore, assume that a pretest cutoff score of 50 was (more or less arbitrarily) chosen as the assignment criterion or that all those scoring lower than 50 on the pretest are to be given the new treatment protocol while those with scores greater than or equal to 50 are given the standard treatment.

It is useful to begin by considering what the data might look like if you did not administer the treatment protocol but instead only measured all participants at two points in time. Figure 8.9a shows the hypothetical bivariate distribution for this situation. Each dot on the figure indicates a single person's pretest and posttest scores. The blue *X*s to the left of the cutoff show the program cases. They are more severely ill on both the pretest, and posttest. The green circles show the comparison group that is comparatively healthy on both measures. The vertical line at the pretest score of 50 indicates the cutoff point. (In Figure 8.9a, the assumption is that no treatment has been given.) The solid line through the bivariate distribution is the linear *regression line*. The distribution depicts a strong positive relationship between the pretest and posttest; in general, the more healthy a person is at the pretest, the more healthy he or she is on the posttest, and the more severely ill a person is at the pretest, the more ill that person is on the posttest.

Consider what the outcome might look like if the new treatment protocol is administered and has a positive effect (see Figure 8.9b). For simplicity, assume that the treatment had a constant effect that raised each treated person's health score by ten points.

Figure 8.9b is identical to Figure 8.9a except that all points to the left of the cutoff (that is, the treatment group) have been raised by 10 points on the posttest. The dashed line in Figure 8.9b shows what you would expect the treated group's regression line to look like if the program had no effect (as was the case in Figure 8.9a).

It is sometimes difficult to see the forest for the trees in these types of bivariate plots. So, let's remove the individual data points and look only at the regression lines. The plot of regression lines for the treatment effect case of Figure 8.9b is shown in Figure 8.9c.

On the basis of Figure 8.9c, you can now see how the RD design got its name; a program effect is suggested when you observe a *jump* or *discontinuity* in the regression lines at the cutoff point. This is illustrated in Figure 8.9d.

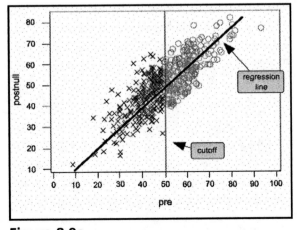

Figure 8.9a
Pre-post distribution for a RD design with no treatment effect.

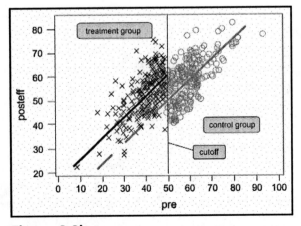

Figure 8.9b
The RD design with ten-point treatment effect.

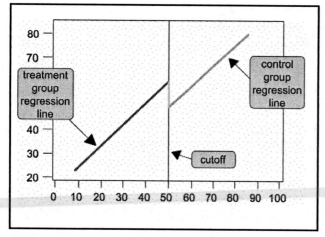

Figure 8.9c
Regression lines for the data shown in Figure 8.9b.

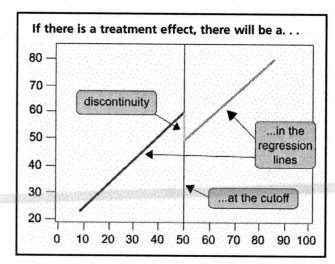

Figure 8.9d
How the RD design got its name.

The Logic of the RD Design

The previous discussion indicates what the key feature of the RD design is: *assignment based on a cutoff value on a pre-program measure*. The cutoff rule for the simple two-group case is essentially as follows:

- All persons on one side of the cutoff are assigned to one group.
- All persons on the other side of the cutoff are assigned to the other group and need a continuous quantitative pre-program measure.

The choice of cutoff value is usually based on one of two factors. It can be made solely on the basis of the program resources that are available. For instance, if a program can only handle 25 persons and 70 people apply, you can choose a cutoff point that distinguishes the 25 most needy persons from the rest. Alternatively, you can choose the cutoff on substantive grounds. If the pre-program assignment measure is an indication of severity of illness measured on a 1 to 7 scale and physicians or other experts believe that all patients scoring 5 or more are critical and fit well the criteria defined for program participants, you might use a cutoff value of 5.

To interpret the results of an RD design, you must know the nature of the assignment variable and the outcome measure, as well as who received the program. Without this information, no distinct outcome pattern directly indicates whether an effect is positive or negative.

To illustrate this, consider a new hypothetical example of an RD design. Assume that a hospital administrator would like to improve the quality of patient care through the institution of an intensive quality-of-care training program for staff. Because of financial constraints, the program is too costly to implement for all employees and so instead it will be administered to the entire staff from specifically targeted units or wards that seem most in need of improving quality of care. Two general measures of quality of care are available. The first is an aggregate rating of quality of care based on observation and rating by an administrative staff member and will be labeled here the QOC rating. The second is the ratio of the number of recorded patient complaints relative to the number of patients in the unit over a fixed period of time and will be termed here the Complaint Ratio. In this scenario, the administrator could use either the QOC rating or Complaint

Ratio as the basis for assigning units to receive the training. Similarly, the effects of the training could be measured on either variable. Figures 8.10a through 8.10d show four outcomes of alternative RD implementations possible under this scenario.

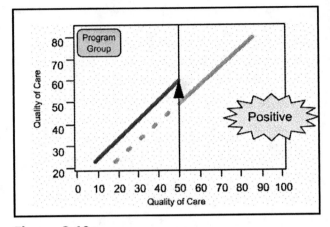

Figure 8.10a
Regression lines in hypothetical outcome 1 for an RD design.

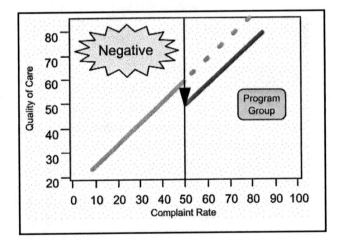

Figure 8.10b
Regression lines in hypothetical outcome 2 for an RD design.

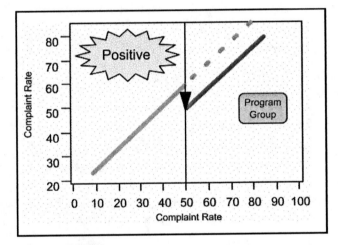

Figure 8.10c
Regression lines in hypothetical outcome 3 for an RD design.

Figure 8.10d
Regression lines in hypothetical outcome 4 for an RD design.

Only the regression lines are shown in Figures 8.10a through 8.10d. It is worth noting that even though all four outcomes have the same pattern of regression lines, they do not imply the same result. In Figure 8.10a and Figure 8.10b, hospital units were assigned to training because they scored *below* some cutoff score on the QOC rating. In Figure 8.10c and Figure 8.10d, units received training because they scored *above* the cutoff score value on the Complaint Ratio measure. In each graph, the dashed line indicates the regression line you would expect to find for the training group if the training had no effect. This dashed line represents the no-discontinuity projection of the comparison-group regression line into the region of the program group pretest scores.

You can clearly see that even though the outcome regression lines are the same in all four groups, you would interpret the four graphs differently. Figure 8.10a depicts a positive effect because training raised the program group's regression line on the QOC rating over what would have been expected. Figure 8.10b however shows a negative effect because the program raised training group scores on the Complaint Ratio, indicating increased complaint rates. Figure 8.10c shows a positive effect because the regression line was lowered on the Complaint Ratio relative to what you would have expected. Finally, Figure 8.10d shows a negative effect where the training resulted in lower QOC ratings than you would expect otherwise. The point here is a simple one. A discontinuity in regression lines indicates a program effect in the RD design; but the discontinuity alone is not sufficient to tell you whether the effect is positive or negative. To make this determination, you need to know who received the program and how to interpret the direction of scale values on the outcome measures.

The Role of the Comparison Group in RD Designs

With this introductory discussion of the design in mind, you can now see what constitutes the benchmark for comparison in the RD design. In experimental or other *quasi-experimental designs*, you either assume or try to provide evidence that the program and comparison groups are equivalent prior to the program so that post-program differences can be attributed to the manipulation. The RD design involves no such assumption. Instead, with RD designs you assume that in the absence of the program the pre-post relationship would be equivalent for the two groups. Thus, the strength of the RD design is dependent on two major factors. The first is the assumption that there is no spurious discontinuity in the pre-post relationship that happens to coincide with the cutoff point. The second factor concerns the degree to which you can know and correctly model the pre-post relationship and constitutes the major problem in the statistical analysis of the RD design, which will be discussed in Chapter 10, "Analysis."

The Internal Validity of the RD Design

Internal validity refers to whether one can infer that the treatment or program being investigated caused a change in outcome indicators. Internal validity is not concerned with your ability to generalize but rather focuses on whether a *causal* relationship can be demonstrated for the immediate research context. Research designs that address causal questions are often compared on their relative ability to yield internally valid results.

In most causal-hypothesis tests, the central inferential question is whether any observed outcome differences between groups are attributable to the program or instead to some other factor. To argue for the internal validity of an inference, the analyst must attempt to demonstrate that the program—and not some plausible alternative explanation—is responsible for the effect. In the literature on internal validity, these plausible alternative explanations or factors are often termed *threats to internal validity*. Many threats can be ruled out by including a *control group*. Assuming that the control group is equivalent to the program group prior to the study, the control group pre-post gain shows you what would have happened in the program group if it had not had the program. A different rate of gain in the program group provides evidence for the relative effect of the program itself. Thus, randomized-experimental designs are considered strong in internal validity because they give you confidence in the probabilistic, pre-program equivalence between groups that results from *random assignment* and helps ensure that the control group provides a legitimate reflection of all nonprogram factors that might affect outcomes.

RD designs contain several selection threats to internal validity because of the deliberate pre-program differences between groups. (These are discussed in Chapter 6, "Design.") These threats might, at first glance, appear to be a problem. For instance, a ***selection-maturation threat*** implies that different rates of maturation between groups explain outcome differences. For the sake of argument, let's consider a pre-post distribution with a linear relationship having a slope equal to two units. This implies that on average, a person with a given pretest score will have a posttest score two times higher. Clearly there is maturation in this situation; that is, people are getting consistently higher scores over time. If a person has a pretest score of 10 units, you would predict a posttest score of 20 for an absolute gain of 10. However, if a person has a pretest score of 50, you would predict a posttest score of 100 for an absolute gain of 50. Thus, the second person naturally gains or matures more in absolute units; although the rate of gain relative to the pretest score is constant. Along these lines, in the RD design, you expect that all participants may mature and that in absolute terms this maturation might be different for the two groups on average. Nevertheless, a program effect in the RD design is not indicated by a difference between the posttest averages of the groups, but rather by a change in the pre-post relationship at the cutoff point. In this example, although you might expect different absolute levels of maturation, a single, continuous regression line with a slope equal to 2 describes these different maturational rates perfectly. More to the point, for selection-maturation to be a threat to internal validity in RD designs, it must induce a discontinuity in the pre-post relationship that happens to coincide with the cutoff point—an unlikely scenario in most studies.

Another selection threat to internal validity that might intuitively seem likely in the RD design concerns the possibility of differential ***regression to the mean*** or a selection-regression threat. The phenomenon of regression to the mean arises when you asymmetrically sample groups from a distribution. On any subsequent measure, the obtained sample group mean will be closer to the population mean for that measure (in standardized units) than the sample mean from the original distribution is to its population mean. In RD designs, you deliberately create asymmetric samples through the cutoff assignment and consequently expect regression towards the mean in both groups. In general, you should expect the low-scoring pretest group to evidence a relative gain on the posttest and the high-scoring pretest group to show a relative loss. As with selection-maturation, even though you expect to see differential regression to the mean, it poses no problem for the internal validity of the RD design. Regression to the mean does not result in a discontinuity in the bivariate relationship coincidental with the cutoff point. In fact, the regression to the mean that occurs is continuous across the range of the pretest scores and is described by the regression line itself. (The term regression was originally coined by Galton to refer to the fact that a regression line describes regression to the mean.)

Although the RD design might initially seem susceptible to selection biases, it is not. The previous discussion demonstrates that only factors that would naturally induce a discontinuity in the pre-post relationship could be considered threats to the internal validity of inferences from the RD design. In principle then, the RD design is as strong in internal validity as its randomized experimental alternatives. In practice, however, the validity of the RD design depends directly on how well you can model the true pre-post relationship, certainly a nontrivial statistical problem.

8-2b The RD Design and Accountability

It makes sense intuitively that the accountability of a program is largely dependent on the explicitness of the assignment or allocation of the program to recipients. Lawmakers and administrators need to recognize that programs are more evaluable and accountable when the allocation of the program is more public and verifiable. The three major pre-post designs—the Pre-Post Randomized Experiments (Chapter 7, "Experimental Design"), the RD design, and the NEGD design (both discussed earlier in this chapter)—are analogous to the three types of program allocation schemes that legislators or administrators might choose. Randomized experiments are analogous to the use of a lottery for allocating the program. RD designs can be considered explicit, accountable methods for assigning programs based on need or merit. NEGD designs might be considered a type of political allocation because they enable the use of unverifiable, subjective, or politically motivated assignment. Most social programs are politically allocated. Even when programs are allocated primarily based on need or merit, the regulatory agency usually reserves some discretionary capability in deciding who receives the program. Without debating the need for such discretion, it is clear that the methodological community should encourage administrators and legislators who want their programs to be accountable so they can make explicit their criteria for program eligibility by either using probabilistically based lotteries or by relying on *quantitative* eligibility ratings and cutoff values as in the RD design. To the extent that legislators and administrators can be convinced to move toward more explicit assignment criteria, both the potential utility of the RD design and the accountability of the programs will be increased.

8-2c Statistical Power and the RD Design

The previous discussion argues that the RD design is strong in *internal validity*, certainly stronger than the *NEGD* design, and perhaps as strong as the randomized-experiments design; but the RD designs are not as statistically powerful as the randomized experiments (see Chapter 10, "Analysis," for a discussion of statistical power). That is, to achieve the same level of statistical accuracy, an RD design needs as much as 2.75 times the participants as a randomized experiment. For instance, if a randomized experiment needs 100 participants to achieve a certain level of power, the RD design might need as many as 275.

8-2d Ethics and the RD Design

So why would you ever use the RD design instead of a randomized one? The real allure of the RD design is that it allows you to assign the treatment or program to those who most need or deserve it. Thus, the real attractiveness of the design is ethical; you don't have to deny the program or treatment to participants who might need it as you do in randomized studies.

8-3 Other Quasi-Experimental Designs

There are many different types of *quasi-experimental designs* that have a variety of applications in specific contexts. Here, I'll briefly present a number of the more interesting or important quasi-experimental designs. By studying the features of these designs, you can gain a deeper understanding of how to tailor design components to address threats to *internal validity* in your own research contexts.

8-3a The Proxy Pretest Design

The *Proxy-Pretest design* (see Figure 8.11) looks like a standard pre-post design with an important difference. The pretest in this design is collected after the program is given! But how can you call it a pretest if it's collected after the program? Because you use a proxy variable to estimate where the groups would have been on the pretest. There are essentially two variations of this design. In the first, you ask the participants to estimate where their pretest level would have been. This can be called the Recollection Proxy-Pretest design. For instance, you might ask participants to complete your measures by estimating how they would have answered the questions six months ago. This type of proxy pretest is not good for estimating actual pre-post changes because people may forget where they were at some prior time or they may distort the pretest estimates to make themselves look better. However, at times, you might be interested not so much in where they were on the pretest but rather in where they think they were. The Recollection Proxy Pretest would be a sensible way to assess participants' perceived gain or change.

$$N\ O_1\ X\ O_2$$
$$N\ O_1\ \ \ O_2$$

Figure 8.11
The Proxy-Pretest design.

The other Proxy-Pretest design uses archived records to stand in for the pretest. This design is called the Archived Proxy-Pretest design. For instance, imagine that you are studying the effects of an educational program on the math performance of eighth graders. Unfortunately, you were brought in to do the study after the program had already been started (a too-frequent case, I'm afraid). You are able to construct a posttest that shows math ability after training, but you have no pretest. Under these circumstances, your best bet might be to find a proxy variable that would estimate pretest performance. For instance, you might use the students' grade point average in math from the seventh grade as the proxy pretest.

The Proxy-Pretest design is not one you should ever select by choice; but, if you find yourself in a situation where you have to evaluate a program that has already begun, it may be the best you can do and would almost certainly be better than relying only on a posttest-only design.

8-3b The Separate Pre-Post Samples Design

The basic idea in the *Separate Pre-Post Samples* design (and its variations) is that the people you use for the pretest are not the same as the people you use for the posttest (see Figure 8.12). Take a close look at the design notation for the first variation of this design. There are four groups (indicated by the four lines) but two of the groups come from a single nonequivalent group and the other two also come from a single nonequivalent group (indicated by the subscripts next to N). Imagine that you have two agencies or organizations that you think are similar. You want to implement your study in one agency and use the other as a control. The program you are looking at is an agency-wide one and you expect the outcomes to be most noticeable at the agency level. For instance, let's say the program is designed to improve customer satisfaction. Because customers routinely cycle through your agency, you can't measure the same customers pre-post. Instead, you measure customer satisfaction in each agency at one point in time, implement your program, and then measure customer satisfaction in the agency at another point in time after the program. Notice that the customers will be different within each agency for the pretest and posttest. This design is not a particularly strong one because you cannot match individual participant responses from pre to post; you can only look at the change in average customer satisfaction. Here, you always run the risk that you have nonequivalence not only between the agencies but within the pre and post groups as well. For instance, if you have different types of clients at different times of the year, this could bias the results. You could also look at this as having a proxy pretest on a different group of people.

Figure 8.12
The Separate Pre-Post
Samples design.

$$
\begin{array}{llll}
N_1 & O & & \\
N_1 & & X & O \\
N_2 & O & & \\
N_2 & & & O
\end{array}
$$

The second example of the Separate Pre-Post Sample design is shown in design notation in Figure 8.13. Again, there are four groups in the study. This time, however, you are taking random samples from your agency or organization at each point in time. This is essentially the same design as the one in Figure 8.12 except for the random sampling. Probably the most sensible use of this design would be in situations where you routinely do sample surveys in an organization or community. For instance, assume that every year two similar communities do a community-wide survey of residents to ask about satisfaction with city services. Because of costs, you randomly sample each community each year. In one of the communities, you decide to institute a program of community policing and you want to see whether residents feel safer and have changed in their attitudes towards police. You would use the results of last year's survey as the pretest in both communities and this year's results as the posttest. Again, this is not a particularly strong design. Even though you are taking random samples from each community each year, it may still be the case that the community changes fundamentally from one year to the next and that the random samples within a community cannot be considered equivalent.

Figure 8.13
The Separate Pre-Post
Sample design with
random sampling.

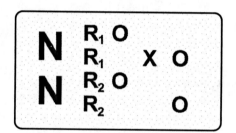

8-3c The Double-Pretest Design

The Double-Pretest design (see Figure 8.14) is a strong quasi-experimental design with respect to internal validity. Why? Recall that the Pre-Post NEGD is especially susceptible to selection threats to internal validity. In other words, the nonequivalent groups may be different in some way before the program is given and you may incorrectly attribute posttest differences to the program. Although the pretest helps you assess the degree of pre-program similarity, it does not determine whether the groups are changing at similar rates prior to the program. Thus, the NEGD is especially susceptible to *selection-maturation threats*.

Figure 8.14
The Double-Pretest design.

The ***Double-Pretest design*** includes two measures prior to the program. Consequently, if the program and comparison group are maturing at different rates, you should detect this as a change from pretest 1 to pretest 2. Therefore, this design explicitly controls for selection-maturation threats. The design is also sometimes referred to as a dry-run, quasi-experimental design because the double pretests simulate what would happen in the ***null case***.

The Switching-Replications quasi-experimental design is also strong with respect to internal validity, and because it allows for two independent implementations of the program, it may enhance external validity or generalizability (see Figure 8.15). The ***Switching-Replications design*** has two groups and three waves of measurement. In the first phase of the design, both groups are given pretests, one is given the program, and both are posttested. In the second phase of the design, the original comparison group is given the program while the original program group serves as the control. This design is identical in structure to its randomized experimental version (described in Chapter 7, "Experimental Design") but lacks the random assignment to group. It is certainly superior to the simple ***NEGD***. In addition, because it ensures that all participants eventually get the program, it is probably one of the most ethically feasible quasi-experiments.

8-3d The Switching-Replications Design

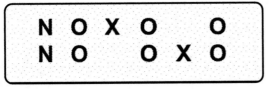

Figure 8.15
The Switching-Replications design.

The ***Nonequivalent Dependent Variables (NEDV) design*** is a deceptive one. In its simple form, it is an extremely weak design with respect to ***internal validity***. However, in its ***pattern-matching*** variations (covered later in this chapter), it opens the door to an entirely different approach to ***causal*** assessment that is extremely powerful. The design notation shown in Figure 8.16 is for the simple two-variable case. Notice that this design has only *a single group of participants*. The two lines in the notation indicate separate ***variables***, not separate groups.

8-3e The Nonequivalent Dependent Variables (NEDV) Design

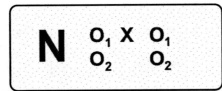

Figure 8.16
The NEDV design.

The idea in this design is that you have a program designed to change a specific outcome. For instance, assume you are training for first-year high-school students in algebra. Your training program is designed to affect algebra scores; but it is not designed to affect geometry scores. You reasonably expect pre-post geometry performance to be affected by other internal validity factors such as history or maturation. In this case, the pre-post geometry performance acts like a ***control group;*** it models what would likely have happened to the algebra pre-post scores if the program hadn't been given. The key is that the control variable has to be similar enough to the target variable to be affected in the same way by history, maturation, and the other single group internal validity threats, but not so similar that it is affected by the program.

Figure 8.17 shows the results you might get for the two-variable, algebra-geometry example. Note that this design only works if the geometry variable is a reasonable proxy for what would have happened on the algebra scores in the absence of the program. The real allure of this design is the possibility that you don't need a control group; you can give the program to your entire sample. The problem is that in its two-variable simple version, the assumption of the control variable is a difficult one to meet. (Note that a double-pretest version of this design would be considerably stronger.)

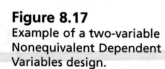

Figure 8.17
Example of a two-variable Nonequivalent Dependent Variables design.

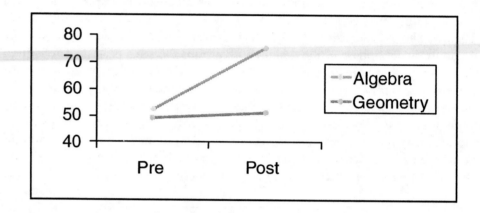

The Pattern-Matching NEDV Design

Although the two-variable NEDV design is quite weak, you can make it considerably stronger by adding multiple outcome variables. In this variation, you need many outcome variables and a theory that tells *how affected* (from most to least) each variable will be by the program. Let's reconsider the example from the algebra program in the previous discussion. Now, instead of having only an algebra and geometry score, imagine you have ten measures that you collect pre and post. You would expect the algebra measure to be most affected by the program (because that's what the program was most designed to affect). However, in this variation, you recognize that geometry might also be affected because training in algebra might be relevant, at least tangentially, to geometry skills. On the other hand, you might theorize that creativity would be much less affected, even indirectly, by training in algebra and so you predict the creativity measure to be the least affected of the ten measures.

Now, line up your theoretical expectations against your pre-post gains for each variable. You can see in Figure 8.18 that the expected order of outcomes (on the left) is mirrored well in the actual outcomes (on the right).

Figure 8.18
Example of a Pattern Matching variation of the NEDV design.

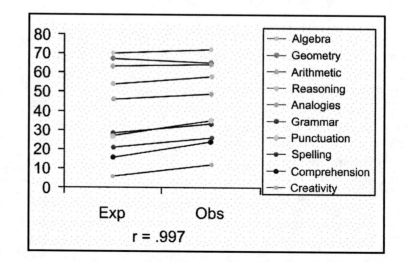

Depending on the circumstances, the ***Pattern-Matching NEDV design*** can be quite strong with respect to ***internal validity***. In general, the design is stronger if you have a larger set of variables and your expectation pattern matches well with the observed results. What are the threats to internal validity in this design? Only a factor (such as an historical event or maturational pattern) that would yield the same outcome pattern can act as an alternative explanation. Furthermore, the more complex the predicted pattern, the less likely it is that some other factor would yield it. The problem is, the more complex the predicted pattern, the less likely it is that you will find it matches your observed data as well.

The Pattern-Matching NEDV design is especially attractive for several reasons. It requires you to specify expectations prior to institution of the program. Doing so can be a sobering experience. Often researchers make naive assumptions about how programs or interventions will work. When you're forced to look at the programs in detail, you begin to see that your assumptions may be unrealistic. The design also requires a detailed measurement net—a large set of outcome variables and a detailed sense of how they are related to each other. Developing this level of detail about your measurement constructs is liable to improve the ***construct validity*** of your study. Increasingly, methodologies can help researchers empirically develop construct networks that describe the expected interrelationships among outcome variables. (See the section, "Concept Mapping," for more information about how to do this, in Chapter 1, "Foundations.") Finally, the Pattern-Matching NEDV is especially intriguing because it suggests that it is possible to assess the effects of programs even if you only have a treated group. Assuming the other conditions for the design are met, control groups are not necessarily needed for ***causal*** assessment. Of course, you can also couple the Pattern-Matching NEDV design with standard experimental or quasi-experimental control group designs for even more enhanced validity. Additionally, if your experimental or quasi-experimental design already has many outcome measures as part of the measurement protocol, the design might be considerably enriched by generating variable-level expectations about program outcomes and testing the match statistically.

One of my favorite questions to my statistician friends goes to the heart of the potential of the Pattern-Matching NEDV design. I ask them, "Suppose you have ten outcome variables in a study and that you find that all ten show no statistically significant treatment effects when tested individually (or even when tested as a multivariate set). And suppose, like the desperate graduate students who find in their initial analysis that nothing is significant, that you decide to look at the direction of the effects across the ten variables. You line up the variables in terms of which should be most to least affected by your program. And, miracle of miracles, you find that there is a strong and statistically significant correlation between the expected and observed *order* of effects even though no individual effect was statistically significant. Is this finding interpretable as a treatment effect?" My answer is "Yes." I think the graduate student's desperation-driven intuition to look at order of effects is a sensible one. I would conclude that the reason you did not find statistical effects on the individual variables is that you didn't have sufficient statistical power. (You can find more about this in the discussion on statistical power in Chapter 10, "Analysis.") Of course, the results will only be interpretable as a treatment effect if you can rule out any other plausible factor that could have caused the ordering of outcomes. Nonetheless, the more detailed the predicted pattern and the stronger the correlation to observed results, the more likely it becomes that the treatment effect is the most plausible explanation. In such cases, the expected pattern of results is like a unique fingerprint, and the observed pattern that matches it can only be due to that unique source pattern.

I believe that the *pattern-matching* notion implicit in the NEDV design opens the way to an entirely different approach to causal assessment, one that is closely linked to detailed prior explication of the program and to detailed mapping of constructs. It suggests a much richer model for causal assessment than one that relies only on a simplistic dichotomous treatment-control model. In fact, I'm so convinced of the importance of this idea that I've staked a major part of my career on developing pattern-matching models for conducting research!

8-3f The Regression Point Displacement (RPD) Design

The *Regression Point Displacement (RPD)* design is a simple quasi-experimental strategy that has important implications, especially for community-based research. The problem with community-level interventions is that it is difficult to do causal assessment to determine whether your program made a difference as opposed to other potential factors. Typically, in community-level interventions, program costs preclude implementation of the program in more than one community. You look at pre-post indicators for the program community and see whether there is a change. If you're relatively enlightened, you seek out another similar community and use it as a comparison. However, because the intervention is at the community level, you only have a single unit of measurement for your program and comparison groups.

The RPD design (see Figure 8.19) attempts to enhance the single program unit situation by comparing the performance on that single unit with the performance of a large set of comparison units. In community research, you would compare the pre-post results for the intervention community with a large set of other communities. The advantage of doing this is that you don't rely on a single nonequivalent community; you attempt to use results from a heterogeneous set of nonequivalent communities to model the comparison condition and then compare your single site to this model. For typical community-based research, such an approach may greatly enhance your ability to make causal inferences.

Figure 8.19
The Regression Point Displacement (RPD) design.

I'll illustrate the RPD design with an example of a community-based AIDS education program to be implemented in one particular community in a state, perhaps a county. The state routinely publishes annual HIV positive rates by county for the entire state. So, the remaining counties in the state function as control counties. Instead of averaging all the control counties to obtain a single control score, you use them as separate units in the analysis. Figure 8.20a shows the bivariate pre-post distribution of HIV positive rates per 1000 people for all the counties in the state. The program county—the one that gets the AIDS education program—is shown as an X and the remaining control counties are shown as Os. You compute a regression line for the control cases (shown in blue on the figure) to model your predicted outcome for a count with any specific pretest rate. To estimate the effect of the program you test whether the displacement of the program county from the control county regression line is statistically significant.

Figure 8.20b shows why the RPD design was given its name. In this design, you know you have a treatment effect when there is a significant *displacement* of the program *point* from the control group *regression* line.

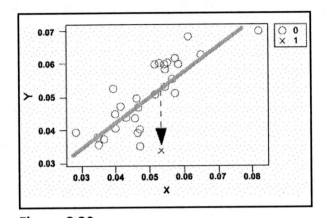

Figure 8.20a
An example of the RPD design.

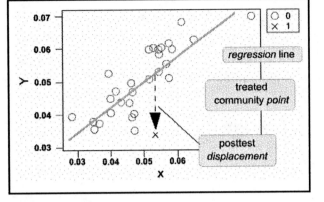

Figure 8.20b
How the RPD design got its name.

The RPD design is especially applicable in situations where a treatment or program is applied in a single geographical unit (such as a state, county, city, hospital, or hospital unit) instead of an individual, where many other units are available as control cases, and where there is routine measurement (for example monthly, or annually) of relevant outcome variables.

The analysis of the RPD design turns out to be a variation of the Analysis of Covariance model.

SUMMARY

This chapter introduced the idea of **quasi-experimental designs**. These designs look a bit like their randomized or true experimental relatives (described in Chapter 7, "Experimental Design,") but they lack their random assignment to groups. Two major types of quasi-experimental designs were explained in detail. Both are pre-post, two-group designs, and they differ primarily in the manner used to assign the groups. In the **NEGD**, groups are assigned naturally or are used intact; the researcher does not control the assignment. In **RD** designs, participants are assigned to groups solely on the basis of a cutoff score on the preprogram measure; the researcher explicitly controls this assignment. Because assignment is explicitly controlled in the RD design and not in **NEGD**, the former is considered stronger with respect to **internal validity**, perhaps comparable in strength to randomized experiments. Finally, the versatility and range of quasi-experimental design was illustrated through brief presentation of a number of lesser-known designs that illustrate various combinations of sampling, measurement, or analysis strategies.

Chapter

9

Advanced Design Topics

This chapter encourages you to think deeply about social research design. Although I've called this chapter "advanced" design topics, don't let that put you off. Just because they're advanced doesn't mean they're hard to understand. Up to now, I have primarily been talking about specific designs and design types. But all three topics in this chapter talk about issues that cut across the entire research design endeavor. The chapter begins by addressing how you go about designing a research design. I might have put this topic before the chapters on specific designs, but I think that it is better to address this issue after you have a firm foundation in design. The second topic discusses the commonalities across all designs that have a pretest and posttest and a treatment and *control group*. These pre-post, two-group designs are the most common designs used for *causal* assessment. If you can understand the underlying similarities and differences of this type of design, you'll be well on your way to mastering research designs in general. Finally, I conclude with considerations of some of the major hot topics in research design today. Hopefully, this will put you on the cutting edge (and hopefully, you won't get cut!).

Key Terms

causal
control group
covariance
external validity
history threat
internal validity
main effect
mortality threat
NEGD design
pattern matching
random assignment
RD design
RE design
selection bias
threats to internal validity

9-1 Designing Designs for Research[1]

Much contemporary social research is devoted to examining whether a program, treatment, or manipulation causes some outcome or result. For example, you might want to know whether a new educational program causes subsequent achievement score gains, whether a special work release program for prisoners causes lower recidivism rates, whether a novel drug causes a reduction in symptoms, and so on. In Chapter 6, "Design," I mentioned that three conditions must be met before you can infer that such a cause-effect relationship exists:

1. **Covariation**—Changes in the presumed cause must be related to changes in the presumed effect. Thus, if you introduce, remove, or change the level of a treatment or program, you should observe some change in the outcome measures.

2. **Temporal precedence**—The presumed cause must occur prior to the presumed effect.

3. **No plausible alternative explanations**—The presumed cause must be the only reasonable explanation for changes in the outcome measures. If other factors could be responsible for changes in the outcome measures, you cannot be confident that the presumed cause-effect relationship is correct.

In most social research the third condition is the most difficult to meet. Any number of factors other than the treatment or program could cause changes in outcome measures. Chapter 6 lists a number of common plausible alternative explanations (or *threats to internal validity*). For example, it may be that some historical event that occurs at the same time that the program or treatment is instituted was responsible for the change in the outcome measures; or, changes in record keeping or measurement systems that occur at the same time as the program might be falsely attributed to the program.

The typical social science methodology textbook (which this book is not, I daresay) usually presents an array of research designs and the alternative explanations these designs rule out or minimize. This tends to foster a "cookbook" approach to research design—an emphasis on the selection of an available design off the shelf, as it were. While standard designs may sometimes fit real-life situations, top-notch researchers (which I'm sure you aspire to be) learn how to tailor a research design to fit the particular needs of the research context and minimize the relevant threats to validity. Furthermore, even if standard textbook designs are used, an understanding of the logic of design construction in general will improve your comprehension of these standard approaches. In this section, I present an approach to how to design a research design. While this is by no means the only strategy for constructing research designs, it helps to clarify some of the basic principles of design logic.

9-1a Minimizing Threats to Validity

Before we get to constructing designs themselves, it would help to think about what designs are designed to accomplish. Good research designs minimize the plausible alternative explanations for the hypothesized cause-effect relationship. But research design is not the only way you can rule out threats. Here, I present five ways to minimize threats to validity, one of which is by research design:

1. **By argument**—The most straightforward way to rule out a potential threat to validity is simply to argue that the threat in question is not a

---

[1] Much of the material for this section is based on Trochim, W. and Land, D. (1982). Designing Designs for Research. *The Researcher,* 1, 1, 1-6.

reasonable one. Such an argument may be made either *a priori* or *a posteriori*. (That's before the fact or after the fact, for those of you who never studied dead languages.) The former is usually more convincing than the latter. For example, depending on the situation, you might argue that an instrumentation threat is not likely because the same test is used for pre- and posttest measurements and did not involve observers who might improve or change over time. In most cases, ruling out a potential threat to validity by argument alone is weaker than using the other following approaches. As a result, the most plausible threats in a study should not, except in unusual cases, be ruled out by argument alone.

2. **By Measurement or Observation**—In some cases it is possible to rule out a threat by measuring it and demonstrating that either it does not occur at all or occurs so minimally as to not be a strong alternative explanation for the cause-effect relationship. Consider, for example, a study of the effects of an advertising campaign on subsequent sales of a particular product. In such a study, history (meaning the occurrence of other events than the advertising campaign that might lead to an increased desire to purchase the product) would be a plausible alternative explanation. For example, a change in the local economy, the removal of a competing product from the market, or similar events could cause an increase in product sales. You can attempt to minimize such threats by measuring local economic indicators and the availability and sales of competing products. If there are no changes in these measures coincident with the onset of the advertising campaign, these threats would be considerably minimized. Similarly, if you are studying the effects of special mathematics training on math achievement scores of children, it might be useful to observe everyday classroom behavior to verify that students were not receiving any math training in addition to that provided in the study.

3. **By design**—Here, the major emphasis is on ruling out alternative explanations by adding treatment or *control groups*, waves of measurement, and the like. I've already covered how you do this in the previous two chapters.

4. **By analysis**—Statistical analysis offers you several ways to rule out alternative explanations. For instance, you could study the plausibility of an attrition or *mortality threat* by conducting a two-way factorial experimental design (see Chapter 7, "Experimental Design"). One factor in this study might be the original treatment group designations (for example program vs. comparison group), while the other factor would be attrition (for example, dropout vs. non-dropout group). The dependent measure could be the pretest or other available pre-program measures. A *main effect* on the attrition factor would be indicative of a threat to external validity or generalizability; whereas an interaction between group and attrition factors would point to a possible threat to internal validity. Where both effects occur, it is reasonable to infer that there is a threat to both internal and *external validity*.

The plausibility of alternative explanations might also be minimized using covariance analysis (see the discussion of *covariance* in Chapter 7, "Experimental Design"). For example, in a study of the effects of workfare programs on social welfare case loads, one plausible alternative explanation might be the status of local economic conditions. Here, it might be possible to construct a measure of economic conditions and include that measure as a covariate in the statistical analysis in order to adjust for or remove this factor from the outcome scores. You must be careful when using covariance adjustments of this type; perfect covariates do not exist in most social research and the use of imperfect covariates does not completely adjust for potential alternative explanations. Nevertheless, demonstrating that treatment effects occur even after adjusting on a number of good covariates strengthens causal assertions.

5. **By preventive action**—When you anticipate potential threats, you can often rule them out by taking some type of preventive action. For example, if the program is a desirable one, it is likely that the comparison group would feel jealous or demoralized. You can take several actions to minimize the effects of these attitudes, including offering the program to the comparison group upon completion of the study or using program and comparison groups that have little opportunity for contact and communication. In addition, you can use auditing methods and quality control to track potential experimental dropouts or to insure the standardization of measurement.

These five methods for reducing the threats to internal validity should not be considered mutually exclusive. The inclusion of measurements designed to minimize threats to validity will obviously be related to the design structure and is likely to be a factor in the analysis. A good research plan should, wherever possible, make use of multiple methods for reducing threats. In general, reducing a particular threat by design or preventive action is stronger than by using one of the other three approaches. Choosing which strategy to use for any particular threat is complex and depends at least on the cost of the strategy and on the potential seriousness of the threat.

9-1b Building a Design

Here is where the rubber meets the road, design-wise. In the next few sections, I'll take a look at the different elements or pieces in a design and then show you how you might think about putting them together to create a tailored design to address your own research context.

Basic Design Elements

Most research designs can be constructed from four basic elements:

1. **Time**—A *causal* relationship, by its very nature, implies that some time has elapsed between the occurrence of the cause and the consequent effect. Although for some phenomena, the elapsed time is measured in microseconds and is therefore unnoticeable to a casual observer, you normally assume that the cause and effect in social science arenas do not occur simultaneously. In design notation, you indicate this temporal element horizontally. You place the symbol used to indicate the presumed cause to the left of the symbol, indicating measurement of the effect. Thus, as you read from left to right in design notation, you are reading across time. Complex designs might involve a lengthy sequence of observations and programs or treatments across time.

2. **Program(s) or Treatment(s)**—The presumed cause may be a program or treatment under the explicit control of the researcher or the occurrence of some natural event or program not explicitly controlled. Recall from Chapter 6, "Design," that in design notation, you usually depict a presumed cause with the symbol X. When multiple programs or treatments are being studied using the same design, you keep the programs distinct by using subscripts such as X_1 or X_2. For a comparison group (one that does not receive the program under study) no X is used.

3. **Observation(s) or Measure(s)**—Measurements are typically depicted in design notation with the symbol O. If the same measurement or observation is taken at every point in time in a design, this O is sufficient. Similarly, if the same set of measures is given at every point in time in this study, the O can be used to depict the entire set of measures. However, if you give different measures at different times, it is useful to subscript the O to distinguish between measurements and points in time.

4. **Groups or Individuals**—The final design element consists of the intact groups or the individuals who participate in various conditions. Typically, there will be one or more program and comparison groups. In design notation, each group is indicated on a separate line. Furthermore, the manner in which groups are assigned to the conditions can be indicated by an appropriate symbol at the beginning of each line. In these cases, R represents a randomly assigned group, N depicts a nonrandomly assigned group (a nonequivalent group or cohort), and C indicates that the group was assigned using a cutoff score on a measurement.

Perhaps the easiest way to understand how these four basic elements become integrated into a design structure is to give several examples. One of the most commonly used designs in social research is the two-group pre-post design, which is shown in Figure 9.1.

```
N   O   X   O
N   O       O
```

Figure 9.1
Design notation for the two-group pre-post non-equivalent groups design.

The two lines in the design indicate that the study was comprised of two groups. The two groups were nonrandomly assigned as indicated by the N. Both groups were measured before the program or treatment occurred as indicated by the first O in each line. Following this pre-observation, the group in the first line received a program or treatment, while the group in the second line did not. Finally, both groups were measured subsequent to the program.

Another common design is the posttest-only randomized experiment. The design can be depicted as shown in Figure 9.2.

```
R   X   O
R       O
```

Figure 9.2
The posttest-only randomized experimental design.

Here, two groups are randomly selected with one group receiving the program and one acting as a comparison group. Both groups are measured after the program is administered.

Expanding a Design

With this brief review of design notation, you are now ready to understand one of the basic procedures you can use to create a tailored design—the idea of expanding basic design elements. Expanding involves combining the four basic design elements in different ways to arrive at a specific design that is appropriate for the setting at hand. As a reference or basis for all expansion, think of a design that includes only a cause and its observed effect (see Figure 9.3).

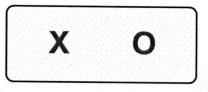

Figure 9.3
The simplest causal design with the cause and its observed effect.

This is the simplest design in causal research and serves as a starting point for the development of tailored strategies. When you add to this basic design, you are essentially expanding one of the four basic elements described previously. Each possible expansion has implications both for the cost of the study and for the threats that might be ruled out. Next I will discuss the four most common ways to expand on this simple design.

Expanding Across Time

You can add to the basic design by including additional observations either before or after the program, or by adding or removing the program or different programs. For example, you might add one or more pre-program measurements and achieve the design shown in Figure 9.4.

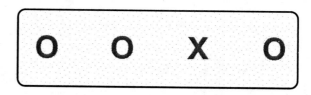

Figure 9.4
A double-pretest single-group design created by expanding across time.

The addition of such pretests provides a baseline that, for instance, helps to assess the potential of a maturation or testing threat. If a change occurs between the first and second pre-program measures, it is reasonable to expect that similar changes might take place between the second pretest and the posttest even in the absence of the program. However, if no change occurs between the two pretests, you might more confidently assume that maturation or testing is not a likely alternative explanation for the cause-effect relationship you hypothesized. Similarly, you could add additional post-program measures, which would be useful for determining whether an immediate program effect decays over time, or whether there is a lag in time between the initiation of the program and the occurrence of an effect. You might also add and remove the program over time as shown in Figure 9.5.

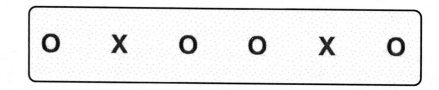

Figure 9.5
An add-remove design formed by expanding program and observation elements over time.

The design notation in Figure 9.5 shows one form of what is sometimes called the ABAB design that is frequently used in clinical psychology and psychiatry. The design is particularly strong against a **history threat** because when you repeat the program, it is less likely that unique historical events are responsible for replicated outcome patterns.

Expanding Across Programs

You have just seen that you can expand the program by adding it or removing it across time. Another way to expand the program would be to partition it into different levels of treatment. For example, in a study of the effect of a novel drug on subsequent behavior, you might use more than one dosage of the drug (see the design notation in Figure 9.6).

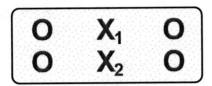

Figure 9.6
A two-treatment design formed by expanding across programs.

This design is an example of a simple factorial design with one factor having two levels. Notice that group assignment is not specified, indicating that any type of assignment might have been used. This is a common strategy in a sensitivity or parametric study where the primary focus is on the effects obtained at various program levels. In a similar manner, you might expand the program by varying specific components of it across groups, which might be useful if you wanted to study different modes of the delivery of the program, different sets of program materials, and the like. Finally, you can expand the program by using theoretically polarized or opposite treatments. A comparison group is one example of such a polarization. Another might involve use of a second program that you expect to have an opposite effect on the outcome measures. A strategy of this sort provides evidence that the outcome measure is sensitive enough to differentiate between different programs.

Expanding Across Observations

At any point in time in a research design, it is usually desirable to collect multiple or redundant measurements. For example, you might add a number of measures that are similar to each other to determine whether their results converge. Or, you might want to add measurements that theoretically should not be affected by the program in question to demonstrate that the program discriminates between effects. Strategies of this type are useful for achieving convergent and discriminant validity of measures as discussed in Chapter 3, "The Theory of Measurement." Another way to expand the observations is by proxy measurements (see the discussion of proxy pretest designs in Chapter 8, "Quasi-Experimental Design"). Assume that you wanted to study a new educational program but neglected to take pre-program measurements. You might use a standardized achievement test for the posttest and grade point average records as a proxy measure of student achievement prior to the initiation of the program. Finally, you might also expand the observations through the use of "recollected" measures. Again, if you were conducting a study and had neglected to administer a pretest or desired information in addition to the pretest information, you might ask participants to recall how they felt or behaved prior to the study and use this information as an additional measure. Different measurement approaches obviously yield data of different quality. What is advocated here is the use of multiple measurements rather than reliance on only a single strategy.

Expanding Across Groups

Often, it will be to your advantage to add additional groups to a design to rule out specific threats to validity. For example, consider the pre-post two-group randomized experimental design in Figure 9.7.

Figure 9.7
The basic pre-post randomized experimental design.

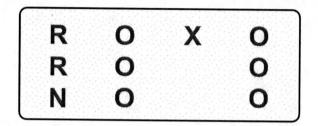

If this design were implemented within a single institution where members of
the two groups were in contact with each other, one might expect intergroup communication, group rivalry, or demoralization of a group denied a desirable treatment or given an undesirable one to pose threats to the validity of the causal
inference. (Social threats to internal validity are covered in Chapter 6, "Design.") In
such a case, you might add an additional nonequivalent group from a similar institution that consists of persons unaware of the original two groups (see Figure 9.8).

Figure 9.8
A randomized experiment
expanded with a nonequiv-
alent control group.

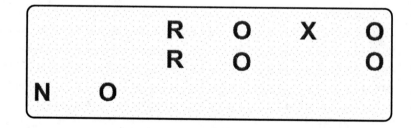

In a similar manner, whenever you use nonequivalent groups in a study it is
usually advantageous to have multiple replications of each group. The use of many
nonequivalent groups helps minimize the potential of a particular selection bias
affecting the results. In some cases, it may be desirable to include the norm group
as an additional group in the design. Norming group averages are available for
most standardized achievement tests, for example, and might comprise an additional nonequivalent control group. You can also use cohort groups in a number
of ways. For example, you might use a single measure of a cohort group to help
rule out a testing threat (see Figure 9.9).

Figure 9.9
A randomized experiment
expanded with a nonequiv-
alent group to help rule
out a testing threat.

```
              R    O    X    O
              R    O         O

      N    O
```

In this design, the randomized groups might be sixth graders from the same
school year, and the cohort might be the entire sixth grade from the previous academic year. This cohort group did not take the pretest, and if it is similar to the
randomly selected control group, it would provide evidence for or against the
notion that taking the pretest had an effect on posttest scores. You might also use
pre-post cohort groups (see Figure 9.10).

Here, the treatment group consists of sixth graders, the first comparison
group of seventh graders in the same year, and the second comparison group consists of the following year's sixth graders (the fifth graders during the study year).
Strategies of this sort are particularly useful in nonequivalent designs where *selection bias* is a potential problem and where routinely collected institutional data is

available. Finally, one other approach for expanding the groups involves partitioning groups with different assignment strategies. For example, you might randomly divide nonequivalent groups or select nonequivalent subgroups from randomly assigned groups. An example of this sort involving the combination of *random assignment* and assignment by a cutoff is discussed in detail in the following section.

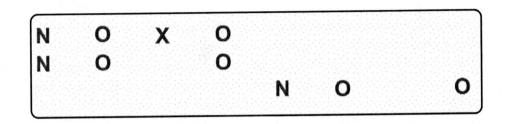

Figure 9.10
A nonequivalent group design expanded with an additional nonequivalent group.

Considering the basic elements of a research design or the possibilities for expansion are not alone sufficient. You need to be able to integrate these elements with an overall strategy. Additionally you need to decide which potential threats are best handled by design rather than by argument, measurement, analysis, or preventive action.

9-1c A Simple Strategy for Design Construction

While no definitive approach for designing designs exists, I suggest a tentative strategy based on the notion of expansion discussed previously. First, you begin the designing task by setting forth a design that depicts the simple hypothesized causal relationship. Second, you deliberately over-expand this basic design by expanding across time, program, observations, and groups. At this step, the emphasis is on accounting for as many likely alternative explanations or threats to validity as possible using the design. Finally, you scale back this over-expanded version considering the effect of eliminating each design component. It is at this point that you face the difficult decisions concerning the costs of each design component and the advantages of ruling out specific threats using other approaches.

Several advantages result from using this type of approach to design construction. First, you are forced to be explicit about the decisions you create. Second, the approach is conservative in nature. The strategy minimizes the chance of your overlooking a major threat to validity in constructing your design. Third, you arrive at a design that is tailored to the situation at hand. Finally, the strategy is cost-efficient. Threats you can account for by some other, less costly, approach need not be accounted for in the design itself.

9-1d An Example of a Hybrid Design

Some of the ideas discussed in the previous sections can be illustrated in an example. To my knowledge, the design I'm presenting here has never been used, although it has strong features to commend it.

Let us assume that you want to study the effects of a new compensatory education program on subsequent student achievement. The program is designed to help students who are poor in reading improve reading skills. You can begin with the simple hypothesized cause-effect relationship (see Figure 9.11).

Here, the X represents the reading program and the O stands for a reading achievement test. Assume you decide that it is desirable to add a pre-program measure so that you might investigate whether the program improves reading test scores. You also decide to expand across groups by adding a comparison group. At this point, you have the typical notation shown in Figure 9.12.

Figure 9.11
The cause-effect relationship: the starting point for
tailoring a design.

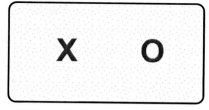

Figure 9.12
A pre-post two-group
design.

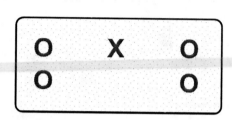

The next problem concerns how to assign the two groups. Since the program is specifically designed to help students who need special assistance in reading, you rule out random assignment because it would require denying the program to students in need. You considered the possibility of offering the program to one randomly assigned group in the first year and to the control group in the second, but ruled that out on the grounds that it would require two years of program expenses and the denial of a potentially helpful program for half of the students for a period of a year. Instead, you decide to assign students by means of a cutoff score on the pretest. All students scoring below a preselected percentile on the reading pretest would be given the program while those above that percentile would act as controls. (The RD design is covered in Chapter 8, "Quasi-Experimental Design.") However, previous experience with this strategy shows that it is difficult to adhere to a single cutoff score for assignment to a group. Of special concern is the fact that teachers or administrators might allow students who score slightly above the cutoff point into the program because they have lit-tle confidence in the ability of the achievement test to make fine distinctions in reading skills for children who score close to the cutoff. To deal with this potential problem, you decide to partition the groups using a particular combination of assignment by a cutoff and random assignment as shown in Figure 9.13.

Figure 9.13
A randomized experimen-
tal design nested within a
regression-discontinuity
design.

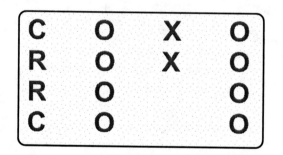

This design has two cutoff points. All those scoring below a certain percentile are assigned to the program group automatically by this cutoff. All those scoring above another higher percentile are automatically assigned to the comparison group by this cutoff. Finally, all those who fall in the interval between the cutoffs on the pretest are randomly assigned to either the program or comparison group.

This strategy has several advantages. It directly addresses the concern to teachers and administrators that the test may not be able to discriminate well between students who score immediately above or below a cutoff point. For example, a student whose true ability in reading would place him or her near the cutoff might have a bad day and therefore might be placed into the treatment or comparison group by chance factors. The design outlined in Figure 9.13 is defensible. You can agree with the teachers and administrators that the test is fallible. Nevertheless, since you need some criterion to assign students to the program, you can argue that the fairest approach would be to assign borderline cases by lottery. In addition, by combining two excellent strategies (the randomized experiment and the regression-discontinuity) you can analyze results separately for each and address the possibility that design factors might bias results.

Many other worthwhile strategies are not mentioned in the previous scenario. For example, instead of using simple randomized assignment within the cutoff interval, you might use a weighted random assignment so that students scoring lower in the interval have a greater probability of being assigned to the program. In addition, you might consider expanding the design in a number of other ways, by including double pretests or multiple posttests; multiple measures of reading skills; additional replications of the program or variations of the programs and additional groups such as norming groups; controls from other schools, and the like. Nevertheless, this brief example serves to illustrate the advantages of explicitly constructing a research design to meet the specific needs of a particular situation.

Throughout the design construction task, it is important to have in mind some endpoint—some criteria that you should try to achieve before finally accepting a design strategy. The criteria discussed in the following sections are only meant to be suggestive of the characteristics found in good research design. It is worth noting that all of these criteria point to the need to individually tailor research designs rather than accepting standard textbook strategies as is.

9-1e The Nature of Good Design

- **Theory-Grounded**—Good research strategies reflect the theories that you are investigating. When you hypothesize specific theoretical expectations, you should then incorporate them into the design. For example, when theory predicts a specific treatment effect on one measure but not on another, the inclusion of both in the design improves discriminant validity and demonstrates the predictive power of the theory.
- **Situational**—Good research designs reflect the settings of the investigation. This was illustrated in the previous section where a particular need of teachers and administrators was explicitly addressed in the design strategy. Similarly you can assess intergroup rivalry, demoralization, and competition through the use of additional comparison groups not in direct contact with the original group.
- **Feasible**—Good designs can be implemented. You must carefully plan the sequence and timing of events. You need to anticipate potential problems in measurement, adherence to assignment, database construction, and the like. Where needed, you should include additional groups or measurements in the design to explicitly correct for such problems.
- **Redundant**—Good research designs have some flexibility built into them. Often, this flexibility results from duplication of essential design features. For example, multiple replications of a treatment help to ensure that failure to implement the treatment in one setting will not invalidate the entire study.
- **Efficient**—Good designs strike a balance between redundancy and the tendency to overdesign. Where it is reasonable, other, less costly strategies for ruling out potential threats to validity are utilized.

This is by no means an exhaustive list of the criteria by which to judge good research design. Nevertheless, goals of this sort help to guide you toward a final design choice and emphasize important components that should be included.

The development of a theory of research methodology for the social sciences has largely occurred over the past half century and most intensively within the past two decades. It is not surprising, in such a relatively recent effort, that an emphasis on a few standard research designs has occurred. Nevertheless, by moving away from the notion of design selection and towards an emphasis on design construction, there is much to be gained in our understanding of design principles and in the quality of our research.

9-2 Relationships among Pre-Post Designs

Now that you are getting more sophisticated in understanding the idea of research design, you are ready to think more methodologically about some of the underlying principles that cut across design types. Here I show how the most frequently used design structures can be understood in relation to each other (see Figure 9.14).

Figure 9.14
The basic pre-post two-group design structure.

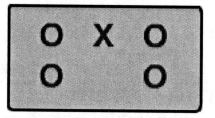

There are three major types of pre-post program-comparison group designs all sharing the basic design structure shown in Figure 9.14:

- The *RE design*
- The *NEGD design*
- The *RD design*

The designs differ only in the method by which participants are assigned to the two groups. In the RE, participants are assigned randomly. In the RD design, they are assigned using a cutoff score on the pretest. In the NEGD, assignment of participants is not explicitly controlled; they might self-select into either group, or other unknown or unspecified factors might determine assignment.

Because these three designs differ so critically in their assignment strategy, they are often considered distinct or unrelated. However, it is useful to look at them as forming a continuum, both in terms of assignment and in terms of their strength with respect to *internal validity*.

You can look at the similarity of the three designs in terms of their assignment by graphing their assignment functions with respect to the pretest variable. In Figure 9.15, the vertical axis is the probability that a specific unit (such as a person) will be assigned to the treatment group. These values, because they are probabilities, range from 0 to 1. The horizontal axis is an idealized pretest score. Each line on the graph is an assignment function for a design.

Let's first examine the assignment function for the simple pre-post randomized experiment. Because units are assigned randomly, the probability that a unit will be assigned to the treatment group is always 1/2 or .5 (assuming equal assignment probabilities are used). This function is indicated by the horizontal red line at .5 in the figure. For the RD design, I've arbitrarily set the cutoff value at the midpoint of the pretest variable and assigned units scoring below that value to the treatment and those scoring at or above that value to the control condition. (The arguments made here would generalize to the case of high-scoring treatment cases as well.) In this case, the assignment function is a simple step function, with the probability of assignment to the treatment = 1 for the pretest scores below the cutoff and = 0 for those above. It is important to note that for both the RE and RD designs it is an easy matter to plot assignment functions because assignment is explicitly controlled. This is not the case for the NEGD. Here, the idealized assignment function differs depending on the degree to which the groups are nonequivalent on the pretest. If they are extremely nonequivalent (with the treatment group scoring lower on the pretest), the assignment function would approach the step function of the RD design. If the groups are hardly nonequivalent at all, the function would approach the flat-line function of the randomized experiment.

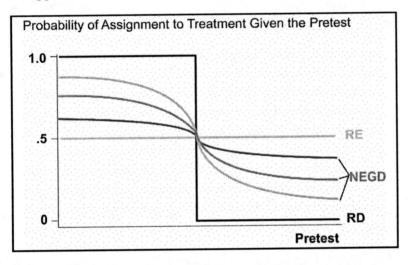

Figure 9.15
Probability of assignment to treatment for the RE, NEGD, and RD design.

The graph of assignment functions points out an important issue about the relationships among these designs: The designs are not distinct with respect to their assignment functions; they form a continuum (see Figure 9.16). On one end of the continuum is the RE design and at the other is the RD. The NEGD can be viewed as a degraded RD or RE depending on whether the assignment function more closely approximates one or the other.

You can also view the designs as differing with respect to the degree to which they generate a pretest difference between the groups.

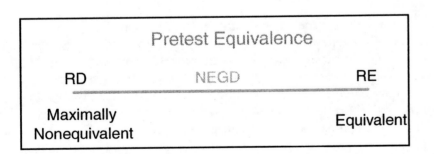

Figure 9.16
The continuum of pre-post two-group designs in terms of preprogram equivalence.

Figure 9.16 shows that the RD design induces the maximum possible pretest difference. The RE design induces the smallest pretest difference (the most equivalent). The NEGD fills in the gap between these two extreme cases. If the groups are extremely nonequivalent, the design is closer to the RD design. If they're extremely similar, it's closer to the RE design.

Finally, you can also distinguish the three designs in terms of the *a priori* knowledge they give about assignment. It should be clear that in the RE design you know perfectly the probability of assignment to treatment; it is .5 for each participant. Similarly, with the RD design, you also know perfectly the probability of assignment. In this case, it is precisely dependent on the cutoff assignment rule. It is dependent on the pretest where the RE design is not. In both these designs, you know the assignment function perfectly, and it is this knowledge that enables you to obtain unbiased estimates of the treatment effect with these designs. This is why I conclude that, with respect to internal validity, the RD design is as strong as the RE design. With the NEGD, however, you do not know the assignment function perfectly. Because of this, you need to model this function either directly or indirectly (for example, through reliability corrections).

The major point is that you should not look at these three designs as entirely distinct. They are related by the nature of their assignment functions and the degree of pretest nonequivalence between groups. This continuum has important implications for understanding the statistical analyses of these designs. (To learn more about statistical analysis, read Chapter 10, "Analysis.")

9-3 Contemporary Issues in Research Design[2]

It is fitting to end this section on research design by reflecting on where the research design endeavor stands today and trying to identify what the major, cutting-edge issues in design currently are. Of course, cutting-edge issues can always turn into a two-edged sword, so let's be careful!

Research design is a relatively recent invention. It really didn't exist in any formal sense prior to the 20th century and didn't really become delineated until the 1950s and 1960s. In the last half of the 20th century, this area has primarily involved explication of two interrelated topics: the theory of the validity of casual inferences and a taxonomy of the research designs that allow the examination of causal hypotheses.

Here I want to make the case that in the past decade traditional thinking has moved beyond the traditional thinking about design as simply a collection of specific designs and threats to validity has been replaced with a more integrated, synthetic view of design as part of a general logical and epistemological framework for research. To support this view that the notion of research design is evolving toward increasing integration, I will present a number of themes that seem to characterize current thinking and that cut across validity typologies and design taxonomies. This list of themes may also be viewed as a tentative description of the advances in thinking about research design in social research.

9-3a The Role of Judgment

One theme that underlies most of the others and that illustrates the increasing awareness of the tentativeness and frailty of research concerns the importance of human judgment in research. I know it's probably obvious to you that the personal subjective judgments of researchers has a major effect on research, but believe it or not, I and a lot of my colleagues really seemed to lose sight of this fact over the past half century and are only rediscovering it now. We were lured by the idea that we might be able to mechanize the research design process, to automate it in a sense to minimize the role of human judgment and (we thought) improve the objectivity of our work. But I think we now realize that objectivity (at least in the old-fashioned positivist sense) isn't all it was cracked up to be and that it is heavily dependent on human judgment itself. Researchers are beginning to think

[2] Parts of this section were based on Trochim, W. (Ed.), (1986). Editor's Notes. *Advances in Quasi-Experimental Design and Analysis. New Directions for Program Evaluation Series*, Number 31, San Francisco, CA: Jossey-Bass.

about the psychological components of cause-effect relationships and causal reasoning and are increasingly incorporating models of the judgmental process into their research designs and analyses. And researchers are also recognizing more clearly the sociological bases of scientific thought and the fact that science is at root a human enterprise. We increasingly recognize that scientific communities have social norms and customs and often operate like tribal groups (and, unfortunately, are sometimes as primitive). The positivist, mechanistic view is all but gone from contemporary design thinking, and what remains is a more judgmental and ironically, a more scientifically sensible perspective.

In the early days, methodologists took a taxonomic approach to design, laying out a collection of relatively discrete research designs and discussing how weak or strong they were for valid causal inference. Presentations of research designs were full of discussions of classification issues and specialized design notation systems (a lot like the X and O system of notation I present here and which my students fondly refer to as the tic-tac-toe school of design notation). Almost certainly, these early design proponents recognized that there was a virtual infinity of design variations and that validity was more complexly related to theory and context than their presentations implied. Nonetheless, what seemed to evolve was a cookbook approach to design that largely involved picking a design off the shelf and checking off lists of validity threats.

In the past few decades, we've gotten a little more sophisticated than that, constructing tailored research designs as combinations of more elemental units (for example, assignment strategies, measurement occasions) based on the specific contextual needs and plausible alternative explanations for a treatment effect (as described in the first section in this chapter). The implication for you is that you should focus on the advantages of different combinations of design features rather than on a relatively restricted set of prefabricated designs. In writing this text, I try (without always succeeding) to encourage you to break away from this canned, off-the-shelf, taxonomic design mentality, and I emphasize design principles and issues that cut across the traditional distinctions between true experiments, non-experiments, and quasi-experiments (as in the discussion of the previous section of this chapter).

9-3b The Case for Tailored Designs

Research design has sometimes been criticized for encouraging an atheoretical, black-box research mentality. People are assigned to either complex, convoluted programs, or (often) to equally complex comparison conditions. The machinery of *random assignment* (or our quasi-experimental attempts to approximate random assignment) are the primary means of defining whether the program has an effect. If you think about it, this comparison group mentality is inherently atheoretical and noncontextual. It assumes that the same design mechanism works in exactly the same way whether you apply it in studies of mental health, criminal justice, income maintenance, or education.

There is nothing inherently wrong with this program-group-versus-comparison-group logic. The problem is that it may be a rather crude, uninformative approach. In the two-group case, you are simply creating a dichotomous input into reality. If you observe a posttest difference between groups, it could be explained by this dichotomous program-versus-comparison-group input or by any number of alternative explanations, including differential attrition rates, intergroup rivalry and communication, initial selection differences among groups, or different group histories. Researchers usually try to deal with these

9-3c The Crucial Role of Theory

alternative explanations by ruling them out through argument, additional measurement, patched-up design features, and auxiliary analysis.

But we now see that there may be another way to approach research that emphasizes theoretical explanation more and simplistic design structure less. For instance, we have begun to emphasize greater use of patterns in research by using more complex theory-driven predictions that, if corroborated, allow fewer plausible alternative explanations for the effect of a program. (*Pattern matching* is covered in Chapter 8, "Quasi-Experimental Design.") Because appropriate theories may not be readily available, especially for the evaluation of contemporary social programs, we are developing methods and processes to help people articulate the implicit theories that program administrators and stakeholder groups have in mind and which presumably guide the formation and implementation of the program.

9-3d Attention to Program Implementation

A theory-driven approach to research will be futile unless we can demonstrate that the program was in fact carried out or implemented as the theory intended. I know this is obvious to you, but once again, it's astonishing how often people like me forget these basic truths. In the past few decades, we have seen the development of program implementation theory that looks at the process of program execution as an important part of research itself. For instance, one approach emphasizes the development of organizational procedures and training systems that accurately transmit the program and that anticipate likely institutional sources of resistance. Another strategy involves the assessment of program delivery through program audits, management information systems, and the like. This emphasis on program implementation has further obscured the traditional distinction between process and outcome evaluation. At the least, it is certainly clear that good research cannot be accomplished without attending to program processes, and we are continuing to develop better notions of how to combine these two efforts.

9-3e The Importance of Quality Control

Over and over, our experience with research has shown that even the best-laid research plans often go awry in practice, sometimes with disastrous results. Okay, I know this is another one of those things that should have been obvious, but at least we're finally beginning to catch on now. Over the past decade, researchers have begun to pay increasing attention to the integrity and quality of research designs in real-world settings. One way to do this is to go to people who know something about data integrity and quality assurance and incorporate techniques used by these other professions: accounting, auditing, industrial quality control. For instance, double-bookkeeping can be used to keep verifiable records of research participation. Acceptance sampling can be an efficient method for checking accuracy in large data collection efforts where an exhaustive examination of records is impractical or excessive in cost. These issues are particularly important in quasi-experimental research design, where it is especially important to demonstrate that sampling, measurement, group assignment, and analysis decisions do not interact with program participation in ways that can confound the final interpretation of results.

9-3f The Advantages of Multiple Perspectives

Researchers have long recognized the importance of replication and systematic variation in research. In the past few years, we have rediscovered this principle. (There does seem to be an awful lot of re-discovering going on in this discussion, doesn't there?) The emphasis on multiple perspectives rests on the notion that no single point of view will ever be sufficient for understanding a phenomenon with validity. Multiple realizations—of research questions, measures, samples, designs, analyses, replications, and so on—are essential for convergence on the truth (and even then we're lucky if we get there). However, such a varied approach can become a methodological and epistemological Pandora's box unless researchers apply critical judgment in deciding which multiples to use in a study or set of studies. That's the challenge, and researchers are only beginning to address it.

The history of research design is inseparable from the development of the theory of the validity of causal inference. For decades researchers have been arguing about the definition of validity and debating whether it's more important to the establishment of a cause-effect relationship (*internal validity*) or whether we should emphasize generalizability (*external validity*). Some researchers argued that it was more important to nail down the cause-effect relationship even for nonrepresentative people in one place at one time and then worry about generalizing in subsequent studies that attempt to replicate the original study. Others worried that it doesn't make sense to pour our resources into intense rigorous studies of a particular group in one place and at one time because this has no generalizability and little policy relevance. Believe it or not, I remember having numerous intense debates about this dilemma as a graduate student. Of course, the obvious solution—that we want to achieve a balance between internal and external validity, between establishing the cause-effect relationship with precision and sampling broadly enough to have some generalizability—has emerged with painful slowness over time. But, at least we got there. More and more, research design is seen as a balancing act, using judgment to allocate precious and scarce resources to blend different levels of validity.

9-3g Evolution of the Concept of Validity

In the past decade, researchers have made considerable progress toward complicating statistical analyses to account for increasingly complex contexts and designs. For all of you who have to take statistics this is, of course, the bad news. In the past 50 years, we have developed more complex statistics for dealing with measurement error, creating dichotomous dependent variables, estimating invisible traits and characteristics, and so on. In fact, I think that many of these advances are among the most important contributions social science has made in the past fifty years. Too bad so few people understand them! Of course, it would help if we could learn how to teach statistics—especially the newer, more complex and exciting approaches—to real people. Who knows, maybe we'll accomplish that in the next century. In the meantime, those of you who have to slog through advanced stats courses can perhaps take heart that the complexity you're grappling with actually represents a legitimate advance.

Parallel to the development of these increasingly complex, realistic statistical models, cynicism has deepened among researchers about the ability of any single model or analysis to be sufficient. (And that's really saying something because researchers started out as a cynical crowd.) Increasingly researchers are calling for multiple statistical analyses and using the results to bracket the likely true estimates. Researchers have virtually abandoned hope of finding a single correct analysis, and have accordingly moved to multiple analyses that are based on systematically distinct assumptional frameworks and that rely in an increasingly direct way on the role of judgment.

9-3h Development of Increasingly Complex Realistic Analytic Models

SUMMARY

So where does this leave all of us who do social research? The good news is that all of these advances suggest that researchers have become much more realistic about what research can accomplish. Gone are the heady days of the 60s and 70s where we hoped to be able to turn applied social research into a branch of science akin to physics or chemistry. The bad news is that this makes our lives considerably more complicated. Researchers have discovered a lot of problems in our initial approaches to social research and we've invented ever more complicated solutions for them. The overall picture that emerges about contemporary research is that research design is judgmental. It is based on multiple and varied sources of evidence; it should be multiplistic in realization; it must attend to process as well as to outcome; it is better off when theory driven; and it leads ultimately to multiple analyses that attempt to bracket the program effect within some reasonable range.

In one sense, this is hardly a pretty picture. Contemporary views about research design and its role in causal inference are certainly more tentative and critical than they were in 1965 or perhaps even in 1979. But, this more integrated and complex view of research has emerged directly from our experiences in the conduct of such studies. Perhaps the social research community is learning how to do this stuff better. At least, that's the hope.

Part

5

Analysis

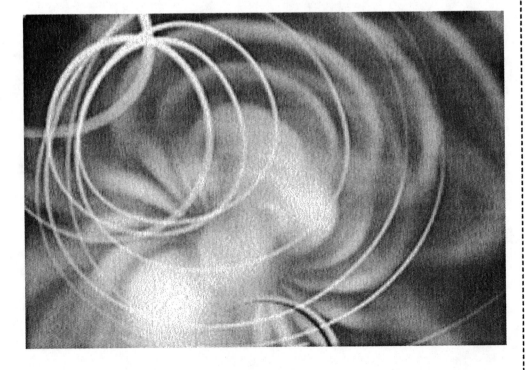

Chapter 10
Analysis

Chapter 11
Analysis for Research Design

Chapter 12
Write-Up

Analysis

By the time you get to the analysis of your data, most of the really difficult work has been done. It's much more difficult to define the research problem; develop and implement a sampling plan; conceptualize, operationalize, and test your measures; and develop a design structure. If you have done this work well, the analysis of the data is usually straightforward.

In most social research, data analysis involves three major steps, performed in roughly this order:

- Data preparation involves checking or logging the data in; checking the data for accuracy; entering the data into the computer; transforming the data; and developing and documenting a database structure that integrates the various measures.
- Descriptive statistics describe the basic features of the data in a study. They provide simple summaries about the sample and the measures. Together with simple graphics analysis, they form the basis of virtually every quantitative analysis of data. With descriptive statistics, you are simply describing what is—what the data shows.
- Statistical analysis of the research design tests your research hypotheses. In experimental and quasi-experimental designs, you use statistics to determine whether the program or treatment has a statistically detectable effect.

In most research projects, descriptions of how the data was prepared tend to be brief and to focus on only the more unique aspects of your study, such as specific data transformations you performed. The descriptive statistics that you actually look at can be voluminous. In most write-ups, you carefully select and organize these statistics into summary tables and graphs that show only the most relevant or important information. After you describe the data, you construct specific analyses for each of the research questions or hypotheses raised in your research design. In most analysis write-ups, it's especially critical that you not miss the forest for the trees. If you present too much detail, the reader may not be able to follow the central line of the results. Often extensive analysis details are appropriately relegated to appendices, reserving only the most critical analysis summaries for the body of the report itself.

This chapter discusses the basics of data analysis. I save the topic of data analysis for your research design for next chapter. However, I'll warn you right now that this is not a statistics text. I'll cover lots of statistics, some elementary and some advanced, but I'm not trying to teach you statistics here. Instead, I'm trying to get you to think about data analysis and how it fits into the broader context of your research.

Key Terms

0.05 level of significance
alpha level
causal
central tendency
codebook
conclusion validity
construct validity
correlation
correlation matrix
degrees of freedom (df)
descriptive statistics
dispersion
distribution
double entry
external validity
fishing and the error rate
  problem
frequency distribution
hypothesis
internal validity
mean
median
mode
Pearson Product Moment
  Correlation
qualitative
quantitative
range
reliability
standard deviation
statistical power
symmetric matrix
threat to conclusion validity
variance

I'll begin this chapter by discussing *conclusion validity*, the validity of inferences you draw from your data analyses. This will give you an understanding of some of the key principles involved in any research analysis. Then I'll cover the often-overlooked issue of data preparation. This includes all of the steps involved in cleaning and organizing the data for analysis. I then introduce the basic descriptive statistics and consider some general analysis issues that set the stage for consideration of the analysis of the major research designs in the Chapter 11, "Analysis for Research Design."

10-1 Conclusion Validity

Of the four types of validity (see also *internal validity, construct validity,* and *external validity*), *conclusion validity* is undoubtedly the least considered and most misunderstood—probably due to the fact that it was originally labeled statistical conclusion validity and you know how even the mere mention of the word *statistics* will scare off most of the human race!

In many ways, conclusion validity is the most important of the four validity types because it is relevant whenever you are trying to decide whether there is a relationship in your observations (and that's one of the most basic aspects of any analysis). Perhaps I should start with an attempt at a definition:

Conclusion validity is the degree to which conclusions you reach about relationships in your data are reasonable.

For instance, if you're doing a study that looks at the relationship between socioeconomic status (SES) and attitudes about capital punishment, you eventually want to reach some conclusion. Based on your data, you might conclude that there is a positive relationship—that persons with higher SES tend to have a more positive view of capital punishment; whereas those with lower SES tend to be more opposed. Conclusion validity in this case is the degree to which that conclusion or inference is credible or believable.

Although conclusion validity was originally thought to be a statistical-inference issue, it has become more apparent that it is also relevant in qualitative research. For example, in an observational field study of homeless adolescents, a researcher might, on the basis of field notes, see a pattern that suggests that teenagers on the street who use drugs are more likely to be involved in more complex social networks and to interact with a more varied group of people than the nondrug users. Although this conclusion or inference may be based entirely on qualitative observational data, you can ask whether it has conclusion validity, that is, whether it is a reasonable conclusion about the relationship inferred from the observations.

Whenever you investigate a relationship, you essentially have two possible conclusions: either there is a relationship in your data, or there isn't. In either case, however, you could be wrong in your conclusion. You might conclude that there is a relationship when in fact, there is not; or you might infer that no relationship exists when in fact one does (but you didn't detect it).

It's important to realize that conclusion validity is an issue whenever you are talking about a relationship, even when the relationship is between some program (or treatment) and some outcome. In other words, conclusion validity also pertains to *causal* relationships. How do you distinguish it from internal validity, which is also involved with causal relationships? Conclusion validity is only concerned with whether there is a relationship; internal validity assumes you have demonstrated a relationship and is concerned with whether that relationship is causal. For instance, in a program evaluation, you might conclude that there is a positive relationship between your educational program and achievement test scores; students in the program get higher scores and students not in the program get lower ones. Conclusion validity is essentially concerned with whether that relationship is a reasonable one or not, given the data. However, it is possible to conclude that, while a relationship exists between the program and outcome, the program didn't cause the outcome. Perhaps some other factor, and not your program, was responsible for the outcome in this study. For instance, the observed differences in the outcome could be due to the fact that the program group was smarter than the comparison group to begin with. Your observed posttest differences between these groups could be due to this initial difference and not be the result of your program. This issue—the possibility that some factor other than your program caused the outcome—is what internal validity is all about. So, it is possible that in a study you can conclude that your program and outcome are related (conclusion validity) and also conclude that the outcome was caused by some factor other than the program (you don't have internal validity).

I'll begin this discussion by considering the major threats to conclusion validity—the different reasons you might be wrong in concluding that there is or isn't a relationship. You'll see that there are several key reasons why reaching conclusions about relationships is so difficult. One major problem is that it is often hard to see a relationship because your measures or observations have low *reliability;* they are too weak relative to all of the noise in the environment. Another issue is that the relationship you are looking for may be a weak one and seeing it is a bit like looking for a needle in the haystack. Sometimes the problem is that you just didn't collect enough information to see the relationship even if it is there. All of these problems are related to the idea of statistical power and so I'll spend some time trying to explain what power is in this context. Finally, you need to recognize that you have some control over your ability to detect relationships, and I'll conclude with some suggestions for improving conclusion validity.

A *threat to conclusion validity* is any factor that can lead you to reach an incorrect conclusion about a relationship in your observations. You can essentially make two kinds of errors about relationships:

10-1a Threats to Conclusion Validity

- You can conclude that there is no relationship when in fact there is. (You missed the relationship or didn't see it.)
- You can conclude that there is a relationship when in fact there is not. (You're seeing things that aren't there!)

Most threats to conclusion validity have to do with the first problem. Why? Maybe it's because it's so hard in most research to find relationships in data in the first place that it's not as big or frequent a problem; researchers tend to have more problems finding the needle in the haystack than seeing things that aren't there! So, I'll divide the threats by the type of error with which they are associated.

Finding No Relationship When There Is One (or, Missing the Needle in the Haystack)

When you're looking for the needle in the haystack, you essentially have two basic problems: the tiny needle and too much hay. You can view this as a signal-to-noise ratio problem (see Figure 10.1). The signal is the needle—the relationship you are trying to see. The noise consists of all of the factors that make it hard to see the relationship.

Figure 10.1
The signal-to-noise ratio is analogous to looking for the needle (signal) in the haystack (noise).

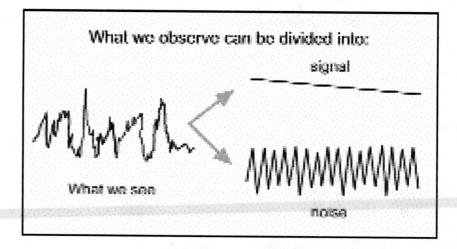

There are several important sources of noise, each of which is a threat to conclusion validity. One important threat is *low reliability of measures* (see the section "Reliability" in Chapter 3, "The Theory of Measurement"). This can be due to many factors including poor question wording, bad instrument design or layout, illegibility of field notes, and so on. In studies where you are evaluating a program, you can introduce noise through *poor reliability of treatment implementation.* If the program doesn't follow the prescribed procedures or is inconsistently carried out, it will be harder to see relationships between the program and other factors like the outcomes. Noise caused by *random irrelevancies in the setting* can also obscure your ability to see a relationship. In a classroom context, the traffic outside the room, disturbances in the hallway, and countless other irrelevant events can distract the researcher or the participants. The types of people you have in your study can also make it harder to see relationships. The threat here is due to the *random heterogeneity of respondents.* If you have a diverse group of respondents, group members are likely to vary more widely on your measures or observations. Some of their variability may be related to the phenomenon you are looking at, but at least part of it is likely to constitute individual differences that are irrelevant to the relationship you observe.

All of these threats add variability into the research context and contribute to the noise relative to the signal of the relationship you are looking for; but noise is only one part of the problem. You also have to consider the issue of the signal—the true strength of the relationship. One broad threat to conclusion validity tends to subsume or encompass all of the noise-producing factors mentioned and also takes into account the strength of the signal, the amount of information you collect, and the amount of risk you're willing to take in making a decision about whether a relationship exists. This threat is called *low statistical power.* Because this idea is so important in understanding how to make decisions about relationships, I have included a separate discussion of statistical power later in this chapter.

Finding a Relationship When There Is Not One (or Seeing Things That Aren't There)

In anything but the most trivial research study, the researcher spends a considerable amount of time analyzing the data for relationships. Of course, it's important to conduct a thorough analysis, but most people are well aware of the fact that if you play with the data long enough, you can often turn up results that support or corroborate your hypotheses. In more everyday terms, you fish for a specific result by analyzing the data repeatedly under slightly differing conditions or assumptions.

In statistical analysis, you attempt to determine the probability that your finding is a real one or a chance finding. In fact, you often use this probability to decide whether to accept the statistical result as evidence that there is a relationship. In the social sciences, researchers often use the rather arbitrary value, known as the *0.05 level of significance*, to decide whether their result is credible or could be considered a fluke. Essentially, the value 0.05 means that the result you got could be expected to occur by chance at least 5 times out of every 100 times you ran the statistical analysis.

The probability assumption that underlies most statistical analyses assumes that each analysis is independent of the other. However, that may not be true when you conduct multiple analyses of the same data. For instance, let's say you conduct 20 statistical tests and for each one you use the 0.05 level criterion for deciding whether you are observing a relationship. For each test, the odds are 5 out of 100 that you will see a relationship even if there is not one there. (That's what it means to say that the result could be due to chance.) Odds of 5 out of 100 are equal to the fraction 5/100 which is also equal to 1 out of 20. Now, in this example, you conduct 20 separate analyses. Let's say that you find that of the twenty results, only one is statistically significant at the 0.05 level. Does that mean you have found a statistically significant relationship? If you had only done the one analysis, you might conclude that you found a relationship in that result. However, if you did 20 analyses, you would expect to find one of them significant by chance alone, even if no real relationship exists in the data. This threat to conclusion validity is called the *fishing and the error rate problem*. The basic problem is that you were fishing by conducting multiple analyses and treating each one as though it was independent. Instead, when you conduct multiple analyses, you should adjust the error rate (the significance level) to reflect the number of analyses you are doing. The bottom line here is that you are more likely to see a relationship when there isn't one when you keep reanalyzing your data and don't take your fishing into account when drawing your conclusions.

Problems That Can Lead to Either Conclusion Error

Every analysis is based on a variety of assumptions about the nature of the data, the procedures you use to conduct the analysis, and the match between these two. If you are not sensitive to the assumptions behind your analysis, you are likely to draw erroneous conclusions about relationships. In *quantitative* research, this threat is referred to as the violated assumptions of statistical tests. For instance, many statistical analyses are based on the assumption that the data is distributed normally—that the population from which it is drawn would be distributed according to a normal or bell-shaped curve. If that assumption is not true for your data and you use that statistical test, you are likely to get an incorrect estimate of the true relationship. It's not always possible to predict what type of error you might make—seeing a relationship that isn't there or missing one that is.

I believe that the same problem can occur in *qualitative* research as well. There are assumptions, some of which you may not even realize, behind all qualitative methods. For instance, in interview situations you might assume that the respondents are free to say anything they wish. If that is not true—if the respondent is under covert pressure from supervisors to respond in a certain way—you may erroneously see relationships in the responses that aren't real and/or miss ones that are.

The threats discussed in this section illustrate some of the major difficulties and traps that are involved in one of the most basic areas of research—deciding whether there is a relationship in your data or observations. So, how do you attempt to deal with these threats? The following section details a number of strategies for improving conclusion validity through minimizing or eliminating these threats.

10-1b Statistical Power

Warning! I am about to launch into some technical, statistical gibberish. I think I can explain *statistical power* in a way that is understandable, but you will need to have a little patience. This is probably a good section for you read while intermittently applying some classic relaxation techniques—deep breathing, meditation, and so on. I highly recommend reading this in small doses with frequent meditative breaks. So here goes... .

Four interrelated components influence the conclusions you might reach from a statistical test in a research project:

- **Sample size**, or the number of units (people) accessible to the study
- **Effect size**, or the salience of the treatment relative to the noise in measurement
- **Alpha level** (α, or significance level), or the odds that the observed result is due to chance
- **Power**, or the odds that you will observe a treatment effect when it occurs

If you know the values for any three of these components, it is possible to compute the value of the fourth. For instance, you might want to determine what a reasonable sample size would be for a study. If you could make reasonable estimates of the effect size, alpha level, and power, it would be simple to compute (or, more likely, look up in a table) the sample size.

Some of these components are easier to manipulate than others are, depending on the project's circumstances. For example, if the project is an evaluation of an educational program or counseling program with a specific number of available consumers, the sample size is set or predetermined, or, if the drug dosage in a program has to be small due to its potential negative side effects, the effect size may consequently be small. The goal is to achieve a balance of the four components that allows the maximum level of power to detect an effect if one exists, given programmatic, logistical, or financial constraints on the other components.

Figure 10.2 shows the basic decision matrix involved in any statistical conclusion. What do I mean by a decision matrix? It is a table that shows what decisions or conclusions you can reach from any statistical analysis and how these are related to reality. All statistical conclusions involve constructing two mutually exclusive hypotheses, termed the null (labeled H_0) and alternative (labeled H_1) hypothesis (see Chapter 1, "Foundations"). Together, the hypotheses describe all possible outcomes with respect to the inference. The central decision involves determining which *hypothesis* to accept and which to reject. (Because the two are mutually exclusive and exhaustive, you will always have to accept one and reject the other.) For instance, in the typical case, the null hypothesis might be

H_0: Program Effect = 0

whereas the alternative might be

H_1: Program Effect <> 0

When you conduct a statistical analysis to test this hypothesis, you have to accept one of these: either your program works (H_1) or it doesn't (H_0). When you accept one, you automatically reject the other. This is what you conclude; but things are a little more complicated than this. Just because you conclude something doesn't make it true. (Remember your parents telling you this at some point?) Reality often has a way of being different from what we think it is. So, the other aspect of your decision has to do with the reality of the conclusion. Like your statistical conclusion, this can be expressed in only two ways—the null hypothesis is true or the alternative one is true. That's it. Those are the only options.

You should now be getting an inkling of where I am going with this somewhat convoluted presentation. The statistical decision matrix shown in Figure 10.2 shows the four possible options made by combining each possible conclusion with each possible reality.

In reality → / ↓ What we conclude	Null true / Alternative false / In reality... / • There is no real program effect / • There is no difference, gain / • Our theory is wrong	Null false / Alternative true / In reality... / • There is a real program effect / • There is a difference, gain / • Our theory is correct
Accept null / Reject alternative / We say... / • There is no real program effect / • There is no difference, gain / • Our theory is wrong	$1 - \alpha$ / THE CONFIDENCE LEVEL / The odds of saying there is no effect or gain when in fact there is none / # of times out of 100 when there is no effect, we'll say there is none	β / TYPE II ERROR / The odds of saying there is no effect or gain when in fact there is one / # of times out of 100 when there is an effect, we'll say there is none
Reject null / Accept alternative / We say... / • There is a real program effect / • There is a difference, gain / • Our theory is correct	α / TYPE I ERROR / The odds of saying there is an effect or gain when in fact there is none / # of times out of 100 when there is no effect, we'll say there is one	$1 - \beta$ / POWER / The odds of saying there is an effect or gain when in fact there is one / # of times out of 100 when there is an effect, we'll say there is one

Figure 10.2
The statistical inference decision matrix.

Figure 10.2 is a complex figure that you should take some time to study. In fact, I think you should prop it up on a table, sit down in front of it cross-legged and just stare at it for a few hours.

First, look at the header row (the shaded area). This row depicts reality—whether there really is a program effect, difference, or gain. Of course, the problem is that you never know for sure what is really happening (unless you're God). Nevertheless, because you have set up mutually exclusive hypotheses, one must be right and one must be wrong. Therefore, consider this the view from God's position, knowing which hypothesis is correct—isn't it great to get a chance to play God? The first column of the 2 × 2 table shows the case where the program does not have an effect; the second column shows where it does have an effect or make a difference.

The left header column describes the world mortals live in. Regardless of what's true, you have to make decisions about which of your hypotheses is correct. This header column describes the two decisions you can reach—that your program had no effect (the first row of the 2 × 2 table) or that it did have an effect (the second row).

Now, let's examine the cells of the 2 × 2 table. The first thing to recognize is that two of the cells represent a correct conclusion and two of them represent an error. If you say there is no relationship or effect (accept the null) and there is in reality no relationship or effect, you're in the upper-left cell and you are correct. If you say a program effect exists (accept the alternative) and there is in reality a program effect, you're in the lower-right cell and you are correct. Those are the two possible correct conclusions. Now consider the two errors. If you say there is a relationship or effect and there is not, you're in the cell on the lower left and you're wrong. We call this type of error a Type I error. (Pretty original, huh?) It is like seeing things that aren't there (as described earlier in this chapter). You're seeing an effect but you're wrong. If you say there is no effect and in fact there is an effect, you're in the cell on the upper right and you're wrong. We call this type of error—guess what—a Type II error. This type of error is like not seeing the needle in the haystack as described earlier in this chapter. There is an effect in reality, but you couldn't see it.

Each cell shows the Greek symbol used to name that cell. (You knew there had to be Greek symbols here. Statisticians can't even write their own names without using Greek letters.) Notice that the columns sum to 1 ($\alpha + (1 - \alpha) = 1$ and $\beta + (1 - \beta) = 1$). (Having trouble adding in Greek? Just keep in mind that $\alpha - \alpha = 0$, no matter what language you use for the symbol α.) Why can you sum down the columns, but not across the rows? Because if one column is true, the other is irrelevant; if the program has a real effect (the right column), it can't, at the same time, not have one. Reality can only be in one column or the other (even though, given the reality, you could be in either row). Therefore, the odds or probabilities have to sum to 1 for each column because the two rows in each column describe the only possible decisions (accept or reject the null/alternative) for each possible reality.

Below the Greek symbol is a typical value for that cell. You should especially note the values in the bottom two cells. The value of α is typically set at .05 in the social sciences. A newer, but growing, tradition is to try to achieve a standard for statistical power of at least .80. Below the typical values is the name typically given for that cell (in caps). If you weren't paying attention a few paragraphs ago, I'll give you one more chance to note that two of the cells describe errors—you reach the wrong conclusion—and in the other two cells, you reach the correct conclusion. Sometimes it's hard to remember which error is Type I and which is Type II. If you keep in mind that Type I is the same as the α or significance level, it might help you to remember that both involve seeing things that aren't there. People are more likely to be susceptible to a Type I error because they almost always want to conclude that their program works. If they find a statistical effect, they tend to advertise it loudly. On the other hand, people probably check more thoroughly for Type II errors because when they find that the program was not demonstrably effective, they immediately want to find out why. (In this case, you might hope to show that you had low power and high β—that the odds of saying there was no treatment effect even when there was were too high.) Following the capitalized common name are two ways of describing the value of each cell: one in terms of outcomes and one in terms of theory testing. In italics, I give an example of how to express the numerical value in words.

To better understand the strange relationships between the two columns, think about what happens if you want to increase your power in a study. As you increase power, you increase the chances that you are going to find an effect if it's there (wind up in the bottom row). However, if you increase the chances of winding up in the bottom row, you must, at the same time, increase the chances of making a Type I error! Although you can't sum to 1 across rows, there is clearly a relationship. Since you usually want high power *and* low Type I error, you should be able to appreciate that you have a built-in tension here. (Now might be a good moment for a meditation break. Reread the last paragraph over and over until it begins to make sense!)

We often talk about alpha (α) and beta (β) using the language of higher and lower. For instance, you might talk about the advantages of a higher or lower α-level in a study. You have to be careful about interpreting the meaning of these terms. When you talk about *higher* α-levels, you mean that you are *increasing* the chance of a Type I error. Therefore, a *lower* α-level actually means that you are conducting a *more rigorous* test.

With all of this in mind, let's consider a few common associations evident in the table. You should convince yourself of the following (each of these is it's own little meditation exercise):

- The lower the α, the lower the power. The higher the α, the higher the power.
- The lower the α, the less likely it is that you will make a Type I error (reject the null when it's true).
- The lower the α, the more rigorous the test.
- An α of .01 (compared with .05 or .10) means the researcher is being relatively careful and is only willing to risk being wrong 1 in a 100 times in rejecting the null when it's true (saying there's an effect when there really isn't).
- An α of .01 (compared with .05 or .10) limits the chances of ending up in the bottom row, of concluding that the program has an effect. This means that statistical power and the chances of making a Type I error are lower.
- An α of .01 means there is a 99 percent chance of saying there is no difference when there in fact is no difference (being in the upper-left box).
- Increasing α (for example from .01 to .05 or .10) increases the chances of making a Type I error (saying there is a difference when there is not), decreases the chances of making a Type II error (saying there is no difference when there is), and decreases the rigor of the test.
- Increasing α (for example from .01 to .05 or .10) increases power because you will be rejecting the null more often (accepting the alternative) and consequently, when the alternative is true, there is a greater chance of accepting it (power).

10-1c Improving Conclusion Validity

So let's say you have a potential problem ensuring that you reach credible conclusions about relationships in your data. What can you do about it? Here are some general guidelines you can follow in designing your study that will help improve conclusion validity.

- **Good statistical power**—The rule of thumb in social research is that you want *statistical power* to be greater than 0.8 in value (see the previous discussion on statistical power). That is, you want to have at least 80 chances out of 100 of finding a relationship when there is one. As pointed out in the discussion of statistical power, several factors interact to affect power. One thing you can usually do is collect more information—use a larger sample size. Of course, you have to weigh the gain in power against the time and expense of having more participants or gathering more data. The second thing you can do is increase your risk of making a Type I error—increase the chance that you will find a relationship when it's not there. In practical terms, you can do that statistically by raising the alpha level. For instance, instead of using a 0.05 significance level, you might use 0.10 as your cutoff point. Finally, you can increase the effect size. Since the effect size is a ratio of the signal of the relationship to the noise in the context, there are two broad strategies here. To raise the signal, you can increase the salience of the relationship itself. This is especially true in experimental contexts where you are looking at the effects of a program or treatment. If you increase the dosage of the program (for example, increase the hours spent in training or the number of training sessions), it will be easier to see the effect when the treatment is stronger. The other option is to decrease the noise (or, put another way, increase reliability).

- **Good reliability**—*Reliability* (see discussion in Chapter 3, "The Theory of Measurement") is related to the idea of noise or error that obscures your ability to see a relationship. In general, you can improve reliability by doing a better job of constructing measurement instruments, by increasing the number of questions on a scale, or by reducing situational distractions in the measurement context. When you improve reliability, you reduce noise, which increases your statistical power and improves ***conclusion validity***.

- **Good implementation**—When you are studying the effects of interventions, treatments, or programs, you can improve conclusion validity by ensuring good implementation. You accomplish this by training program operators and standardizing the protocols for administering the program.

10-2 Data Preparation

Data preparation involves checking or logging the data in; checking the data for accuracy; entering the data into the computer; transforming the data; and developing and documenting a database structure that integrates the various measures.

10-2a Logging the Data

In any research project, you might have data coming from several different sources at different times as in the following examples:

- Mail survey returns
- Coded-interview data
- Pretest or posttest data
- Observational data

In all but the simplest of studies, you need to set up a procedure for logging the information and keeping track of it until you are ready to do a comprehensive data analysis. Different researchers differ in how they keep track of incoming data. In most cases, you will want to set up a database that enables you to assess, at any time, which data is already entered and which still needs to be entered. You could do this with any standard computerized database program (such as Microsoft Access or Claris Filemaker), although this requires familiarity with such programs, or you can accomplish this using standard statistical programs (for example, SPSS, SAS, Minitab, or Datadesk) and running simple descriptive analyses to get reports on data status. It is also critical that the data analyst retain the original data records—returned surveys, field notes, test protocols, and so on—for a reasonable period of time. Most professional researchers retain such records for at least five to seven years. For important or expensive studies, the original data might be stored in a data archive. The data analyst should always be able to trace a result from a data analysis back to the original forms on which the data was collected. A database for logging incoming data is a critical component in good research record keeping.

10-2b Checking the Data for Accuracy

As soon as you receive the data, you should screen it for accuracy. In some circumstances, doing this right away allows you to go back to the sample to clarify any problems or errors. You should ask the following questions as part of this initial data screening:

- Are the responses legible/readable?
- Are all important questions answered?
- Are the responses complete?
- Is all relevant contextual information included (for example, data, time, place, and researcher)?

In most social research, quality of measurement is a major issue. Ensuring that the data collection process does not contribute inaccuracies helps ensure the overall quality of subsequent analyses.

The database structure is the manner in which you intend to store the data for the study so that it can be accessed in subsequent data analyses. You might use the same structure you used for logging in the data; or in large complex studies, you might have one structure for logging data and another for storing it. As mentioned previously, there are generally two options for storing data on computer: database programs and statistical programs. Usually database programs are the more complex of the two to learn and operate, but they allow you greater flexibility in manipulating the data.

In every research project, you should generate a printed ***codebook*** that describes the data and indicates where and how it can be accessed. Minimally the codebook should include the following items for each variable:

- Variable name
- Variable description
- Variable format (number, data, text)
- Instrument/method of collection
- Date collected
- Respondent or group
- Variable location (in database)
- Notes

The codebook is an indispensable tool for the analysis team. Together with the database, it should provide comprehensive documentation that enables other researchers who might subsequently want to analyze the data to do so without any additional information.

10-2c Developing a Database Structure

You can enter data into a computer in a variety of ways. Probably the easiest is to just type the data in directly. To ensure a high level of data accuracy, you should use a procedure called ***double entry***. In this procedure, you enter the data once. Then, you use a special program that allows you to enter the data a second time and checks the second entries against the first. If there is a discrepancy, the program notifies you and enables you to determine which is the correct entry. This double-entry procedure significantly reduces entry errors. However, these double-entry programs are not widely available and require some training. An alternative is to enter the data once and set up a procedure for checking the data for accuracy. For instance, you might spot check records on a random basis.

After you enter the data, you will use various programs to summarize the data that enable you to check that all the data falls within acceptable limits and boundaries. For instance, such summaries enable you to spot whether there are persons whose age is 601 or whether anyone entered a 7 where you expect a 1-to-5 response.

10-2d Entering the Data into the Computer

10-2e Data Transformations

After the data is entered, it is almost always necessary to transform the raw data into variables that are usable in the analyses. This is often accomplished by using a transformation, that is, by transforming the original data into a form that is more useful or usable. There are a variety of transformations that you might perform. The following are some of the more common ones:

- **Missing values:** Many analysis programs automatically treat blank values as missing. In others, you need to designate specific values to represent missing values. For instance, you might use a value of -99 to indicate that the item is missing. You need to check the specific program you are using to determine how to handle missing values.

- **Item reversals:** On scales and surveys, the use of reversal items (see Chapter 4, "Survey Research and Scaling") can help reduce the possibility of a response set. When you analyze the data, you want all scores for scale items to be in the same direction where high scores mean the same thing and low scores mean the same thing. In these cases, you have to reverse the ratings for some of the scale items. For instance, let's say you had a five-point response scale for a self-esteem measure where 1 meant strongly disagree and 5 meant strongly agree. One item is "I generally feel good about myself." If respondents strongly agree with this item, they will put a 5, and this value would be indicative of higher self-esteem. Alternatively, consider an item like "Sometimes I feel like I'm not worth much as a person." Here, if a respondent strongly agrees by rating this a 5, it would indicate low self-esteem. To compare these two items, you would reverse the scores. (Probably you'd reverse the latter item so that high values always indicate higher self-esteem.) You want a transformation where if the original value was 1, it's changed to 5; 2 is changed to 4; 3 remains the same; 4 is changed to 2; and 5 is changed to 1. Although you could program these changes as separate statements in most programs, it's easier to do this with a simple formula like the following:

  New Value = (High Value + 1) - Original Value

  In our example, the *high value* for the scale is 5; so to get the new (transformed) scale value, you simply subtract the *original value* on each reversal item from 6 (that is, 5 + 1).

- **Scale totals:** After you transform any individual scale items, you will often want to add or average across individual items to get a total score for the scale.

- **Categories:** You will want to collapse many variables into categories. For instance, you may want to collapse income estimates (in dollar amounts) into income ranges.

10-3 Descriptive Statistics

Descriptive statistics describe the basic features of the data in a study. They provide simple summaries about the sample and the measures. Together with simple graphics analysis, they form the basis of virtually every quantitative analysis of data.

Descriptive statistics present quantitative descriptions in a manageable form. In a research study, you may have many measures, or you might measure a large number of people on any given measure. Descriptive statistics help you summarize large amounts of data in a sensible way. Each descriptive statistic reduces data into a simpler summary. For instance, consider a simple number used to summarize how well a batter is performing in baseball, the batting average. This single number is the number of hits divided by the number of times at bat (reported to three significant digits). A batter who is hitting .333 is getting a hit one time in every three at bats. One batting .250 is hitting one time in four. The single number describes a large number of discrete events. Or, consider the scourge of many students: the grade point average (GPA). This single number describes the general performance of a student across a potentially wide range of course experiences.

Every time you try to describe a large set of observations with a single indicator, you run the risk of distorting the original data or losing important detail. The batting average doesn't tell you whether batters hit home runs or singles. It doesn't tell whether they've been in a slump or on a streak. The GPAs don't tell you whether the students were in difficult courses or easy ones, or whether the courses were in their major field or in other disciplines. Even given these limitations, descriptive statistics provide a powerful summary that enables comparisons across people or other units.

A single variable has three major characteristics that are typically described as follows:

- The distribution
- The central tendency
- The dispersion

In most situations, you would describe all three of these characteristics for each of the variables in your study.

10-3a The Distribution

The **distribution** is a summary of the frequency of individual values or ranges of values for a variable. The simplest distribution lists every value of a variable and the number of persons who had each value. For instance, a typical way to describe the distribution of college students is by year in college, listing the number or percent of students at each of the four years. Or, you describe gender by listing the number or percent of males and females. In these cases, the variable has few enough values that you can list each one and summarize how many sample cases had the value. But what do you do for a variable like income or GPA? These variables have a large number of possible values, with relatively few people having each one. In this case, you group the raw scores into categories according to ranges of values. For instance, you might look at GPA according to the letter grade ranges, or you might group income into four or five ranges of income values.

One of the most common ways to describe a single variable is with a **frequency distribution**. Depending on the particular variable, all of the data values might be represented, or you might group the values into categories first. (For example, with age, price, or temperature variables, it is usually not sensible to determine the frequencies for each value. Rather, the values are grouped into ranges and the frequencies determined.) Frequency distributions can be depicted in two ways, as a table or as a graph. Figure 10.3a shows an age frequency distribution with five categories of age ranges defined. The same frequency distribution can be depicted in a graph as shown in Figure 10.3b. This type of graph is often referred to as a histogram or bar chart.

Distributions can also be displayed using percentages. For example, you could use percentages to describe the following:

- Percentage of people in different income levels
- Percentage of people in different age ranges
- Percentage of people in different ranges of standardized test scores

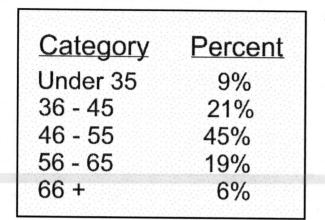

Category	Percent
Under 35	9%
36 - 45	21%
46 - 55	45%
56 - 65	19%
66 +	6%

Figure 10.3a
A frequency distribution in table form.

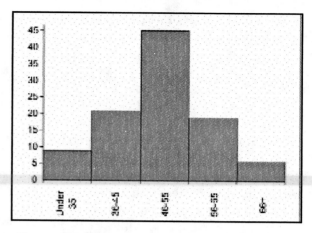

Figure 10.3b
A frequency distribution bar chart.

10-3b Central Tendency

The *central tendency* of a distribution is an estimate of the center of a distribution of values. There are three major types of estimates of central tendency:

- Mean
- Median
- Mode

The *mean* or average is probably the most commonly used method of describing central tendency. To compute the mean all you do is add up all the values and divide by the number of values. For example, the mean or average quiz score is determined by summing all the scores and dividing by the number of students taking the exam. Consider the test score values:

15, 20, 21, 20, 36, 15, 25, 15

The sum of these eight values is 167, so the mean is 167/8 = 20.875.

The *median* is the score found at the exact middle of the set of values. One way to compute the median is to list all scores in numerical order and then locate the score in the center of the sample. For example, if there are 500 scores in the list, score number 250 would be the median. If you order the eight scores shown previously, you would get

15, 15, 15, 20, 20, 21, 25, 36

There are eight scores and score number 4 and number 5 represent the halfway point. Since both of these scores are 20, the median is 20. If the two middle scores had different values, you would have to interpolate to determine the median.

The *mode* is the most frequently occurring value in the set of scores. To determine the mode, you might again order the scores as shown previously and then count each one. The most frequently occurring value is the mode. In our example, the value 15 occurs three times and is the mode. In some distributions, there is more than one modal value. For instance, in a bimodal distribution, two values occur most frequently.

Notice that for the same set of eight scores, we got three different values—20.875, 20, and 15—for the mean, median, and mode, respectively. If the distribution is truly normal (bell-shaped), the mean, median, and mode are all equal to each other.

Dispersion refers to the spread of the values around the central tendency. The two common measures of dispersion are the range and the standard deviation. The *range* is simply the highest value minus the lowest value. In the previous example distribution, the high value is 36 and the low is 15, so the range is 36 - 15 = 21.

The **standard deviation** is a more accurate and detailed estimate of dispersion because an outlier can greatly exaggerate the range (as was true in this example where the single outlier value of 36 stands apart from the rest of the values). The standard deviation shows the relation that set of scores has to the mean of the sample. Again lets take the set of scores:

15, 20, 21, 20, 36, 15, 25, 15

To compute the standard deviation, you first find the distance between each value and the mean. You know from before that the mean is 20.875. So, the differences from the mean are

15 - 20.875 = -5.875
20 - 20.875 = -0.875
21 - 20.875 = +0.125
20 - 20.875 = -0.875
36 - 20.875 = 15.125
15 - 20.875 = -5.875
25 - 20.875 = +4.125
15 - 20.875 = -5.875

Notice that values that are below the mean have negative discrepancies and values above it have positive ones. Next, you square each discrepancy:

-5.875 × -5.875 = 34.515625
-0.875 × -0.875 = 0.765625
+0.125 × +0.125 = 0.015625
-0.875 × -0.875 = 0.765625
15.125 × 15.125 = 228.765625
-5.875 × -5.875 = 34.515625
+4.125 × +4.125 = 17.015625
-5.875 × -5.875 = 34.515625

Now, you take these squares and sum them to get the Sum of Squares (SS) value. Here, the sum is 350.875. Next, you divide this sum by the number of scores minus 1. Here, the result is 350.875 / 7 = 50.125. This value is known as the **variance**. To get the standard deviation, you take the square root of the variance (remember that you squared the deviations earlier). This would be SQRT(50.125) = 7.079901129253.

Although this computation may seem convoluted, it's actually quite simple. To see this, consider the formula for the standard deviation shown in Figure 10.4.

In the top part of the ratio, the numerator, notice that each score has the mean subtracted from it, the difference is squared, and the squares are summed. In the bottom part, you take the number of scores minus 1. The ratio is the variance and the square root is the standard deviation. In English, the standard deviation is described as follows:

The square root of the sum of the squared deviations from the mean divided by the number of scores minus one.

Although you can calculate these univariate statistics by hand, it becomes quite tedious when you have more than a few values and variables. Every statistics program is capable of calculating them easily for you. For instance, I put the eight scores into SPSS and got the results shown in Table 10.1.

Figure 10.4
Formula for the standard deviation.

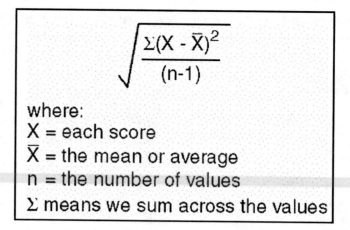

where:
X = each score
$\overline{X}$ = the mean or average
n = the number of values
Σ means we sum across the values

T A B L E **10.1**   **Table of descriptive statistics.**

N	8
Mean	20.8750
Median	20.0000
Mode	15.00
Std. deviation	7.0799
Variance	50.1250
Range	21.00

This table confirms the calculations I did by hand previously.

The standard deviation allows you to reach some conclusions about specific scores in your distribution. Assuming that the distribution of scores is normal or bell-shaped (or close to it), you can reach the following conclusions:

- Approximately 68 percent of the scores in the sample fall within one standard deviation of the mean.
- Approximately 95 percent of the scores in the sample fall within two standard deviations of the mean.
- Approximately 99 percent of the scores in the sample fall within three standard deviations of the mean.

For instance, since the mean in our example is 20.875 and the standard deviation is 7.0799, you can use the statement listed previously to estimate that approximately 95 percent of the scores will fall in the range of 20.875 (2 × 7.0799) to 20.875 + (2 × 7.0799) or between 6.7152 and 35.0348. This kind of information is critical in enabling you to compare the performance of individuals on one variable with their performance on another, even when the variables are measured on entirely different scales.

10-3d Correlation

The correlation is one of the most common and most useful statistics. A **correlation** is a single number that describes the degree of relationship between two variables. Let's work through an example to show you how this statistic is computed.

Correlation Example

Let's assume that you want to look at the relationship between two variables, height (in inches) and self-esteem. Perhaps you have a hypothesis that how tall you are affects your self-esteem. (Incidentally, I don't think you have to worry about the direction of causality here; it's not likely that self-esteem causes your height.) Let's say you collect some information on twenty individuals—all male. (The average height differs for males and females; so to keep this example simple, I'll just use males.) Height is measured in inches. Self-esteem is measured based on the average of 10, 1-to-5 rating items (where higher scores mean higher self-esteem). See Table 10.2 for the data for the 20 cases. (Don't take this too seriously; I made this data up to illustrate what a correlation is.)

T A B L E 10.2 Hypothetical data to demonstrate the correlation between height and self-esteem.

Person	Height	Self-Esteem
1	68	4.1
2	71	4.6
3	62	3.8
4	75	4.4
5	58	3.2
6	60	3.1
7	67	3.8
8	68	4.1
9	71	4.3
10	69	3.7
11	68	3.5
12	67	3.2
13	63	3.7
14	62	3.3
15	60	3.4
16	63	4.0
17	65	4.1
18	67	3.8
19	63	3.4
20	61	3.6

Now, let's take a quick look at the histogram for each variable (see Figure 10.5 and Figure 10.6).

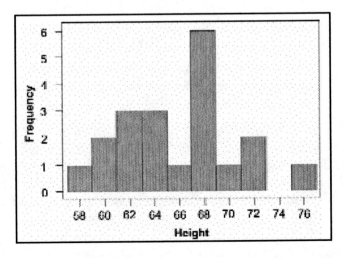

Figure 10.5
Histogram for the height variable in the example correlation calculation.

Figure 10.6
Histogram for the self-esteem variable in the example correlation calculation.

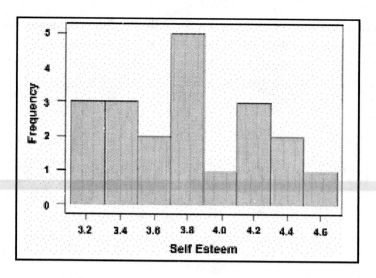

Table 10.3 shows the descriptive statistics.

TABLE 10.3 Descriptive statistics for correlation calculation example.

Variable	Mean	St Dev	Variance	Sum	Minimum	Maximum	Range
Height	65.4	4.40574	19.4105	1308	58	75	17
Self-Esteem	3.755	0.426090	0.181553	75.1	3.1	4.6	1.5

Finally, look at the simple bivariate (two-variable) plot (see Figure 10.7).

Figure 10.7
Bivariate plot for the example correlation calculation.

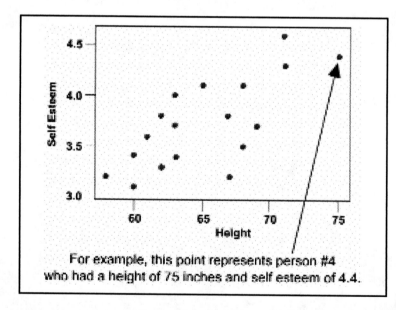

You should immediately see in the bivariate plot that the relationship between the variables is a positive one because if you were to fit a single straight line through the dots it would have a positive slope or move up from left to right. (If you can't see the positive relationship, review the section "Types of Relationships" in Chapter 1.) Since the correlation is nothing more than a quantitative estimate of the relationship, you would expect a positive correlation.

What does a positive relationship mean in this context? It means that, in general, higher scores on one variable tend to be paired with higher scores on the other and that lower scores on one variable tend to be paired with lower scores on the other. You should confirm visually that this is generally true in the plot in Figure 10.7.

Calculating the Correlation

Now you're ready to compute the correlation value. The formula for the correlation is shown in Figure 10.8.

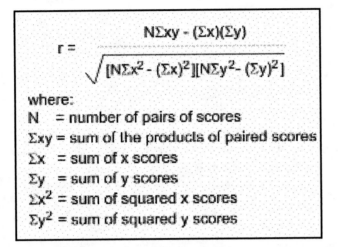

$$r = \frac{N\Sigma xy - (\Sigma x)(\Sigma y)}{\sqrt{[N\Sigma x^2 - (\Sigma x)^2][N\Sigma y^2 - (\Sigma y)^2]}}$$

where:
N = number of pairs of scores
Σxy = sum of the products of paired scores
Σx = sum of x scores
Σy = sum of y scores
Σx^2 = sum of squared x scores
Σy^2 = sum of squared y scores

Figure 10.8
The formula for the correlation.

The symbol **r** stands for the correlation. Through the magic of mathematics, it turns out that r will always be between -1.0 and +1.0. If the correlation is negative, you have a negative relationship; if it's positive, the relationship is positive. (Pretty clever, huh?) You don't need to know how I came up with this formula unless you want to be a statistician. But you probably will need to know how the formula relates to real data—how you can use the formula to compute the correlation. Let's look at the data you need for the formula. Table 10.4 shows the original data with the other necessary columns.

TABLE **10.4** **Computations for the example correlation calculation.**

Person	Height (x)	Self-Esteem (y)	xy	x^2	y^2
1	68	4.1	278.8	4624	16.81
2	71	4.6	326.6	5041	21.16
3	62	3.8	235.6	3844	14.44
4	75	4.4	330	5625	19.36
5	58	3.2	185.6	3364	10.24
6	60	3.1	186	3600	9.61
7	67	3.8	254.6	4489	14.44
8	68	4.1	278.8	4624	16.81
9	71	4.3	305.3	5041	18.49
10	69	3.7	255.3	4761	13.69

continues →

TABLE **10.4**   Continued.

Person	Height (x)	Self-Esteem (y)	xy	x²	y²
11	68	3.5	238	4624	12.25
12	67	3.2	214.4	4489	10.24
13	63	3.7	233.1	3969	13.69
14	62	3.3	204.6	3844	10.89
15	60	3.4	204	3600	11.56
16	63	4	252	3969	16
17	65	4.1	266.5	4225	16.81
18	67	3.8	254.6	4489	14.44
19	63	3.4	214.2	3969	11.56
20	61	3.6	219.6	3721	12.96
Sum =	**1308**	**75.1**	**4937.6**	**85912**	**285.45**

The first three columns are the same as those in Table 10.2. The next three columns are simple computations based on the height and self-esteem data in the first three columns. The bottom row consists of the sum of each column. This is all the information you need to compute the correlation. Figure 10.9 shows the values from the bottom row of the table (where N is 20 people) as they are related to the symbols in the formula:

Figure 10.9
The parts of the correlation formula with the numerical values from the example.

$$
\begin{aligned}
N &= 20 \\
\Sigma xy &= 4937.6 \\
\Sigma x &= 1308 \\
\Sigma y &= 75.1 \\
\Sigma x^2 &= 85912 \\
\Sigma y^2 &= 285.45
\end{aligned}
$$

Now, when you plug these values into the formula in Figure 10.8, you get the following. (I show it here tediously, one step at a time in Figure 10.10.)

Figure 10.10
Example of the computation of the correlation.

$$
r = \frac{20(4937.6) - (1308)(75.1)}{\sqrt{[20(85912) - (1308 * 1308)][20(285.45) - (75.1 * 75.1)]}}
$$

$$
r = \frac{20(4937.6) - (1308)(75.1)}{\sqrt{[1718240 - 1710864][5709 - 5640.01]}}
$$

$$
r = \frac{521.2}{\sqrt{[7376][68.99]}}
$$

$$
r = \frac{521.2}{\sqrt{508870.2}}
$$

$$
r = \frac{521.2}{713.3514}
$$

$$
r = .73
$$

So, the correlation for the 20 cases is .73, which is a fairly strong positive relationship. I guess there is a relationship between height and self-esteem, at least in this made-up data!

Testing the Significance of a Correlation

After you've computed a correlation, you can determine the probability that the observed correlation occurred by chance. That is, you can conduct a significance test. Most often, you are interested in determining the probability that the correlation is a real one and not a chance occurrence. When you are interested in that, you are testing the mutually exclusive hypotheses:

$H_0: r = 0$

$H_1: r \neq 0$

The easiest way to test this hypothesis is to find a statistics book that has a table of critical values of r. (Most introductory statistics texts would have a table like this.) As in all hypothesis testing, you need to first determine the significance level you will use for the test. Here, I'll use the common significance level of $\alpha = .05$. This means that I am conducting a test where the odds that the correlation occurred by chance are no more than 5 out of 100. Before I look up the critical value in a table, I also have to compute the *degrees of freedom or df.* The df for a correlation is simply equal to N - 2 or, in this example, is 20 - 2 = 18. Finally, I have to decide whether I am doing a one-tailed or two-tailed test (see the discussion in Chapter 1, "Foundations"). In this example, since I have no strong prior theory to suggest whether the relationship between height and self-esteem would be positive or negative, I'll opt for the two-tailed test. With these three pieces of information—the significance level (alpha = .05), degrees of freedom (df = 18), and type of test (two-tailed)—I can now test the significance of the correlation I found. When I look up this value in the handy little table at the back of my statistics book, I find that the critical value is .4438. This means that if my correlation is greater than .4438 or less than -.4438 (remember, this is a two-tailed test) I can conclude that the odds are less than 5 out of 100 that this is a chance occurrence. Since my correlation of .73 is actually quite a bit higher, I conclude that it is not a chance finding and that the correlation is statistically significant (given the parameters of the test). I can reject the null hypothesis and accept the alternative—I have a statistically significant correlation.

The Correlation Matrix

All I've shown you so far is how to compute a correlation between two variables. In most studies, you usually have more than two variables. Let's say you have a study with 10 interval-level variables and you want to estimate the relationships among all of them (between all possible pairs of variables). In this instance, you have 45 unique correlations to estimate (more later on how I knew that). You could do the computations just completed 45 times to obtain the correlations, or you could use just about any statistics program to automatically compute all 45 with a simple click of the mouse.

I used a simple statistics program to generate random data for 10 variables with 20 cases (persons) for each variable. Then, I told the program to compute the correlations among these variables. The results are shown in Table 10.5.

TABLE **10.5**   **Hypothetical correlation matrix for ten variables.**

	C1	C2	C3	C4	C5	C6	C7	C8	C9	C10
C1	1.000									
C2	0.274	1.000								
C3	-0.134	-0.269	1.000							
C4	0.201	-0.153	0.075	1.000						
C5	-0.129	-0.166	0.278	-0.011	1.000					
C6	-0.095	0.280	-0.348	-0.378	-0.009	1.000				
C7	0.171	-0.122	0.288	0.086	0.193	0.002	1.000			
C8	0.219	0.242	-0.380	-0.227	-0.551	0.324	-0.082	1.000		
C9	0.518	0.238	0.002	0.082	-0.015	0.304	0.347	-0.013	1.000	
C10	0.299	0.568	0.165	-0.122	-0.106	-0.169	0.243	0.014	0.352	1.000

This type of table is called a ***correlation matrix***. It lists the variable names (in this case, C1 through C10) down the first column and across the first row. The diagonal of a correlation matrix (the numbers that go from the upper-left corner to the lower right) always consists of ones because these are the correlations between each variable and itself (and a variable is always perfectly correlated with itself). The statistical program I used shows only the lower triangle of the correlation matrix. In every correlation matrix, there are two triangles: the values below and to the left of the diagonal (lower triangle) and above and to the right of the diagonal (upper triangle). There is no reason to print both triangles because the two triangles of a correlation matrix are always mirror images of each other. (The correlation of variable x with variable y is always equal to the correlation of variable y with variable x.) When a matrix has this mirror-image quality above and below the diagonal, it is referred to as a ***symmetric matrix***. A correlation matrix is always a symmetric matrix.

To locate the correlation for any pair of variables, find the value in the table for the row and column intersection for those two variables. For instance, to find the correlation between variables C5 and C2, look for where row C2 and column C5 is (in this case, it's blank because it falls in the upper triangle area) and where row C5 and column C2 is and, in the second case, the correlation is -.166.

Okay, so how did I know that there are 45 unique correlations when there are 10 variables? There's a simple little formula that tells how many pairs (correlations) there are for any number of variables (see Figure 10.11).

Figure 10.11
Formula for determining the number of unique correlations given the number of variables.

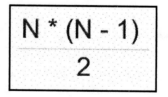

$$\frac{N * (N - 1)}{2}$$

N is the number of variables. In the example, I had 10 variables, so I know I have (10 * 9)/2 = 90/2 = 45 pairs.

Other Correlations

The specific type of correlation I've illustrated here is known as the ***Pearson Product Moment Correlation***. It is appropriate when both variables are measured at an interval level (see the discussion of level of measurement in Chapter 3, "The Theory of Measurement"). However there are other types of correlations for other circumstances. For instance, if you have two ordinal variables, you could use the Spearman Rank Order Correlation (rho) or the Kendall Rank Order Correlation (tau). When one measure is a continuous, interval level one and the other is dichotomous (two-category), you can use the Point-Biserial Correlation. The formulas for these various correlations differ because of the type of data you're feeding into the formulas, but the idea is the same; they estimate the relationship between two variables as a number between −1 and +1.

SUMMARY

This chapter introduced the basics involved in data analysis. ***Conclusion validity*** is the degree to which inferences about ***relationships*** in data are reasonable. Conclusions from data involve accepting one ***hypothesis*** and thereby rejecting its mutually exclusive and exhaustive alternative, and in reaching a conclusion, you can either be correct or incorrect. You can make two types of errors. A Type I error occurs when you conclude there is a relationship when in fact there is not (seeing something that's not there). A Type II error occurs when you conclude there is no effect when in fact there is (missing the needle in the haystack). Data preparation involves checking or logging the data in; checking the data for accuracy; entering the data into the computer; transforming the data; and developing and documenting a database structure that integrates the various measures. ***Descriptive statistics*** describe the basic features of the data in a study. The basic descriptive statistics include descriptions of the data distributions, measures of central tendency and dispersion or variability, and the different forms of correlation.

Analysis for Research Design

The heart of the data analysis—the part where you answer the major research questions—is inextricably linked to the research design. Especially in causal research, the research design frames the entire endeavor, specifying how the measures and participants are brought together. So, it shouldn't surprise you that the research design also frames the data analysis, determining the type of analysis that you can and cannot do.

This chapter describes the relationship between design and analysis. I begin with inferential statistics, which differ from *descriptive statistics* in that they are explicitly constructed to address a research question or *hypothesis*. I then present the General Linear Model (GLM). Even though each specific design has its own unique design quirks and idiosyncrasies, things aren't as confusing as they may at first seem. The GLM underlies all of the analyses presented here, so if you get a good understanding of what that's all about, the rest should be a little easier to handle. (Note that I said a little easier. I didn't say it was going to be easy.) I then move on to consider the basic randomized experimental designs, starting with the simplest—the two-group posttest-only experiment—and moving to more complex designs. Finally, I take you into the world of quasi-experimental analysis where the quasi nature of the design leads to all types of analytic problems (some of which may even make you queasy). You'll learn that you pay a price, analytically speaking, when you move away from *random assignment*. By the time you're through with all of this, you'll have a pretty firm grasp on how analysis is crafted to your research design and about the perils of applying the analysis that seems most obvious to the wrong design structure.

Key Terms

ACOVA
alpha level
ANOVA
 (Analysis of
 Variance)
bell curve
causal
confidence
 interval
control group
covariate
Cronbach's
 Alpha
degrees of
 freedom (df)
descriptive
 statistics
distribution
dummy
 variable
error term
GLM (General
 Linear Model)
hypothesis
inferential
 statistics
interaction
 effect
least squares
linear model
main effects
mean
measurement
 error
model
 specification
Nonequivalent
 Groups design
 (NEGD)

null case
null hypothesis
quasi-
 experimental
 designs
random
 assignment
Randomized
 Block design
 (RD)
regression
 analysis
regression line
Regression
 Point
 Displacement
 design(RPD)
relationship
reliability
residual
selection threat
slope
standard
 deviation
standard error
standard error
 of the
 difference
true score
 theory
t-test
t-value
variables
variance

11-1 Inferential Statistics

Inferential statistics is the process of trying to reach conclusions that extend beyond the immediate data. You are trying to use the data as the basis for drawing broader inferences (thus, the name). For instance, you use inferential statistics to try to infer from the sample data what the population might think. Or, you use inferential statistics to make judgments about the probability that an observed difference between groups is a dependable one or one that might have happened by chance in your study. Thus, you use inferential statistics to make inferences from your data to general conditions; you use descriptive statistics simply to describe what's going on in the data.

In this chapter, I concentrate on inferential statistics, which are useful in experimental and *quasi-experimental research design* or in program-outcome evaluation. To understand inferential statistics there are two issues I need you to consider, one somewhat general and theoretical and the other more concrete and methodological.

First, you can't get much more general than the *GLM*. Virtually all the major inferential statistics come from a general family of statistical models known as the GLM. This includes the t-test, Analysis of Variance (ANOVA), Analysis of Covariance (ANCOVA), regression analysis, and many of the multivariate methods like factor analysis, multidimensional scaling, cluster analysis, discriminant function analysis, and so on. Given the importance of the GLM, it's a good idea for any serious social researcher to become familiar with it. The discussion of the GLM here is elementary and only considers the simplest straight-line model; but it will familiarize you with the idea of the linear model and help prepare you for the more complex analyses described in the rest of this chapter.

Second, on a more concrete and methodological note, you can't truly understand how the GLM is used to analyze data from research designs unless you learn what a dummy variable is and how it is used. The name doesn't suggest that you are using *variables* that aren't smart or, even worse, that the analyst who uses them is a dummy! Perhaps these variables would be better described as proxy variables. Essentially a *dummy variable* is one that uses discrete numbers, usually 0 and 1, to represent different groups in your study in the equations of the GLM. The concept of dummy variables is a simple idea that enables some complicated things to happen. For instance, by including a simple dummy variable in a model, you can model two separate lines (one for each treatment group) with a single equation.

11-2 General Linear Model

The GLM underlies most of the statistical analyses that are used in applied and social research. It is the foundation for the t-test, ANOVA, ANCOVA, regression analysis, and many of the multivariate methods including factor analysis, cluster analysis, multidimensional scaling, discriminant function analysis, canonical correlation, and others. Because of its generality, the model is important for students of social research. Although a deep understanding of the GLM requires some advanced statistical training, I will attempt here to introduce the concept and provide a nonstatistical description.

11-2a The Two-Variable Linear Model

The easiest point of entry into understanding the GLM is with the two-variable case. Figure 11.1a shows a bivariate plot of two variables. These may be any two continuous variables, but in the discussion that follows, think of them as a pretest (on the x-axis) and a posttest (on the y-axis). Each dot on the plot represents the pretest and posttest score for an individual. The pattern clearly shows a positive relationship because, in general, people with higher pretest scores also have higher posttests, and vice versa.

The goal in data analysis is to summarize or describe accurately what is happening in the data. The bivariate plot shows the data. How might you best summarize this data? Figure 11.1b shows that a straight line through the cloud of data points would effectively describe the pattern in the bivariate plot. Although the line does not perfectly describe any specific point (because no point falls precisely on the line), it does accurately describe the pattern in the data. When you fit a line to data, you are using a ***linear model***. The term linear refers to the fact that you are fitting a line. The term model refers to the equation that summarizes the line that you fit. A line like the one shown in Figure 11.1b is often referred to as a ***regression line*** (a description of the relationship between two variables) and the analysis that produces it is often called ***regression analysis***.

Figure 11.1c shows the equation for a straight line. You may remember this equation from your high school algebra classes where it is often stated in the form $y = mx + b$. This equation has the following components:

y = the y-axis variable, the outcome or posttest
x = the x-axis variable, the pretest
b_0 = the intercept (value of y when x = 0)
b_1 = the slope of the line

The slope of the line is the change in the posttest given in pretest units. As mentioned previously, this equation does not perfectly fit the cloud of points in Figure 11.1a. If it did, every point would fall on the line. You need one more component to describe the way this line fits to the bivariate plot.

Figure 11.1d shows the equation for the two-variable or bivariate linear model. The component added to the equation in Figure 11.1d is an ***error term*** that describes the vertical distance from the straight line to each point. This component is called error because it is the degree to which the line is in error in describing each point. When you fit the two-variable linear model to your data, you have an x and y score for each person in your study. You input these value pairs into a computer program. The program estimates the b_0 and b_1 values as indicated in Figure 11.1e. You will actually get two numbers back that are estimates of those two values.

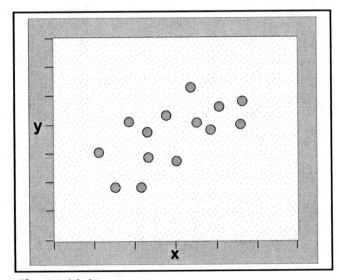

Figure 11.1a
A bivariate plot.

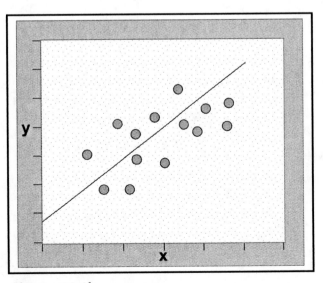

Figure 11.1b
A straight-line summary of the data.

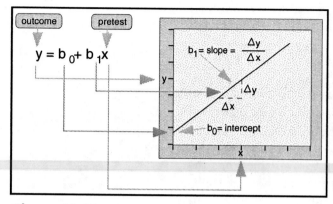

Figure 11.1c
The straight-line model.

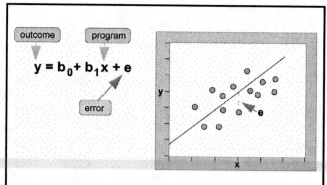

Figure 11.1d
The two-variable linear model.

Figure 11.1e
What the model estimates.

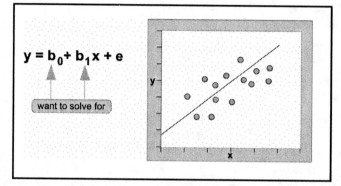

You can think of the two-variable regression line like any other descriptive statistic; it simply describes the relationship between two variables much as a **mean** describes the central tendency of a single variable. Just as the **mean** does not accurately represent every value in a distribution, the regression line does not accurately represent every value in the bivariate distribution. You use these summaries because they show the general patterns in your data and allow you to describe these patterns in more concise ways than showing the entire distribution would allow.

11-2b Extending the General Linear Model to the General Case

After this brief introduction to the two-variable case, let's extend the model to its most general case—the GLM. Essentially the GLM looks the same as the two-variable model shown in Figure 11.1e; it is an equation. The big difference is that each of the four terms in the GLM can represent a set of variables instead of representing only a single variable. So, the general linear model can be written as follows:

$$y = b_0 + bx + e$$

where
y = a set of outcome variables
x = a set of pre-program variables or covariates
b_0 = the set of intercepts (value of each y when each x = 0)
b = a set of coefficients, one each for each x

This model allows you to include an enormous amount of information. In an experimental or quasi-experimental study, you would represent the program or treatment with one or more dummy-coded variables, each represented in the equation as an additional x-value. (Although the convention is to use the symbol **Z** to indicate that the variable is a dummy-coded x.) If your study has multiple outcome variables, you can include them as a set of y-values. If you have multiple pretests, you can include them as a set of x-values. For each x-value (and each **Z**-value), you estimate a b-value that represents an x,y relationship. The estimates of these b-values and the statistical testing of these estimates is what enables you to test specific research hypotheses about *relationships* between variables or differences between groups.

The GLM allows you to summarize a variety of research outcomes. The major problem for the researcher who uses the GLM is *model specification,* which the user must enact to specify the exact equation that best summarizes the data for a study. If the model is misspecified, the estimates of the coefficients (the b-values) are likely to be biased (wrong) and the resulting equation will not describe the data accurately. In complex situations, this model specification problem can be a serious and difficult one (see, for example, the discussion of model specification in the statistical analysis of the regression-discontinuity design later in this chapter).

The GLM is one of the most important tools in the statistical analysis of data. It represents a major achievement in the advancement of social research in the twentieth century.

A *dummy variable* is a numerical *variable* used in *regression analysis* to represent subgroups of the sample in your study. It is not a variable used by dummies. In fact, you have to be pretty smart to figure out how to use dummy variables. In research design, a dummy variable is typically used to distinguish different treatment groups. In the simplest case, you would use a 0,1 dummy variable where a person is given a value of 0 if placed in the *control group* or a 1 if in the treated group.

11-2c Dummy Variables

Dummy variables are useful because they enable you to use a single regression equation to represent multiple groups. This means that you don't need to write out separate equation models for each subgroup. The dummy variables act like *switches* that turn various parameters on and off in an equation. Another advantage of a 0,1 dummy-coded variable is that even though it is a nominal-level variable, you can treat it statistically like an interval-level variable. (If this made no sense to you, you probably should refresh your memory on levels of measurement covered in Chapter 3, "The Theory of Measurement.") For instance, if you take an average of a 0,1 variable, the result is meaningful—the proportion of 1s in the distribution.

To illustrate dummy variables, consider the simple regression model for a posttest-only two-group randomized experiment shown in Figure 11.2. This model is mathematically identical to conducting a t-test on the posttest means for two groups or conducting a one-way ANOVA (as described later in this chapter). The key term in the model is β_1, the estimate of the difference between the groups. To see how dummy variables work, I'll use this simple model to show you how dummy variables can be used to pull out the separate subequations for each subgroup. Then I'll show how to estimate the difference between the subgroups by subtracting their respective equations. You'll see that you can pack an enormous amount of information into a single equation using dummy variables. All I want to show you here is that β_1 is the difference between the treatment and control groups.

Figure 11.2
Use of a dummy variable in
a regression equation.

$$y_i = \beta_0 + \beta_1 Z_i + e_i$$

where:

y_i = outcome score for the ith unit

β_0 = coefficient for the *intercept*

β_1 = coefficient for the *slope*

Z_i = 1 if i^{th} unit is in the treatment group
0 if i^{th} unit is in the control group

e_i = residual for the ith unit

To see this, the first step is to compute what the equation would be for each of the two groups separately (see Figure 11.3). For the control group, Z = 0. When you substitute that into the equation, and recognize that by assumption the error term averages to 0, you find that the predicted value for the control group is β_0, the intercept. Now, to figure out the treatment-group line, you substitute the value of 1 for Z, again recognizing that by assumption, the error term averages to 0. The equation for the treatment group indicates that the treatment group value is the sum of the two beta values.

Figure 11.3
Using a dummy variable to
create separate equations
for each dummy variable
value.

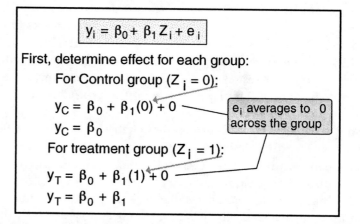

$$y_i = \beta_0 + \beta_1 Z_i + e_i$$

First, determine effect for each group:

For Control group ($Z_i = 0$):

$$y_C = \beta_0 + \beta_1(0) + 0$$
$$y_C = \beta_0$$

For treatment group ($Z_i = 1$):

$$y_T = \beta_0 + \beta_1(1) + 0$$
$$y_T = \beta_0 + \beta_1$$

e_i averages to 0 across the group

Now you're ready to move on to the second step—computing the difference between the groups. How do you determine that? Well, the difference must be the difference between the equations for the two groups that you worked out previously. In other words, to find the difference between the groups, you find the difference between the equations for the two groups! It should be obvious from Figure 11.4 that the difference is β_1. Think about what this means. The difference between the groups is β_1. Okay, one more time just for the sheer heck of it: the difference between the groups in this model is β_1!

Whenever you have a regression model with dummy variables, you can always see how the variables are being used to represent multiple subgroup equations by following the two steps described in Figures 11.3 and 11.4 as follows:

- Create separate equations for each subgroup by substituting the dummy values (as in Figure 11.3).
- Find the difference between groups by finding the difference between their equations (as in Figure 11.4).

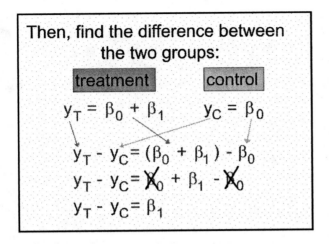

Figure 11.4
Determine the difference between two groups by subtracting the equations generated through their dummy variables.

I turn now to the discussion of the experimental designs and how they are analyzed. Perhaps one of the simplest inferential tests is used when you want to compare the average performance of two groups on a single measure to see whether there is a difference. This simple two-group posttest-only randomized experiment is usually analyzed with the simple *t-test*, which is actually just the simplest variation of the one-way ANOVA. You might want to know whether eighth-grade boys and girls differ in math test scores or whether a program group differs on the outcome measure from a control group. The factorial experimental designs are usually analyzed with the ANOVA model. *Randomized Block designs (RD)* use a special form of the ANOVA-blocking model that uses dummy-coded variables to represent the blocks. The Analysis of Covariance Experimental design uses, not surprisingly, the Analysis of Covariance statistical model.

To analyze the two-group posttest-only randomized experimental design you need an analysis that meets the following requirements:

- Has two groups
- Uses a post-only measure
- Has two distributions (measures), each with an average and variation
- Assesses treatment effect = statistical (non-chance) difference between the groups

The t-test fits the bill perfectly. The t-test assesses whether the means of two groups are *statistically* different from each other. Why is it called the t-test? Because when the statistician who invented this analysis first wrote out the formula, he used the letter "t" to symbolize the value that describes the difference between the groups. Why? Beats me. You remember the formula for the straight line from your high school algebra? You know, the one that goes y = mx + b? Well, using the name t-test is like calling that formula the y-formula. Maybe the statisticians decided they would come up with more interesting names later. Maybe they were in the same fix as the astronomers who had so many stars to name they just assigned temporary numbers until someone noteworthy enough came along. Whatever the reason, don't lose any sleep over it. The t-test is just a name and, as the bard says, what's in a name?

Before you can proceed to the analysis itself, it is useful to understand what the difference means in the question, "Is there a difference between the groups?" Each group can be represented by a bell-shaped curve that describes the group's distribution on a single variable. You can think of the **bell curve** as a smoothed histogram or bar graph describing the frequency of each possible measurement response.

11-3 Experimental Analysis

11-3a The t-Test

Figure 11.5 shows the distributions for the treated (blue) and control (green) groups in a study. Actually, the figure shows the idealized or smoothed *distribution*—the actual distribution would usually be depicted with a histogram or bar graph. The figure indicates where the control and treatment group *means* are located. The question the t-test addresses is whether the means are statistically different.

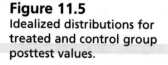

Figure 11.5
Idealized distributions for treated and control group posttest values.

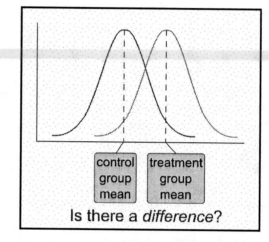

What does it mean to say that the averages for two groups are statistically different? Consider the three situations shown in Figure 11.6. The first thing to notice about the three situations is that *the difference between the means is the same in all three.* But, you should also notice that the three situations don't look the same; they tell different stories. The top example shows a case with moderate variability of scores within each group. The second situation shows the high-variability case. The third shows the case with low variability. Clearly, you would conclude that the two groups appear most different or distinct in the bottom or low-variability case. Why? Because there is relatively little overlap between the two bell-shaped curves. In the high-variability case, the group difference appears least striking (even though it is identical) because the two bell-shaped distributions overlap so much.

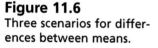

Figure 11.6
Three scenarios for differences between means.

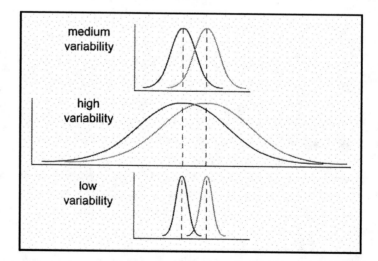

This leads to an important conclusion: when you are looking at the differences between scores for two groups, you have to judge the difference between their means relative to the spread or variability of their scores. The t-test does just this.

Statistical Analysis of the t-Test

So how does the t-test work? The formula for the t-test is a ratio. The top part of the ratio is the difference between the two means or averages. The bottom part is a measure of the variability or dispersion of the scores. This formula is essentially another example of the signal-to-noise metaphor in research; the difference between the means is the signal that, in this case, you think your program or treatment introduced into the data; the bottom part of the formula is a measure of variability that is essentially noise that might make it harder to see the group difference. The ratio that you compute is called a **t-value** and describes the difference between the groups relative to the variability of the scores in the groups. Figure 11.7a shows the formula for the t-test and how the numerator and denominator are related to the distributions.

The top part of the formula is easy to compute—just find the difference between the means. The bottom part is called the **standard error of the difference.** To compute it, take the **variance** (see Chapter 10, "Analysis") for each group and divide it by the number of people in that group minus 1. You add these two values and then take their square root. The specific formula is given in Figure 11.7b. Remember, that the variance is simply the square of the **standard deviation.** The final formula for the t-test is shown in Figure 11.7c.

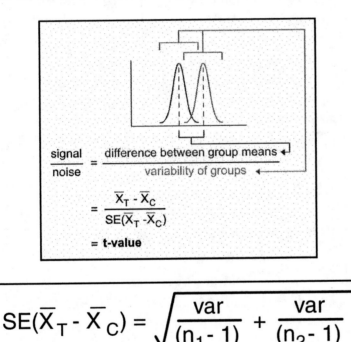

$$\frac{\text{signal}}{\text{noise}} = \frac{\text{difference between group means}}{\text{variability of groups}}$$

$$= \frac{\overline{X}_T - \overline{X}_C}{SE(\overline{X}_T - \overline{X}_C)}$$

$$= \text{t-value}$$

Figure 11.7a
Formula for the t-test.

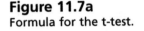

$$SE(\overline{X}_T - \overline{X}_C) = \sqrt{\frac{var}{(n_1 - 1)} + \frac{var}{(n_2 - 1)}}$$

Figure 11.7b
Formula for the standard error of the difference between the means.

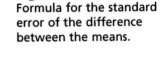

$$t = \frac{\overline{X}_T - \overline{X}_C}{\sqrt{\frac{var_1}{(n_1 - 1)} + \frac{var_2}{(n_2 - 1)}}}$$

Figure 11.7c
Formula for the t-test.

The t-value will be positive if the first mean is larger than the second value and negative if it is smaller. After you compute the t-value, you have to look it up in a table of significance to test whether the ratio is large enough to say that the difference between the groups is not likely to have been a chance finding. To test the significance, you need to set a risk level (called the **alpha level**, as described in Chapter 10, "Analysis"). In most social research, the rule of thumb is to set the alpha level at .05. This means that five times out of a hundred, you would find a statistically significant difference between the means even if there were none (meaning by chance). You also need to determine the **degrees of freedom (df)** for the test. In the t-test, the df is the sum of the persons in both groups minus 2. Given the alpha level, the df, and the **t-value,** you can look the t-value up in a standard table of significance to determine whether the t-value is large enough to be significant. If it is, you can conclude that the difference between the means for the two groups is different (even given the variability). Fortunately, statistical computer programs routinely print the significance test results and save you the trouble of looking them up in a table.

You can estimate the treatment effect for the posttest-only randomized experiment in three ways. All three yield mathematically equivalent results, a fancy way of saying that they give you the exact same answer. So why are there three different ones? In large part, these three approaches evolved independently and only after that was it clear that they are essentially three ways to do the same thing. So, what are the three ways? First, you can compute an independent t-test as described here. Second, you could compute a one-way ANOVA between two independent groups. Finally, you can use regression analysis to regress the posttest values onto a dummy-coded treatment variable. Of these three, the regression analysis approach is the most general. In fact, I describe the statistical models for all the experimental and quasi-experimental designs in regression-model terms. You just need to be aware that the results from all three methods are identical. Okay, so here's the statistical model for the t-test in regression form (see Figure 11.8).

Figure 11.8
The regression formula for the t-test or the two-group one-way Analysis of Variance (ANOVA).

$$y_i = \beta_0 + \beta_1 Z_i + e_i$$

where:
y_i = outcome score for the ith unit
β_0 = coefficient for the *intercept*
β_1 = coefficient for the *slope*
Z_i = 1 if i^{th} unit is in the treatment group
         0 if i^{th} unit is in the control group
e_i = residual for the ith unit

Look familiar? It is identical to the formula I showed in Figure 11.2 to introduce **dummy variables.** Also, you may not realize it (although I hope against hope that you do), but essentially this formula is the equation for a straight line with a random **error term** (e_i) thrown in. Remember high school algebra? Remember high school? Okay, for those of you with faulty memories, you may recall that the equation for a straight line is often given as follows:

$$y = mx + b$$

which, when rearranged can be written as follows:

$$y = b + mx$$

(The complexities of the commutative property make you nervous? If this gets too tricky, you may need to stop for a break. Have something to eat, make some coffee, or take the poor dog out for a walk.) Now you should see that in the statistical model y_i is the same as y in the straight line formula, β_0 is the same as b, β_1 is the same as m, and Z_i is the same as x. In other words, in the statistical formula, β_0 is the intercept and β_1 is the slope (see Figure 11.9).

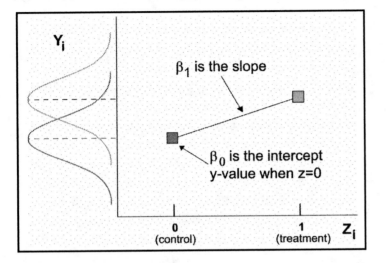

Figure 11.9
The elements of the equation in Figure 11.8 in graphic form.

It is critical that you understand that the slope, β_1, is the same thing as the posttest difference between the means for the two groups. How can a slope be a difference between means? To see this, you have to look at a graph of what's going on, which I provided for you in Figure 11.9. The graph shows the posttest on the vertical axis. This is exactly the same as the two bell-shaped curves shown in Figures 11.5 and 11.6 except that here they're turned on their sides and are graphed on the vertical dimension. On the horizontal axis, the Z variable is plotted. This variable has only two possible values: a 0 if the person is in the **control group** or a 1 if the person is in the program group. This kind of variable is a **dummy variable** because it is a stand-in variable that represents the program or treatment conditions with its two values (see the discussion of dummy variables earlier in this chapter). The two points in the graph indicate the average posttest value for the control (Z = 0) and treated (Z = 1) cases. The line that connects the two dots is only included for visual enhancement purposes; because there are no Z values between 0 and 1, there can be no values plotted where the line is. Nevertheless, you can meaningfully speak about the slope of this line—the line that would connect the posttest means for the two values of Z. Do you remember the definition of slope? (Here we go again, back to high school!) The **slope** is the change in y over the change in x (or, in this case, Z). Remember, the change in Z between the groups is always equal to 1 (for example, 1 - 0 = 1). Therefore, the slope of the line must be equal to the difference between the average y-values for the two groups. That's what I set out to show (reread the first sentence of this paragraph). β_1 is the same value that you would get if you subtracted the two means from each other. (In this case, because the treatment group equals 1, you are subtracting the control group out of the treatment group value. A positive value implies that the treatment-group mean is higher than the control-group mean; a negative value means it's lower.)

But remember at the beginning of this discussion, I pointed out that just knowing the difference between the means was not good enough for estimating the treatment effect because it doesn't take into account the variability or spread of the scores. So how do you do that here? Every regression-analysis program will give, in addition to the beta values, a report on whether each beta value is statistically significant. They report a **t-value** that tests whether the beta value differs from zero. It turns out that the t-value for the β_1 coefficient is the exact same number that you would get if you did a t-test for independent groups. And, it's the same as the square root of the F value in the two-group one-way ANOVA (because $t^2 = F$).

Here's a few conclusions from all this:

- The t-test, one-way ANOVA, and regression analysis all yield *same* results in this case.
- The regression-analysis method utilizes a dummy variable (Z) for treatment.
- Regression analysis is the most *general* model of the three.

11-3b Factorial Design Analysis

Now that you have some understanding of the **GLM** and dummy variables, I can present the models for other experimental designs rather easily. Figure 11.10 shows the regression model for a simple 2 × 2 factorial design.

Figure 11.10
Regression model for a 2 × 2 factorial design.

$$y_i = \beta_0 + \beta_1 Z_{1i} + \beta_2 Z_{2i} + \beta_3 Z_{1i} Z_{2i} + e_i$$

where:
y_i = outcome score for the ith unit
β_0 = coefficient for the intercept
β_1 = mean difference on factor 1
β_2 = mean difference on factor 2
β_3 = interaction of factor 1 and factor 2
Z_{1i} = dummy variable for factor 1
         (0 = 1 hr/wk, 1 = 4 hrs/wk)
Z_{2i} = dummy variable for factor 2
         (0 = in class, 1 = pull-out)
e_i = residual for the ith unit

In this design, you have one factor for time in instruction (1 hour/week versus 4 hours/week) and one factor for setting (in-class or pull-out). The model uses a dummy variable (represented by a Z) for each factor. In two-way factorial designs like this, you have two **main effects** and one **interaction effect**. In this model, the main effects are the statistics associated with the beta values that are adjacent to the Z-variables. The interaction effect is the statistic associated with β_3 (that is, the t-value for this coefficient) because it is adjacent in the formula to the multiplication of (interaction of) the dummy-coded Z variables for the two factors. Because there are two dummy-coded variables, and each has two values, you can write out 2 × 2 = 4 separate equations from this one general model. (Go ahead, I dare you. If you need to refresh your memory, check back to the discussion of dummy variables presented earlier in this chapter.) You might want to see if you can write out the equations for the four cells. Then, look at some of the differences between the groups. You can also write two equations for each Z variable. These equations represent the main effect equations. To see the difference between levels of a factor, subtract the equations from each other.

11-3c Randomized Block Analysis

The statistical model for the ***Randomized Block design (RD)*** can also be presented in regression analysis notation. Figure 11.11 shows the model for a case where there are four blocks or homogeneous subgroups.

$$y_i = \beta_0 + \beta_1 Z_{1i} + \beta_2 Z_{2i} + \beta_3 Z_{3i} + \beta_4 Z_{4i} + e_i$$

where:
y_i = outcome score for the ith unit
β_0 = coefficient for the intercept
β_1 = mean difference for treatment
β_2 = blocking coefficient for block 2
β_3 = blocking coefficient for block 3
β_4 = blocking coefficient for block 4
Z_{1i} = dummy variable for treatment (0 = control, 1 = treatment)
Z_{2i} = 1 if block 2, 0 otherwise
Z_{3i} = 1 if block 3, 0 otherwise
Z_{4i} = 1 if block 4, 0 otherwise
e_i = residual for the ith unit

Figure 11.11
Regression model for a Randomized Block design.

Notice that a number of ***dummy variables*** are used to specify this model. The dummy variable Z_1 represents the treatment group. The dummy variables Z_2, Z_3, and Z_4 indicate blocks 2, 3, and 4 respectively. Analogously, the beta values (βs) reflect the treatment and blocks 2, 3, and 4. What happened to Block 1 in this model? To see what the equation for the Block 1 comparison group is, fill in your dummy variables and multiply through. In this case, all four Zs are equal to 0, and you should see that the intercept (β_0) is the estimate for the Block 1 control group. For the Block 1 treatment group, $Z_1 = 1$ and the estimate is equal to $\beta_0 + \beta_1$. By substituting the appropriate dummy variable switches, you should be able to figure out the equation for any block or treatment group.

The data matrix that is entered into this analysis would consist of five columns and as many rows as you have participants: the posttest data and one column of 0s or 1s for each of the four dummy variables.

11-3d Analysis of Covariance

The statistical model for the ***ANCOVA***, which estimates the difference between the groups on the posttest after adjusting for differences on the pretest, can also be given in regression analysis notation. The model shown in Figure 11.12 is for a case where there is a single covariate, a treated group, and a control group.

$$y_i = \beta_0 + \beta_1 X_i + \beta_2 Z_i + e_i$$

where:
y_i = outcome score for the ith unit
β_0 = coefficient for the intercept
β_1 = pretest coefficient
β_2 = mean difference for treatment
Z_i = dummy variable for treatment (0 = control, 1 = treatment)
e_i = residual for the ith unit

Figure 11.12
Regression model for the ANCOVA.

The dummy variable Z_i represents the treatment group. The beta values (βs) are the parameters being estimated. The value β_0 represents the intercept. In this model, it is the predicted posttest value for the control group for a given X value (and, when X = 0, it is the intercept for the control-group regression line). Why? Because a control group case has a Z = 0, and since the Z variable is multiplied with β_2, that whole term would drop out.

The data matrix that is entered into this analysis would consist of three columns—the posttest data, one column of 0s or 1s to indicate which treatment group the participant is in, and the *covariate* score—and as many rows as you have participants.

This model assumes that the data in the two groups are well described by straight lines that have the same slope. If this does not appear to be the case, you have to modify the model appropriately. How do you do that? Well, I'll tell you the short answer, but for the complete one you need to take an advanced statistics course. The short answer is that you add the term $b_i X_i Z_i$ to the model in Figure 11.12. If you've been following along, you should be able to create the separate equations for the different values of the dummy variable Z_i and convince yourself that the addition of this term will allow for the two groups to have different *slopes*.

11-4 Quasi-Experimental Analysis

The *quasi-experimental designs* differ from the experimental ones in that they don't use *random assignment* to assign units (people) to program groups. The lack of random assignment in these designs tends to complicate their analysis considerably. For example, to analyze the *Nonequivalent Groups design (NEGD)*, you have to adjust the pretest scores for *measurement error* in what is often called a Reliability-Corrected Analysis of Covariance model. In the *RD design*, you need to be especially concerned about curvilinearity and model misspecification. Consequently, I recommend a conservative analysis approach based on polynomial regression that starts by overfitting the likely true function and then reduces the model based on the results. The *Regression Point Displacement design (RPD)* has only a single treated unit. Nevertheless, the analysis of the RPD design is based directly on the traditional ANCOVA model.

In all fairness, I have to warn you that this section is not for the faint-of-heart. The experimental designs discussed previously have fairly straightforward analysis models. You'll see here that you pay a price for not using random assignment like they do; the analyses are considerably more complex.

11-4a Nonequivalent Groups Analysis

The design notation for the NEGD shows two groups—a program and comparison group—and each is measured pre and post (see Figure 11.13). The statistical model that you might intuitively expect to be used in this situation would have a pretest variable, posttest variable, and a *dummy variable* that describes which group the person is in. These three variables would be the input for the statistical analysis.

Figure 11.13
Design notation for the NEGD

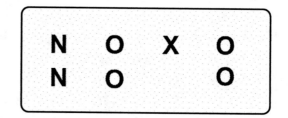

In this example, assume you are interested in estimating the difference between the groups on the posttest after adjusting for differences on the pretest.

This is essentially the ANCOVA model as described in connection with randomized experiments. (Review the discussion "Covariance Designs" and how to adjust for pretest differences in Chapter 7, "Experimental Design.") There's only one major problem with this model when used with the NEGD; it doesn't work! Here, I'll tell you the story of why the ANCOVA model fails and what you can do to adjust it so it works correctly.

A Simulation Example

To see what happens when you use the ANCOVA analysis on data from a NEGD, I created a computer simulation to generate hypothetical data. I created 500 hypothetical persons, with 250 in the program and 250 in the comparison condition. Because this is a nonequivalent design, I made the groups nonequivalent on the pretest by adding five points to each program group person's pretest score. Then, I added 15 points to each program person's posttest score. When I take the initial 5-point advantage into account, I should find a 10-point program effect. The bivariate plot in Figure 11.14 shows the data from this simulation.

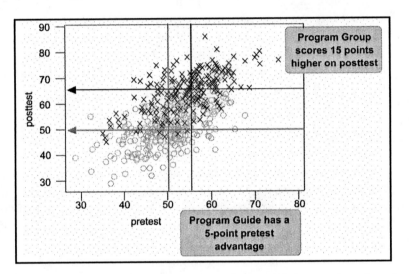

Figure 11.14
Simulated data for the NEGD.

I then analyzed the data with the ANCOVA model. Remember that the way I set this up, I should observe approximately a 10-point program effect if the ANCOVA analysis works correctly. The results are presented in Figure 11.15.

In this analysis, I put in three scores for each person: a pretest score (X), a posttest score (Y), and either a 0 or 1 to indicate whether the person was in the program (Z = 1) or comparison (Z = 0) group. The table in Figure 11.15 shows the equation that the ANCOVA model estimates.

$$y_i = 18.7 + .626X_i + 11.3Z_i$$

Predictor	Coef	StErr	t	p
Constant	18.714	1.969	9.50	0.000
pretest	0.62600	0.03864	16.20	0.000
Group	11.2818	0.5682	19.85	0.000

$$
\begin{aligned}
\bullet\, CI_{.95(\beta_2 = 10)} &= \beta_2 \pm 2SE(\beta_2) \\
&= 11.2818 \pm 2(.5682) \\
&= 11.2818 \pm 1.1364
\end{aligned}
$$

$\bullet\, CI = 10.1454 \text{ to } 12.4182$

Figure 11.15
Results of the original ANCOVA analysis of the simulated data in Figure 11.14.

The equation has the three values I put in (X, Y, and Z) and the three coefficients that the program estimates. The key coefficient is the one next to the program variable Z (labeled Group in the table). This coefficient estimates the average difference between the program and comparison groups (because it's the coefficient paired with the **dummy variable** indicating what group the person is in). The value should be 10 because I put in a 10-point difference. In this analysis, the actual value I got was 11.3 (or 11.2818, to be more precise). Well, that's not too bad, you might say. It's fairly close to the 10-point effect I created. But I need to determine whether the obtained value of 11.2818 is statistically different from the true value of 10. To see whether it is, I have to construct a **confidence interval** around the estimate and examine the difference between 11.2818 and 10 relative to the variability in the data. Fortunately, the program does this automatically. If you look in the table in Figure 11.15, you'll see that the third line shows the coefficient associated with the difference between the groups, the **standard error** for that coefficient (an indicator of variability), the t-value, and the probability value. All the **t-value** shows is that the coefficient of 11.2818 is statistically different from zero. But I want to know whether it is different from the true treatment effect value of 10. To determine this, I construct a confidence interval around the t-value, using the standard error. The 95 percent confidence interval is the coefficient plus or minus two times the standard error value. The calculation shows that the 95 percent confidence interval for the 11.2818 coefficient is 10.1454 to 12.4182. Any value falling within this range can't be considered different beyond a 95 percent level from the obtained value of 11.2818. But the true value of 10 points falls outside the range. In other words, the estimate of 11.2818 is significantly different from the true value. In still other words, the results of this analysis are biased. I got the wrong answer. In this example, the estimate of the program effect is significantly larger than the true program effect (even though the difference between 10 and 11.2818 doesn't seem that much larger, it exceeds chance levels). So, you have a problem when you apply the analysis model that intuitively makes the most sense for the NEGD. To understand why this bias occurs, look a little more deeply at how the statistical analysis works in relation to the NEGD.

The Problem

Take a look at Figure 11.16, which shows the regression lines for simulated data presented originally in Figure 11.14. These lines may look like they fit the data well. But in the previous section, I showed that they give a biased estimate—in this case an overestimate—of the treatment effect.

Figure 11.16
Bivariate plot for a non-equivalent groups design showing the group regression lines.

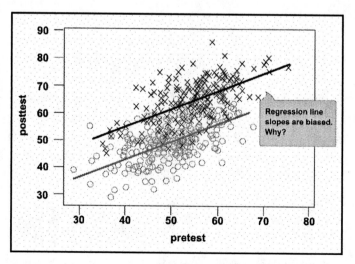

Why is the ANCOVA analysis biased when used with the NEGD? And, why isn't it biased when used with a pretest-posttest randomized experiment? Actually, several things happen to produce the bias, which is why it's somewhat difficult to understand (and counterintuitive). Here are the two reasons for the bias:

- Pretest ***measurement error*** leads to the attenuation or flattening of the slopes in the regression lines.
- Groups are nonequivalent.

The first problem actually also occurs in randomized studies, but it doesn't lead to biased treatment effects because the groups are equivalent (at least probabilistically). The combination of both these conditions causes the problem. And, understanding the problem is what leads us to a solution in this case.

Regression and Measurement Error

I begin my attempt to explain the source of the bias by asking you to consider how error in measurement affects ***regression analysis***. I'll provide three different measurement-error scenarios to demonstrate what the error does.[1] In all three scenarios, assume that there is no true treatment effect, that the ***null hypothesis*** is true.

The first scenario is the case of no measurement error at all. In this hypothetical case, all of the points fall right on the ***regression lines*** themselves. The second scenario introduces ***measurement error*** on the posttest, but not on the pretest. Figure 11.17 shows that when you have posttest error, you are disbursing the points vertically—up and down—from the regression lines. Imagine a specific case, one person in a study. Without measurement error, the person would be expected to score on the regression line itself. With posttest measurement error, that person would do better or worse on the posttest than he or she should. This would lead the score to be displaced vertically. In the third scenario, measurement error occurs only on the pretest. It stands to reason in this scenario that the cases would be displaced horizontally—left and right—off of the regression lines. For these three hypothetical cases, none of which would occur in reality, you can see how data points would be disbursed.

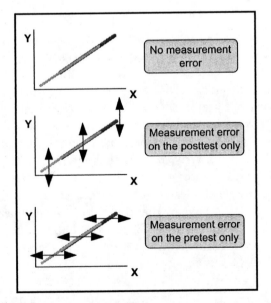

Figure 11.17
Measurement error in non-equivalent group designs.

---

[1] This discussion of measurement error in nonequivalent group designs draws heavily from Charles Reichardt's Chapter 4 in Cook, T.D. and Campbell, D.T. (1979). *Quasi-experimentation: Design and Analysis Issues for Field Settings.* Houghton Mifflin, Boston. Chip (Charles' nickname) and I were in graduate school together at Northwestern with him preceding me by a few years. He spent many an afternoon patiently trying to explain these complex statistical issues to me. He gets all the credit for anything I might have right and none of the blame for any of my errors.

How Regression Fits Lines

Regression analysis is a **least squares** analytic procedure. The actual criterion for fitting the line is to fit it so that you minimize the sum of the squares of the residuals from the regression line. Let's deconstruct this sentence a bit. The key term is residual. The **residual** is the vertical distance from the regression line to each point.

Figure 11.18 shows four residuals: two for each group. Two of the residuals fall above their regression line and two fall below. What is the criterion for fitting a line through the cloud of data points? Take all of the residuals within a group. (Fit separate lines for the program and comparison group.) If the data points are above the line, they will be positive; and if they're below, they'll be negative values. Square all the residuals in the group. Compute the sum of the squares of the residuals—just add them. That's it. Regression analysis fits a line through the data that yields the smallest sum of the squared residuals. How it does this is another matter; but you should now understand what it's doing. The key thing to notice is that *the regression line is fit in terms of the residuals, and the residuals are always and only vertical displacements from the regression line.*

Figure 11.18
Regression analysis as a least squares procedure.

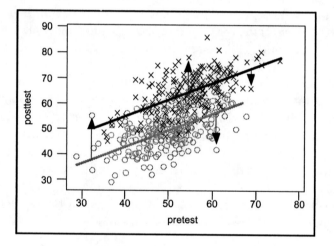

How Measurement Error Affects Slope

Now let's put the ideas of the previous two sections together. Consider the three measurement-error scenarios described previously. When there is no measurement error, the **slopes** of the regression lines are unaffected. Figure 11.17 shows the regression lines in this no-error condition. Notice that there is no treatment effect in any of the three graphs shown in the figure. (There would be a treatment effect only if there was a vertical displacement between the two lines.) Now, consider the case where there is measurement error on the posttest. Will the slopes be affected? The answer is no. Why? Because in **regression analysis**, you fit the line relative to the vertical displacements of the points. Posttest **measurement error** affects the vertical dimension, and, if the errors are random, you would get as many **residuals** pushing up as down and the slope of the line would, on average, remain the same as in the **null case**. There would, in this posttest measurement-error case, be more variability of data around the regression line, but the line would be located in the same place as in the no-error case.

Now let's consider the case of measurement error on the pretest (the bottom panel in Figure 11.17). In this scenario, errors are added along the horizontal dimension; but regression analysis fits the lines relative to vertical displacements. So how will this affect the slope?

Figure 11.19 illustrates what happens. If there is no error, the lines would overlap as indicated for the null case in the figure. When you add in pretest measurement error, you are in effect elongating the horizontal dimension without changing the vertical. Since regression analysis fits to the vertical, this would force the regression line to stretch to fit the horizontally elongated distribution. The only way it can do this is by rotating around its center point. The result is that the line has been flattened or attenuated; the slope of the line will be lower when there is pretest measurement error than it should actually be. You should be able to see that flattening the line in each group by rotating it around its own center introduces a displacement between the two lines that was not there originally. Although there was no treatment effect in the original case, false or pseudo effect was introduced. The biased estimate of the slope that results from pretest measurement error introduces a phony treatment effect. In this example, it introduced an effect where there was none. In the simulated example shown earlier, it exaggerated the actual effect that was constructed for the simulation.

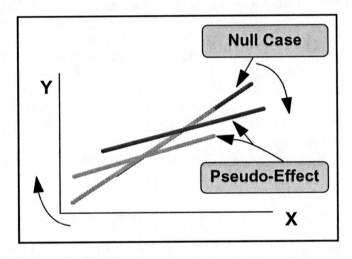

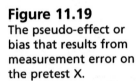

Figure 11.19
The pseudo-effect or bias that results from measurement error on the pretest X.

Why Doesn't the Problem Occur in Randomized Designs?

So, why doesn't this pseudo-effect occur in the randomized ANCOVA design? Figure 11.20 shows that even in the randomized design, pretest measurement error *does* cause the slopes of the lines to be flattened.

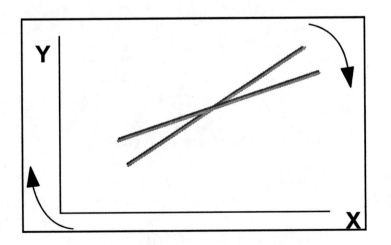

Figure 11.20
Pretest measurement error in a randomized experiment does attenuate slopes but does not lead to biased estimates of the treatment effect.

But, a pseudo-effect in the randomized case doesn't occur even though the attenuation does. Why? Because in the randomized case, the two groups are equivalent on the pretest; there is no horizontal difference between the lines. The lines for the two groups overlap perfectly in the null case. So, when the attenuation occurs, it occurs the same way in both lines (and around the same rotation point) and there is no vertical displacement introduced between the lines. Compare Figures 11.19 and 11.20. You should now see that the difference is the **NEGD** case shows the attenuation of slopes and the initial nonequivalence between the groups. Under these circumstances, the flattening of the lines introduces a displacement. In the randomized case, flattening also occurs, but there is no displacement because there is no nonequivalence between the groups initially.

Summary of the Problem

So where does this leave us? The **ANCOVA** statistical model seemed at first glance to have all of the right components to correctly model data from the **NEGD;** but it didn't work correctly. The estimate of the treatment effect was biased. Upon examination, you saw that the bias was due to two major factors: the attenuation of slope that results from pretest **measurement error** coupled with the initial nonequivalence between the groups. The problem is not caused by posttest measurement error because of the criterion that is used in **regression analysis** to fit the line. It does not occur in randomized experiments because there is no pretest nonequivalence. You might also guess from these arguments that the bias will be greater with greater nonequivalence between groups; the less similar the groups, the bigger the problem. In real-life research, as opposed to simulations, you can count on measurement error in all measurements. Measurement is never perfect. Therefore, in nonequivalent group designs the ANCOVA analysis that seemed intuitively sensible can be expected to yield incorrect results!

The Solution

Now that you understand the problem in the analysis of the NEGD, you can go about trying to fix it. Since the problem is caused in part by measurement error on the pretest, one way to deal with it would be to address the measurement-error issue. If you could remove the pretest measurement error and approximate the no pretest error case, there would be no attenuation or flattening of the regression lines and no pseudo-effect introduced. To see how you might adjust for pretest measurement error, you need to recall what you know about measurement error and its relation to **reliability** of measurement.

Recall from reliability theory (Chapter 3, "The Theory of Measurement") and the idea of **true score theory** that reliability can be defined as the ratio shown in Figure 11.21.

Figure 11.21
Reliability defined in terms of true score theory.

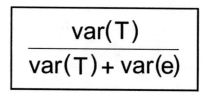

$$\frac{var(T)}{var(T) + var(e)}$$

In this ratio, T is the true ability or level on the measure and e is measurement error. It follows that the reliability of the pretest is directly related to the amount of measurement error. If there is no measurement error on the pretest, the var(e) term in the denominator is zero and reliability = 1. If the pretest is nothing but measurement error, the Var(T) term is 0 and the reliability is 0. That is, if the measure is nothing but measurement error, it is totally unreliable. If half of the measure is true score and half is measurement error, the reliability is .5. This shows that there is a direct relationship between measurement error and reliability; reliability reflects the proportion of measurement error in your measure. Since measurement error on the pretest is a necessary condition for bias in the NEGD (if there is no pretest measurement error there is no bias even in the NEGD), if you correct for the measurement error, you correct for the bias. But, you can't see measurement error directly in your data. (Remember, only God can see how much of a score is true score and how much is error, and she isn't telling.) However, you can estimate the reliability. Since reliability is directly related to measurement error, you can use the reliability estimate as a proxy for how much measurement error is present, and you can adjust pretest scores using the reliability estimate to correct for the attenuation of slopes and remove the bias in the NEGD.

The Reliability-Corrected ANCOVA

To solve the bias in ANCOVA treatment effect estimates for the NEGD, you use a reliability correction that adjusts the pretest for measurement error. Figure 11.22 shows what a reliability correction looks like.

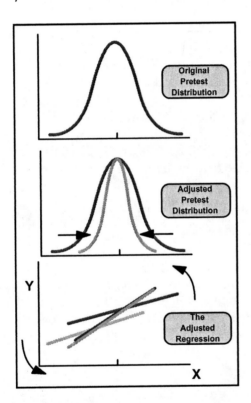

Figure 11.22
How adjusting for pretest reliability narrows the distribution of the pretest and "sharpens" the slope of the regression lines back to their true level.

The top graph shows the pretest distribution as you observe it, with measurement error included in it. Remember that I said previously that adding measurement error widens or elongates the horizontal dimension in the bivariate distribution. In the frequency distribution shown in the top graph, the distribution is wider than it would be if there were no error in measurement. The second graph shows that what you really want to do to adjust the pretest scores is squeeze the pretest distribution inwards by an amount proportionate to the amount that measurement error elongated or widened it. You make this adjustment separately for the program and comparison groups. The third graph shows what effect squeezing the pretest would have on the *regression lines;* it would increase their *slopes* rotating them back to where they truly belong and remove the bias that was introduced by the measurement error. In effect, you are doing the opposite of what *measurement error* did so that you can correct for the measurement error.

All you need to know is how much to squeeze the pretest distribution in to adjust for measurement error correctly. The answer is in the reliability coefficient. Since *reliability* is an estimate of the proportion of your measure that is true score relative to error, it should tell you how much you have to squeeze. In fact, the formula for the adjustment is simple (see Figure 11.23).

Figure 11.23
Formula for adjusting pretest values for unreliability in the reliability-corrected ANCOVA.

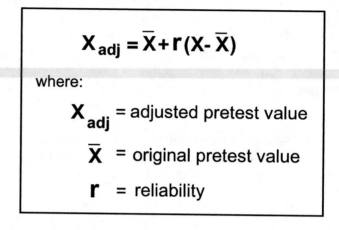

$$X_{adj} = \bar{X} + r(X - \bar{X})$$

where:

X_{adj} = adjusted pretest value

$\bar{X}$ = original pretest value

r = reliability

The idea in this formula is that you are going to construct new pretest scores for each person. These new scores will be adjusted for pretest unreliability by an amount proportional to the reliability. Each person's score will be closer to the pretest mean for that group. The formula tells you how much closer. Let's look at a few examples. First, let's look at the case where there is no pretest measurement error. Here, reliability would be 1. In this case, you actually don't want to adjust the data at all. Imagine that you have a person with a pretest score of 40, where the mean of the pretest for the group is 50. You would get the following adjusted score:

$X_{adj} = 50 + 1(40-50)$
$X_{adj} = 50 + 1(-10)$
$X_{adj} = 50 - 10$
$X_{adj} = 40$

Or, in other words, you wouldn't make any adjustment at all. That's what you want in the no-measurement-error case.

Now, let's assume that reliability was relatively low, say .5. For a person with a pretest score of 40 where the group *mean* is 50, you would get the following:

$X_{adj} = 50 + .5(40-50)$
$X_{adj} = 50 + .5(-10)$
$X_{adj} = 50 - 5$
$X_{adj} = 45$

Or, when reliability is .5, you would move the pretest score halfway in towards the mean—halfway from its original value of 40 towards the mean of 50, or to 45.

Finally, let's assume that for the same case the reliability was stronger at .8. The reliability adjustment would be as follows:

$X_{adj} = 50 + .8(40-50)$
$X_{adj} = 50 + .8(-10)$
$X_{adj} = 50 - 8$
$X_{adj} = 42$

That is, with reliability of .8 you would want to move the score in 20 percent towards its mean (because if reliability is .8, the amount of the score due to error is $1 - .8 = .2$).

You should be able to see that if you make this adjustment to all of the pretest scores in a group, you would be squeezing the pretest distribution in by an amount proportionate to the measurement error (1 - reliability). It's important to note that you need to make this correction separately for your program and comparison groups.

You're now ready to take this adjusted pretest score and substitute it for the original pretest score in the ANCOVA model (see Figure 11.24).

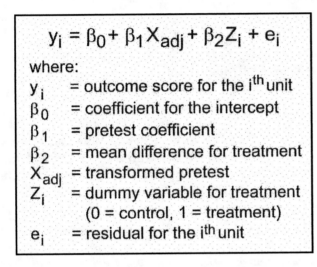

Figure 11.24
The regression model for the reliability-corrected ANCOVA.

Notice that the only difference is that the X in the original ANCOVA is changed to the term X_{adj}.

The Simulation Revisited

So, let's go see how well these adjustments work. I'll use the same simulated data that I used earlier. The results are shown in Figure 11.25.

$$y_i = -3.14 + 1.06X_{adj} + 9.30Z_i$$

Predictor	Coef	StErr	t	p
Constant	-3.141	3.300	-0.95	0.342
adjpre	1.06316	0.06557	16.21	0.000
Group	9.3048	0.6166	15.09	0.000

- $CI_{.95(\beta_2 = 10)}$ = $\beta_2 \pm 2SE(\beta_2)$
  = $9.3048 \pm 2(.6166)$
  = 9.3048 ± 1.2332
- CI = 8.0716 to 10.5380

Figure 11.25
Results of the reliability-corrected ANCOVA for the simulated data.

This time the estimate of the treatment effect is 9.3048 (instead of 11.2818). This estimate is closer to the true value of 10 points that I put into the simulated data. When I construct a 95 percent *confidence interval* for the adjusted estimate, the true value of 10 falls within the interval. That is, the analysis estimated a treatment effect that is not statistically different from the true effect; it is an unbiased estimate.

You should also compare the *slope* of the lines in this adjusted model with the original slope. Now the slope is nearly 1 at 1.06316, whereas before it was .626—considerably lower or flatter. The slope in the adjusted model approximates the expected true slope of the line (which is 1) in the simulated data. The original slope showed the attenuation that the pretest measurement error caused.

So, the reliability-corrected ANCOVA model is used in the statistical analysis of the NEGD to correct for the bias that would occur as a result of measurement error on the pretest.

Which Reliability Should You Use?

There's really only one more major issue to settle to finish this story. You know from reliability theory that you can't calculate the true reliability; you can only estimate it. A variety of reliability estimates exist, and they're likely to give you different values. *Cronbach's Alpha* tends to be a high estimate of reliability. The test-retest reliability tends to be a lower-bound estimate of reliability. So which do you use in a correction formula? The answer is both! When analyzing data from the *NEGD*, it's safest to do two analyses: one with an upper-bound estimate of reliability and one with a lower-bound one. If you find a significant treatment effect estimate with both, you can be fairly confident that you have found a significant effect.

This certainly doesn't feel like a satisfying conclusion to this rather convoluted story about the analysis of the NEGD, and it's not. In some ways, I look at this as the price you pay when you give up *random assignment* and use intact groups in a NEGD: your analysis becomes more complicated as you deal with adjustments that are needed, in part, because of the nonequivalence between the groups. Nevertheless, there are also benefits in using nonequivalent groups instead of randomly assigning. You have to decide whether the tradeoff is worth it.

11-4b Regression-Discontinuity Analysis

The basic **RD** design is a two-group pretest-posttest model as indicated in the design notation (see Figure 11.26). As in other versions of this design structure (see the sections the Analysis of Covariance Randomized Experiment and the Nonequivalent Groups Design in this chapter), you will need a statistical model that includes a term for the pretest, one for the posttest, and a dummy-coded variable to represent the program.

Figure 11.26
Notation for the Regression-Discontinuity (RD) design.

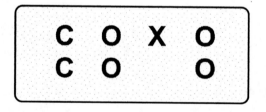

Assumptions in the Analysis

Before discussing the specific analytic model, it's important to understand the assumptions that must be met. This presentation assumes that you are dealing with the basic RD design as described earlier. Variations in the design will be discussed later. There are five central assumptions that must be made for the analytic model that is presented as appropriate, each of which is discussed in turn:

1. **The cutoff criterion**—The cutoff criterion must be followed without exception. When there is an incorrect assignment relative to the cutoff value (unless it is known to be random), a *selection threat* arises and

estimates of the effect of the program are likely to be biased. An incorrect assignment relative to the cutoff, often termed a fuzzy RD design, introduces analytic complexities that are outside the scope of this discussion.

2. **The pre-post distribution**—It is assumed that the pre-post distribution is describable as a polynomial function. If the true pre-post relationship is logarithmic, exponential, or some other function, the following model is specified incorrectly and estimates of the effect of the program are likely to be biased. Of course, if the data can be transformed to create a polynomial distribution prior to analysis, the following model may be appropriate although it is likely to be more problematic to interpret. It is also sometimes the case that even if the true relationship is not polynomial, a sufficiently high-order polynomial will adequately account for whatever function exists. However, you are not likely to know whether this is the case.

3. **Comparison group pretest variance**—There must be a sufficient number of pretest values in the comparison group to enable adequate estimation of the true relationship (for example, the pre-post regression line) for that group. It is usually desirable to have variability in the program group as well although this is not strictly enforced because you can project the comparison group line to a single point for the program group.

4. **Continuous pretest distribution**—Both groups must come from a single, continuous pretest distribution with the division between groups determined by the cutoff. In some cases, you might be able to find intact groups (for example, two groups of patients from two different geographic locations) that serendipitously divide on some measure so as to imply some cutoff. Such naturally discontinuous groups must be used with caution because of the greater likelihood that if they differed naturally at the cutoff prior to the program such a difference could reflect a selection bias that could introduce natural pre-post discontinuities at that point.

5. **Program implementation**—It is assumed that the program is uniformly delivered to all recipients, that is, that they all receive the same dosage, length of stay, amount of training, or whatever. If this is not the case, it is necessary to model explicitly the program as implemented, thus complicating the analysis somewhat.

The Curvilinearity Problem

The major problem in analyzing data from the RD design is incorrect model specification. As I will show, when you specify the statistical model incorrectly, you are likely to get biased estimates of the treatment effect. To introduce this idea, let's begin by considering what happens if the data (the bivariate, pre-post relationship) is curvilinear and you fit a straight-line model to the data.

Figure 11.27a shows a simple curvilinear relationship. If the curved line in Figure 11.27a describes the pre-post relationship, you need to take this into account in your statistical model. Notice that, although there is a cutoff value at 50 in the figure, there is no jump or discontinuity in the line at the cutoff. This indicates that there is no effect of the treatment.

Now look at Figure 11.27b. The figure shows what happens when you fit a straight-line model to the curvilinear relationship of Figure 11.27a. In the model, *slopes* of both straight lines are restricted and so must be the same. (For example, you did not allow for any interaction between the program and the pretest.) You can see that the straight-line model suggests that there is a jump at the cutoff, even though you can see that in the true function there is no discontinuity.

Even allowing the straight-line slopes to differ doesn't solve the problem (although it does help). Figure 11.27c shows what happens in this case. Although the pseudo-effect in this case is smaller than when the slopes are forced to be equal, you still obtain a pseudo-effect.

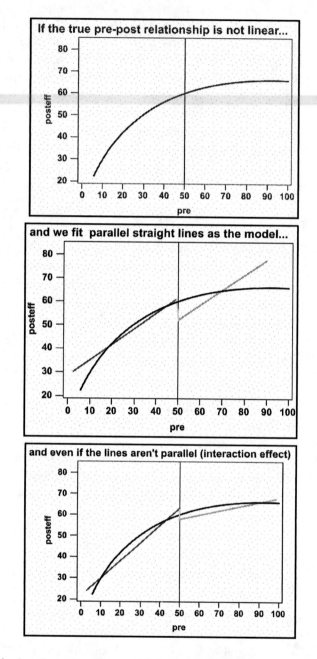

Figure 11.27a
A curvilinear relationship.

Figure 11.27b
Misspecification of the regression model in an RD design by fitting straight lines to a true curvilinear relationship.

Figure 11.27c
A curvilinear relationship fit with a straight-line model with different slopes for each line (an interaction effect).

The conclusion is a simple one. If the true model is curved and you fit only straight lines, you are likely to conclude incorrectly that the treatment made a difference when it did not. This is a specific instance of the more general problem of model specification.

Model Specification

To understand the **model specification** issue and how it relates to the **RD** design, you must try to distinguish three types of specifications. Figure 11.28a shows the case where the true model is *exactly specified*. What does "exactly specified" mean? The top equation describes the truth for the data. It describes a simple straight-line, pre-post relationship with a treatment effect. Notice that it includes terms for the posttest Y, the pretest X, and the dummy-coded treatment variable Z. The bottom equation shows the model that you specify in the analysis. It too includes a term for the posttest Y, the pretest X, and the dummy-coded treatment variable Z. That's all it includes; there are no unnecessary terms in the model that you specify. When you exactly specify the true model, you get unbiased and efficient estimates of the treatment effect.

Now, let's look at the situation in Figure 11.28b. The true model is the same as in Figure 11.28a. However, this time an analytic model that includes an extra and unnecessary term is specified. In this case, because all of the necessary terms are included, the estimate of the treatment effect will be unbiased. However, you pay a price for including unneeded terms in your analysis; the treatment effect estimate will not be efficient. What does this mean? It means that the chance that you will conclude your treatment doesn't work when it in fact does increases. Including an unnecessary term in the analysis is like adding unnecessary noise to the data; it makes it harder to see the effect of the treatment even if it's there.

Finally, consider the example shown in Figure 11.28c. Here, the truth is more complicated than the model. In reality, two terms are included in the analysis. In this case, the treatment effect estimate is both biased and inefficient.

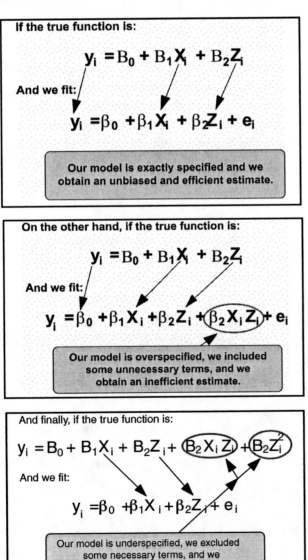

Figure 11.28a
An exactly specified model.

Figure 11.28b
An overspecified model.

Figure 11.28c
An underspecified model.

Analysis Strategy

Given the discussion of model misspecification, you can develop a modeling strategy that is designed first, to guard against biased estimates and second, to ensure maximum efficiency of estimates. The best option would obviously be to specify the true model exactly. However this is often difficult to achieve in practice because the true model is often obscured by the error in the data and because you're not God and don't know what the true model is. If you have to make a mistake—if you must specify the model incorrectly—the discussion of misspecification suggests you should overspecify the true model rather than underspecify. Overspecification ensures that you have included all necessary terms even at the expense of unnecessary ones. It will yield an unbiased estimate of the effect, even though it will be inefficient. Underspecification is the situation you most want to avoid because it yields both biased and inefficient estimates.

Given this preference sequence, you should begin your general analysis by specifying a model that you are fairly certain is overspecified. The treatment effect estimate for this model is likely to be unbiased although it will be inefficient. Then, in successive analyses, gradually remove higher-order terms until the treatment-effect estimate appears to differ from the initial one, or until the model diagnostics (for example the residual plots) indicate that the model fits poorly.

Steps in the Analysis

The basic RD analysis involves five steps:

1. **Transform the pretest**—The analysis begins by subtracting the cutoff value from each pretest score, creating the modified pretest term shown in Figure 11.29. This is done to set the intercept equal to the cutoff value. How does this work? If you subtract the cutoff from every pretest value, the modified pretest will be equal to 0 where it was originally at the cutoff value. Since the intercept is by definition the Y-value when X = 0, what you have done is set X to 0 at the cutoff, making the cutoff the intercept point.

Figure 11.29
Transforming the pretest by subtracting the cutoff value.

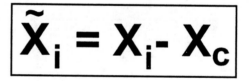

$$\tilde{X}_i = X_i - X_c$$

2. **Examine relationship visually**—You should look for two major things in a graph of the pre-post relationship. First it is important to determine whether there is any visually discernable discontinuity in the relationship at the cutoff. The discontinuity could be a change in level vertically (***main effect***), a change in *slope* (***interaction effect***), or both. If it is visually clear that there is a discontinuity at the cutoff, you should not be satisfied with analytic results that indicate no program effect. However, if no discontinuity is visually apparent, it may be that variability in the data is masking an effect and you must attend carefully to the analytic results.

   The second thing to look for in the bivariate relationship is the degree of polynomial that may be required as indicated by the bivariate slope of the distribution, particularly in the comparison group. A good approach is to count the number of flexion points (that is, the number of times the distribution flexes or bends) that are apparent in the distribution. If the distribution appears linear, there are no flexion points. A single flexion point could be indicative of a second (quadratic) order polynomial. You use this information to determine the initial model that will be specified.

3. **Specify higher-order terms and interactions**—Depending on the number of flexion points detected in step 2, you next create transformations of the modified assignment variable, X. The rule of thumb here is that you go two orders of polynomial higher than was indicated by the number of flexion points. Thus, if the bivariate relationship appeared linear (there were no flexion points), you would want to create transformations up to a second-order (0 + 2) polynomial. This is shown in Figure 11.30. There do not appear to be any inflexion points or bends in the bivariate distribution of Figure 11.30.

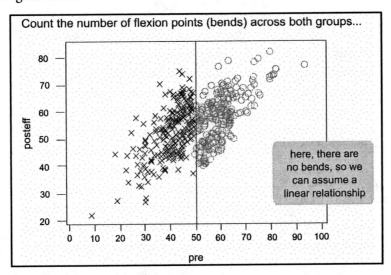

Figure 11.30
Bivariate distribution with no flexion points.

The first-order polynomial already exists in the model (X) and so you would only have to create the second-order polynomial by squaring X to obtain X^2. For each transformation of X, you also create the interaction term by multiplying the polynomial by Z. In this example, there would be two interaction terms: X_iZ_i and $X_i^2Z_i$. Each transformation can be easily accomplished through straightforward multiplication on the computer. If there appeared to be two flexion points in the bivariate distribution, you would create transformations up to the fourth (2 + 2) power and their interactions.

Visual inspection need not be the only basis for the initial determination of the degree of polynomial that is needed. Certainly, prior experience modeling similar data should be taken into account. The rule of thumb given here implies that you should err on the side of overestimating the true polynomial function that is needed for reasons outlined previously in discussing *model specification*. For whatever power is initially estimated from visual inspection, you should construct all transformations and their interactions up to that power. Thus if the fourth power is chosen, you should construct all four terms X to X^4 and their interactions.

4. **Estimate initial model**—At this point, you can begin the actual analysis. You can use any acceptable multiple-regression program on the computer to accomplish this. You simply regress the posttest scores, Y, on the modified pretest, X, the treatment variable, Z, and all higher-order transformations and interactions created in step 3. The regression coefficient associated with the Z term (the group-membership variable) is the estimate of the main effect of the program. If there is a vertical discontinuity

at the cutoff, it will be estimated by this coefficient. You can test the significance of the coefficient (or any other) by constructing a standard **t-test** using the standard error of the coefficient, which is invariably supplied in the computer program output. For the data in Figure 11.30, you would use the model given in Figure 11.31.

Figure 11.31
The initial model for the case of no flexion points (full quadratic model specification).

$$y_i = \beta_0 + \beta_1 \tilde{X}_i + \beta_2 Z_i + \beta_3 \tilde{X}_i Z_i + \beta_4 \tilde{X}_i^2 + \beta_5 \tilde{X}_i^2 Z_i + e_i$$

where:
y_i = outcome score for the ith unit
β_0 = coefficient for the intercept
β_1 = pretest coefficient
β_2 = mean difference for treatment
β_3 = linear interaction
β_4 = quadratic pretest coefficient
β_5 = quadratic interaction
X_i = transformed pretest
Z_i = dummy variable for treatment
(0 = control, 1 = treatment)
e_i = residual for the ith unit

If during step 3, you correctly overestimated the polynomial function required to model the distribution, the estimate of the program effect will at least be unbiased. However, by including terms that may not be needed in the true model, the estimate is likely to be inefficient; that is, standard error terms will be inflated and hence the significance of the program effect may be underestimated. Nevertheless, if at this point in the analysis the coefficient is highly significant, it would be reasonable to conclude that there is a program effect. The direction of the effect is interpreted based on the sign of the coefficient and the direction of scale of the posttest. Interaction effects can also be examined. For instance, a linear interaction would be implied by a significant regression coefficient for the XZ term.

5. **Refining the Model**—On the basis of the results of step 4, you might want to attempt to remove apparently unnecessary terms and re-estimate the treatment effect with greater efficiency. This is a tricky procedure and should be approached cautiously to minimize the possibility of bias. To accomplish this, you should certainly examine the output of the regression analysis in step 4, noting the degree to which the overall model fits the data, the presence of any insignificant coefficients, and the pattern of residuals. A conservative way to decide how to refine the model would be to begin by examining the highest-order term in the current model and its interaction. If both coefficients are nonsignificant, and the goodness-of-fit measures and pattern of residuals indicate a good fit, you might drop these two terms and re-estimate the resulting model. Thus, if you estimated up to a fourth-order polynomial, and found the coefficients for X^4 and X^4Z were nonsignificant, you could drop these terms and respecify the third-order model. You would repeat this procedure until either of the coefficients is significant; the goodness-of-fit measure drops appreciably, or the pattern of residuals indicates a poorly fitting model. The final model may still include unnecessary terms, but there are likely to be fewer of these and consequently, efficiency should be greater. Model-specification procedures that involve dropping any term at any stage of the

analysis are more dangerous and more likely to yield biased estimates because of the considerable multicolinearity that will exist between the terms in the model.

Example Analysis

Okay, so I've thrown a lot at you in this section. Here's where I think it will begin to make a little more sense. It's easier to understand how data from a *RD* design is analyzed by looking an example. The data for this example is shown in Figure 11.32.

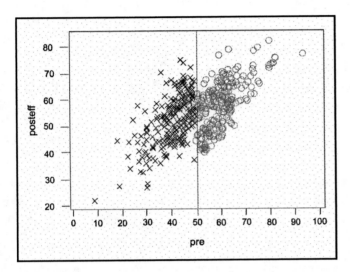

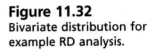

Figure 11.32
Bivariate distribution for example RD analysis.

Several things are apparent visually. First, there is a whopping treatment effect in this simulated data. You'll never see an effect like this in real life! Figure 11.32 shows simulated data where the true treatment effect is 10 points. Second, both groups are well described by straight lines; there are no flexion points apparent. Thus, the initial model to specify is the full quadratic one shown in Figure 11.31.

The results of the initial specification are shown in Figure 11.33. The treatment effect estimate is the one next to the group variable. This initial estimate is 10.231 (SE = 1.248)—close to the true value of 10 points—but notice that there is evidence that several of the higher-order terms are not statistically significant and may not be needed in the model. Specifically, the linear interaction term linint (XZ), and both the quadratic (X^2) and quadratic interaction (X^2Z) terms are not significant.

The regression equation is

posteff = 49.1 + 0.972*precut + 10.2*group -0.236*linint - 0.00539*quad + 0.00276 quadint

Predictor	Coef	Stdev	t-ratio	p
Constant	49.1411	0.8964	54.82	0.000
precut	0.9716	0.1492	6.51	0.000
Group	10.231	1.248	8.20	0.000
linint	-0.2363	0.2162	-1.09	0.275
quad	-0.005391	0.004994	-1.08	0.281
quadint	0.002757	0.007475	0.37	0.712

• s = 6.643   • R - sq = 47.4%   • R - sq (adj) = 47.1%

Figure 11.33
Regression results for the full quadratic model.

Although you might be tempted (and perhaps even justified) to drop all three terms from the model, if you follow the guidelines given in step 5, you begin by dropping only the two quadratic terms quad and quadint. The results for this model are shown in Figure 11.34.

Figure 11.34
Regression results for initial model without quadratic terms.

The regression equation is

posteff = 49.8 + 0.824*precut + 9.89*group -0.0196*linint

Predictor	Coef	Stdev	t-ratio	p
Constant	49.7508	0.6957	71.52	0.000
precut	0.82371	0.05889	13.99	0.000
Group	9.8939	0.9528	10.38	0.000
linint	-0.01963	0.08284	-0.24	0.813

• s = 6.639   • R - sq = 47.5%   • R - sq (adj) = 47.2%

You can see that in this model the treatment effect estimate is now 9.89 (SE = .95). Again, this estimate is close to the true 10-point treatment effect. Notice, however, that the standard error (SE) is smaller than it was in the original model. This is the gain in efficiency you get when you eliminate the two unneeded quadratic terms. You can also see that the linear interaction term linint is still not significant. This term would be significant if the *slopes* of the lines for the two groups were different. Visual inspection shows that the slopes are the same and so it makes sense that this term is not significant.

Finally, let's drop out the nonsignificant linear interaction term and respecify the model. These results are shown in Figure 11.35.

Figure 11.35
Regression results for final model.

The regression equation is

posteff = 49.8 + 0.814*precut + 9.89*group

Predictor	Coef	Stdev	t-ratio	p
Constant	49.8421	0.5786	86.14	0.000
precut	0.81379	0.04138	19.67	0.000
Group	9.8875	0.9515	10.39	0.000

• s = 6.633   • R - sq = 47.5%   • R - sq (adj) = 47.3%

You see in these results that the treatment effect and SE are almost identical to the previous model and that the treatment effect estimate is an unbiased estimate of the true effect of 10 points. You can also see that all the terms in the final model are statistically significant, suggesting that they are needed to model the data and should not be eliminated.

So, what does our model look like visually? Figure 11.36 shows the original bivariate distribution with the fitted regression model.

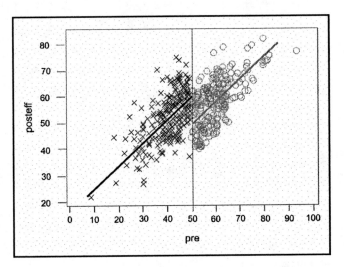

Figure 11.36
Bivariate distribution with final regression model.

Clearly, the model fits well, both statistically and visually.

11-4c Regression Point Displacement Analysis

I come now to the last of the *quasi-experimental* designs I want to discuss in reference to analysis—the *Regression Point Displacement (RDP)* design. At this point in the chapter, you should be able to anticipate the kind of analysis I'm going to suggest. You'll see that the principles are the same here as for all of the other analyses, especially in that this analysis also relies on the *GLM* and *regression analysis*.

The notation for the RPD design (see Figure 11.37) shows that the statistical analysis requires the following:

- A posttest score
- A pretest score
- A variable to represent the treatment group (where 0 = comparison and 1 = program)

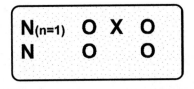

Figure 11.37
Notation for the Regression Point Displacement design.

These requirements are identical to the requirements for the *ANCOVA* model and should look very familiar by now. The only difference is that the RPD design has only a single treated group score.

Figure 11.38 shows a bivariate (pre-post) distribution for a hypothetical RPD design of a community-based AIDS education program. The new AIDS-education program is piloted in one particular county in a state, with the remaining counties acting as controls. The state routinely publishes annual HIV positive rates by county for the entire state. The x-values show the HIV-positive rates per 1000 people for the year preceding the program, while the y-values show the rates for the year following it. Our goal is to estimate the size of the vertical displacement of the treated unit from the *regression line* of all of the control units, indicated on the graph by the dashed arrow. The model I'll use is the now-familiar ANCOVA model stated in regression model form (see Figure 11.39).

Figure 11.38
Bivariate plot for the RPD
design.

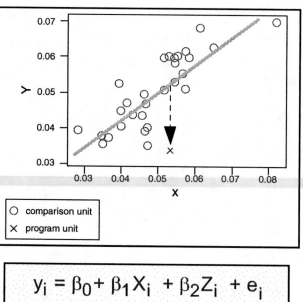

Figure 11.39
The regression model for
the RPD design assuming a
linear pre-post relation-
ship.

$$y_i = \beta_0 + \beta_1 X_i + \beta_2 Z_i + e_i$$

where:
y_i = outcome score for the ith unit
β_0 = coefficient for the intercept
β_1 = pretest coefficient
β_2 = mean difference for treatment
X_i = covariate
Z_i = dummy variable for treatment
      (0 = control, 1 = treatment [n=1])
e_i = residual for the ith unit

When you fit the model to the simulated data, you obtain the regression table shown in Figure 11.40.

Figure 11.40
Results of applying the
regression model of
Figure 11.39 to the data
of Figure 11.38.

The regression equation is

Y = 0.0120 + 0.784 X - 0.0199 Z

Predictor	Coef	Stdev	t-ratio	p
Constant	0.011956	0.004965	2.41	0.023
X	0.78365	0.09864	7.94	0.000
Z	-0.019936	0.005800	-3.44	0.002

• s = 0.005689   • R - sq = 72.6%   • R - sq (adj) = 70.6%

The coefficient associated with the dichotomous treatment variable is the estimate of the vertical displacement from the line. In this example, the results show
that the program lowers HIV positive rates by .019 and that this amount is statistically significant. This displacement is shown in the results graph in Figure 11.41.

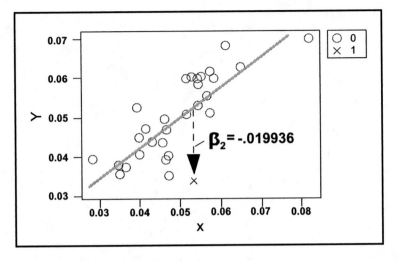

Figure 11.41
The results of the RPD
analysis showing the size
of the treatment effect.

Phew! I'm hoping for your sake that you weren't assigned to read this chapter in a single night. And, I'm hoping you didn't put this off until the night before the exam. However, in case you did, let me summarize the salient points.

This chapter described data analysis as it relates to research design. When I talk about statistical analysis of research design, I'm in the area usually referred to as *inferential statistics*. With inferential statistics, we attempt to draw inferences (often *causal*) from the data based on our research design. To understand inferential statistics, you need to be familiar with the *GLM*, which underlies virtually all of the statistics presented in this chapter. The GLM is the basic structure of the *t-test*, *ANOVA*, *ANCOVA*, *regression analysis*, and many of the multivariate methods like factor analysis, multidimensional scaling, cluster analysis, discriminant function analysis, and so on. GLM is a deceptively simple formula that describes how a set of independent variables is related mathematically to a set of dependent variables. To understand how the GLM works in research design you have to grasp the idea of *dummy variables* that are used to represent the various treatment and *control groups* in the regression models for the different designs. The analyses of the different experimental designs are straightforward regression models that range from the simple t-test to the multiple dummy variable factorial and blocking models to the ANCOVA that includes both a dummy variable and a continuous pretest. The *quasi-experimental designs* make for more difficult and challenging modeling problems. While it might seem intuitively that the usual ANCOVA model would be appropriate for both the *NEGD* and the regression-discontinuity, it will often yield biased estimates if not appropriately modified.

SUMMARY

Chapter 12

Write-Up

So now that you've completed the research project, what do you do? I know you won't want to hear this, but your work is still far from done. In fact, this final stage—writing up your research—may be one of the most difficult. Developing a good, effective, and concise report is an art form in itself, and in many research projects, you will need to write multiple reports that present the results at different levels of detail for different audiences.

There are several general considerations to keep in mind when generating a report:

- The Audience—Who is going to read the report? Reports will differ considerably depending on whether the audience will want or require technical detail, whether they are looking for a summary of results, or whether they are about to examine your research in a Ph.D. exam.

- The Story—I believe that every research project has at least one major story in it. Sometimes the story centers around a specific research finding. Sometimes it is based on a methodological problem or challenge. When you write your report, you should attempt to tell the story to your reader. Even in formal journal articles where you will be required to be concise and detailed at the same time, a good storyline can help make an otherwise dull report interesting to the reader.

  The hardest part of telling the story in your research is finding the story in the first place. Usually when you come to writing up your research you have been steeped in the details for weeks or months (and sometimes even for years). You've been worrying about sampling responses, struggling with operationalizing your measures, dealing with the details of design, and wrestling with the data analysis. You're a bit like the ostrich that has its head in the sand. To find the story in your research, you have to pull your head out of the sand and look at the big picture. You have to try to view your research from your audience's perspective. You may have to let go of some of the details that you obsessed so much about and leave them out of the write-up or bury them in technical appendices or tables.

- Formatting Considerations—Are you writing a research report to submit for publication in a journal? If so, you should be aware that every journal requires articles that you follow specific formatting guidelines. Thinking of writing a book? Again, every publisher requires specific formatting. Writing a term paper? Most faculty members require you to follow specific guidelines.

Doing your thesis or dissertation? Every university I know of has strict policies about formatting and style. There are legendary stories that circulate among graduate students about the dissertation that was rejected because the page margins were a quarter inch off or the figures weren't labeled correctly.

To illustrate what a set of research report specifications might include, I present in this section general guidelines for the formatting of a research write-up for a class term paper. These guidelines are similar to the types of specifications you might be required to follow for a journal article. However, you need to check the specific formatting guidelines for the report you are writing; the ones presented here are likely to differ in some ways from any other guidelines that may be required in other contexts.

I've also included a sample research paper write-up that illustrates these guidelines. This sample paper is for a make-believe research project; but it illustrates how a final research report might look using the guidelines given here.

12-1 Key Elements

This page describes the elements or criteria that you must typically address in a research paper. The assumption here is that you are addressing a causal hypothesis in your paper.

I. Introduction

1. **Statement of the problem:** State the general problem area clearly and unambiguously. Discuss the importance and significance of the problem area.

2. **Statement of causal relationship:** Clearly state cause-effect relationship to be studied and relate it sensibly to the problem area.

3. **Statement of constructs:** Explain each key construct in the research/evaluation project (minimally, both the cause and effect). Ensure that explanations are readily understandable (that is, jargon-free) to an intelligent reader.

4. **Literature citations and review:** Cite literature cited from reputable and appropriate sources (such as professional journals and books, and not *Time, Newsweek,* and so on) and supply a minimum of five references. Condense the literature in an intelligent fashion and include only the most relevant information. Ensure that all citations are in the correct format.

5. **Statement of hypothesis:** Clearly state the hypothesis (or hypotheses) and specify what the paper predicts. The relationship of the hypothesis to both the problem statement and literature review must be readily understood from reading the text.

II. Methods

Sample section:

1. **Sampling procedure specifications:** Describe the procedure for selecting units (such as subjects and records) for the study and ensure that it is appropriate. State which sampling method you used and why. Describe the population and sampling frame. In an evaluation, the program participants are frequently self-selected (volunteers) and if so, should be described as such.

2. **Sample description:** Describe the sample accurately and ensure that it is appropriate. Anticipate problems in contacting and measuring the sample.

3. **External validity considerations:** Consider generalizability from the sample to the sampling frame and population.

Measurement section:

1. **Measures:** Describe each outcome measurement construct briefly. (A minimum of *two* outcome constructs is required.) For each construct, briefly describe the measure or measures and include an appropriate citation and reference (unless you created the measure). You describe briefly the measure you constructed and *provide the entire measure* in an appendix. The measures that are used are relevant to the hypotheses of the study and are included in those hypotheses. Wherever possible, use multiple measures of the same construct.
2. **Construction of measures:** Clearly word questionnaires, tests, and interviews. They should be specific, appropriate for the population, and follow in a logical fashion. Follow the standards for good questions. For archival data, describe original data collection procedures adequately and construct indices (for example, combinations of individual measures) correctly. For scales, you must describe briefly which scaling procedure you used and how you implemented it. Describe the procedures you used for collecting the qualitative measures in detail.
3. **Reliability and validity:** You must address both the reliability and validity of *all* of your measures. For reliability, you must specify what estimation procedure(s) you used. For validity, you must explain how you assessed construct validity. Wherever possible, you should minimally address both convergent and discriminant validity. The procedures that are used to examine reliability and validity are appropriate for the measures.

Design and Procedures section:

1. **Design:** Clearly present the design in both notational and text form. Ensure that the design is appropriate for the problem and addresses the hypothesis.
2. **Internal validity:** Discuss threats to internal validity and how they are addressed by the design. Also consider any threats to internal validity that are not well controlled.
3. **Description of procedures:** Include an overview of how the study will be conducted. Describe the sequence of events and ensure that it is appropriate to the design. Include sufficient information so that the essential features of the study could be replicated by a reader.

III.   Results

1. **Statement of Results:** State the results concisely and ensure that they are plausible for the research described.
2. **Tables:** Format a table (or tables) correctly to present part of the analysis accurately and concisely.
3. **Figures:** Design figure(s) clearly to accurately describe a relevant aspect of the results.

IV.   Conclusions, Abstract, and Reference Sections

1. **Implications of the study:** Assuming the expected results are obtained, discuss the implications of these results. Briefly mention any remaining problems that you anticipate in the study.

2. **Abstract:** The abstract is 125 words or less and presents a concise picture of the proposed research. Include major constructs and hypotheses. The abstract is the first section of the paper.

3. **References:** Include all citations in the correct format and ensure that they are appropriate for the study described.

Stylistic Elements

I. Professional Writing

Avoid first person and sex-stereotyped forms. Present material in an unbiased and unemotional (for example, no feelings about things), but not necessarily uninteresting, fashion.

II. Parallel Construction

Keep tense parallel within and between sentences (as appropriate).

III. Sentence Structure

Use correct sentence structure and punctuation. Avoid incomplete and run-on sentences.

IV. Spelling and Word Usage

Make sure that spelling and word usage are appropriate. Correctly capitalize and abbreviate words.

V. General Style

Ensure that the document is neatly produced and reads well. The format for the document has been correctly followed.

12-2 Formatting

The instructions provided here are for a research article or a research report (generally these guidelines follow the formatting guidelines of the American Psychological Association documented in *Publication Manual of the American Psychological Association*, 5th Edition). Please consult the specific guidelines that are required by the publisher for the type of document you are producing.

All sections of the paper should be typed, double-spaced on white 8 1/2 x 11 inch paper with 12-pitch typeface with all margins set to 1 inch. *Remember to consult the APA publication manual, fourth edition, pages 306–320 to see how text should appear.* Every page must have a header in the upper-right corner with the running header right-justified on the top line and the page number right-justified and double-spaced on the line below it. The paper must have all the following sections in the order given, following the specifications outlined for each section (all pages numbers are approximate):

- Title Page
- Abstract (on a separate single page)
- The Body (no page breaks between sections in the body)
  - Introduction (2-3 pages)
  - Methods (7-10 pages)
    - Sample (1 page)
    - Measures (2-3 pages)
    - Design (2-3 pages)
    - Procedures (2-3 pages)
  - Results (2-3 pages)
  - Conclusions (1-2 pages)
- References

- Tables (one to a page)
- Figures (one to a page)
- Appendices

On separate lines and centered, the title page has the title of the study, the author's name, and the institutional affiliation. At the bottom of the title page, you should have the words (in caps) RUNNING HEADER: followed by a short identifying title (2-4 words) for the study. This running header should also appear on the top-right of every page of the paper.

12-2a Title Page

The abstract is limited to one page, double-spaced. At the top of the page, centered, you should have the word "Abstract." The abstract itself should be written in paragraph form and should be a concise summary of the entire paper including the problem, major hypotheses, sample and population, a brief description of the measures, the name of the design or a short description (no design notation here), the major results, and the major conclusions. Obviously, to fit this all on one page you will have to be extremely concise.

12-2b Abstract

The first page of the body of the paper should have, centered, the complete title of the study.

12-2c Body

The first section in the body is the introduction. Do not include a heading that says, "Introduction." You simply begin the paper in paragraph form following the title. Every introduction will have the following (roughly in this order): a statement of the problem being addressed; a statement of the cause-effect relationship being studied; a description of the major constructs involved; a brief review of relevant literature (including citations); and a statement of hypotheses. The entire section should be in paragraph form with the possible exception of the hypotheses, which may be indented.

12-2d Introduction

The next section of the paper has four subsections: Sample, Measures, Design, and Procedures. The Methods section should begin immediately after the introduction (no page break) and should have the centered title, "Methods." Each of the four subsections should have an underlined, left-justified section heading.

12-2e Methods

This section should describe the population of interest, the sampling frame, the method for selecting the sample, and the sample itself. A brief discussion of external validity is appropriate here; that is, you should state the degree to which you believe results will be generalizable from your sample to the population. Sampling is covered in Chapter 2, "Sampling."

12-2f Sample

This section should include a brief description of your constructs and all measures used to operationalize them. You may present short instruments in their entirety in this section. If you have more lengthy instruments, you may present some typical questions to give the reader a sense of what you will be doing (and include the full measure in an appendix). You may include any instruments in full in appendices rather than in the body. Appendices should be labeled by letter (for example Appendix A) and cited appropriately in the body of the text. For pre-existing instruments, you should cite any relevant information about reliability and validity if it is available. For all instruments, you should briefly state how you

12-2g Measures

determined reliability and validity, report the results, and discuss them. For reliability, you must describe the methods you used and report results. A brief discussion of how you have addressed construct validity is essential. In general, you should try to demonstrate both convergent and discriminant validity. You must discuss the evidence in support of the validity of your measures. Measurement is covered in Chapter 3, "The Theory of Measurement."

12-2h Design

You should state the name of the design used and tell whether it is a true or quasi-experiment, nonequivalent group design, and so on. You should also present the design structure in X and O notation. (This should be indented and centered, not put into a sentence.) You should also include a discussion of internal validity that describes the major likely threats in your study and how the design accounts for them, if at all. (Be your own study critic here and provide enough information to show that you understand the threats to validity, whether you've been able to account for them all in the design or not.)

12-2i Procedures

Generally, this section ties together the sampling, measurement, and research design. In this section, you should briefly describe the overall plan of the research, the sequence of events from beginning to end (including sampling, measurement, and use of groups in designs), how participants will be notified, and how their confidentiality will be protected (where relevant). An essential part of this subsection is a description of the program or independent variable that you are studying.

12-2j Results

The heading for this section is centered with upper and lower-case letters. You should indicate concisely what results you found in this research. Your results don't have to confirm your hypotheses. In fact, the common experience in social research is the finding of no effect.

12-2k Conclusions

Here you should describe the conclusions you reach (assuming you got the results described in the Results section). You should relate these conclusions back to the level of the construct and the general problem area that you described in the introduction. You should also discuss the overall strength of the research proposed (for example a general discussion of the strong and weak validity areas) and should present some suggestions for possible future research that would be sensible based on the results of this work.

12-2l References

There are really two parts to a reference citation. First, there is the way you cite the item in the text when you are discussing it. Second, there is the way you list the complete reference in the reference section in the back of the report.

Reference Citations in the Text of Your Paper

Cited references appear in the text of your paper and are a way of giving credit to the source of the information you quoted or used in your paper. They generally consist of the following bits of information:

The author's last name, unless first initials are needed to distinguish between two authors with the same last name. If there are six or more authors, the first author is listed followed by the term, et al., and then the year of the publication is given in parenthesis. Year of publication in parenthesis. Page numbers are given with a quotation or when only a specific part of a source was used.

"To be or not to be" (Shakespeare, 1660, p. 241)

One Work by One Author:

Rogers (1994) compared reaction times...

One Work by Multiple Authors:

Wasserstein, Zappulla, Rosen, Gerstman, and Rock (1994) [first time you cite in text]

Wasserstein et al. (1994) found [subsequent times you cite in text]

Reference List in Reference Section

There are a wide variety of reference citation formats. Before submitting any research report, you should check to see which type of format is considered acceptable for that context. If there is no official format requirement, the most sensible thing is for you to select one approach and implement it consistently. (There's nothing worse than a reference list with a variety of formats.) Here, I'll illustrate by example some of the major reference items and how they might be cited in the reference section.

The references list all the articles, books, and other sources used in the research and preparation of the paper and cited with a parenthetical (textual) citation in the text. These items are entered in alphabetical order according to the authors' last names; if a source does not have an author, alphabetize according to the first word of the title, disregarding the articles *a*, *an*, and *the* if they are the first word in the title.

EXAMPLES

BOOK BY ONE AUTHOR:

Jones, T. (1940). *My life on the road.* New York: Doubleday.

BOOK BY TWO AUTHORS:

Williams, A., & Wilson, J. (1962). *New ways with chicken.* New York: Harcourt.

BOOK BY THREE OR MORE AUTHORS:

Smith, J., Jones, J., & Williams, S. (1976). *Common names.* Chicago: University of Chicago Press.

BOOK WITH NO GIVEN AUTHOR OR EDITOR:

Handbook of Korea (4th ed.). (1982). Seoul: Korean Overseas Information, Ministry of Culture & Information: Author.

TWO OR MORE BOOKS BY THE SAME AUTHOR:

Oates, J.C. (1990). *Because it is bitter, and because it is my heart.* New York: Dutton.

Oates, J.C. (1993). *Foxfire: Confessions of a girl gang.* New York: Dutton.

Note: Entries by the same author are arranged chronologically by the year of publication, the earliest first. References with the same first author and different second and subsequent authors are listed alphabetically by the surname of the second author, and then by the surname of the third author. References with the same authors in the same order are entered chronologically by year of publication, the earliest first. References by the same author (or by the same two or more authors in identical order) with the same publication date are listed alphabetically by the first word of the title following the date; lower case letters (a, b, c, and so on) are included after the year, within the parentheses.

BOOK BY A CORPORATE (GROUP) AUTHOR:

President's Commission on Higher Education. (1977). *Higher education for American democracy.* Washington, DC: U.S. Government Printing Office.

BOOK WITH AN EDITOR:

Bloom, H. (Ed.). (1988). *James Joyce's Dubliners.* New York: Chelsea House.

A TRANSLATION:

Dostoevsky, F. (1964). *Crime and punishment* (J. Coulson, Trans.). New York: Norton. (Original work published 1866).

AN ARTICLE OR READING IN A COLLECTION OF PIECES BY SEVERAL AUTHORS (ANTHOLOGY):

O'Connor, M.F. (1975). *Everything that rises must converge.* In J.R. Knott, Jr., & C.R. Raeske (Eds.), *Mirrors: An introduction to literature* (2nd ed., pp. 58–67). San Francisco: Canfield.

EDITION OF A BOOK:

Tortora, G.J., Funke, B.R., & Case, C.L. (1989). *Microbiology: An introduction* (3rd ed.). Redwood City, CA: Benjamin/Cummings.

DIAGNOSTIC AND STATISTICAL MANUAL OF MENTAL DISORDERS:

American Psychiatric Association. (1994). *Diagnostic and statistical manual of mental disorders* (4th ed.). Washington, DC: Author.

A WORK IN SEVERAL VOLUMES:

Churchill, W.S. (1957). *A history of the English speaking peoples: Vol. 3. The age of revolution.* New York: Dodd, Mead.

ENCYCLOPEDIA OR DICTIONARY:

Cockrell, D. (1980). Beatles. In *The new Grove dictionary of music and musicians* (6th ed., Vol. 2, pp. 321–322). London: Macmillan.

ARTICLE FROM A WEEKLY MAGAZINE:

Jones, W. (1970, August 14). Today's kids. *Newseek, 76,* 10–15.

ARTICLE FROM A MONTHLY MAGAZINE:

Howe, I. (1968, September). James Baldwin: At ease in apocalypse. *Harper's, 237,* 92–100.

ARTICLE FROM A NEWSPAPER:

Brody, J.E. (1976, October 10). Multiple cancers termed on increase. *New York Times (national ed.),* p. A37.

ARTICLE FROM A SCHOLARLY ACADEMIC OR PROFESSIONAL JOURNAL:

Barber, B.K. (1994). Cultural, family, and personal contexts of parent-adolescent conflict. *Journal of Marriage and the Family, 56,* 375–386.

GOVERNMENT PUBLICATION:

U.S. Department of Labor. Bureau of Labor Statistics. (1980). *Productivity.* Washington, DC: U.S. Government Printing Office.

PAMPHLET OR BROCHURE:

Research and Training Center on Independent Living. (1993). *Guidelines for reporting and writing about people with disabilities* (4th ed.) [Brochure]. Lawrence, KS: Author.

Any tables should have a heading with "Table #" (where # is the table number), followed by the title for the heading that describes concisely what is contained in the table. Tables and figures are typed on separate sheets at the end of the paper after the references and before the appendices. In the text you should put a reference where each table or figure should be inserted using this form:

12-2m Tables

Insert Table 1 about here

Figures are drawn on separate sheets at the end of the paper after the references and tables, and before the appendices. In the text you should put a reference where each figure will be inserted using this form:

12-2n Figures

Insert Figure 1 about here

Appendices should be used only when absolutely necessary. Generally, you will only use them for presentation of extensive measurement instruments, for detailed descriptions of the program or independent variable, and for any relevant supporting documents that you don't include in the body. Even if you include such appendices, you should briefly describe the relevant material in the body and give an accurate citation to the appropriate appendix (for example, see Appendix A).

12-2o Appendices

This paper should be used only as an example of a research paper write-up. For sample references that are not included with this paper, you should consult the *Publication Manual of the American Psychological Association, 5th Edition.*

This paper is provided only to give you an idea of what a research paper might look like. You are not allowed to copy any of the text of this paper in writing your own report.

12-3 Sample Paper

The Effects of a Supported Employment Program on Psychosocial Indicators

for Persons with Severe Mental Illness

William M. K. Trochim

Cornell University

Running head: SUPPORTED EMPLOYMENT

Abstract

This paper describes the psychosocial effects of a program of supported employment (SE) for persons with severe mental illness. The SE program involves extended individualized supported employment for clients through a Mobile Job Support Worker (MJSW) who maintains contact with the client after job placement and supports the client in a variety of ways. A 50% simple random sample was taken of all persons who entered the Breakthroughs Agency between 3/1/93 and 2/28/95 and who met study criteria. The resulting 484 cases were randomly assigned to either the SE condition (treatment group) or the usual protocol (control group), which consisted of life-skills training and employment in an in-house sheltered workshop setting. All participants were measured at intake and at three months after beginning employment, on two measures of psychological functioning (the BPRS and GAS) and two measures of self-esteem (RSE and ESE). Significant treatment effects were found on all four measures, but they were in the opposite direction from what was hypothesized. Instead of functioning better and having more self-esteem, persons in SE had lower functioning levels and lower self-esteem. The most likely explanation is that people who work in low-paying service jobs in real-world settings generally do not like them and experience significant job stress, whether they have severe mental illness or not. The implications for theory in psychosocial rehabilitation are considered.

The Effects of a Supported Employment Program on Psychosocial Indicators for Persons with Severe Mental Illness

Over the past quarter century a shift has occurred from traditional institution-based models of care for persons with severe mental illness (SMI) to more individualized community-based treatments. Along with this, there has been a significant shift in thought about the potential for persons with SMI to be rehabilitated toward lifestyles that more closely approximate those of persons without such illness. A central issue is the ability of a person to hold a regular full-time job for a sustained period of time. There have been several attempts to develop novel and radical models for program interventions designed to assist persons with SMI to sustain full-time employment while living in the community. The most promising of these have emerged from the tradition of psychiatric rehabilitation with its emphases on individual consumer goal setting, skills training, job preparation, and employment support (Cook, Jonikas, & Solomon, 1992). These are relatively new and field evaluations are rare or have only recently been initiated (Cook, 1992; Cook & Razzano, 1992). Most of the early attempts to evaluate such programs have naturally focused almost exclusively on employment outcomes. However, theory suggests that sustained employment and living in the community may have important therapeutic benefits in addition to the obvious economic ones. To date, there have been no formal studies of the effects of psychiatric rehabilitation programs on key illness-related outcomes. To address this issue, this study seeks to examine the effects of a new program of supported employment on psychosocial outcomes for persons with SMI.

Over the past several decades, the theory of vocational rehabilitation has experienced two major stages of evolution. Original models of vocational rehabilitation were based on the idea of sheltered workshop employment. Clients were paid a piece rate and worked only with other individuals who were disabled. Sheltered workshops tended to be "end points" for persons with severe and profound mental retardation since few ever moved from sheltered to competitive employment (Woest, Klein, & Atkins,

1986). Controlled studies of sheltered workshop performance of persons with mental illness suggested only minimal success (Griffiths, 1974) and other research indicated that persons with mental illness earned lower wages, presented more behavior problems, and showed poorer workshop attendance than workers with other disabilities (Ciardiello, 1981; Whitehead, 1977).

In the 1980s, a new model of services called Supported Employment (SE) was proposed as less expensive and more normalizing for persons undergoing rehabilitation (Wehman, 1985). The SE model emphasizes first locating a job in an integrated setting for minimum wage or above and then placing the person on the job and providing the training and support services needed to remain employed (1985). Services such as individualized job development, one-on-one job coaching, advo-cacy with co-workers and employers, and "fading" support were found to be effective in maintaining employment for individuals with severe and profound mental retardation (1985). The idea that this model could be generalized to persons with all types of severe disabilities, including severe mental illness, became commonly accepted (Chadsey-Rusch & Rusch, 1986).

One of the more notable SE programs was developed at Breakthroughs, the site for the present study, which created a new staff position called the mobile job support worker (MJSW) and removed the common six-month time limit for many placements. MJSWs provide ongoing, mobile support and intervention at or near the work site, even for jobs with high degrees of independence (Cook & Hoffschmidt, 1993). Time limits for many placements were removed so that clients could stay on as permanent employees if they and their employers wished. The suspension of time limits on job placements, along with MJSW support, became the basis of SE services delivered at Breakthroughs.

There are two key psychosocial outcome constructs of interest in this study. The first is the overall *psychological functioning* of the person with SMI. This would include the specification of severity of cognitive and affective symptomotology as well as the overall level of psychological functioning. The second is the level of self-reported *self-esteem* of the person. This was measured both generally and with specific reference to employment.

The key hypothesis of this study is:

H_O: A program of supported employment will result in either *no change or negative effects* on psychological functioning and self-esteem.

which will be tested against the alternative:

H_A: A program of supported employment will lead to *positive effects* on psychological functioning and self-esteem.

Methods

Sample

The population of interest for this study is all adults with SMI residing in the United States in the early 1990s. The population that is accessible to this study consists of all persons who were clients of the Breakthroughs Agency in Chicago, Illinois between the dates of March 1, 1993 and February 28, 1995 who met the following criteria: 1) a history of severe mental illness (e.g., either schizophrenia, severe depression, or manic-depression); 2) a willingness to achieve paid employment; 3) their primary diagnosis must not include chronic alcoholism or hard drug use; and 4) they must be 18 years of age or older. The sampling frame was obtained from records of the agency. Because of the large number of clients who pass through the agency each year (e.g., approximately 500 who meet the criteria) a simple random sample of 50% was chosen for inclusion in the study. This resulted in a sample size of 484 persons over the two-year course of the study.

On average, study participants were 30 years old and high school graduates (average education level = 13 years). The majority of participants (70%) were male. Most had never married (85%), few (2%) were currently married, and the remainder had been formerly married (13%). Just over half (51%) are African

American, with the remainder Caucasian (43%) or other minority groups (6%). In terms of illness history, the members in the sample averaged four prior psychiatric hospitalizations and spent a lifetime average of nine months as patients in psychiatric hospitals. The primary diagnoses were schizophrenia (42%) and severe chronic depression (37%). Participants had spent an average of almost two and one-half years (29 months) at the longest job they ever held.

The study sample cannot be considered representative of the original population of interest. Generalizability was not a primary goal; the major purpose of this study was to determine whether a specific SE program *could* work in an accessible context. Any effects of SE evident in this study can be generalized to urban psychiatric agencies that are similar to Breakthroughs, have a similar clientele, and implement a similar program.

Measures

All but one of the measures used in this study are well-known instruments in the research literature on psychosocial functioning. All of the instruments were administered as part of a structured interview that an evaluation social worker had with study participants at regular intervals.

Two measures of psychological functioning were used. The Brief Psychiatric Rating Scale (BPRS) (Overall & Gorham, 1962) is an 18-item scale that measures perceived severity of symptoms ranging from "somatic concern" and "anxiety" to "depressive mood" and "disorientation." Ratings are given on a 0-to-6 Likert-type response scale where 0 = "not present" and 6 = "extremely severe" and the scale score is simply the sum of the 18 items. The Global Assessment Scale (GAS) (Endicott, Spitzer, Fleiss, & Cohen, 1976) is a single 1-to-100 rating on a scale where each ten-point increment has a detailed description of functioning (higher scores indicate better functioning). For instance, one would give a rating between 91-100 if the person showed "no symptoms, superior functioning..." and a value between 1-10 if the person "needed constant supervision..."

Two measures of self-esteem were used. The first is the Rosenberg Self Esteem (RSE) Scale (Rosenberg, 1965), a 10-item scale rated on a 6-point response format where 1 = "strongly disagree" and 6 = "strongly agree" and there is no neutral point. The total score is simply the sum across the ten items, with five of the items being reversals. The second measure was developed explicitly for this study and was designed to measure the Employment Self Esteem (ESE) of a person with SMI. This is a 10-item scale that uses a 4-point response format where 1 = "strongly disagree" and 4 = "strongly agree" and there is no neutral point. The final ten items were selected from a pool of 97 original candidate items, based upon high item-total score correlations and a judgment of face validity by a panel of three psychologists. This instrument was deliberately kept simple—a shorter response scale and no reversal items—because of the difficulties associated with measuring a population with SMI. The entire instrument is provided in Appendix A.

All four of the measures evidenced strong reliability and validity. Internal consistency reliability estimates using Cronbach's alpha ranged from .76 for ESE to .88 for SE. Test-retest reliabilities were nearly as high, ranging from .72 for ESE to .83 for the BPRS. Convergent validity was evidenced by the correlations within construct. For the two psychological functioning scales, the correlation was .68; while for the self-esteem measures it was somewhat lower at .57. Discriminant validity was examined by looking at the cross-construct correlations, which ranged from .18 (BPRS-ESE) to .41 (GAS-SE).

Design

A pretest-posttest two-group randomized experimental design was used in this study. In notational form, the design can be depicted as:

R O X O

R O O

where:

R = the groups were randomly assigned

O = the four measures (i.e., BPRS, GAS, RSE, and ESE)

X = supported employment

The comparison group received the standard Breakthroughs protocol, which emphasized in-house training in life skills and employment in an in-house sheltered workshop. All participants were measured at intake (pretest) and at three months after intake (posttest).

This type of randomized experimental design is generally strong in internal validity. It rules out threats of history, maturation, testing, instrumentation, mortality, and selection interactions. Its primary weaknesses are in the potential for treatment-related mortality (i.e., a type of selection-mortality) and for problems that result from the reactions of participants and administrators to knowledge of the varying experimental conditions. In this study, the drop-out rate was 4% (N = 9) for the control group and 5% (N = 13) in the treatment group. Because these rates are low and are approximately equal in each group, it is not plausible that there is differential mortality. There is a possibility that there were some deleterious effects due to participant knowledge of the other group's existence (e.g., compensatory rivalry, resentful demoralization). Staff members were debriefed at several points throughout the study and were explicitly asked about such issues. There were no reports of any apparent negative feelings from the participants in this regard. Nor is it plausible that staff might have equalized conditions between the two groups. Staff members were given extensive training and were monitored throughout the course of the study. Overall, this study can be considered strong with respect to internal validity.

Procedures

Between 3/1/93 and 2/28/95, each person admitted to Breakthroughs who met the study inclusion criteria was immediately assigned a random number that gave him or her a 50/50 chance of being selected into the study sample. For those selected, the purpose of the study was explained, including the nature of the two treatments, and the need for and use of random assignment. Participants were assured confidentiality and were given an opportunity to decline to participate in the study. Only 7 people (out of 491) refused to participate. At intake, each selected sample member was assigned a random number giving them a 50/50 chance of being assigned to either the Supported Employment condition or the standard in-agency sheltered workshop. In addition, all study participants were given the four measures at intake.

All participants spent the initial two weeks in the program in training and orientation. This consisted of life skill training (e.g., handling money, getting around, cooking, and nutrition) and job preparation (employee roles and coping strategies). At the end of that period, each participant was assigned to a job site—at the agency sheltered workshop for those in the control condition, and to an outside employer if in the Supported Employment group. Control participants were expected to work full-time at the sheltered workshop for a three-month period, at which point they were posttested and given an opportunity to obtain outside employment (either Supported Employment or not). The Supported Employment participants were each assigned a case worker—called a Mobile Job Support Worker (MJSW)—who met with the person at the job site two times per week for an hour each time. The MJSW could provide any support or assistance deemed necessary to help the person cope with job stress, including counseling or working beside the person for short periods of time. In addition, the MJSW was always accessible by cellular telephone, and could be called by the participant or the employer at any time. At the end of three months, each participant was posttested and given the option of staying with their current job (with or without Supported Employment) or moving to the sheltered workshop.

Results

There were 484 participants in the final sample for this study, 242 in each treatment. There were 9 dropouts from the control group and 13 from the treatment group, leaving a total of 233 and 229 in each group, respectively, from whom both pretest and posttest were obtained. Due to unexpected difficulties in coping with job stress, 19 Supported Employment participants had to be transferred into the sheltered workshop prior to the posttest. In all 19 cases, no one was transferred prior to week 6 of employment, and 15 were transferred after week 8. In all analyses, these cases were included with the Supported Employment group (intent-to-treat analysis) yielding treatment effect estimates that are likely to be conservative.

The major results for the four outcome measures are shown in Figure 1.

Insert Figure 1 about here

It is immediately apparent that in all four cases the null hypothesis has to be accepted; contrary to expectations, Supported Employment cases did significantly *worse* on all four outcomes than did control participants.

The mean gains, standard deviations, sample sizes, and t-values (t-test for differences in average gain) are shown for the four outcome measures in Table 1.

Insert Table 1 about here

The results in the table confirm the impressions in the figures. Note that all t-values are negative except for the BPRS, where high scores indicate greater severity of illness. For all four outcomes, the t-values were statistically significant ($p < .05$).

Conclusions

The results of this study were clearly contrary to initial expectations. The alternative hypothesis suggested that SE participants would show improved psychological functioning and self-esteem after three months of employment. Exactly the reverse happened; SE participants showed significantly worse psychological functioning and self-esteem.

There are two major possible explanations for this outcome pattern. First, it seems reasonable that there might be a delayed positive or "boomerang" effect of employment outside of a sheltered setting. SE cases may have to go through an initial difficult period of adjustment (longer than three months) before positive effects become apparent. This "you have to get worse before you get better" theory is commonly held in other treatment-contexts like drug addiction and alcoholism. But a second explanation seems more plausible — that people working full-time jobs in real-world settings are almost certainly going to be under greater stress and experience more negative outcomes than those who work in the relatively safe confines of an in-agency sheltered workshop. Put more succinctly, the lesson here might very well be that work is hard. Sheltered workshops are generally nurturing work environments where virtually all employees share similar illness histories and where expectations about productivity are relatively low. In contrast, getting a job at a local hamburger shop or as a shipping clerk puts the person in contact with co-workers who may not be sympathetic to their histories or forgiving with respect to low productivity. This second explanation seems even more plausible in the wake of informal debriefing sessions held as focus groups with the staff and selected research participants. It was clear in the discussion that SE persons experienced significantly higher job stress levels and more negative consequences. However, most of them also felt that the experience was a good one overall and that even their "normal" co-workers "hated their jobs" most of the time.

One lesson we might take from this study is that much of our contemporary theory in psychiatric rehabilitation is naive at best and, in some cases, may be seriously misleading. Theory led us to believe that outside work was a "good" thing that would naturally lead to "good" outcomes   like increased psychological functioning and self-esteem. But for most people (SMI or not) work is at best tolerable, especially for the types of low-paying service jobs available to study participants. While people with SMI may not function as well or have high self-esteem, we should balance this with the desire they may have to "be like other people," including struggling with the vagaries of life and work that others struggle with.

Future research in this area needs to address the theoretical assumptions about employment outcomes for persons with SMI. It is especially important that attempts to replicate this study also try to measure how SE participants feel about the decision to work, even if traditional outcome indicators suffer. It may very well be that negative outcomes on traditional indicators can be associated with a "positive" impact for the participants and for the society as a whole.

References

Chadsey-Rusch, J. & Rusch, F.R. (1986). *The ecology of the workplace.* In J. Chadsey-Rusch, C. Haney-Maxwell, L.A. Phelps, & F.R. Rusch (Eds.), *School-to-work transition issues and models* (pp. 59–94). Champaign, IL: Transition Institute at Illinois.

Ciardiello, J.A. (1981). Job placement success of schizophrenic clients in sheltered workshop programs. *Vocational Evaluation and Work Adjustment Bulletin, 14,* 125–128, 140.

Cook, J.A. (1992). Job ending among youth and adults with severe mental illness. *Journal of Mental Health Administration, 19*(2), 158–169.

Cook, J.A., & Hoffschmidt, S. (1993). Psychosocial rehabilitation programming: A comprehensive model for the 1990's. In R.W. Flexer & P. Solomon (Eds.), *Social and community support for people with severe mental disabilities: Service integration in rehabilitation and mental health.* Andover, MA: Andover Publishing.

Cook, J.A., Jonikas, J., & Solomon, M. (1992). Models of vocational rehabilitation for youth and adults with severe mental illness. *American Rehabilitation, 18,* 3, 6–32.

Cook, J.A., & Razzano, L. (1992). Natural vocational supports for persons with severe mental illness: Breakthroughs supported competitive employment program. In L. Stein (Ed.), *New directions for mental health services, 56,* 23–41. San Francisco: Jossey-Bass.

Endicott, J.R., Spitzer, J.L., Fleiss, J.L..,& Cohen, J. (1976). The Global Assessment Scale: A procedure for measuring overall severity of psychiatric disturbance. *Archives of General Psychiatry, 33,* 766–771.

Griffiths, R.D. (1974). Rehabilitation of chronic psychotic patients. *Psychological Medicine, 4,* 316–325.

Overall, J.E., & Gorham, D.R. (1962). The Brief Psychiatric Rating Scale. *Psychological Reports, 10,* 799–812.

Rosenberg, M. (1965). *Society and adolescent self image.* Princeton, NJ: Princeton University Press.

Wehman, P. (1985). Supported competitive employment for persons with severe disabilities. In P. McCarthy, J. Everson, S. Monn, & M. Barcus (Eds.), *School-to-work transition for youth with severe disabilities* (pp. 167–182). Richmond, VA: Virginia Commonwealth University.

Whitehead, C.W. (1977). *Sheltered workshop study: A nationwide report on sheltered workshops and their employment of handicapped individuals* (Workshop Survey, Volume 1). U.S. Department of Labor Service Publication. Washington, DC: U.S. Government Printing Office.

Woest, J., Klein, M., & Atkins, B.J. (1986). An overview of supported employment strategies. *Journal of Rehabilitation Administration, 10*(4), 130–135.

Figure 1. Pretest and posttest means for treatment (SE) and control groups for the four outcome measures.

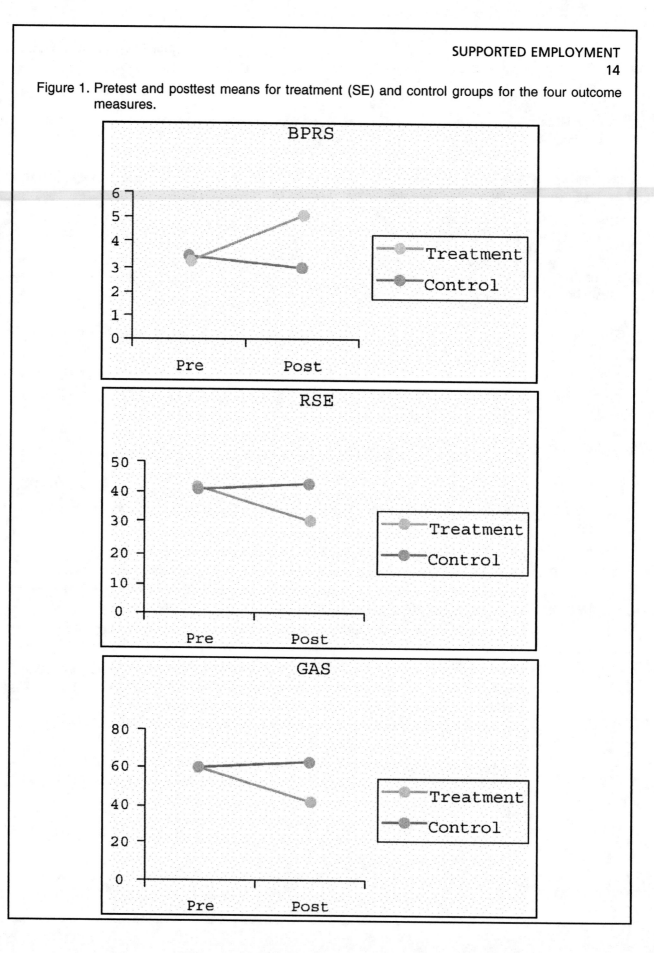

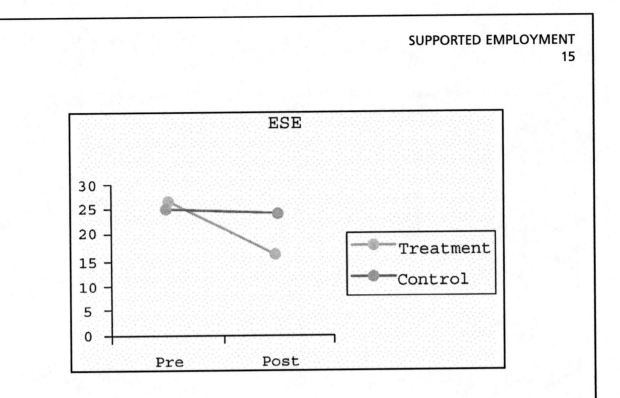

Table 1. Means, standard deviations and Ns for the pretest, posttest, and gain scores for the four outcome variables and t-test for difference between average gains.

BPRS		Pretest	Posttest	Gain
Treatment	Mean	3.2	5.1	1.9
sd	2.4	2.7	2.55	
N	229	229	229	
Control	Mean	3.4	3.0	-0.4
sd	2.3	2.5	2.4	
N	233	233	233	
t =	9.979625	p<.05		
GAS		Pretest	Posttest	Gain
Treatment	Mean	59	43	-16
sd	25.2	24.3	24.75	
N	229	229	229	
Control	Mean	61	63	2
sd	26.7	22.1	24.4	
N	233	233	233	
t =	-7.87075	p<.05		
RSE		Pretest	Posttest	Gain
Treatment	Mean	42	31	-11
sd	27.1	26.5	26.8	
N	229	229	229	
Control	Mean	41	43	2
sd	28.2	25.9	27.05	
N	233	233	233	
t =	-5.1889	p<.05		
ESE		Pretest	Posttest	Gain
Treatment	Mean	27	16	-11
sd	18.6	20.3	19.45	
N	233	233	233	
Control	Mean	25	24	-1
sd	18.6	20.3	19.45	
N	233	233	233	
t =	-5.41191	p<.05		

Appendix A

The Employment Self-Esteem Scale

Please rate how strongly you agree or disagree with each of the following statements.

| Strongly Disagree | Somewhat Disagree | Somewhat Agree | Strongly Agree | 1. I feel good about my work on the job. |

| Strongly Disagree | Somewhat Disagree | Somewhat Agree | Strongly Agree | 2. On the whole, I get along well with others at work. |

| Strongly Disagree | Somewhat Disagree | Somewhat Agree | Strongly Agree | 3. I am proud of my ability to cope with difficulties at work. |

| Strongly Disagree | Somewhat Disagree | Somewhat Agree | Strongly Agree | 4. When I feel uncomfortable at work, I know how to handle it. |

| Strongly Disagree | Somewhat Disagree | Somewhat Agree | Strongly Agree | 5. I can tell that other people at work are glad to have me there. |

| Strongly Disagree | Somewhat Disagree | Somewhat Agree | Strongly Agree | 6. I know I'll be able to cope with work for as long as I want. |

| Strongly Disagree | Somewhat Disagree | Somewhat Agree | Strongly Agree | 7. I am proud of my relationship with my supervisor at work. |

| Strongly Disagree | Somewhat Disagree | Somewhat Agree | Strongly Agree | 8. I am confident that I can handle my job without constant assistance. |

| Strongly Disagree | Somewhat Disagree | Somewhat Agree | Strongly Agree | 9. I feel like I make a useful contribution at work. |

| Strongly Disagree | Somewhat Disagree | Somewhat Agree | Strongly Agree | 10. I can tell that my co-workers respect me. |

Glossary

A

0.05 level of significance See alpha level.

alpha level The significance level. Specifically, alpha is the Type I error, or the probability of concluding that there is a treatment effect when in reality there is not.

alternative hypothesis A specific statement of prediction that usually states what you expect will happen in your study.

ANCOVA (Analysis of Covariance) An analysis that estimates the difference between the groups on the posttest after adjusting for differences on the pretest.

anonymity The assurance that no one, including the researchers, will be able to link data to a specific individual.

ANOVA (Analysis of Variance) An analysis that estimates the difference between groups on a posttest. The ANOVA could estimate the difference between a treatment and control group (thus being equivalent to the t-test) or can examine both main and interaction effects in a factorial design.

area random sampling (see Cluster random sampling)

attribute A specific value of a variable. For instance, the variable sex or gender has two attributes: male and female.

B

bell curve Smoothed histogram or bar graph describing the expected frequency for each value of a variable. The name comes from the fact that such a distribution often has the shape of a bell.

C

case study An intensive study of a specific individual or specific context.

causal Pertaining to a cause-effect relationship.

causal relationship A cause-effect relationship. For example, when you evaluate whether your treatment or program causes an outcome to occur, you are examining a causal relationship.

cause construct Your abstract idea or theory of what the cause is in a cause-effect relationship you are investigating.

central tendency An estimate of the center of a distribution of values. The most usual measures of central tendency are the mean, median, and mode.

cluster random sampling A sampling method that involves dividing the population into groups called clusters, randomly selecting clusters, and then sampling each element in the selected clusters. This method is useful when sampling a population that is spread across a wide area geographically.

codebook A written description of the data that describes each variable and indicates where and how it can be accessed.

coding The process of categorizing qualitative data.

compensatory equalization of treatment A social threat to internal validity that occurs when the control group is given a program or treatment (usually by a well-meaning third party) designed to make up for or "compensate" for the treatment the program group gets. This threat diminishes the researcher's ability to evaluate the program effect by equalizing the group's experiences.

compensatory program A program given to only those who need it on the basis of some screening mechanism.

compensatory rivalry A social threat to internal validity that occurs when one group knows the program another group is getting and, because of that, develops a competitive attitude with the other group. Often it is the comparison group knowing that the program group is receiving a desirable program (e.g., new computers) that generates the rivalry.

concept maps Two dimensional graphs of a group's ideas where ideas that are more similar are located closer together and those judged less similar are more distant. Concept maps are often used by a group to develop a conceptual framework for a research project.

conclusion validity The degree to which conclusions you reach about relationships in your data are reasonable.

concurrent validity An operationalization's ability to distinguish between groups that it should theoretically be able to distinguish between.

confidence interval Technically, 1 - alpha. The confidence interval is the probability of correctly concluding that there is no treatment effect.

confidentiality An assurance made to study participants that identifying information about them acquired through the study will not be released to anyone outside of the study.

construct validity The degree to which inferences can legitimately be made from the operationalizations in your study to the theoretical constructs on which those operationalizations are based.

constructivisim The belief that you construct your view of the world based on your experiences and perceptions.

content analysis The analysis of text documents. The analysis can be quantitative, qualitative, or both. Typically, the major purpose of content analysis is to identify patterns in text.

content validity A check of the operationalization against the relevant content domain for the construct.

control group A group, comparable to the program group, that didn't receive the program.

convergent validity The degree to which the operationalization is similar to (converges on) other operationalizations to which it should be theoretically similar.

correlation A single number that describes the degree of relationship between two variables.

correlation matrix A table of correlations showing all possible relationships among a set of variables. The diagonal of a correlation matrix (the numbers that go from the upper-left corner to the lower right) always consists of ones because these are the correlations between each variable and itself (and a variable is always perfectly correlated with itself). Off-diagonal elements are the correlation of the variables represented by that row and column in the matrix.

correlational relationship Two variables that perform in a synchronized manner.

covariates Variables you adjust for in your study.

criterion-related validity The validation of a measure based on its relationship to another independent measure as predicted by your theory of how the measures should behave.

critical realism The belief that there is an external reality independent of a person's thinking (realism) but that we can never know that reality with perfect accuracy (critical).

Cronbach's Alpha One specific method of estimating the reliability of a measure. Although not calculated in this manner, Cronbach's Alpha can be thought of as analogous to the average of all possible split-half correlations.

cross-sectional A study that takes place at a single point in time.

cumulative or Guttman scale A method of scaling in which the items are assigned scale values that allow them to be placed in a cumulative ordering with respect to the construct being scaled.

D

data audit The process of reviewing data collection procedures and data to make judgments about the potential for bias or distortion.

deductive Top-down reasoning that works from the more general to the more specific.

degrees of freedom (df) A statistical term that is a function of the sample size. In the t-test formula, for instance, the df is the sum of the persons in both groups minus 2.

dependent variable The variable affected by the independent variable, for example the outcome.

descriptive statistics Statistics used to describe the basic features of the data in a study.

dichotomous question A question with two possible responses.

diffusion or imitation of treatment A social threat to internal validity that occurs because a comparison group learns about the program either directly or indirectly from program group participants. In a school context, children from different groups within the same school might share experiences during lunch hour. Or, comparison group students, seeing what the program group is getting, might set up their own experience to try to imitate that of the program group.

direct observation The process of observing a phenomenon to gather information about it. This process is distinguished from participant observation in that a direct observer doesn't typically try to become a participant in the context and does strive to be as unobtrusive as possible so as not to bias the observations.

discriminant validity The degree to which concepts that should not be related theoretically are, in fact, not interrelated in reality.

dispersion The spread of the values around the central tendency. The two common measures of dispersion are the range and the standard deviation.

distribution The manner in which a variable takes different values in your data.

double entry An automated method for checking data-entry accuracy in which you enter data once and then enter it a second time, with the software automatically stopping each time a discrepancy is detected until the data enterer resolves the discrepancy. This procedure assures extremely high rates of data entry accuracy, although it requires twice as long for data entry.

double pretest design A design that includes two waves of measurement prior to the program.

dummy variable A variable that uses discrete numbers, usually 0 and 1, to represent different groups in your study in the equations of the GLM.

E

ecological fallacy Faulty reasoning that results from making conclusions about individuals based only on analyses of group data.

effect construct Your abstract idea or theory of what the outcome is in a cause-effect relationship you are investigating.

empirical Based on direct observations and measurements of reality.

epistemological assumptions The assumptions that underlie the theory of methods.

epistemology The philosophy of knowledge or of how you come to know about the world.

error term A term in a regression equation that captures the degree to which the line is in error (for example, the residual) in describing each point.

ethnography Study of a culture using qualitative field research.

exception dictionary A dictionary that includes all nonessential words like is, and, and of, in a content analysis study.

exception fallacy A faulty conclusion reached as a result of basing a conclusion on exceptional or unique cases.

exhaustive The property of a variable that occurs when you include all possible answerable responses.

expert sampling A sample of people with known or demonstrable experience and expertise in some area.

external validity The degree to which the conclusions in your study would hold for other persons in other places and at other times.

F

face validity A validity that checks that "on its face" the operationalization seems like a good translation of the construct.

factor A major independent variable.

factorial designs Designs that focus on the program or treatment, its components, and its major dimensions and enable you to determine whether the program has an effect, whether different subcomponents are effective, and whether there are interactions in the effects caused by subcomponents.

field research A research method in which the researcher goes into the field to observe the phenomenon in its natural state.

filter or contingency question A question you ask the respondents to determine whether they are qualified or experienced enough to answer a subsequent one.

fishing and the error rate problem A problem that occurs as a result of conducting multiple analyses and treating each one as independent.

formative evaluation Evaluations that strengthen or improve the object being evaluated. Formative evaluations are used to improve programs while they are still under development.

frequency distribution A summary of the frequency of individual values or ranges of values for a variable.

fully-crossed factorial design A design that includes the pairing of every combination of factor levels.

G

GLM (General Linear Model) A system of equations that is used as the mathematical framework for most of the statistical analyses used in applied social research.

gradient of similarity The dimension along which your study context can be related to other potential contexts to which you might wish to generalize. Contexts that are closer to yours along the gradient of similarity of place, time, people, and so on can be generalized to with more confidence that ones that are further away.

grounded theory A theory rooted in observation about phenomena of interest. Also, a method for achieving such a theory.

H

heterogeneity sampling Sampling for diversity or variety.

hierarchical modeling The incorporation of multiple units of analysis within a single analytic model. For instance, in an educational study, you might want to compare student performance with teacher expectations. To examine this relationship would require averaging student performance for each class because each teacher has multiple students and you are collecting data at both the teacher and student level.

history threat A threat to internal validity that occurs when some historical event affects your study outcome.

hypothesis A specific statement of prediction.

hypothetical-deductive model A model in which two hypotheses are tested and so that all possible outcomes exist and so that if one hypotheses is accepted the second must therefore be rejected.

I

idiographic Laws or rules that relate to individuals.

incomplete factorial design A design in which some cells or combinations in a fully-crossed factorial design are intentionally left empty.

independent variable The variable that you manipulate. For instance, a program or treatment is typically an independent variable.

indirect measure An unobtrusive measure that occurs naturally in a research context.

inductive Bottom-up reasoning that begins with specific observations and measures and ends up as general conclusion or theory.

inferential statistics Statistical analyses used to reach conclusions that extend beyond the immediate data alone.

informed consent A policy of informing study participants about the procedures and risks involved in research that ensures that all participants must give their consent to participate.

Institutional Review Board (IRB) A panel of people who review grant proposals with respect to ethical implications and decide whether additional actions need to be taken to assure the safety and rights of participants.

instrumentation threat A threat to internal validity that arises when the instruments (or observers) used on the posttest and the pretest differ.

interaction effect An effect that occurs when differences on one factor depend on which level you are on another factor.

internal validity The approximate truth about inferences regarding cause-effect or causal relationships.

interval level response A response measured on an interval level, where the size of the interval between potential response values is meaningful. Most 1-to-5 rating responses can be considered interval level.

inverse relationship (see negative relationship).

L

least squares The criterion for fitting a regression line so that you minimize the sum of the squares of the residuals from the regression line.

level A subdivision of a factor into components or features.

Likert scale A method of scaling in which the items are assigned interval-level scale values and the responses are gathered using an interval level response format.

linear model Any statistical model that uses equations to estimate lines.

longitudinal A study that takes place over time.

M

main effect An outcome that shows consistent differences between all levels of a factor.

maturation threat A threat to validity that occurs as a result of natural maturation that occurs between pre- and post-measurement.

mean A description of the central tendency in which you add up all the values and divide by the number of values.

measurement error Any influence on an observed score not related to what you are attempting to measure.

median The middle number in a series of numbers. For example in Thurstone scaling the median is the value above and below which 50 percent of the ratings fall.

median The score found at the exact middle or fiftieth percentile of the set of values. One way to compute the median is to list all scores in numerical order and then locate the score in the center of the sample.

memoing A process for recording your thoughts and ideas as they evolve throughout the study.

methodology The methods you use to try to understand the world better.

modal instance sampling Sampling for the most typical case.

mode The most frequently occurring value in the set of scores.

model specification The process of stating the equation that you believe best summarizes the data for a study.

mono-method bias A threat to construct validity that occurs because you use only a single method of measurement.

mono-operation bias A threat to construct validity that occurs when you rely on only a single implementation of your independent variable, cause, program, or treatment in your study.

mortality threat A threat to validity that occurs because a significant number of participants drop out.

multimethod matrix (MTMM) A matrix of correlations arranged to facilitate the assessment of construct validity.

multioption variable A question format in which the respondent can pick multiple variables from a list.

multiple group threat An internal validity threat that occurs in studies that use multiple groups, for instance, a program and a comparison group.

multi-stage sampling The combining of several sampling techniques to create a more efficient or effective sample than the use of any one sampling type can achieve on its own.

mutually exclusive The property of a variable that ensures that the respondent is not able to assign two attributes simultaneously. For example, gender is a variable with mutually exclusive options if it is impossible for the respondents to simultaneously claim to be both male and female.

N

natural selection theory of knowledge A theory that ideas have survival value and that knowledge evolves through a process of variation, selection, and retention.

negative relationship A relationship between variables in which high values for one variable are associated with low values on another variable.

nominal response format A response format that has a number beside each choice where the number has no meaning except as a placeholder for that response.

nomological network A network that includes the theoretical framework for what you are trying to measure, an empirical framework for how you are going to measure it, and specification of the linkages among and between these two frameworks.

nomothetic Refers to laws or rules that pertain to the general case.

Nonequivalent Dependent Variables (NEDV) design A single-group pre-post quasi-experimental design with two outcome measures where only one measure is theoretically predicted to be affected by the treatment and the other is not.

Nonequivalent-Groups design (NEGD) A pre-post two-group quasi-experimental design structured like a pretest-posttest randomized experiment, but lacking random assignment to group.

nonprobability sampling Sampling that does not involve random selection.

nonproportional quota sampling A sampling method where you sample until you achieve a specific number of sampled units for each subgroup of a population, where the proportions in each group are not the same.

null case A situation in which the treatment has no effect.

null hypothesis The hypothesis that describes the possible outcomes other than the alternative hypothesis. Usually the null hypothesis predicts there will be no effect of a program or treatment you are studying.

O

one-tailed hypothesis A hypothesis that specifies a direction, for example, when your hypothesis predicts that your program will increase the outcome.

ontological assumptions The assumptions you hold about reality. For instance, realism is an ontological assumption that holds that there is an external reality apart from your experience of it.

open coding A phase of the grounded theory method where you consider the data in minute detail while developing some initial categories.

operationalization The act of translating a construct into its manifestation, for example translating the idea of your treatment or program into the actual program, or translating the idea of what you want to measure into the real measure. The result is also referred to as an operationalization, that is, you might describe your actual program as an operationalized program.

operationalization Your translation of an idea or construct into something real and concrete.

ordinal response format A response format in which respondents are asked to rank the possible answers in order of preference.

P

participant observation A method of qualitative observation where the researcher becomes a participant in the culture or context being observed.

pattern matching The degree of correspondence between two data items. For instance, you might look at a pattern match of a theoretical expectation pattern with an observed patten to see if you are getting the outcomes you expect.

Pattern-Matching NEDV design A single-group pre-post quasi-experimental design with multiple outcome measures where there is a theoretically-specified pattern of expected effects across the measures. To assess the treatment effect, the theoretical pattern of expected outcomes is correlated or matched with the observed pattern of outcomes as measured.

Pearson Product Moment Correlation A particular type of correlation used when both variables can be assumed to be measured at an interval level of measurement.

phenomenology A philosophical perspective as well as an approach to qualitative methodology that focuses on people's subjective experiences and interpretations of the world.

population The group you want to generalize to and the group you sample from in a study.

population parameter The mean or average you would obtain if you were able to sample the entire population.

positive relationship A relationship between variables in which high values for one variable are associated with high values on another variable and low values are associated with low values.

positivism The philosophical position that the only meaningful inferences are ones that can be verified through experience or direct measurement. Positivism is often associated with the stereotype of the hard-headed, lab-coat scientist who refuses to believe in something if it can't be seen or measured directly.

post-positivism The rejection of positivism in favor of a position that one can make reasonable inferences about phenomena based upon theoretical reasoning combined with experience-based evidence.

posttest-only nonexperimental design A research design in which only a posttest is given. It is referred to as nonexperimental because no control group exists.

posttest-only randomized experiment An experiment in which the groups are randomly assigned and receive only a posttest.

predictive validity A type of construct validity based on the idea that your measure is able to predict what it theoretically should be able to predict.

pre-post nonequivalent groups quasi-experiment A research design in which groups receive both a pre- and posttest and group assignment is not randomized and therefore the groups may be nonequivalent, making it a quasi-experiment.

probabilistic Based on probabilities.

probabilistic equivalence The notion that two groups, if measured infinitely, would on average perform identically. Note that two groups that are probabilistically equivalent would seldom obtain the exact same average score.

probability sampling Method of sampling that utilizes some form of *random selection.*

projective question A hypothetically framed question. For example, you might ask the respondent how much money people they know typically give in a year to charitable causes.

proportional quota sampling A sampling method where you sample until you achieve a specific number of sampled units for each subgroup of a population, where the proportions in each group are the same.

Proximal Similarity Model A model for generalizing from your study to other contexts based upon the degree to which the other context is similar to your study context.

Proxy-Pretest design A post-only design in which, after the fact, a pretest measure is constructed from pre-existing data. This is usually done to make up for the fact that the research did not include a true pretest.

Q

qualitative data Data in which the variables are not in a numerical form, but are in the form of text, photographs, sounds bytes, and so on.

qualitative measures Data not recorded in numerical form.

qualitative variable A variable that is not in numerical form.

quantitative data Data that appears in numerical form.

quantitative variable Data in the form of numbers.

quasi-experimental designs Research designs that look like randomized or true experiments (they have multiple groups and pre-post measurement) but use nonrandom assignment to assign the groups.

quasi-experimental designs Research designs that have several of the key features of randomized experimental designs, such as pre-post measurement and treatment-control group comparisons, but lack random assignment to treatment group.

quota sampling Any sampling method where you sample until you achieve a specific number of sampled units for each subgroup of a population.

R

random assignment Process of assigning your sample into two or more subgroups by chance. Procedures for random assignment can vary from flipping a coin to using a table of random numbers to using the random number capability built into a computer.

random selection Process or procedure that assures that the different units in your population are selected by chance.

Randomized Block design Experimental designs in which the sample is grouped into relatively homogeneous subgroups or blocks within which your experiment is replicated. This procedure reduces noise or variance in the data.

range The highest value minus the lowest value.

regression artifact See Regression threat.

regression line A line that describes the relationship between two or more variables.

regression analysis A general statistical analysis that enables us to model relationships in data and test for treatment effects. In regression analysis, we model relationships that can be depicted in graphic form with lines that are called regression lines.

Regression Point Displacement (RPD) A pre-post quasi-experimental research design where the treatment is given to only one unit in the sample with all remaining units acting as controls. This design is particularly useful to study the effects of community-level interventions where outcome data is routinely collected at the community level.

Regression Point Displacement (RDP) A pre-post quasi-experimental design where the program or treatment is given to only a single unit (for example, person or school) but many units are used as a comparison group.

regression threat A statistical phenomenon that causes a group's average performance on one measure to regress toward or appear closer to the mean of that measure than anticipated or predicted. Regression occurs whenever you have a nonrandom sample from a population and two measures that are imperfectly correlated. A regression threat will bias your estimate of the group's posttest performance and can lead to incorrect causal inferences.

regression to the mean See Regression threat.

Regression-Discontinuity (RD) A pretest-posttest, program-comparison group quasi-experimental design in which a cutoff criterion on the preprogram measure is the method of assignment to group.

relationship Refers to the correspondence between two variables.

reliability The degree to which a measure is consistent or dependable; the degree to which it would give you the same result over and over again, assuming the underlying phenomenon is not changing.

repeated measures Two or more waves of measurement over time.

Requests For Proposals (RFPs) These RFPs, published by government agencies and some companies, describe some problem that the agency would like researchers to address. Typically, the RFP describes the problem that needs addressing, the contexts in which it operates, the approach they would like you to take to investigate to address the problem, and the amount they would be willing to pay for such research.

research question The central issue being addressed in the study, which is typically phrased in the language of theory.

resentful demoralization A social threat to internal validity that occurs when the comparison group knows what the program group is getting and instead of developing a rivalry, control group members become discouraged or angry and give up.

residual The vertical distance from the regression line to each point. The residual in regression analysis refers to the portion of the outcome or dependent variable that you cannot predict with your regression equation.

response A specific measurement value that a sampling unit supplies.

response brackets A question response type that includes groups of answers, such as between 30 and 40 years old, or between $50,000 and $100,000 annual income.

response format The format you use to collect the answer from the respondent.

response scale A sequential numerical response format, such as a 1-to-5 rating format.

right to service The ethical issue involved when participants do not receive a service that they would be eligible for if they were not in your study. For example, the member of a control group might not receive a drug because they are in a study.

S

sample The actual units you select to participate in your study.

sampling distribution The theoretical distribution of an infinite number of samples of the population of interest in your study.

sampling error Error in measurement associated with sampling.

sampling frame The list from which you draw your sample. In some cases, there is no list; you draw your sample based upon an explicit rule. For instance, when doing quota sampling of passers-by at the local mall, you do not have a list per se, and the sampling frame is the population of people who pass by within the time frame of your study and the rule(s) you use to decide whom to select.

sampling model A model for generalizing in which you identify your population, draw a fair sample and conduct your research, and finally generalize your results to other populations groups.

scaling The branch of measurement that involves the construction of an instrument that associates qualitative constructs with quantitative metric units.

secondary analysis Analysis that makes use of already existing data sources.

selection bias Any factor other than the program that leads to posttest differences between groups.

selection threat See selection bias.

selection-history threat A threat to internal validity that results from any other event that occurs between pretest and posttest that the groups experience differently.

selection-instrumentation A threat to internal validity that results from differential changes in the test used for each group from pretest to posttest.

selection-maturation threat A threat to internal validity that arises from any differential rates of normal growth between pretest and posttest for the groups.

selection-mortality A threat to internal validity that arises when there is differential nonrandom dropout between pretest and posttest.

selection-regression A threat to internal validity that occurs when there are different rates of regression to the mean in the two groups.

selection-testing threat A threat to internal validity that occurs when a differential effect of taking the pretest exists between groups on the posttest.

selective coding Systematic coding with respect to a previously developed core concept.

semantic differential A scaling method in which an object is assessed by the respondent on a set of bipolar adjective pairs.

Separate Pre-Post Samples A design in which the people who receive the pretest are not the same as the people who take the posttest.

simple random sampling A method of sampling that involves drawing a sample from a population so that every possible sample has an equal probability of being selected.

simple random sampling bell curve The histogram or bar chart graph describing the frequency of each possible measurement response.

single-group threat A threat to internal validity that occurs in a study that uses only a single program or treatment group and no comparison or control.

single-option variable A question response list from which the respondent can check only one response.

slope The change in y for a change in x of one unit.

snowball sampling A sampling method in which you sample participants based upon referral from prior participants.

social threats to internal validity Threats to internal validity that arise because social research is conducted in real-world human contexts where people will react to not only what affects them, but also to what is happening to others around them.

Solomon Four-Group design This design has four groups. Two of the groups receive the treatment and two do not. Furthermore, one of the treatment groups and one of the controls receive a pretest and the other two do not. By explicitly including testing as a factor in the design, you can assess experimentally whether a testing threat is operating.

standard deviation The spread or variability of the scores around their average in a *single sample.*

standard deviation The square root of the variance. The standard deviation and variance both measure dispersion, but because the standard deviation is measured in the same units as the original measure and the variance is measured in squared units, the standard deviation is usually the more directly interpretable and meaningful.

standard error The spread of the averages around the average of averages in a sampling distribution.

standard error of the difference A statistical estimate of the standard deviation one would obtain from the distribution of an infinite number of estimates of the difference between the means of two groups.

statistic A value that is estimated from data.

statistical power The probability of correctly concluding that there is a treatment or program effect in your data.

stratified random sampling A method of sampling that involves dividing your population into homogeneous subgroups and then taking a simple random sample in each subgroup.

structured response formats A response format that is predetermined prior to administration.

subjectivist The belief that there is no external reality and that the world as you see it is solely a creation of your own mind.

summative evaluations Evaluations that examine the effects or outcomes of some program or treatment.

Switching-Replications design A two-group design in two phases defined by three waves of measurement. The implementation of the treatment is repeated in both phases. In the repetition of the treatment, the two groups *switch* roles; the original control group in phase 1 becomes the treatment group in phase 2; whereas the original treatment acts as the control. By the end of the study, all participants have received the treatment.

symmetric matrix A square table where the value for each numbered row and column is identical to the value for the same numbered column and row.

systematic random sample A sampling method where you determine randomly where you want to start selecting in the sampling frame and then follow a rule to select every x^{th} element in the sampling frame list (where the ordering of the list is assumed to be random).

T

t-test A statistical test of the difference between the means of two groups, often a program and comparison group. The t-test is the simplest variation of the one-way Analysis of Variance (ANOVA).

t-value The estimate of the difference between the groups relative to the variability of the scores in the groups.

temporal precedence One criterion for establishing a causal relationship that holds that the cause must occur before the effect.

testing threat A threat to internal validity that occurs when taking the pretest affects how participants do on the posttest.

theoretical Pertaining to theory. Social research is theoretical, meaning that much of it is concerned with developing, exploring, or testing the theories or ideas that social researchers have about how the world operates.

third-variable problem An unobserved variable that accounts for a correlation between two variables.

threat to conclusion validity Any factor that can lead you to reach an incorrect conclusion about a relationship in your observations.

threats to validity Reasons your conclusion or inference might be wrong.

time series Many waves of measurement over time.

translation validity A type of construct validity related to how well you translated the idea of your measure into its operationalization.

true score theory A theory that maintains that every measurement is an additive composite of two components: the true ability of the respondent and random error.

two-group posttest-only randomized experiment A research design in which two randomly assigned groups participate. Only one group receives the program and both groups receive a posttest.

two-tailed hypothesis A hypothesis that does not specify a direction. For example in a study on self-esteem, you do not predict whether your assisted-living program will have a positive or negative effect on the self-esteem of the respondents in your study.

U

unit of analysis The entity that you are analyzing in your analysis: for example individuals, groups, or social interactions.

unobtrusive measures Methods used to collect data without interfering in the lives of the respondents.

unstructured interviewing An interviewing method that uses no predetermined interview protocol or survey and where the interview questions emerge and evolve as the interview proceeds.

unstructured response formats A response format that is not predetermined and allows the respondent or interviewer to determine. An open-ended question is a type of unstructured response format.

V

validity The best available approximation of the truth of a given proposition, inference, or conclusion.

variable Any entity that can take on different values. For instance, age can be considered a variable because age can take different values for different people at different times.

variance The spread of the scores around the mean of a distribution. Specifically, the variance is the sum of the squared deviations from the mean divided by the number of observations minus 1.

voluntary participation For ethical reasons, researchers must ensure that study participants are taking part in a study voluntarily and are not coerced.

Index

Numbers

0.05 level of significance (conclusion validity), 261
2 × 3 variation (factorial designs), 202-203
65, 95, 99 percent rule, 48-49

A

a priori, 239
abstracts
    reports, 319, 321
    sample paper, 328-331
accessible population, 44
accidental sampling, 56
accuracy of data logging, 266-267
administrative issues (in survey research), 112-113
Allport, Gordon (psychologist), 4
alternative explanations (causal relationships), 174-175
alternative hypothesis, 9
analysis, 257, 281
    ANCOVA, 293-294
    conclusion validity, 258-259
        0.05 level of significance, 261
        "fishing and the error rate problem," 261
            improving, 265-266
            threats, 259-260
        "violated assumptions of statistical tests," 261-262
    correlation, 272-277
        calculating, 275-277
        matrix, 277-279
        Pearson Product Moment Correlation, 279
        symmetric matrix, 278
        testing, 277
    data preparation, 266
        accuracy, 266-267
        data entry, 267
        data transformations, 268
        database structure, 267
        logging data, 266
    descriptive statistics, 268-269
        distribution, 269-272

experimental designs, 287
    t-Test, 287-292
factorial designs, 292
hierarchical modeling, 13
inferential statistics, 282
    dummy variables, 282-286
    GLM, 282-284
minimizing threats to validity, 239
NEGD, 294
quasi-experimental, 294
    nonequivalent groups, 294-304
RD, 304
    assumptions, 304-305
    designs, 293
    example, 311-313
    model specification, 306-310
    problems, 305-306
    steps, 308-311
regression, 283, 285
RPD, 294, 313-314
statistical power, 262, 265
    hypotheses, 262-263
    inference decision matrix, 263-265
unit of analysis, 13
Analysis of Covariance Design (ANCOVA), 207
    covariates, 208-211
analytical models, design issues, 253
ANCOVA (Analysis of Covariance Design), 207
    analysis, 293-294
        simulation example, 295-304
    covariates, 208-211
anonymity, 24
appendices
    reports, 325
    sample paper, 343
area random sampling, 54
arguments, minimizing threats to validity, 239
assignments to groups, 187-188
assumptions
    epistemological, 158
    ontological, 158
    qualitative data, 158
    quantitative data, 158
    RD design analysis, 304-305
attributes, variables, 8
audience (reports), 317
average inter-term correlation, 99

B

basic 2 × 2 factorial design, 198-199
bell curve, 46, 287
bias
    interviewers, 126
    mono-method, 75
    mono-operation, 75
    sampling, 45
    selection, 183
        NEGD, 217
    survey research, 112
        writing questions, 118
    systematic error, 91
bivariate distribution
    NEGD, 217-219
    RD design analysis, 311
blocking designs, 197
    Randomized Block, 205-207
blocks
    hetero-method, 81
    mono-method, 81
body (of reports), 321
bracket responses, 118

C

calculations, correlation, 275-277
Campbell, Don (author's mentor), 215
case studies, qualitative measurement, 161
categories (data transformations), 268
causal relationships, 6
    alternative explanations, 174-175
    conclusion validity, 258
    covariation, 174
    design, 238
        minimizing threats to validity, 238-240
    establishing cause and effect, 173
    internal validity, 172-173, 192
    programs, 240
    temporal precedence, 173
    time, 240
causal studies, 4-5
    research structure, 15-17
    validity, 21-23
        cause constructs, 21-22
        effect constructs, 21-22

cause constructs, 21-22
central tendency, 270
   dispersion, 271-272
check the answer response format, 120-121
circle the answer response format, 121
classifications
   experimental designs, 196-197, 205-207
      blocking designs, 197, 205-207
      covariance designs, 197, 207-211
      factorial designs, 197-200, 202-204
cluster random sampling, 54
cluster sampling, 55
codebook, 267
coding, 160
comparison groups, RD design, 226
compensatory equalization of treatment, 186
compensatory programs, 175
compensatory rivalry, 185
concept mapping, 25-28, 30, 43
conceptualizing, 25
   concept mapping, 25-28, 30
   dense theory, 160
   problem formulation, 25-26
      feasibility, 26
      literature review, 27
conclusion validity, 22-23, 258-259
   0.05 level of significance, 261
   "fishing and the error rate problem," 261
   improving, 265-266
   threats, 259-260
   "violated assumptions of statistical
      tests," 261-262
conclusions
   interviews, 131
   reports, 319, 322
   sample paper, 337-338
concurrent validity, 68
conditions, 16
confidence interval, 296
confidentiality, 24
confirmability, qualitative validity, 163-164
confirmations, 17
consent, informed, 24
construct validity, 22, 64, 66, 69-71, 73-75,
   103, 172
   convergent, 71-72
   definitionalist perspective, 69
   discriminant, 71-73
   interaction issues, 76-77
      confounding constructs, 77
      testing and treatment, 76
   multitrait-multimethod matrix, 79-84
   NEVD, 233
   nomological network, 65, 74, 78-79
   operationalization, 75
   pattern matching, 65, 74, 84, 86-87
      advantages/disadvantages, 88
      concept mapping, 86
      hypothesis, 86
      operationalizations, 85
   relationalist perspective, 70
   social threats, 77
      evaluation apprehension, 77-78
      experimenter expectancies, 78
      hypothesis guessing, 77

   threats, 75
      mono-method bias, 75
      mono-operation bias, 75
      preoperational explication
         of constructs, 75
constructivists, 20
constructs, 16
   cause, 21-22
   effect, 21-22
   operationalization, 21-22
content
   analysis, 165
   survey research, 111-112
      questions, 117-118
      truthful answers, 118-119
contingency questions, 116-117
control groups
   experimental design, 192
   minimizing threats to validity, 239
convenience sampling, 56
convergent validity, 68, 71-72, 80
correlational relationships, 6
correlations, 272-277
   average inter-term, 99
   average item-total, 99
   calculating, 275-277
   matrix, 277-279
   Pearson Product Moment Correlation, 279
   symmetric matrix, 278
   testing, 277
costs, survey research, 112
covariance designs, 197
   ANCOVA, 207, 208-211
covariates, 208-211
covariation, 238
   causal relationships, 174
credibility, qualitative validity, 162
criterion-related validity, 66-68
   concurrent, 68
   convergent, 68, 80
   discriminant, 68, 80
   predictive, 68
critical realism, 19
Cronbach's Alpha, 100
   reliability, 304
Cronbach, Lee (author and psychologist), 78-79
cross-over pattern, NEGD, 220-221
cross-sectional studies, 5
culture
   ethnography, 159
   evaluation research, 34-37
cumulative response format, 115
cumulative scaling, 147-150

D

data
   analysis. See analysis
   audits, 163
   entry, 267
   preparation, 266
      accuracy, 266-267
      data entry, 267
      data transformations, 268
      database structure, 267
      logging data, 266

qualitative, 11-12, 154-159
   assumptions, 158
   coding, 160
quantitative, 11-12, 154-157
   assumptions, 158
   transformations, 268
database structure, 267
deductive reasoning, 17-18
definitionalist perspective (construct validity), 69
degrees of freedom (df), 277, 290
dependability, qualitative validity, 162
dependent variables, 8
descriptive statistics, 268-269
   distribution, 269-272
descriptive studies, 5
design, 171, 186
   ANCOVA, 293-304
      analysis, 293—304
      covariates, 208-211
   building, 240-241, 245
      hybrid designs, 245-247
   cause-effect relationships, 238
      minimizing threats to validity, 238-240
   contemporary issues, 250
      analytical models, 253
      evolution of validity, 253
      judgment, 250-251
      multiple perspectives, 252
      program implementation, 252
      quality control, 252
      tailored designs, 251
      theories, 251-252
   efficiency, 247
   expanding, 241
      across groups, 243-245
      across observations, 243
      across programs, 243
      across time, 242
   experimental, 191
      analysis, 287-292
      classifications, 196-211
      control group, 192
      hybrid, 211-214
      internal validity, 191-193
      probabilistic equivalence, 193-196
      quasi-experimental, 215-219
      random assignment, 193-194, 196
      random selection, 196
      Randomized Block, 205-207
      two-group, 193-195
      two-group posttest-only, 287-288
   factorial, 292
   feasibility, 247
   groups, 187
   NEGD, 295-304
   notation, 187-188
   observations, 186
   posttest-only nonexperimental, 189
   posttest-only randomized, 189, 241
   pre-post nonequivalent groups quasi-
      experiment, 189
   quasi-experimental, 189
      analysis, 294-304
      double-pretest, 230-231
      NEDV, 231-234
      proxy-pretest, 228-229

RD, 304-313
    regression-discontinuity, 221-228
    RPD, 234-235, 313-314
    separate pre-post samples, 229-230
    Switching-Replications, 231
quasi-experimental designs, 228
RD, 293, 304-313
redundancy, 247
relationships, 248-250
reports, 319, 322
RPD, 313-314
sample paper, 333-334
situational, 247
theory-grounded, 247
time, 187
treatments, 186
two-group pre-post, 241
types, 188
validity. *See* validity
df (degrees of freedom), 277, 290
diagrams, integrative, 160
dichotomous response formats, 114, 119-120
dichotomous response scales, 133
diffusion, 185
dimensionality, scaling, 134-136
    Guttman, 147-150
    Likert, 145-147
    Method of Equal-Appearing Intervals,
        136-140, 144-145
    Thurstone, 136
direct observation, 159
    qualitative measurement, 161
discriminant validity, 68, 71-73, 80
dispersion, 271-272
distribution sampling, 46-47
    65, 95, 99 percent rule, 48-49
    bell curve, 46
    standard deviation, 47
distributions, 269, 288
    bivariate, RD design analysis, 311
    central tendency, 270
    dispersion, 271-272
    sampling, standard error, 47
documents, content analysis, 165
doorstep technique (interviews), 128
double entry, 267
double-pretest design, 230-231
dummy variable, 282-286

E

ecological fallacies, 13
effects
    constructs, 21-22
    interaction, 292
    main, 292
efficiency, design, 247
elaboration, interview responses, 130
empirical research, 4
empiricism, 19
epistemological assumptions, 158
epistemology, 18
error terms, 283, 290

errors
    measurement, 90-92, 297
        random, 90
        systematic, 91
    regression, 297
    sampling, 47-48
    standard, 47-48, 296
estimators, reliability, 101
ethics, 23-24
    jargon, 24-25
    RD design, 228
ethnography, 159
evaluation, definition, 3
evaluation research, 30
    culture, 34-37
    definitions, 30-31
    formative, 32
    goals, 31
    methods, 33
    planning-evaluation cycle, 34
    questions, 33
    strategies, 31-32
    summative, 32-33
exception dictionaries, 165
exception fallacies, 13
exhaustive variables, 8
expanding designs, 241
    across groups, 243-245
    across observations, 243
    across programs, 243
    across time, 242
experimental designs, 191
    analysis, 287-292
    classifications, 196-197
        blocking designs, 197, 205-207
        covariance designs, 197, 207-211
        factorial designs, 197-204
    control group, 192
    hybrid, 211-214
    internal validity, 191-193
    pattern matching, 252
    probabilistic equivalence, 193-196
        two-group experiments, 194
    quasi-experimental, 215
        NEGD, 216-220
        random assignment, 215
    random assignment, 193, 196, 251
    random selection, 196
    Randomized Block, 205-207
    selection regression threat, 219-220
    two-group, 193-195
        mortality, 194
        multi-group threats, 194
        selection testing, 194
        selection-instrumentation threats, 194
        single-group threats, 194
        social threats, 194
    two-group posttest-only randomized,
        287-288
expert sampling, 57
external validity, 22, 42-43, 58, 64-66
    generalizations, 42
    improving, 43
    random selection, 196
    social threats, 185
    threats, 43

F

facilities, survey research, 113
factorial designs, 197
    analysis, 292
    basic 2 × 2, 198-199
    interaction effects, 200-202
    main effects, 199-202
    null case, 199
    variations, 202
        2 × 3 example, 202-203
        incomplete designs, 204
        three-factor example, 203-204
factors, 198
    interaction effects, 200-202
    main effects, 199-202
fallacies
    ecological, 13
    exception, 13
feasibility
    design, 247
    problem formulation, 26
field research, 159
    qualitative research, 160
figures
    reports, 325
    sample paper, 340
fill-in-the-blank response formats, 119-120
filters response format, 116-117
"fishing and the error rate problem," conclusion
    validity, 261
formative evaluations, 32
formatting reports, 317, 320
    abstract, 319, 321
    appendices, 325
    body, 321
    conclusions, 322
    design, 322
    figures, 325
    introduction, 321
    measures, 321
    methods, 321
    procedures, 322
    references, 319, 322-324
    results, 322
    sampling, 321
    tables, 325
    title page, 321
fully-crossed factorial designs, 204
funding qualitative measurements, 153-154

G

General Linear Model. *See* GLM
generalizations
    external validity, 42
    qualitative measurements, 152-153
generation, concept mapping, 29
generative questions, 160
GLM (General Linear Model), 282
    two-variable linear model, 282-284
Golden Rule surveys, 125
grounded theory, 160-161
group phenomenon, regression threats, 179
group-administered questionnaires, 108
groups
    design, 187, 241
    expanding designs across, 243-245
Guttman scaling, 115, 147-150

H

haphazard sampling, 56
heterogeneity sampling, 58
heteromethod blocks (MTMM matrix), 81
heterotrait-heteromethod triangles
  (MTMM matrix), 81
heterotrait-monomethod triangles
  (MTMM matrix), 81
hierarchical modeling, 13
history threats, 174, 176
household drop-off surveys, 108
hybrid designs, 245-247
hybrid experiments, 211
  Solomon Four-Group, 211-212
  Switching-Replications, 213-214
hypotheses, 9, 11, 16
  alternative, 9
  confirmations, 17
  guessing, construct validity, 77
  hypothetical-deductive model, 11
  null, 9
  observations, 17
  one-tailed, 9
  pattern matching, 86
  qualitative measurements, 152
  statistical power, 262-263
  theories, 17
  two-tailed, 10

I

idiographic research, 4
imitation of treatment, 185
in-depth interviews, 159
incomplete factorial designs, 204
independent variables, 8
indexes, 165
indirect measures, 164-165
individuals, design, 241
inductive reasoning, 17-18
inferential statistics, 282
  dummy variables, 282-286
  GLM, 282-284
informed consent, 24
Institutional Review Board (IRB), 25
instrumentation threats, 176
integrative diagrams, 160
inter-observer reliability, 96-97
inter-rater reliability, 96-97
interaction (of programs), 76
  confounding constructs, 77
  restricted generalizability, 76-77
  testing and treatment interaction, 76
interaction effects, 200, 202, 292
internal consistency reliability, 96, 99
  average inter-item correlation, 99
  average item-total correlation, 99
  Cronbach's Alpha, 100
  split-half, 100
internal validity, 22, 172-173, 231
  causal relationships, 192
  design relationships, 248
  experimental designs, 191-193
  NEGD, 217
  NEVD, 233
  quasi-experimental designs, 215

random selection, 196
  RD design, 222, 226-227
  social threats, 185
interpretation, concept mapping, 29
interpretation principles, MTMM, 81-82
interval level response format, 115
interval measurement, 104
interval response scales, 133
interval validity, threats, 176-177
interviews, 108-109, 125
  concluding, 131
  conducting, 127
    asking questions, 129-130
    opening remarks, 128-129
  doorstep technique, 128
  in-depth, 159
  interviewers, 126-127
  introductions, 128
  personal, 109
  qualitative measurements, 152
  responses, 130-131
  tasks, 125
  telephone, 109
  training interviewers, 126-127
  unstructured, qualitative measurement, 161
introduction, reports, 318, 321
IRB (Institutional Review Board), 25
item reversals (data transformations), 268
iterative processes, 160

J

jargon
  ethics, 24-25
  research, 4-5
  sampling, 44-45
judgment, contemporary design issues, 250-251

K – L

least squares, 298
levels, 198-199
  interaction effects, 200-202
  main effects, 199-202
levels of measurement, 103-105
Likert scaling, 115, 145-147
literature citations (reports), 318
literature review, problem formulation, 27
logging data, 266
longitudinal studies, 5
  repeated measures, 5
  time series, 5
low statistical power, 260

M

mail surveys, 108
main effects, 199-200, 202, 239, 292
management-oriented models, 31
maps, interviews, 126
maturation threats, 176
mean scores, 270
  regression, 178-182
means, slopes, 291
measurement, 63, 65. See also validity
  construct validity, 64, 66, 69-71, 73-75
    definitionalist, 69
    discriminant, 71-73

nomological network, 65, 74, 78-79
  pattern matching, 65, 74, 84-88
  relationalist, 70
  threats, 75-78
construct validity, convergent, 71-72
criterion-related validity, 66-68
  concurrent, 68
  convergent, 68, 80
  discriminant, 68, 80
  predictive, 68
design, 241
errors, 297-298
external validity, 66
interaction issues, 76
  confounding constructs, 77
  restricted generalizability, 76-77
  testing and treatment, 76
interval, 104
levels, 103-105
minimizing threats to validity, 239
nominal, 104
operationalization, 64-65, 69
qualititative, 151-152
  compared to quantitative, 154-158
  ethnography, 159
  field research, 160
  funding, 153-154
  generalizations, 152-153
  grounded theory, 160-161
  hypotheses, 152
  interviewing, 152
  phenomenology, 159
qualitative methods, 154-158, 161
ordinal, 104
ratio, 104
reliability, 88, 96
  inter-rater, 96-97
  internal consistency, 96, 99-100
  measurement error, 90-92
  parallel-forms, 96, 98
  systematic error, 91
  test-retest, 96-98
  theories, 92-96
  true score theory, 89-90
reports, 319, 321
sample paper, 332-333
translation validity, 66
  content validity, 67, 74
  face validity, 67, 74
unobtrusive, 151, 164
  content analysis, 165
  indirect measures, 164-165
  secondary analysis, 166
median scores, 140, 270
Meehl, Paul (author and psychologist), 78-79
memoing, 160
Method of Equal-Appearing Intervals scaling,
  136-140, 144-145
methodology, 18
methods
  evaluation research, 33
  qualitative, 161
  reports, 318-319, 321
  sample paper, 331-332
  surveys, 132
    population, 109-110
missing values (data transformations), 268

modal instance sampling, 56-57
mode, 270
models
    management-oriented experimental, 31
    participant-oriented, 32
    Proximal Similarity, 42
    qualitative/anthropological, 31
    scientific experimental, 31
    specification, RD analysis, 306-310
mono-method bias, 75
mono-method blocks (MTMM matrix), 81
mono-operation bias, 75
mortality threats, 176
MTMM (multitrait-multimethod matrix), 79-80
    advantages/disadvantages, 83-84
    blocks, 81
    interpretation principles, 81-82
    shapes, 80-81
multi-stage sampling, 55
multi-group threats, two-group
    experiments, 194
multioption variable, 120-121
multiple-group threats, 173, 182-185
multitrait-multimethod matrix. See MTMM
mutually exclusive variables, 8

N

natural selection theory of knowledge, 20
NEDV design, 231
    construct validity, 233
    internal validity, 233
    pattern matching, 232-234
negative instances, 163
negative relationships, 7
NEGD (Nonequivalent-Groups Design), 216
    analysis, 294-304
    bivariate distribution, 217-219
    cross-over pattern, 220-221
    internal validity, 217
    selection bias, 217
    selection instrumentation, 219
    selection threats, 218
    selection-history threat, 218
    selection-maturation threat, 218
    selection-regression threat, 219-220
noise
    noise-reducing experimental designs, 197
        ANCOVA, 207-211
        Randomized Block design, 205-207
    random error, 90
    reducing in data, 206-207
nominal measurement, 104
nominal response format, 114
nomological network, 65, 74, 78-79
nomothetic research, 4
Nonequivalent Dependent Variables. See NEDV
nonequivalent groups, analysis, 294-295
    simulation example, 295-304
Nonequivalent-Groups Design. See NEGD
nonprobability sampling, 55-56
nonproportional quota sampling, 57
notation, design, 187-188
null case, 199
null hypothesis, 9
Nuremberg War Crimes Trial, 23

O

objectivity, 20
observations, 17, 186
    design, 241
    direct, qualitative measurement, 161
    expanding designs across, 243
    minimizing threats to validity, 239
    participant, 159, 161
one-tailed hypothesis, 9
ontological assumptions, 158
open coding, 160
opening questions in surveys, 124
opening remarks in interviews, 128-129
operationalizations, 16, 64-65, 69
    construct validity, 75
    constructs, 21-22
    pattern matching, 85
ordinal measurement, 104
ordinal response format, 114-115
outcomes, 16
overt encouragement, interview responses, 130

P

parallel-forms reliability, 96, 98
participant observation, 159
    qualitative measurement, 161
participant-oriented models, 32
participation types, 24
pattern matching, 65, 74, 84-87, 252
    advantages/disadvantages, 88
    concept mapping, 86
    hypothesis, 86
    NEDV design, 232-234
    operationalizations, 85
    variations, 231
patterns
    cross-over, NEGD, 220-221
    relationships, 6
Pearson Product Moment Correlation, 278-279
personal interviews, 109
personnel survey research, 113
phases, 14
phenomenology, 159
philosophy of research, 14
placement, questions in surveys, 124
planning-evaluation cycle, 34
population, 44
    accessible, 44
    parameter, 45, 48
    survey methods, 109-110
    theoretical, 44
positive relationships, 7
Positivism, 4, 18-20
    B.F. Skinner, 18
    empiricism, 19
Post-Positivism, 4, 18-20
    constructivists, 20
    critical realism, 19
    objectivity, 20
    quantitative research, 158
posteriori, 239
posttest-only nonexperimental design, 189
posttest-only randomized design, 189
    experiment, 241
pre-post nonequivalent groups quasi-experiment
    design, 189

pre-post two-group design, 245, 248
predictive validity, 68
procedures, reports, 322
preoperational explication of constructs, 75
preparation, concept mapping, 29
preventive action, minimizing threats to
    validity, 240
probabilistic equivalence, 193-196
probabilistic research, 4
probability sampling, 50, 55
problem formulation, 25-26
    feasibility, 26
    literature review, 27
procedures, reports, 319
processes, iterative, 160
programs
    causal relationships, 240
    expanding designs across, 243
    implementation, 252
    interaction, 76
        confounding constructs, 77
        restricted generalizability, 76-77
        testing and treatment, 76
proportional quota sampling, 57
proximal similarity, 43
Proximal Similarity Model, 42
proxy variables, 282, 284-286
proxy-pretest design, 228-229
purposive sampling, 56

Q

quality control, design issues, 252
qualitative data, 11-12, 154-157, 159
    assumptions, 158
    coding, 160
qualitative measurement, 151-152
    compared to quantitative, 154-158
    ethnography, 159
    field research, 160
    funding, 153-154
    generalizations, 152-153
    grounded theory, 160-161
    hypotheses, 152
    interviewing, 152
    methods, 161
    phenomenology, 159
qualitative research, 261
qualitative validity, 162
    confirmability, 163-164
    credibility, 162
    dependability, 162
    transferability, 162
quantitative indicators, 221
quantitative data, 11-12, 154-157
    assumptions, 158
quantitative descriptive analysis, 165
quantitative measurement, 154-158
quantitative research, 261
quantitative variables, 8
quasi-experimental designs, 189, 215, 228
    analysis, 294-304
    double-pretest, 230-231
    internal validity, 215
    NEDV, 231
        internal validity, 233
        pattern matching, 232-234

NEGD, 216
    bivariate distribution, 217-219
    cross-over pattern, 220-221
    internal validity, 217
    selection bias, 217
    selection instrumentation, 219
    selection threats, 218-220
    proxy-pretest design, 228-229
    random assignment, 215
    RD, analysis, 304-313
    regression-discontinuity, 221-224
        accountability, 228
        comparison groups, 226
        ethics, 228
        internal validity, 222, 226-227
        logic, 224-226
        regression line, 223
        statistics, 228
    RPD, 234-235
        analysis, 313-314
    separate pre-post samples design, 229-230
    Switching-Replications, 231
questionnaires, 109
    group-administered, 108
    household drop-offs, 108
    mail, 108
questions
    evaluation research, 33
    generative, 160
    interviews, 129-130
    survey research, 111
        bias, 118
        checklist, 124
        content, 117-118
        contingency questions, 116-117
        dichotomous response formats, 114
        Golden Rule, 125
        Guttman scale, 115
        interval response formats, 115
        Likert scale, 115
        nominal response formats, 114
        opening, 124
        ordinal response formats, 114-115
        placement, 124
        semantic differential, 115
        sensitive questions, 124
        structured, 113
        truthful answers, 118-119
        unstructured, 113
        wording, 122-123
quota sampling, 57

R

random assignment, 188, 251
    experimental designs, 193, 196
        two-group experiments, 194
    quasi-experimental designs, 215
random digital-dialing, 45
random error, 90
random selection, 50
    experimental designs, 196
    external validity, 196
    internal validity, 196
Randomized Block design, 205-207
    analysis, 293
range, 271
ratio measurement, 104

RD (regression-discontinuity), 221-224
    accountability, 228
    analysis, 293-294, 304
        assumptions, 304-305
        example, 311-313
        model specification, 306-310
        problems, 305-306
        steps, 308-311
    comparison groups, 226
    ethics, 228
    internal validity, 222, 226-227
    logic, 224-226
    regression line, 223
    statistics, 228
reasoning
    deductive, 17-18
    inductive, 17-18
redundancy, design, 247
references
    reports, 322-324
    sample paper, 339
    sections, reports, 319
regression
    analysis, 283, 285
    errors, 297
    least squares analytic procedure, 298
    lines, 297
        RD design, 223
        scopes, 301
        simulated data, 296
        slopes, 298
    residual, 298
    threats, 177-182
regression point displacement (RPD) design, 234-235
Regression Point Displacement. *See* RPD
regression to the mean
    NEGD, 218
    RD design, 227
regression-discontinuity design, 221-224
    accountability, 228
    comparison groups, 226
    ethics, 228
    internal validity, 222, 226-227
    logic, 224-226
    regression line, 223
    statistics, 228
rehabilitation programs, construct validity, 75
rehearsals, interviews, 127
relational studies, 5
relationalist perspective, construct validity, 70
relationships, 6
    causal, 5-6
        alternative explanations, 174-175
        conclusion validity, 258
        covariation, 174
        establishing cause and effect, 173
        internal validity, 172-173, 192
        programs, 240
        temporal precedence, 173
        time, 240
    cause-effect, design, 238-240
    correlational, 6
    designs, 248-250
    nature of, 6
    negative, 7
    patterns, 6
    positive, 7

    third variable problem, 6
    variables, 6-7
reliability diagonal (MTMM matrix), 80
reliability, 88, 96, 266, 302, 304
    Cronbach's Alpha, 304
    estimators, 101
    inter-rater, 96-97
    internal consistency, 96, 99
        average inter-item correlation, 99
        Cronbach's Alpha, 100
        item total correlation, 99
        split-half, 100
    measurement error, 90-92
        random error, 90
        systematic error, 91
    parallel-forms, 96, 98
    reports, 319
    test rated, 96-98
    theories, 92-96
    true score theory, 89-90
    validity, 101-103
repeated measures (longitudinal studies), 5
repetition, interview responses, 130
response formats
    dichotomous, 114, 119-120
    interval level, 115
    nominal, 114
    ordinal, 114-115
reports, 317-318
    audience, 317
    conclusions, 319
    design, 319
    formatting, 317, 320
        abstract, 319, 321
        appendices, 325
        body, 321
        conclusions, 322
        design, 322
        figures, 325
        introduction, 321
        measures, 321
        methods, 321
        procedures, 322
        reference sections, 319
        references, 322-324
        results, 322
        sampling, 321
        tables, 325
        title page, 321
    introduction, 318
    methods, 318-319
    procedures, 319
    results, 319
    sample paper, 325
        abstract, 328-331
        appendices, 343
        conclusions, 337-338
        designs, 333-334
        figures, 340
        measures, 332-333
        method, 331-332
        procedures, 334-335
        references, 339
        results, 335-336
        tables, 342
        title page, 327
    story, 317
    stylistic elements, 320

representation, concept mapping, 29
Requests for Proposals (RFPs), 26
research, 3
    analysis. *See* analysis
    conceptualizing. *See* conceptualizing
    ethics, 23-24
    evaluation. *See* evaluation research
    fallacies. *See* fallacies
    jargon, 4-5
        ethics, 24-25
    phases, 14
    philosophy, 14
    qualitative, 261
    quantitative, 261
    structure, 14-17
    studies. *See* studies
    survey. *See* survey research
resentful demoralization, 185
residual, 298
response formats (surveys), 119
    brackets, 118
    check the answer, 120-121
    circle the answer, 121
    contingency questions, 116-117
    fill-in-the-blank, 119-120
    Guttman scale, 115
    Likert scale, 115
    multioption variable, 120-121
    semantic differential, 115
    single-option variable, 121
    structured, 119-121
    unstructured, 121-122
responses
    interviews, 130-131
    sampling, 45
    scales, 133
results
    reports, 319, 322
    sample paper, 335-336
reviews, reports, 318
RFPs (Requests for Proposals), 26
right of service, 24
RPD (regression point displacement), 234-235
    analysis, 294, 313-314

S

sample paper, 325
    abstract, 328-331
    appendices, 343
    conclusions, 337-338
    designs, 333-334
    figures, 340
    measures, 332-333
    method, 331-332
    procedures, 334-335
    references, 339
    results, 335-336
    tables, 342
    title page, 327
sampling, 16, 41
    accidental, 56
    bias, 45
    cluster, 55
    cluster random, 54
    convenience, 56

distribution, 46-47
    65, 95, 99 percent rule, 48-49
    bell curve, 46
    standard deviation, 47
    standard error, 47
errors, 47-48
expert, 57
external validity, 42
    improving, 43
    threats, 43
frame, 45, 50, 53, 111
haphazard, 56
heterogeneity, 58
modal instance, 56-57
model, 42
multi-stage, 55
nonprobability, 55-56
nonproportional quota, 57
probability, 50, 55
proportional quota, 57
purposive, 56
quota, 57
random stratified, 205-207
report specifications, 318
reports, 321
simple random, 50-51, 55
snowball, 58
statistics, 45
stratified random, 51-52
surveys, 110-111
systematic random, 53-55
terminology, 44-45
scale totals (data transformations), 268
scaling, 132-133
    dichotomous, 133
    dimensionality, 134-136
        Guttman, 147-150
        Likert, 145-147
        Method of Equal-Appearing Intervals,
            136-140, 144-145
        Thurstone, 136
    interval response scales, 133
    purposes, 134
    response scales, 133
    unidimensional, 132
scientific experimental models, 31
scopes, regression lines, 301
secondary analysis, 166
select mortality, two-group experimental
  designs, 194
selection
    bias, 183, 217
    instrumentation
        NEGD, 219
        two-group experiments, 194
    random, 50
    regression, 218-220
    testing, 194, 219
    threats, 183, 218
    mortality, 184, 219
selective coding, 160
semantic differential response format, 115
semantic differential theory, 135
semantic net, 71
sensitivity, questions in surveys, 124
separate pre-post samples design, 229-230

SES (socioeconomic status), 258
shapes, MTMM, 80-81
signal-enhancing experimental designs, 197
    Basic 2 × 2 factorial design, 198-199
    interaction effects, 200-202
    main effects, 199-202
    nullcase, 199
    variations, 202-204
signal-to-noise ratio metaphor, 196-197
    blocking designs, 197, 205-207
    covariance designs, 197, 207
    factorial designs, 197
        Basic 2 × 2, 198-199
        interaction effects, 200-202
        main effects, 199-202
        nullcase, 199
        variations, 202-204
silent probing, interview responses, 130
simple random sampling, 50-51, 55
simulation example, non-equivalent group
  analysis, 295-304
single-group threats, 173, 175
    two-group experimental designs, 194
single-option variable response format, 121
situational design, 247
Skinner, B.F. (psychologist), 18
slopes
    means, 291
    measurement errors, 298
    regression lines, 298
snowball sampling, 58
social research. *See* research
social threats, 173, 185
    compensatory equalization of treatment, 186
    compensatory rivalry, 185
    construct validity, 77
        evaluation apprehension, 77-78
        experimenter expectancies, 78
        hypothesis guessing, 77
    diffusion, 185
    resentful demoralization, 185
    two-group experiments, 194
socioeconomic status (SES), 258
Solomon Four Group design, 211-212
split-half reliability, 100
standard deviation, 47-48, 94, 271
standard error, 47-48, 289, 296
statistics
    analysis
        ANCOVA, 293-304
        factorial designs, 292
        NEGD, 295-304
        Randomized Block (RD) designs, 293
        t-Test, 289-292
    descriptive. *See* descriptive statistics
    inference decision matrix, 263-265
    inferential, 282
        dummy variables, 282, 284-286
        GLM, 282-284
    NEGD, 217
    phenomenon, regression threats, 179
    power, 262, 265
        hypotheses, 262-263
        inference decision matrix, 263-265
    RD design, 228
    sampling, 45

Stevens, S.S., 133
stories, reports, 317
stratified random sampling, 51-52, 205-207
structure, 14-17
  concept mapping, 29
  surveys, 113
structured response formats, 119-121
studies, 5
  case. *See* case studies
  causal, 5
    research structure, 15-17
    validity, 21-23
  cross-sectional, 5
  descriptive, 5
  longitudinal, 5
  relational, 5
  Tuskegee Syphilis Study, 24
stylistic elements (reports), 320
subjectivist, 19
summative evaluations, 32-33
survey research, 107
  administration issues, 112-113
  bias issues, 112, 118
  constructing surveys, 113
    consideration checklist, 124
    Golden Rule, 125
    questions, 113-119, 122-124
    response formats. *See* response formats
  content issues, 111-112
  interviews, 108-109, 125
    concluding, 131
    conducting, 127-130
    doorstep technique, 128
    interviewer kit, 127
    introductions, 128
    personal, 109
    responses, 130-131
    tasks, 125
    telephone, 109
    training interviewers, 126-127
  methods, 132
  questionnaires, 109
    group-administered, 108
    household drop-off, 108
    mail surveys, 108
  questions, 111
    bias, 118
    checklist, 124
    content, 117-118
    dichotomous response formats, 114
    interval response formats, 115
    Likert scale, 115
    nominal response formats, 114
    opening, 124
    ordinal response formats, 114-115
    placement, 124
    semantic differential response formats, 115
    sensitivity, 124
    structured, 113
    truthful answers, 118-119

    unstructured, 113
    wording, 122-123
  sampling, 110-111
  selecting methods, population, 109-110
Switching-Replications design, 213-214, 231
symmetric correlation, 278
systematic error, 91
systematic random sampling, 53-55

T

t-Test, 287-288
  statistical analysis, 289-292
t-value, 289, 292, 296
tables
  reports, 325
  sample paper, 342
tailored designs, contemporary design issues, 251
telephone interviews, 109
temporal precedence, 238
  causal relationships, 173
Terkel, Studs (writer), 153
terminology. *See* jargon
test-rated reliability, 96-98
testing
  interaction with treatment, 76
  threats, 176
thematic analysis, 165
theoretical population, 44
theoretical research, 4
theories, 247
  conceptually dense, 160
  contemporary design issues, 251-252
  grounded, 160-161
  measurement. *See* measurement
  natural selection theory of knowledge, 20
  proximal similarity, 43
  reliability, 92-96
  semantic differential, 135
  true score, 89-90, 196, 300
third variable problem, 6
threats
  conclusion validity, 259-260
  construct validity, 75
    mono-method bias, 75
    mono-operation bias, 75
    preoperational explication of constructs, 75
  external validity, 43
  minimizing, 238-240
  multi-group, experimental two-group designs, 194
  selection. *See* selection
  social
    construct validity, 77-78
    experimental two-group designs, 194
  validity, 23, 176-177
    history, 174, 176
    instrumentation, 176
    maturation, 176
    mortality, 176
    multiple-group, 173, 182-185

    regression, 177-182
    selection, 183-184
    single-group, 173, 175
    social, 173, 185-186
    testing, 176
three-dimensional scales, 135
three-factor example (factorial designs), 203-204
Thurstone scaling, 136
time
  causal relationships, 240
  design, 187
  expanding designs across, 242
  survey research, 113
time series (longitudinal studies), 5
title page
  reports, 321
  sample paper, 327
transferability, qualitative validity, 162
transformations, data, 268
translation validity, 66
  content, 67, 74
  face, 67, 74
treatments, 186
  causal relationships, 240
  interaction with testing, 76
triangulation, 19
true score theory, 89-90, 196, 300
Tuskegee Syphilis Study, 24
two-dimensional scales, 135
two-group experimental designs, 193-195
  mortality, 194
  multi-group threats, 194
  selection-instrumentation threats, 194
  selection-testing, 194
  single-group threats, 194
  social threats, 194
two-group posttest-only randomized experimental design, 287-288
two-group pre-post design, 241
two-tailed hypothesis, 10
two-variable linear model, 282-284

U

unidimensional scales, 134, 136
  Likert, 145-147
  Method of Equal-Appearing Intervals, 136-140, 144-145
  Thurstone, 136
unidimensional scaling, 132
unit of analysis, 13
unobtrusive measurement, 151, 164
  content analysis, 165
  indirect measures, 164-165
  secondary analysis, 166
unstructured interviewing, qualitative measurement, 161
unstructured questions, surveys, 113
unstructured response formats, 121-122
utilization, concept mapping, 30

V

validity, 14, 20, 22. *See also* measurement
    causal studies, 21-23
        cause constructs, 21-22
        effect constructs, 21-22
    conclusion, 22-23, 258-259
        improving, 265-266
        threats, 259-262
    construct, 22, 64, 66, 69-75, 103, 172
        convergent, 71-72
        definitionalist perspective, 69
        discriminant, 71-73
        interaction issues, 76-77
        multitrait-multimethod matrix, 79-84
        NEVD, 233
        nomological network, 65, 74, 78-79
        operationalization, 75
        pattern matching, 65, 74, 84-88
        relationalist perspective, 70
        social threats, 77-78
        threats, 75
    content, 67, 74
    convergent, 71-72
    criterion-related, 66-68
        concurrent, 68
        convergent, 68, 80
        discriminant, 68, 80
        predictive, 68
    diagonals (MTMM matrix), 81
    discriminant, 71-73
    evolution, 253
    external, 22, 42-43, 58, 64, 66
        generalizations, 42
        improving, 43
        random selection, 196
        social threats, 185
        threats, 43
    face, 67, 74
    internal, 22, 172-173, 231
        causal relationships, 192
        design relationships, 248
        experimental designs, 191-193
        NEGD, 217
        NEVD, 233
        quasi-experimental designs, 215
        random selection, 196
        RD design, 222, 226-227
        social threats, 185

    interval, threats, 176-177
    minimizing threats to, 238-240
    qualitative, 162
        confirmability, 163-164
        credibility, 162
        dependability, 162
        transferability, 162
    reliability, 101-103
    reports, 319
    threats, 23
        history, 174, 176
        instrumentation, 176
        maturation, 176
        mortality, 176
        multiple-group, 173, 182-185
        regression, 177-182
        selection, 183-184
        single-group, 173, 175
        social, 173, 185-186
        testing, 176
    translation, 66
variability
    Randomized Block design, 205
    true score theory, 196
variables, 8-9
    attributes, 8
    correlation, 272-277
        calculating, 275-277
        matrix, 277-279
        Pearson Product Moment
            Correlation, 279
        symmetric matrix, 278
        testing, 277
    definition, 8
    dependent, 8
    dummy, 282, 284-286
    exhaustive, 8
    independent, 8
    mutually exclusive, 8
    quantitative, 8
    regression threats, 179
    relationships, 6-7
variance, 271
variations, pattern matching, 231
"violated assumptions of statistical tests,"
    conclusion validity, 261-262

vocabulary
    ethics, 24-25
    research, 4-5
    sampling, 44-45
voluntary participation, 24

W-Z

wording, questions in surveys, 122-123
write-ups, 317-318
    audience, 317
    conclusions, 319
    design, 319
    formatting, 317, 320
        abstract, 319, 321
        appendices, 325
        body, 321
        conclusions, 322
        design, 322
        figures, 325
        introduction, 321
        measures, 321
        methods, 321
        procedures, 322
        references, 319, 322-324
        results, 322
        sampling, 321
        tables, 325
        title page, 321
    introduction, 318
    methods, 318-319
    procedures, 319
    results, 319
    sample paper, 325
        abstract, 328-331
        appendices, 343
        conclusions, 337-338
        designs, 333-334
        figures, 340
        measures, 332-333
        method, 331-332
        procedures, 334-335
        references, 339
        results, 335-336
        tables, 342
        title page, 327
    story, 317
    stylistic elements, 320
writing survey questions, 122-123